Acknowledgements

The editors wish to acknowledge the work of the chapter authors. Their contributions have required time and energy that could have been devoted to their own projects, their families, and loved ones. All were open to the suggestions from the editors not only in framing their chapters, but also in their presentations. This book would not have been possible without their cooperation.

Special recognition goes to our publisher who has been committed to the project from the beginning and who has spent countless hours behind the scenes.

We want to dedicate this book to those who paved the way and whose lives provided the guidance and inspiration to recognize and include all people regardless of creed, religion, and color.

William B. Talley
Valerie E. D. Russell
Carl R. Flowers

TABLE OF CONTENTS

Acknowledgements... v

The Editors.. viii

Preface..x

Chapter 1 Multicultural Rehabilitation: An Historical Perspective..........1
    Bryan O. Gere, Jennifer Hale Gallardo, Paul Leung, Bobbie Atkins

Chapter 2 Legislative Aspects of Rehabilitation............................24
    Keisha G. Rogers & Jennifer D. Shoffner

Chapter 3 Ethical Issues in Rehabilitation Counseling.....................53
    Paige N. Dunlap, Quintin Boston, & Kaye Cole

Chapter 4 Health disparities in Racial-Ethnic Minority Groups:
    Implications for Rehabilitation and
    Allied Health Professional..70
    Valerie E. D. Russel, Allen N. Lewis, Jr.,
    & Lawanda Ford-Johnson

Chapter 5 Religion, Spirituality, and Secularism, and its relevance to
    Preparing Health Care Professionals................................90
    William Talley & Joyce Bell

Chapter 6 Power and Privilege..119
    Allen N. Lewis, Jr., Brigitte Desport, Margart Kaplan,
    Loraine Antoine, Shushawna DeOliveira, & Joanne Katz

Chapter 7 Counselor Cultural Competence: Facilitating Services for
    People with Disabilities in the United States.....................136
    Keith B. Wilson, Abdoulaye Diallo, & Allen Lewis

Chapter 8 Preparing Culturally Competent Practitioners for
    Rehabilitation and Allied Health..................................156
    William Talley, Chandra Donnell Carey, Benson Cooke, &
    Ngozi Chima

Chapter 9 Case Management and Vocational Rehabilitation
          Counseling...193
          Keith B. Wilson, Tyra N. Turner Whittaker, & Virginia Black

Chapter 10 Diversity Issues in Psychological Assessment...............211
          Chow S. Lam, Debra B. Homa, & Amy Buser

Chapter 11 Addressing the Independent Living Needs of Ethnic-
          Racial Minority Groups...235
          Joan Looby

Chapter 12 Human Resources Development and Issues
          in Rehabilitation..257
          Michelle P. Pointer

Chapter 13 Partnering with Families for Successful Career
          Outcomes...278
          Stacie L. Robertson & Carl R. Flowers

Chapter 14 Rehabilitation Research from a Multiculture
          Perspective...297
          Paul Leung, Catherine Marshall, & Keith Wilson

THE EDITORS

WILLIAM B. TALLEY, PH.D., CRC

Dr. Talley received his bachelor's degree in Psychology and a master's degree in Rehabilitation Counseling from South Carolina State College. He obtained his Doctorate in Rehabilitation from Southern Illinois University Carbondale as well as advanced Certificates of study in Management and Development from Harvard University, School of Education. Among the accomplishments that he considers most notable are that he was the first African American to serve as a Director for a Regional Rehabilitation Continuing Education Program (RRCEP) and he was the first African American to Chair an academic unit at Assumption College. During his career he has served as the principal investigator and or author of more than twelve grants that have netted over five million dollars of funding for the entities he has worked for.

Dr. Talley has published articles on a variety of topics including research related to Private Sector Rehabilitation, Multicultural Counseling, Mentoring, and the Recruitment and Retention of faculty. He is also known for his excellent grant writing skills. He has conducted workshops on grants development and management and his recently funded grant is a Long Term Training Grant in Rehabilitation Counseling, submitted to the Department of Education; Rehabilitation Services Administration (FY 2020-2025).

Dr. Talley has served as a site reviewer for the accrediting body which accredits Graduate Programs in Rehabilitation, The Council on Rehabilitation Education (CORE), and he has reviewed materials for the joint "CORE-CACREP" Conversion process. He has served as a peer reviewer for the US Department of Education and he is a Certified Rehabilitation Counselor.

Dr. Talley and Dr. Lisa Zheng were invited to conduct a three day workshop in China, for local Rehabilitation Professionals.

He has received several notable awards including a Congressional Award from the U. S. House of Representatives, a Citation from the Governor of the State of Maryland, a Citation from The City of Baltimore, Mayor's Office, and a Diversity Enhancement Award from The National Aeronautics and Space Administration (NASA).

While he is a published author and accomplished speaker, he considers his greatest achievement to be the fact that he is the father of two well-rounded sons that he is exceedingly proud of.

VALERIE E. DIXON-RUSSELL, PH.D., CRC, LMHC, LCPC, NCC, PVE

Dr. Dixon-Russell is Program Coordinator of Rehabilitation Counseling, Principal Investigator, and Project Director of multiple federally funded grants and core faculty in the Counselor Education Program at Florida International University.

Dr. Dixon-Russell has two decades of experience working in the counseling profession and has consulted with county, state, and federal governmental agencies. She has published and presented on topics associated with effective interventions for underrepresented populations (i.e. persons with disabilities, offenders, minority cultures), counseling supervision and staff development and training.

Dr. Dixon-Russell serves on the American Rehabilitation Counseling Association (ARCA) board as the Director of the Organization, Administration and Management Council and is the Student Association of Rehabilitation Counseling Association (SARCA@ FIU) faculty advisor. She is a member of several other education and social issue focused organizations.

CARL R. FLOWERS, RH.D., CRC, LCPC

Dr. Flowers is an Emeritus Professor and Director of the Rehabilitation Institute, in the College of Education and Human Services at Southern Illinois University, Carbondale. His research interests include Ethics and Public Policy in Rehabilitation Administration, Leadership, and Multicultural Issues in rehabilitation administration and counseling. Dr. Flowers is a past president of the National Rehabilitation Association (NRA) and the National Association of Multicultural Rehabilitation Concerns (NAMRC). He is a Certified Rehabilitation Counselor (CRC) and a Licensed Clinical Professional Counselor (LCPC).

Dr. Flowers published more than 50 articles, book chapters and monographs, and has 50+ presentations at academic conferences and training seminars at the local, state, national, and international levels. He served on the editorial board of three professional journals, *Journal of Research, Policy and Education, Rehabilitation Counselors and Educators (RCEA) Journal* and the *Journal of Rehabilitation*. Additionally, he has served as Guest Editor for the *Journal of Rehabilitation Administration* (JRA) and *Psychological Record (PR)* and is the Editor of the *Journal of Rehabilitation Administration (JRA)*.

PREFACE

The 2nd edition of the *Multicultural Issues in Rehabilitation and Allied Health* is the culmination of the efforts of several practitioners and professionals in the field. These authors and the editors have done a remarkable job in the design and presentation of the subject areas, which collectively and comprehensively address the multicultural issues related to service delivery in rehabilitation and allied health settings. As the America society continues to evolve in diversity in complex ways, issues related to multiculturalism continue to be front and center for professional service delivery. The examination of diversity issues in service delivery help us to understand the ways in which we can view, appreciate, interact with, and communicate with people of diverse backgrounds and cultures within the society.

Since its first edition, this text has been widely accepted as a resource and reference for scholars and students on multicultural issues in service delivery in rehabilitation and allied health. This is because multicultural competence and evidence-based practice in diverse populations are important issues in contemporary discourse in rehabilitation, mental health, and allied health service delivery. Additionally, what sets this text apart from others is that it contains the rich and unique contributions of academics and practitioners with expertise in the area of multiculturalism.

The current edition of the book has been updated to contain many innovative features, which will be of immense benefit to practitioners in many rehabilitation and allied health fields. Perhaps, the most significant changes in the current edition are the addition of topics *on power and privilege, health disparities, cross-cultural competence, discourse on disability*. Additionally, each of the chapters have a summary and conclusion. Dr. Flowers and Dr. Talley, the editors, have done a wonderful job of updating the chapters in this edition.

Although the current edition, similar to previous editions, does not cover all the issues multiculturalism and diversity (e.g., ageism, sexual orientation, or disability itself), the text has a done a great job in highlighting some of the most important areas in which competence in multicultural practice is important and relevant for rehabilitation and allied health practice.

It is my expectation this book will provoke you to think and to act to better serve the lives of diverse individuals, especially persons with disabilities. I, therefore, wholeheartedly endorse this invaluable text for graduate students in rehabilitation and allied health.

Bryan Gere, Ph.D. MBA
Asst. Professor & Asst. Graduate Clinical Coordinator
University of Maryland Eastern Shores

CHAPTER 1

MULTICULTURAL REHABILITATION:
AN HISTORICAL PERSPECTIVE

JENNIFER HALE GALLARDO
BRYAN GERE
PAUL LEUNG
BOBBIE ATKINS

CHAPTER TOPICS

- Historical Overview of Culture
- Culture, Racism, and Discrimination in U.S
- Multiculturalism
- Multiculturalism in Counseling, Rehabilitation and Mental Health
- Contemporary Issues on Race, Culture and Multiculturalism in America
- Summary and Conclusion

HISTORICAL OVERVIEW OF CULTURE

While the word "culture" has become one of the most trafficked words today, a lot of confusion remains regarding what the term actually means.[46,32] With linguistic roots in several European languages, originally the word was derived from the Latin "cultura," which translated means having to do with the tending of crops and animals.[40] In Roman antiquity, Cicero used the term "cultura animi" as an agricultural metaphor referring to the development of a "philosophical soul" or the cultivation of the mind. The term then largely disappeared from use during Europe's medieval period until in the 17th century European Renaissance. Cicero's notion of the term was revived to denote "the betterment or refinement of individuals, particularly through educational means."[44, p4]

This meaning continues to this day in the use of the term *culture* as aesthetic sensibilities that have been cultivated through moral and intellectual development, and the artistic or literary products of such processes.[27] However, in the 19th and 20th century, an important turn took place in the use of the term when it emerged as a key concept in anthropology that is used to explain a range of human phenomena not directly attributable to genetic inheritance.[46] While the idea that human societies differ in customs and practices is an old one, the term *culture* was used for the first time to try to explain these differences.[44] As anthropology became the central intellectual problem in European colonial expansion, differences in human groups led to the desire to pinpoint the conceptual components of culture.[42]

Perhaps the most famous definition of culture is that of English anthropologist E. B. Tylor,[47] which is still widely used in textbooks today. According to Tylor, culture is defined as "...that complex whole which includes knowledge, belief, art, morals, law, custom, and any other capabilities and habits acquired by man as a member of society."[p.1] However, Tylor used culture interchangeably with *civilization,* which was for him and his contemporaries the highest stage in an explicitly formulated sequence of progressive human development, which began in *savagery* and moved through *barbarism.*[47] Tylor was largely influenced by Darwinian theories of biological evolutionism that featured a succession of biological types, Enlightenment philosophy that divided the world into stages of human progress, and his own Quaker upbringing that assumed a universal humanity. Thus, Tylor conceptualized culture as a universal sequence and hierarchy of values, which placed all human societies on a ladder of successive progression towards cultural and technological advancement, with Western European culture at the summit.

Tylor, unlike most of his contemporaries, did not believe race—the idea of naturally occurring divisions of humanity based on skin color, phenotype, moral character, and intelligence— was a scientifically valid concept. As evident in the views of other anthropologists and writers, this universal classification of humanity has been challenged as a racist classification of human diversity.[19] Franz Boas, an American anthropologist of the early 20th century, brought a radical change to the elitist and Eurocentric view of culture of the previous era, rejecting both evolutionism and hierarchically value-laden categorizations of civilization.[19] Instead, Boas' generation rejected the then popular evolutionary approaches to understanding culture, and conceptualized cultures as the existence of diverse, local, functionally integrated units of society, which developed through social interaction with other groups and diffusion of ideas.[19]

In addition, Boaz also argued against the idea of a higher stage of culture, and introduced the ideology of cultural relativism, or that cultures cannot be ranked in any objective fashion as higher or lower, but that all humans perceive the world through their own cultural lens and judge it according to their own culturally-sanctioned norms and values.[19] In more recent years, social scientists have come to commonly use the term *culture* to describe the beliefs and behaviors that we learn within social groupings, including the rules by which we order our lives, and the meanings by which we interpret our world and place in it.[41] While there has been a close association of culture with ethnicity (population with a common national tradition or shared language), as well as arguments as to how ethnicity often overlaps with cultural difference, culture is by no means limited to differences in ethnicity.[48]

Many scholars, researchers, and theorists have thus extended this definition to describe all kinds of social groupings of people, beyond those with a shared ethnic background. For instance, some cultural study theorists define culture as both general values and the creation and maintenance of group boundaries and identities, as well as relationships of power and authority.[43]

Moreover, theories of intercultural communication conceptualize culture as comprising "verbal and nonverbal language, attitudes, values, perceptions, stereotypes and group identity that are accepted by an identifiable group of people," and widely applicable to any kind of social grouping.[1, p.34] Today, culture is used to describe attitudes and behavior characteristic of shared groupings of ideas or issues, such as culture of transparency, celebrity culture, consumer culture, or marching band culture.[28] There are limits to the concept, however. For instance, as the late Harry F. Wolcott warned, "statements about how a people's culture makes them do this-or-that are highly suspect; humans do things, cultures do not."[50 p.101] Such distinction is valid given popular sentiments and views that sometimes ascribe negative behaviors expressed by individuals from a particular culture as representative of the values and beliefs of the entire society.

The cultural lenses or perspectives from which people view themselves and others and how they are situated within the society are important in the discussion of culture, especially for persons with disability. In the general population, cultural beliefs and practices influence perceptions of persons with disability. Negative perceptions of persons with disability by non-disabled individuals often leads to stigma and discrimination.[31] Stigma and discrimination of persons with disabilities is pervasive and interferes with the ability of persons with disabilities to have access to opportunities, equal treatment, and better community inclusion. Jones, et al.,[39] define Stigma as a 'mark' that distinguishes a person as being deviant, flawed, 'spoiled,' or generally undesirable.[p.24] Stigma can therefore be seen as an undesirable or discrediting attribute that an individual possesses, that reduces that individual's status in the eyes of society. Discrimination refers to negative actions and behaviors that are directed at others due to perceived differences. Stigma and discrimination, therefore, include negative attitudes and behaviors directed at persons with disabilities, their families and friends due to their disability. Negative and discriminatory attitudes towards persons with disabilities reinforce and magnify social differences in class, race, and gender.[1]

Stigma and discriminatory behavior towards persons with disability is heightened by a phenomenon known as hierarchy of disability stigma. The *hierarchy of disability stigma* is a social construct that makes certain kinds of disabilities more acceptable than others. Although, the hierarchy of disability is totally arbitrary, many individuals including professionals unintentionally internalize, ascribe to, and use it in their interactions with persons with disabilities. In its general form, disabilities are placed on a hierarchy, such that the more significant the perception of the disabling condition, the more likely that the individual is placed on a lower level of the hierarchy. Thus, persons without disabilities use disability hierarchy to create, maintain, and heighten group boundaries and identities, as well as relationships of power and authority with persons with disabilities.

According to the hierarchy of disability stigmatization, physical disabilities are on the top of the hierarchy because these disabilities are easier to understand in terms of onset, cause, and limitations, and therefore generally acceptable, thus making persons with physical disabilities to experience less stigma or discrimination. The next group in the hierarchy is cognitive disabilities, followed by intellectual disabilities. Psychiatric disabilities are at the bottom of the hierarchy with the greatest amount of stigma, prejudice, and discrimination.[37] Included in this category are different types of mental illness as well as alcohol abuse and substance abuse. Individuals with abuse and substance abuse are often shamed for being weak and lacking will power. Such discriminatory attitudes are sometimes held by professionals who provide treatment services to persons with these conditions.

For persons with disabilities, the definition of culture has implications for perceptions of self and group identity within society.[17] Persons with disabilities ascribe more to disability culture than the dominant culture within their societies. Peters[36] defined disability culture as "the sum total of behaviors, beliefs, ways of living, and material artifacts that are unique to persons affected by disability."[p.1] Thus, beyond the dominant culture in which persons with disabilities live alongside those without disabilities, persons with disabilities also live in a culture that is unique to the experience of having, and living with a disability.[31] Disability culture thus offer ways for people with different disabilities to forge an identity, and pursue individual and shared goals. Understanding how people with diverse disabilities perceive themselves and their disabilities within the society is central to how health and human services or allied health professionals, can best intervene to provide services, provide advocacy, and address problems that are related to stigma and discrimination.

CULTURAL IDENTITY, RACISM, AND DISCRIMINATION IN THE U.S.

CULTURAL IDENTITY

Cultural identity is a complex, and multifaceted concept related to an individual's self-conception and perception.[24] Collier and Thomas[20] define cultural identity as "identification with and perceived acceptance into a group that has shared systems of symbols and meanings as well as norms/rules for conduct."[p.113] Cultural identity is a dynamic component of an individual's self – concept and connects individuals with their heritage, and provides a template for viewing the world and navigating social interactions.[12] This includes visible and invisible domains such as nationality, religion, language, gender, social class, generation, and education that influence self-construction.[23] In diverse or pluralistic societies, individuals from the less dominant cultural groups typically identify with more than one cultural grouping, although, only one cultural identity may be noticeable in a given situation.[24]

In the U.S., the development of cultural identity of several groups is intricately connected to the history of race relations, discrimination, and the process of acculturation.[28] Whereas, racial and cultural groups that were assimilated assume the identity of the dominant group, segregated groups (e.g., Native Americans, Asians, and Blacks) experience separation from the culture of the dominant group as a result of de-legitimization and marginalization of their racial and cultural identities. Consequently, members of these groups embrace and celebrate their cultural identity and values as a parallel to and in resistance to the imposition of the dominant cultural identity. Some examples include Chinese immigrants living and working exclusively in Chinatown, and Latin Americans hosting Latino Night Performances in predominantly white neighborhoods.[28]

The cultural identity to which an individual with disability assumes or ascribes to within a multicultural society may depend on several factors such as the nature and type of disability, racial and ethnic background, socioeconomic status, and the experiences of living with the disability within the society. In some societies, the cultural beliefs, and practices may place the label of disability on individuals. Mainstream cultural understanding and interpretation of the concept of 'disability' sometimes confer the status or position upon persons with disability in a given society. Thus, a persons with disability may only be disabled to the extent that they ascribe to either the mainstream interpretation of the disability or the disability culture typical for their disability group.

RACISM AND DISCRIMINATION

The emergence and the continued emphasis on a dominant culture has contributed to racism and discrimination within the U.S. society. Racial and ethnic minorities as well as people with disabilities in the U.S. have historically been denied the rights, opportunities, and resources for an autonomous cultural life.[21] The predominant culture has been used to spread and impose myths about the intelligence, abilities, and roles of these groups within the society. For instance, racism or ideology of the superiority of one race over another has resulted in cultural suppression, and socioeconomic disparities. African Americans and other minorities have continued to experience racially motivated economic and social marginalization. For instance, the criminal justice system in America continues to reflect the racial marginalization and denigration of minorities especially African Americans in the United States.[9,21] Discrimination based on race is prevalent in the legal process, policing practices, education, credit, consumer markets, and in housing.[35] These experiences are further magnified for minorities with disabilities, and tend to have a significant impact on community inclusion and overall socioeconomic well-being.

Relative to cultural discrimination, acculturation, a concept that involves the subtle or forceful subsummation of the culture of smaller groups into the larger culture is often emphasized.[3,11,40] For persons with disabilities, there is also a demand to acculturate into an ability-focused society in order to function and become successfully integrated into the society. The extent to which a person experiences inclusion and acceptance is based on perceptions of their ability to engage in roles, society talents, skills, knowledge, and other potentials and perform tasks that are typical within the society. Acculturation for individuals who acquire their disabilities later in life may therefore involve changes in values, and identifications.[3]

MULTICULTURALISM

Multiculturalism is a more recent term that has been used to describe several phenomena: cultural diversity within a given society or country; a political philosophy that strives to acknowledge and provide accommodation to diverse groups within a community; and government policies that promote inclusion and citizenship.[13,33] The concept of multiculturalism is also connected to the political and economic power relations within a society. Berry[10] pointed out that the concept of multiculturalism has two important emphases: the maintenance of heritage cultures and identities (the cultural component) and the full and equitable participation of all ethnocultural groups in the life of the larger society (the social component).[p.98]

The United States of America has always been a culturally and racially diverse country due to its history of slavery and the large-scale immigration of people from other countries.[38] However, multiculturalism has not been historically espoused as a policy at the federal level; what has been advanced and practiced prior to 1960 was the idea of the cultural melting pot.[38] The cultural melting pot view encouraged immigrants to assimilate into American culture by abandoning their own cultures, languages, and other traditions. However, the melting pot myth did not give consideration to the significance and consequences of slavery or consider the enduring legacy of racism, prejudice, and intolerance towards immigrants and cultural minorities.[34] The denial of access to white dominated institutions, socioeconomic privilege and power, and racial apartheid galvanized cultural minorities and immigrants to demand for social justice and for sociocultural and political interactions that value and actively supports mutual cultural differences and equal chances and opportunities.[7] More importantly, there was also a portrayal of the American institutions, identity, and core beliefs as those of the Anglo-Saxon. Consequently, many immigrants and cultural immigrants were not accommodated by the cultural melting pot view, and their sociopolitical realities tended instead towards cultural diversity, and pluralism.[26] The focal idea of multiculturalism based on pluralism is the coexistence of different cultural or ethnic groups within a shared political and social framework.[10]

Similar to racial and ethnic minorities, persons with disabilities also fought against discrimination and bias to have equal treatment and access to opportunities and resources within the society. Following the Second World War, disabled veterans prevailed upon the U.S. government to introduce rehabilitation and vocational training for soldiers that were injured or disabled from the war. This led to the birth of physical rehabilitation and vocational rehabilitation services, which was eventually extended to civilians. However, many individuals with disabilities in the U.S. continued to experience marginalization and did not have access to public facilities and services such as office buildings, and worksites, transportation services, telecommunication, etc. Following the success of the civil rights movement in the 1960s, persons with disabilities also commenced a movement for disability rights, which focused on ensuring that persons with disabilities were accorded basic civil rights and given equal access to opportunities within their communities. In the 1970s, individuals, families, disability rights activists, and other civic groups marched on Washington to agitate for disability legislation. This resulted in the passage of the first disability legislation called the Rehabilitation Act. 1973. Since then several laws have been passed to protect the civil rights of people with disabilities.[37]

The challenge within American society today continues to be answering the question of how diverse groups can live together as a multicultural society in a context of institutionalized racism and cultural discrimination. Furthermore, there is evidence that many Americans of European descent do not value cultural diversity within the American society.[45] Nor do they accept that diversity should be valued or that American society has been shaped by diversity. Contemporary views of multiculturalism have expanded the concept to include group identities related to gender, age, religion, socioeconomic class, sexual orientation, and differences in abilities. The current expanded view of multiculturalism focuses on the subordination of these groupings under the mainstream culture. The mainstream culture or what is conventionally considered the "American core culture" is that which was developed, adopted, and perpetuated largely by white-identified Americans of European descent with minimal influence from other immigrant and minority cultures.[2] Thus, the push for multiculturalism within American society is also focused on remediating injustices resulting from a lack of adequate representation and empowerment of disenfranchised groups.

Persons with disabilities are a disenfranchised group within the American society. In many sectors of American society such as the media, sports, industry, and even government, there is a lack of proper representation of persons with disabilities. For instance, persons with disabilities are underrepresented in Television programs, commercials or movies, educational content in schools, as well as in areas of public policy and legislation. Negative perceptions and implicit bias towards persons with disabilities continue to lead to marginalization of persons with disabilities. Researchers[31,50] have suggested that increasing contact and providing education or accurate information improves negative attitudes and discriminatory behavior towards persons with disabilities.

It is important for professionals in allied health and human services to be aware of the marginalization and disenfranchisement of persons with disabilities from many aspects of society in the communities in which they live. As a professional, some of the challenges that you will experience in addressing the needs of your clients may be related to attitudes and behaviors that pertain to inclusion in social and vocational spheres of the society. Being aware of the barriers that your clients face and serving as a good advocate for your client population may be a good step towards increasing access to opportunities and community inclusion.

MULTICULTURALISM IN COUNSELING, REHABILITATION, AND MENTAL HEALTH

Jackson[25] captured the history of the multicultural counseling movement in a chapter written for *The Handbook of Multicultural Counseling*. Jackson[25] suggested that the roots of the guidance and counseling movement are based on the premise of choosing a vocation. Because African Americans and other minorities faced extreme discrimination and prejudice, African Americans had limited choice in selecting a vocation. Some counseling professionals excluded minority clients or only matched clients with employment where it was felt by the counselor that the clients were most likely to be hired.[25] Clearly, this type of career counseling was not in the best interest of consumers who have disabilities, let alone persons of color.

Jackson[25] also suggested that counseling during this era emphasized the assimilation of immigrant and minority populations into the "mainstream" of American society, and that assimilation counseling "proved to be ineffective for a large segment of the American population, as counselors worked with theories and techniques that were at odds with the cultural backgrounds of their clients."[p.6] Jackson's review of the counseling literature found little information on the role of culture or race in counseling prior to the 1960's. Much of the emphasis in those years was not on counseling, but rather on the significance of culture for the administration of standardized tests. This limitation in the literature provides a background for understanding some of the current challenges related to multicultural counseling in rehabilitation and related counseling areas.

The decade of the 1960's was a particularly prescient time for the multicultural counseling movement. The Civil Rights Act of 1964 certainly paved the way for an exploration and discussion of race. Within the counseling profession, special legislation was passed by the 1966 American Personnel and Guidance Association (APGA) that called for the inclusion of guidance and counseling of persons who were *culturally disadvantaged*.[25] The use of the term "culturally disadvantaged" is interesting as the term suggested that cultures of people of color were somehow lacking. Atkinson, et al.,[3] articulated this when they wrote, "The term culturally disadvantaged suggests the person to whom it is applied is at a disadvantage because he/she lacks the cultural background formed by the controlling social structure....we seriously object, however, to any inference that racial/ethnic groups have less culture."[p.10]

Jackson[25] saw this as an indictment of previous counseling practice, and as recognition that a new paradigm would have to emerge. Jackson[25] related other events within the counseling profession including the call for establishing an Office of Non-White Concerns at the 1969 APGA conference. The petition calling for the office was the beginning of the Association's first Black caucus.[25] The office soon led to the Association for Non-White Concerns (ANWC) in 1972 and to the Association for Multicultural Counseling and Development in 1985.

Within the field of rehabilitation, parallel events occurred though again only after long continuing neglect by the primary rehabilitation professional association. In 1969, nine members of the National Rehabilitation Association (NRA), 46 years after the founding of the NRA, presented a document entitled "Non-White Caucus Demands"[p.59] to the NRA Board of Directors.[30] These nine included some early multicultural pioneers including Thomas Washington, George Ayers, Vernon Hawkins, Beth Anderson, and Jose Rodriguez. The document listed issues long ignored by the NRA related to the need for expanding the Non-White voting membership, employing Non-Whites in NRA, increasing Non-White involvement in the NRA legislative agenda, and expanding NRA support related to directing public resources to Non-White rehabilitation and community organizations. The NRA Board accepted the document and agreed on a resolution to be voted on at the NRA Delegate Assembly that year. The passage of Resolution 14 became the first formal recognition by NRA that race and ethnicity were issues[30] in the organization, and more broadly in rehabilitation. This recognition eventually evolved into the current NRA division known as the National Association of Multicultural Rehabilitation Concerns.

The struggle to bring a multicultural perspective to rehabilitation also includes stories of many individuals with and without disabilities who were pioneers in the effort. We reiterate that this chapter can only partially cover this history. It is important to acknowledge the authors' gratitude as well as apology to the many who may have been omitted. It is essential, as rehabilitation professionals, that we appreciate what brought us to where we are today, as it demonstrates our interdependence on each other along with knowing that we are not alone in the struggle. As many pioneers age and gray, it becomes ever more critical that this legacy not be lost, especially to those who are now entering rehabilitation and are emerging to become rehabilitation's new pioneers.

One movement that has had influence repeatedly on rehabilitation is mental health. The multicultural movement within the mental health community also brought recognition that the needs and requirements of ethnic/racial minority groups were not equivalent to the issues and needs that the majority society presented. Researchers such as Stanley Sue found an underutilization of mental health services by different ethnic/racial groups, as well as different help seeking behaviors that affected how various populations accessed, or did not access, mental health services. Atkinson[8] further elaborated that when "sociodemographic data have been controlled; mental illness is not related to ethnicity per se...."[p.75] People of color, however, are often differentiated from their white peers in terms of mental health access, utilization, quality, and research. These disparities provided continuing motivation for exploring and expanding a multicultural emphasis in rehabilitation counseling and related professions.

The United States Department of Health and Human Services funded several centers with the mission of addressing through research the requirements of different racial and ethnic groups. These centers also provided an impetus to look beyond the traditional mental health services, and the one size fits all approach. Each center has made substantial contributions to our understanding that cultural variables are critical and must be addressed in any service delivery system.

> National Center for American Indian and Alaska Native Mental Health Research has explored some of the specific requirements of American Indians and Alaska natives, the populations indigenous to the United States, but often left out of the loop with regard to

appropriate and relevant mental health services. The rates of post-traumatic stress disorder in American Indian and Alaska Native veterans have always been high, but mental health services were not available for the population, according to a study conducted by the National Center for American Indian and Alaska Native Mental Health Research. The findings of this study revealed that current services for American Indian veterans rank low in availability, accessibility, and acceptability. The Center is located at the University of Colorado Health Sciences Center in Denver.

➢ The National Research Center on Asian American Mental Health, also funded by the National Institute for Mental Health (NIMH), conducts research on various Asian groups, including Koreans, Filipinos, and Southeast Asians. The center has looked at mental health problems among Asians including the rates of mental disturbance and factors that affect utilization of health services. Researchers conducted a study looking at whether it is better for therapists and clients to be of the same race and ethnicity. "We found that Asian clients who had Asian therapists stayed in treatment longer and were more likely to have better treatment outcomes," said Stanley Sue, Ph.D., director of the center located at the University of California, Davis, Department of Psychology.

➢ The African American Mental Health Research Center is part of the Program for Research on Black Americans established by an interdisciplinary team of social scientists. The NIMH started the research center with the goal of studying African American mental health and evaluating the way African Americans seek help for mental illness. In 1993, the grant was expanded to study issues surrounding the mental health of children and adolescents, including the plight of the chronically mentally ill in urban areas. The Program for Research on Black Americans is located at the University of Michigan, Institute for Social Research, in Ann Arbor.

➢ The Center for Hispanic Mental Health Research was established through a grant from the NIMH with a charge to explore mental health research and the fast growing Hispanic population. The Mission of the Center is to conduct innovative applied mental health research on Hispanic populations with a goal of generating new knowledge in order to provide improved services. The Center's objectives include conducting epidemiological research identifying mental health needs of Hispanic populations; studying how standard assessment, treatment interventions, and prevention approaches can be modified to enhance outcomes for Hispanics; conducting psychotherapeutic intervention studies testing new culturally competent psychosocial services; and disseminating research findings through scholarly publications, a Center newsletter, colloquia, and conferences. The center is located at Fordham University, New York.

The issues that led to the formation of these research centers have not diminished and a recent release by the U.S. Surgeon General suggests that there is much work yet to be done. The 2001 supplemental report of the Surgeon General pointed out that disparities affecting mental health care of racial and ethnic minorities, compared with whites, continue to exist. The conclusions included the following:

- Minorities have less access to, and availability of, mental health services.
- Minorities are less likely to receive needed mental health services.
- Minorities in treatment often receive a poorer quality of mental health care.
- Minorities are underrepresented in mental health research.

These disparities correspond to those cited by Atkinson[8] specific to the mental health needs of ethnic minority populations. Mental illness continues to affect racial and ethnic populations disproportionately creating disabling conditions that affect their ability to participate fully in society and to be employed. The Supplemental report found that racial and ethnic minorities collectively experience a greater disability burden from mental illness than do whites. The higher level of burden stems from minorities receiving less care and poorer quality of care. This is distinct in contrast to the notion that mental illnesses are inherently more severe or prevalent in minority communities. Awareness of these issues is essential for rehabilitation providers, educators, and researchers if there is to be truly equitable programs and services based on an "asset orientation,"[5] rather than a deficit approach that undermines what consumers of color have to offer. This perspective is akin to the unacceptable use of "disadvantaged" and brings about a negative bias in understanding and relating to various ethnic groups.

ACCESS TO REHABILITATION SERVICES

One of the earliest publications regarding vocational rehabilitation and Blacks appeared in 1938 in the *Journal of Negro Education*[49] regarding participation of Negroes in the Federally-aided Program of Civilian Vocational Rehabilitation. Based on data obtained in 1935-36, Wilkerson and Penn[49] explored the relative extent to which Negro and white persons participate in the rehabilitation services of the 15 Southern states and District of Columbia.[49] In an attempt to make sense of the data, they speculated "One wonders if the predominating practice of rehabilitation agencies is to fit a Negro client with a cork arm or leg, or a pair of spectacles, find him a job, and close his case, without having afforded him the opportunity for vocational training which a similarly handicapped white client would normally injoy"[p.325] and that annual reports be published "showing the extent to which Negroes and other minority racial groups share in the funds and services."[p.329] Recommendations offered by Wilkerson and Penn[49] included the need for Federal laws to "be amended to require a 'just and equitable' distribution of funds and services to minority racial groups" and that annual reports be published "showing the extent to which Negroes and other minority racial groups share in the funds and services." Inequities and disparities obviously existed during these years and continued to be carried over into the 1980's.

A second watershed event in multicultural rehabilitation occurred in 1980, further accentuating the need for attention to minority populations and specifically African Americans. An article based on the doctoral dissertation of Bobbie J. Atkins[7] was published in the *Journal of Rehabilitation.* The Atkins & Wright article had major impact on rehabilitation, and specifically the state federal public vocational rehabilitation program, as Atkins drew attention to inequalities that existed. For example, Atkins and Wright[7] found that "Blacks entered and exited the public VR programs in a proportionately more disadvantaged status than Whites.[p.45] Atkins and Wright[7] further suggested, "fewer VR resources were employed to help improve the overall status of disabled Blacks,"[p.45] Their conclusion was that "while it is clear from this study that Blacks are proportionately in greater need of compensatory VR services, the actual amount of such assistance was generally less for Blacks than Whites."[p.45] Atkins and Wright[7] are significant not only for their findings and subsequent publication, but as the authors of the first of a number of studies and related publications that explored the relationship between service provision and race or ethnicity.[15,16,4]

Dr. Bobbie Atkins, being the first contemporary to draw attention to the treatment of racial minorities in rehabilitation, also encountered obstacles that future researchers were less likely to face. Because Atkins and Wright[7] suggested what many perceived to be a negative reflection on the state federal vocational rehabilitation program, scrutiny at a level seldom seen before or since was placed on the publication of her data. The article was not published after acceptance and left the reader to draw their own conclusions about the validity of the data and their implications, as is generally the case. The *Journal of Rehabilitation* editors sought out two additional reactions or responses. In what was perhaps an unprecedented act, commentary from the RSA Commissioner and Deputy Commissioner, along with invited comments from two other researchers were obtained. Given the implied criticism of the public rehabilitation program by Atkins & Wright,[7] this certainly seemed a somewhat transparent and defensive way to lessen the impact.

The RSA Commissioner's and Deputy RSA Commissioner's response was that the conclusions of Atkins & Wright[7] were possible, but the analysis did not clearly indicate where the problem was. The response from the two researchers, Bolton and Cooper,[14] suggested that statistical differences could be interpreted in a different way than Atkins & Wright.[7] Bolton & Cooper[14] took the position that the percentage of Blacks accepted into the public VR program exceeded the proportion of Blacks in the U.S. and, at the same time, acknowledged that Blacks have higher rates of disability. Bolton and Cooper[14] went on to suggest that clients who lack education be thoroughly assessed to determine who would benefit from "vocational adjustment and/or intensive job placement." In the end, even the responses could not lessen the impact of a study that confirmed what many in the African American community felt to be true.

It was also during this time period that a Rehabilitation Research and Training Center (R&T) was funded through the National Institute on Disability and Rehabilitation Research that was perhaps the only Center that maintained an agenda related to underserved populations. Based in Howard University and directed by Dr. Sylvia Walker, the Center for Access to Rehabilitation and Economic Opportunity was the only federally funded R&T Center with the express mission to study underserved and underrepresented populations, such as African Americans.

Two other R&T Centers were established to explore rehabilitation and the American Indian and were located at the University of Arizona (UA) in Tucson and at Northern Arizona University (NAU). The NAU and UA were both called the Native American Research and Training Center (NARTC). Historically, UA focused on the health and well-being of Native Americans while NAU focused on vocational rehabilitation and independent living of American Indians. Since 1983, the NARTCs have conducted research and training to improve rehabilitation services for American Indians with disabilities. The centers serve as a national resource for Native American communities and for persons working with Native American populations, especially those with chronic diseases or disabilities.

In the early part of 1987, a subproject was funded to NAU and UA to conduct a national study at the request of Congress. Dr. Joanne O'Connell, NAU Research Director was the lead researcher and editor for the subproject and worked with the primary researcher, Dr. Jim Morgan. In the 1988 grant application, the NAU center changed its name from Native American Research and Training Center to American Indian Rehabilitation Research, primarily for the sake of brevity (NIDRR Competitive Grant Application, December 15, 1988, p.4). The research center on the campus of Howard University, founded by Dr. Sylvia Walker, focused on populations that were not well served by rehabilitation programs. Based on the inclusive vision of

Dr. Walker, the R&T Center for Access to Rehabilitation took upon itself to collaborate with not only the African American community, but also the Hispanic American and Asian American communities in its research and training agenda.

A number of significant documents resulted from the research done during those early years. The study titled "Disability Prevalence and Demographic Association Among Race/Ethnic Minority Populations in the United States: Implications for the 21st Century" was perhaps the first major documentation of disability prevalence within diverse communities. In addition, the Research and Training Center at Howard University hosted numerous workshops, training opportunities, and seminars focusing on multicultural issues and concerns. It is especially noteworthy because many of these conferences and meetings were held without widespread support from those who were not people of color. The Howard Center also collaborated with the President's Committee on Employment of People with Disabilities and coordinated numerous sessions in conjunction with the President's Committee annual meeting.

Several rehabilitation educators also sensed a need for an academic base to address issues related to a multicultural approach to rehabilitation counseling. A special issue of the *Journal of Applied Rehabilitation Counseling* appeared in 1988 devoted to the multicultural aspects of rehabilitation counseling.[29] Not long after, Tennyson Wright and William Emener[51] published the first annotated bibliography consisting of entries between 1952-1988 related to ethnic minority populations, disability, and rehabilitation.

At about the same time, the National Council on Disability (NCD), an independent federal agency charged with oversight related to disability and the federal government, identified needs in diverse populations that were not met. With an African American woman, Ethel Briggs as their Executive Director, inroads were made toward examining needs of minority persons with disabilities. This focus by NCD led to a national conference in Jackson, Mississippi, in 1992, targeting the unique needs of minorities with disabilities. One hundred eighty-six persons participated, including a majority from minority communities, and produced 11 major findings along with recommendations for policy for the National Council. In October 1992, the NCD held a daylong meeting in San Francisco as a follow-up to the national conference.

LEGISLATIVE MANDATES

Two pieces of legislation were instrumental in moving the multicultural rehabilitation agenda forward. The first was Section 610(j) of the Individuals with Disabilities Education Act (IDEA), and its mirror in Section 21 of the Rehabilitation Act Amendments of 1992. Both of these pieces of legislation grew from Congressman Major Owens of New York, who was Chair of the Subcommittee on Select Education.[43] Changes mandated by these two pieces of legislation involved funds specifically set aside to ensure outreach and capacity building for institutions such as historically black colleges and universities and other high minority enrollment institutions. The additional emphasis was brought by legislative mandate; suggesting perhaps that the state federal program did not make the needed effort of outreach to those populations that are in particular need of rehabilitation. In addition, it was a strategy that helped keep multicultural issues in the forefront of rehabilitation public policy.

The initial phase for implementing Section 21 by the Rehabilitation Services Administration was through development of the Rehabilitation Cultural Diversity Initiative (RCDI). Housed within San Diego State University and led by Dr. Bobbie Atkins, the RCDI vision was for rehabilitation to reflect the cultural diversity of American society with the mission to promote opportunities to enhance equal access and quality services for individuals who are culturally diverse. The RSA designated the Regional Rehabilitation Continuing Education Programs (RRCEPs) as the avenue for implementation, with each of the ten RRCEPs funded to perform outreach services to minority institutions of higher learning.

Most RRCEPs designated or hired a staff member to serve in the outreach effort. RSA also established a National Rehabilitation Cultural Diversity Initiative (RCDI) Committee composed of individuals from around the country to provide input into policies established by RSA and to provide recommendations for systemic change. Some of the values driving the RCDI were the empowerment of persons with disabilities; perceiving diversity as an asset; partnership and collaboration; awareness that all people have talents and values; realization that all people deserve respect and equal opportunity; and maximizing human resources in rehabilitation organizations. RCDIs' operating principles were articulated to promote diversity in all aspects of rehabilitation; model diversity inclusion in all interaction with other organizations; work in partnership with its constituencies to ensure empowerment and use of talents; practice and promote the highest standard of human behaviors, products, and interactions; and develop and implement policy changes as needed.

The RCDI utilized a lead specialist (experts in diversity issues) approach in each region to obtain baseline data, to establish research agendas, and to develop programmatic strategies. RCDI proposed to extend beyond the quantitative measures of numbers and statistics to attitudinal and systemic changes. The RCDI, in the words of Dr. Atkins, "was not about the Noah's Ark Syndrome (two by two), but rather about system and paradigm shifts and change.[6]

An outgrowth of the RCDI was the establishment of the Consortia of Administrators for Native American Rehabilitation (CANAR) in 1993 by Dr. Ken Galea'I, who was then the RCEP VIII director. CANAR functioned as a national platform for drawing attention to the need for effective rehabilitation service delivery for American Indians and Alaska Natives with disabilities.

CANAR continues to serve as the official voice of Native American rehabilitation programs, which provide VR services to American Indians and Alaska Natives with disabilities who reside on or near Federal or State reservations, Alaska Native villages, rancheros, and pueblos. Under the leadership of Ms. Treva Roanhorse, CANAR has established itself as a viable political voice using a collaborative and cooperative partnership approach. Membership in CANAR includes Indian Country leaders able to work with a wide variety of constituencies. Due in part to CANAR, rehabilitation programs serving American Indians and Alaska natives have grown. After approximately three years, RSA abandoned the RCDI approach involving the RCEP's and followed a system involving a call for proposals to build capacity. These capacity-building projects are doing much to expand rehabilitation services and education through Indian Tribes and minority institutions of higher education, including minority serving institutions, historically black colleges, and universities and American Indian Tribal colleges. Much of the initial effort was directed toward conducting training sessions on how to access and write grants to support rehabilitation efforts. These sessions, along with related technical assistance, continue at this time.

Also, the Rehabilitation Services Administration, perhaps sensing a need to focus more directly on underserved populations, completed three technical assistance centers. These centers were to assist vocational rehabilitation programs and partners to better respond to the cultural requirements that have been documented as barriers for vocational rehabilitation service delivery. The American Indian Disability Technical Assistance Center was located in Montana. Projecto Vision was housed within the World Institute on Disability in California. The National Technical Assistance Center serving Asian Americans and Pacific Islanders was established in Hawaii. With a three-year time frame, the RSA ceased competitions to extend these centers.

CONTEMPORARY ISSUES ON RACE, CULTURE AND MULTICULTURALISM IN AMERICA

Racism continues to be a divisive issue in the United States. Studies consistently show that minorities continue to be disproportionately incarcerated, and more likely to be racially profiled.[22] Similar to the civil rights era, there have been growing racial intolerance characterized by increasing inter-ethnic tensions, blatant discrimination, and violence against minorities and immigrants in recent times. Misdirected white hatred and racially tinged incidents are common every day experiences for African Americans such as the selective and extrajudicial killings of African Americans by law enforcement officers as well as private citizens (as in the case of the Charleston church massacre). Also, there is a conscious fear of the overthrow of the majority white culture, such that conscious efforts are made to devalue and repress minority culture and values. In 2016, the 11th U.S. Circuit Court of Appeals ruled that it was legal for an employer to refuse to hire an African American woman with dreadlocks. A similar attempt was also made in the military pertaining to a black female officer but the decision was later overturned.

Despite the existence of legislation, persons with disabilities continue to experience discrimination in employment.[31] Many inequities abound in hiring practices that impact the employment of persons with disabilities. Additionally, most employers are not willing to advance people with disabilities on their job due to negative conceptions of the abilities and competencies of persons with disabilities.[18]

In the recent 2017 presidential election, many politicians targeted African Americans, Latinos, immigrants, Muslims and even persons with disabilities using inflammatory rhetoric to arouse animosity and intolerance towards them. Similar to the war on crime, race was used as a tool in the purported war on terror with attendant negative consequences for minorities and their communities. As the immigrant population increases in the U.S., there has also been an attack on Affirmative action. Recently, the U.S. Department of Justice announced that it is planning to investigate and sue universities over affirmative action admission policies that are targeted at discriminating against white applicants. However, affirmative action is about opportunities and providing access to resources and a platform for those who are historically, and socioeconomically disadvantaged to have a better starting point for moving forward and having success. Persons of color and especially those with disabilities face more barriers which they have to overcome in order to attend higher education institutions, especially institutions of renown.

SUMMARY AND CONCLUSION

As the U.S. continues to increase in racial and cultural diversity, there is a need to understand the historical and contemporary significance of these constructs within the society and particularly on its institutions. However, as Omi and Winnat[34] pointed out, "racial discourse is now littered with confused and contradictory meanings."[p.245] More importantly, for professionals that are working with minorities, there is a need to clearly understand and articulate how racial and cultural factors intervene on the interactions between individuals, among different groups as well as between individuals from specific racial and cultural groups and the institutions within the U.S. society. Similarly, the culture of the U.S. is undergoing accelerating changes that continue to impact not only the U.S. society but also the rest of the world. The cultural diversity in the U.S. has contributed to a rich cultural heritage but has also threatened the survival of minority cultures which are increasingly subsumed or immersed into the dominant culture. Our focus however in this chapter has nonetheless been on how these constructs negatively position minority groups and lead to their continued marginalization within the U.S. society. This is especially the case for individuals with disabilities that we serve in health and human services agencies, especially those from underrepresented groups (e.g., people with disabilities, women, racial & ethnic groups of color).

People with disabilities from underrepresented groups experience multiple intersectional and discrimination that contributes to their continued marginalization. People with disabilities from underrepresented backgrounds are marginalized in terms of access to health and socioeconomic services or benefits. It is therefore important for professionals that work with these individuals to advocate on behalf of their clients for access to services. Professionals should also demonstrate the right attitudes and behaviors that reflect inclusion. This chapter only scratches the surface regarding the rich and diverse history of multicultural rehabilitation. It is, in many ways, only the reflections of the two authors, based on their own experiences.

What are the lessons of history and rehabilitation? Nothing happens without commitment and struggle for what one believes to be important. A place at the table for persons of color resulted in greater emphasis on the importance of values, family, religion, and other cultural attributes more often found in communities of color. This chapter focused on what has occurred, but we would be remiss not to think about what our legacy means for the future.

We need to always be "asset oriented"[5] and focus on the strengths that are brought to the table by so many diverse groups. Education and research must be inclusive of all, but in particular, those who have been so long ignored. Rehabilitation is not "nice" or even "interesting," but must be meaningful so that there is an improvement in the quality of life for all persons with disabilities. There will be a continuing need to dispel myths about not only disability, but also race and ethnicity.

Finally, there is a need to enlist partners who may have an interest in other issues of civil rights, race, and ethnicity to include disability as part of their agenda. Many organizations continue to leave out disability as part of the consideration of diversity. A major challenge for emerging leaders is not to abandon the struggle for equality. There is a tremendous need for all the talents of persons committed to ensuring that disability is embraced as a natural part of the human experience that includes people of color.

REFERENCES

[1] Aggleton, P., Wood, K., Malcolm, A., & Parker, R. (2005). HIV-related stigma, discrimination, and human rights violations: Case studies of successful Programmes. Switzerland: UNAIDS

[2] Alba, R. D., & Nee, V. (2009). *Remaking the American mainstream: Assimilation and contemporary immigration*. Harvard University Press.

[3] Arends Tóth, J., & Van de Vijver, F. J. (2003). Multiculturalism and acculturation: views of Dutch and Turkish–Dutch. *European Journal of*

[4] Asbury, C. A., Walker, S., Belgrave, F. Z., Maholmes, V. & Green, L. (1994). Psychosocial, cultural, and accessibility factors associated with participation of African Americans in rehabilitation. *Rehabilitation Psychology,* 39 (2), 113-121.

[5] Atkins, B. J. (1988). An asset-oriented approach to cross cultural issues: Blacks in rehabilitation. *Journal of Applied Rehabilitation counseling,* 19(4) 45-49.

[6] Atkins, B. J. (1995). Diversity: A continuing rehabilitation challenge and opportunity in Disability and diversity: New leadership for a new era. President's Committee on Employment of People with Disabilities. Washington, D.C.

[7] Atkins, B. J. & Wright, G.N. (1980). The vocational rehabilitation of blacks, *Journal of Rehabilitation, 42*(2), 40-46. [4] Atkinson, D. R. (2004). *Counseling American Minorities*. Boston: McGraw Hill.

[8] Atkinson, D. R. (2004). *Counseling American Minorities*. Boston: McGraw Hill

[9] Barak, G., Leighton, P., & Flavin, J. (2010). *Class, race, gender, and crime: The social realities of justice in America*. Rowman & Littlefield Publishers.

[10] Berry, J. W. (2010). Mobility and acculturation. In The psychology of global mobility (pp. 193-210). Springer New York.

[11] Berry, J. W. (2006). Mutual attitudes among immigrants and ethnocultural groups in Canada. *International Journal of Intercultural Relations, 30*(6), 719-734.

[12] Berry, T. R., & Candis, M. R. (2013). Cultural identity and education: A critical race perspective. *The Journal of Educational Foundations,* 27(3/4), 43.

[13] Bloemraad, I., Korteweg, A., & Yurdakul, G. (2008). Citizenship and immigration: Multiculturalism, assimilation, and challenges to the nation-state. *Annual Review and Sociology, 34*, 153-179.

[14] Bolton, B., & Cooper, P. G. (1980). Three views: Vocational rehabilitation of Blacks: The comment. *Journal of Rehabilitation, 46*(41) 41-49.

[15] Bowe, F. (1983). Demography and disability: A chartbook for rehabilitation. Fayetteville, AR: Arkansas Rehabilitation Research and Training Center, University of Arkansas.

[16]Bowe, F. (1985) Employment trends in the information age. *Rehabilitation counseling bulletin* 29(1): 19-25.

[17]Brown, S. (2002). What is disability culture? *Disability Studies Quarterly*, 22(2).

[18]Chan, F., McMahon, B. T., Cheing, G., Rosenthal, D. A., & Bezyak, J. (2005). Drivers of workplace discrimination against people with disabilities: The utility of attribution theory. *Work*, 25(1), 77-88.

[19]Clifford, J. (1989). The Predicament of Culture: Twentieth-Century Ethnography, Literature, and Art. Cambridge, Mass.: Harvard University Press.

[20]Collier, V. P., & Thomas, W. P. (1989). How quickly can immigrants become proficient in school English. *Journal of educational issues of language minority students*, 5(1), 26-38.

[21]Greene, H. T., & Gabbidon, S. L. (2011). Race and crime: a text/reader. Sage.

[22]Harris, C. T., Steffensmeier, D., Ulmer, J. T., & Painter-Davis, N. (2009). Are Blacks and Hispanics disproportionately incarcerated relative to their arrests? Racial and ethnic disproportionality between arrest and incarceration. *Race and social problems*, 1(4), 187.

[23]Holliday, A. (2010). Complexity in cultural identity. *Language and Intercultural Communication*, 10(2), 165-177.

[24]Huynh, Q.-L., Nguyen, A.-M., Benet-Martinez, V. (2011). Bicultural Identity Integration. In S. J. Schwartz, K. Luyckx, & V. L. Vignoles (Eds.), Handbook of Identity Theory and Research (pp. 827-842). New York, NY: Springer, New York.

[25] Jackson, M. L. (1995). Multicultural counseling: Historical perspectives. In J. G. Ponterotto, J. M Casas, L. A. Suzuki, & C. M. Alexander (Eds.), *Handbook of multicultural counseling* (pp. 3-16). Thousand Oaks, CA: Sage.

[26]Jones, E. E., Farina, A., Hastorf, A. H., Markus, H., Miller, D. T., & Scott, R. A. (1984). *Social stigma: The psychology of marked relationships*. New York: Freeman.

[27]Kolb, E. (2009). *The Evolution of New York City's Multiculturalism: Melting Pot or Salad Bowl*. BoD–Books on Demand.

[28]Kroeber A.L. and Kluckhohn, C. (1963). Culture : a critical review of concepts and definitions. New York : Vintage Books.

[29]Leal, A., Leung, P., Martin, W.E., & Harrison, O.K. (1988) (Eds.) *Multicultural Aspects of Rehabilitation Counseling, Journal of Applied Rehabilitation Counseling,* 19(4).

[30]Lu, X. (2001). Bicultural identity development and Chinese community formation: Anethnographic study of Chinese schools in Chicago. *Howard Journal of Communication*, 12(4), 203-220.

[31]McConnell, L. R., J. M. Keener, J. Farish (1995). National Association of Multicultural Rehabilitation Concerns - Special Anniversary Issue 1925-1995. *Journal of Rehabilitation* 61(3) 58-60.

[32]Marini, I., Glover-Graf, N. M., & Millington, M. J. (2011). *Psychosocial aspects of disability: Insider perspectives and strategies for counselors.* Springer Publishing Company.

[33]Merriam Webster, 2014 https://www.merriam-webster.com/words-at-play/2014-word-of-the-year/culture.

[34]Ng, E. S., & Bloemraad, I. (2015). A SWOT analysis of multiculturalism in Canada, Europe, Mauritius, and South Korea.

[35]Omi, M., & Winant, H. (2014). *Racial formation in the United States.* Routledge.

[36]Pager, D., & Shepherd, H. (2008). The sociology of discrimination: Racial discrimination in employment, housing, credit, and consumer markets. *Annual Review Sociology, 34,* 181-209.

[37]Perez, A. D., & Hirschman, C. (2009). The changing racial and ethnic composition of the US population: Emerging American identities. *Population and Development Review, 35*(1), 1-51.

[38]Peters, S. (2006). Disability culture. *Encyclopedia of disability,* 412-419.

[39]Ponterotto, J.G., Casas, J.M., Suzuki, L.A., Alexander, C.M. (Eds.) *Handbook of Multicultural Counseling,* Thousand Oaks, CA: Sage.

[40]Rubin, S. & Roessler R. (2008). *Foundations of the vocational rehabilitation process.* 6th ed. Austin, TX: Pro-Ed.

[41]Schwartz, S. J., Vignoles, V. L., Brown, R., & Zagefka, H. (2014). The identity dynamics of acculturation and multiculturalism: Situating acculturation in context. *The Oxford handbook of multicultural identity,* 57-93.

[42]Singer, M. A. (1998). Perception & Identity in Intercultural Communication. Nicholas Brealey Publishing.

[43]Stocking, G. W. (1968). Race, Culture, and Evolution. Essays in the Histor of Anthropology. George W. Stocking, Jr. London: Collier-Macmillan.

[44]Strathern, M. (1978). "The Limits of Auto-anthropology." In Anthropology at Home ed. A Jackson, 16-37. London: Tavistock.

[45]Tanner, K. (1997). Theories of Culture: A New Agenda for Theology. Fortress.

[46]Taylor, D. M., & Lambert, W. E. (1996). The meaning of multiculturalism in a culturally diverse urban American area. *The Journal of social psychology, 136*(6), 727-740.

[47]Tylor, R. B. (1871). Primitive culture: Researches into the development of mythology, philosophy, religion, are, and custom (Vol. 2). J. Murray

[48]Williams, R. (1976). Keywords: A Vocabulary of Culture and Society. 1976. London: Fontana/Croom Helm.

[49]Wilkerson, C. A., & Penn, L. A. (1938). The participation f Negroes in the federally-aided program of civilian vocational rehabilitation. *Journal of Negro Education, 7,* 319-3330.

[50]Wolcott, HF. (1999). Ethnography: A Way of Seeing. Walnut Creek, CA: Altamira Press.

Multicultural Issues in Rehabilitation and Allied Health

PUBLISHED BY
Aspen Professional Services
63 Duffers Drive
Linn Creek, MO 65052

Copyright 2021 by Aspen Professional Services
jandrew@socket.net
All rights reserved.

ISBN: 978-1-7332488-3-9

No part of this publication may be reproduced, stored in a retrieval system, or transmitted in any form or by any means, electronic, mechanical, photocopying, recording, or otherwise, without the prior permission of Aspen Professional Services.

The cover: Many fabrics represent the range of cultures in the global village we all live in. It is the hand of understanding we all lend, to help heal the global issues we face every day.
Cover design by Vincent E. Gardner.

To secure additional copies, contact

Aspen Professional Services
63 Duffers Drive
Linn Creek, MO 65052
jandrew@socket.net
573.286.0418
573.317.0907 (Cellular)
573.873.2116 (Fax)

iv

MULTICULTURAL ISSUES IN REHABILITATION AND ALLIED HEALTH

EDITED BY

WILLIAM B. TALLEY
University of Maryland Eastern Shore

VALERIE E. D. RUSSELL
Florida International University

CARL R. FLOWERS
Southern Illinois University Carbondale

Aspen Professional Services

[51] Wright, T. J., & Emener, W. G. (1989). Ethnic minorities with disabilities: An annotated bibliography of rehabilitation literature. Department of Rehabilitation Counseling, University of South Florida.

[52] Yuker, H. E. (1988). *Attitudes toward persons with disabilities.* Springer Publishing Co.

[53] Zawaiza, T., Walker, S., & Ball, S. (2002, May). *Diversity matters: Infusing issues of people with disabilities from underserved communities into a trans-disciplinary research agenda in the behavioral and social sciences.* Washington, DC: Howard University, Center for Disability and Socioeconomic Policy Studies.

CHAPTER 2

LEGISLATIVE ASPECTS OF REHABILITATION

KEISHA G. ROGERS
JENNIFER D. SHOFFNER

CHAPTER TOPICS

- ➤ The Depression and Pre-World War II Years: 1920-1939
- ➤ Accelerated Growth Era: 1940-1959
- ➤ The Legislative Era: 1960-1979
- ➤ The 1980s and 1990s
- ➤ The American with Disabilities Act and Beyond
- ➤ Summary and Conclusion

This chapter provides a historical overview of legislation in rehabilitation. The early legislation, designed to establish a foundation for rehabilitation, is summarized briefly, and the later legislative mandates are discussed in detail. Prevailing social attitudes and language describing people with disabilities are kept intact, so that the reader has an opportunity to comprehend the socio-political dynamics that moved the field of rehabilitation. The concept of multiculturalism and issues affecting rehabilitation outcomes of people with disabilities of diverse backgrounds are also discussed.

The legislation discussed in this chapter is the basis of both the process of vocational rehabilitation and the cornerstone of professionalism in the field. Legislation can only reflect the spirit of the legislators and their constituents at the time. Many of the acts cited in this chapter do not address issues related to persons of diverse backgrounds and nothing about the cultural context of the United States at the time the legislation was passed is mentioned. The legislation often accurately reflects the spirit of the time. Diversity was not a focus. Multiculturalism was not perceived to be an issue. Therefore, the legislation is barren of language from this perspective. However, that does not mean that there were not multicultural issues underlying the need for rehabilitation legislation during the legislative history. This chapter will look at some of the most critical pieces of legislation that relate to the field of vocational rehabilitation and some of the culturally relevant issues of the time.

The legislative history of vocational rehabilitation begins around 1916, focusing on World War I and the issues of veterans with disabilities who were returning to civilian life in the United States. This early period only occasionally highlights cultural issues, which reflects the country's lack of focus and even denial of diversity during that period. The sections of the chapter beginning in about 1992 to the present reflect a much more culturally rich, diversity-focused legislative period, reflective of the cultural changes taking place in the United States that also reflect the spirit of the times from a cultural perspective.

The National Defense Act of 1916 provided educational and vocational instruction for soldiers in active military service to increase their military efficiency and return to civil life with better occupational skills.

The Smith-Hughes Act of 1917 (Public Law 64-347) created the Federal Board for Vocational Education to administer federal monies on a matching basis to the states for vocational education programs. The Act provided for the physical restoration and vocational retraining of disabled veterans of World War I and dislocated industrial workers.

The Soldier's Rehabilitation Act of 1918 (Public Law 65-178, The Smith-Sears Act) expanded the Federal Board of Vocational Education to offer programs of vocational rehabilitation exclusively to disabled veterans. The disabled veteran had to be vocationally handicapped in a gainful occupation to qualify for services.

It is quite obvious that the early legislative focus was on veterans, and especially those whose contributions to our country's war efforts had caused them serious impairment. Job placement was the obvious goal, with soldiers given an alternative to being on welfare rolls after their war-related disability. Due to industrial and farm mechanization, many could not, with their disabilities, return to their former work.

Cost was an issue and return for the tax dollar has always been the goal. Bitter notes that between 108% and 133% of the tax dollars spent on vocational rehabilitation are returned to the United States coffers from the income taxes of the rehabilitants.[4] This was seen not as a welfare program but a jobs program. Obviously, no money can be returned to government without successful job placement.

THE DEPRESSION AND PRE-WORLD WAR II YEARS: 1920-1939

The Smith-Fess Act of 1920 (Public Law 66-236) established the First Civilian Vocational Rehabilitation Act that provided vocational rehabilitation services to those "physically disabled" due to industrial accidents, or other injuries not related to war injury. It established the state-federal program on a 50-50 matching basis to provide vocational guidance, vocational education, training, occupational adjustment, prostheses, and placement services. The act emphasized services for civilians with physical disabilities and was definitely vocational in nature. Other relevant legislation during this time period included the Social Security Act of 1935 (Public Law 74-271), the Randolph-Sheppard Act of 1936 (Public Law 74-732) that authorized the states to license qualified vending machine operators who were blind, in federal buildings, and the Wagner-O'Day Act of 1938 (Public Law 75-739), later amended by Public Law 92-28 of 1971, that mandated the federal government to purchase items produced in workshops by persons who are blind or visually impaired.[26]

The Great Depression of the 1930s had a severe impact on placement. Even the best placement counseling could not help procure jobs if there were none. Consequently, this was where learning job-seeking skills to sell oneself to the employer became most relevant. "Mr. Employer, you need me because..." helped keep many off the bread lines. Wilkerson and Penn[39] found that, in the years leading up to the World War, disabled African Americans received vocational rehabilitation significantly less than White Americans, although as a group, African Americans had a greater need.

ACCELERATED GROWTH ERA: 1940-1959

As a result of the GI Bill, established by the federal government after World War II to financially assist veterans in their educational endeavors, colleges and universities experienced an increase in enrollment. Retraining and skill development were crucial in this period's unstable job market. In addition to training, the transition from wartime production to peacetime growth increased demand on the educational system. A liberal arts education was now deemed important. An individual needed to possess a basic education to become a "well-rounded" individual. It was believed that this preparation would best serve a peacetime economy. The transition toward long-range goals and individual planning now became reality.

Veterans Administration (VA) physicians made assessments of Black ex-GI's based on racialized concepts of normality, i.e. by assuming that a disability was merely typical of a "normal" African American. In 1948, for example, chief medical officers told black veterans at a VA hospital in Virginia, "there is nothing wrong with your nose, that's your natural look; nature made all Negroes to look that way."[17, p.1104-1105]

Officials at VA hospitals and rehabilitation centers in states such as Mississippi, South Carolina, Georgia, Virginia, Missouri, and Alabama enforced racial segregation and often provided blacks with less than adequate health care, personal adjustment counseling, and physical rehabilitation.[17] African American veterans often found themselves barred from access to the special vocational compensation and rehabilitation allotted to them under Public Law 16 and the GI Bill of Rights.[17] In addition to the persistence of the racism against which they fought, activist black veterans were hampered by the advent of the Cold War and subsequent anticommunist hysteria that forced the protest politics developed by wounded black World War II servicemen, underground.[17]

J. C. Lee wrote to NAACP Executive Secretary Walter White, "Is this the Democracy that I've spent nearly three years defending in the Pacific? I am a disabled veteran, but the deplorable conditions that exist here in this country makes me wonder if I'm going to survive as a Negro."[23] White physician Harold Blackwell commented to NAACP Secretary of Veterans Affairs in 1945 about black disabled veterans "The time that Negro disabled GIs spent in the service does not qualify them for royalties from this man's Army. The only legitimate patients in this hospital are free, white and twenty- one."[23]

The Vocational Rehabilitation Act Amendments of 1943 (Public Law 78-113, Barden-LaFollette Act) superseded the original 1920 Act and brought many significant changes. The new law deleted the word "physical" from the earlier definition and, for the first time, made eligible persons with mental retardation and mental illness. In addition, for the first time, separate state agencies for persons who are blind and visually impaired were established. The concept of rehabilitation was widened by broadening the scope of services to include any services necessary for persons with disabilities to engage in remunerative occupations. These services include medical, surgical, and physical restoration; hospitalization; corrective surgery or therapeutic treatment; prosthetic devices to obtain or retain employment; transportation;

occupational licenses; occupational tools and equipment; maintenance; and books and training materials.[24,26]

The Vocational Rehabilitation Act Amendments of 1954 (Public Law 83-565, Hill-Burton Act) provided training grants to colleges and universities to develop master's degree programs for rehabilitation counselors; in-service grants for staff development of state vocational rehabilitation agencies; and short-term grants for seminars, workshops, specialized institutes, and rehabilitation research fellowships. It expanded resources for restoring persons with disabilities to productive employment. Funds were available to expand community based rehabilitation facilities and workshops as opposed to traditional institutional settings; for research and demonstration grants to state rehabilitation agencies, rehabilitation facilities, universities, and institutions to harness new knowledge for better rehabilitation and information dissemination throughout the country. The act also strengthened the provisions of the Randolph-Sheppard Act with Vending Stand Programs for persons who are blind or visually impaired; expanded services for persons who are mentally ill; provided greater financial support to the states, and established a working relationship between public (state-federal) and private (rehabilitation facilities) agencies for rehabilitation to attain goals for persons with disabilities.[26]

THE LEGISLATIVE ERA: 1960-1979

The 1960s through the 1970s were a time of great social consciousness in the United States. The Great Society of Lyndon B. Johnson and a tremendous amount of social legislation, from civil rights and women's rights issues to environmental concerns, were approved by Congress.

As the United States became more socially conscious during this period, the legislative activity and the acts began to include themes addressing culturally relevant issues. This was particularly true following the assassination of Dr. Martin Luther King in 1968. Rehabilitation legislation finally began to include language about social disadvantages and eventually became honest and bold enough to enumerate the needs of specific populations that had been largely ignored.

The Vocational Rehabilitation Act Amendments of 1965 (Public Law 89-333) eliminated economic need as a prerequisite for vocational rehabilitation services. Services were expanded to include the socially disadvantaged and behavior disorders such as juvenile offenders, adult public offenders, alcoholics, and drug abusers. Six-month evaluation and 18-month extended evaluation services to determine employment potential were established for persons with mental retardation and severe disability. Reader services for the blind and visually impaired and interpreter services for the deaf and hard of hearing were provided. Funds were provided to construct new centers, workshops, and residential accommodations for the mentally retarded; improve existing workshops and facilities to provide better job training, state-wide planning, and project development; and expand working relationships between public and voluntary agencies for vocational rehabilitation services and return to gainful employment for handicapped citizens. Professional training assistance in vocational rehabilitation was extended from two to four years. Finally, the Act created the National Commission on Architectural Barriers to enhance employment opportunities.[24]

Other legislation during this period included the Social Security Amendments of 1965 (of the original Social Security Act of 1935) that targeted state vocational rehabilitation (VR) agencies to assure that insurance beneficiaries who are disabled receive vocational rehabilitation services. The Vocational Rehabilitation Act Amendments of 1968 (Public Law 90-391) broadened eligibility criteria to include persons who are "socially disadvantaged" due to environmental deprivation and provided for vocational evaluation and work adjustment programs.

The Rehabilitation Act of 1973 (Public Law 93-112), which was a major overhaul of the original Vocational Rehabilitation Act of 1920 and its subsequent amendments, emphasized priority services to persons with severe disabilities, client's rights, the individualized written rehabilitation program (IWRP), annual reviews, accountability, post-employment services, the promotion of consumer involvement, and support for research and the advancement of civil rights for person with disabilities.[30]

One of the landmark accomplishments of the 1973 Rehabilitation Act were the title V provisions to advance the *civil rights* of persons with disabilities. Persons with severe disabilities had been barred from *mainstreaming* into society mainly due to discrimination, and inaccessible housing and work sites. Sections 501, 502, 503, and 504 of the title enforced affirmative action, non-discrimination in employment, and accessibility in place of residence and work.

SECTION 501: *Non-discrimination in hiring practices in the Federal government*. It requires each Federal department and agency in the executive branch to submit an Affirmative Action Program plan to the U.S. Civil Service Commission for the hiring, placement, and advancement of workers with disabilities in Federal employment. Such public agency plans should act as a model for other private agencies, businesses, and industries to emulate. An Interagency Committee on Handicapped Employees was established to oversee the effective implementation of affirmative action plans, make reviews and updates annually, and provide sufficient assurances and commitment to the intent of section 501. The committee included the chairman of the Civil Service Commission, the Administrator of Veterans' Affairs, the Secretary of Labor, and the Secretary of Health, Education, and Welfare (now, the Department of Health and Human Resources and the Department of Education).

SECTION 502: Accessibility established the Architectural and Transportation Barriers Compliance Board (ATBCB) that modified the provisions of the Architectural Barriers Act of 1968 (Public Law 90-480), and its subsequent amendment of 1970 (Public Law 91-205). The major functions of the Board were to investigate alternative approaches to the architectural, transportation, and attitudinal barriers confronting the handicapped; determine measures to be taken by federal, state, and local governments and other public or non-profit agencies to eliminate transportation barriers or subsidize travel expenses for those unable to use mass transit to work; and determine the housing needs, availability, and accessibility to handicapped individuals. The Board was empowered to hold public hearings and conduct investigations of those not in compliance with the provisions of the Act, and to report the results and make administrative and legislative recommendations to Congress and to the President to eliminate barriers (Public Law 93-112, p. 36-37).

SECTION 503: Affirmative Action requires any contractor or subcontractor for a federal department or agency receiving in excess of $2,500 to take affirmative action to employ and advance the employment of qualified handicapped individuals. In addition, any contractor or subcontractor for the federal government receiving in excess of $50,000 or employing 50 or more people must develop a written affirmative action plan and submit it to the Employment Standards Administration of the Department of Labor. "Affirmative action under this program requires that qualified handicapped individuals be actively recruited, considered, and employed, and that all qualified handicapped employees not be discriminated against for promotions, training, transfers, and other job opportunities."[34p. 243-244]

Persons with disabilities may not be discriminated against in employment on the basis of physical or mental handicaps and may file complaints with the Department of Labor concerning contractors or subcontractors failing or refusing to comply with the provisions of their contracts.

SECTION 504: Nondiscrimination in programs or institutions receiving federal grants prohibits discrimination on the basis of physical or mental handicap, against otherwise qualified persons with disabilities, from participation in programs or institutions receiving federal financial assistance. Not only employers, but also educational and social services programs (such as vocational schools, training centers, rehabilitation facilities, work-study centers, work-activity centers, day care centers, hospitals, nursing homes, housing programs, transportation programs, school districts, and colleges and universities that receive grants or financial assistance from the federal government are expected to make "reasonable accommodation." Examples of such accommodations are, but are not limited to, the provision of reader services, Braille reading materials, talking books, talking calculators for the blind; large print material for the partially sighted; interpreter services for the deaf and hearing impaired; alternative test-taking procedures for persons with specific learning disabilities; accessibility to buildings, classrooms, and restrooms; designated parking facilities close to buildings; prevention of architectural barriers in new building construction and renovation of inaccessible buildings and facilities.

Employers' hiring criteria should be based on the actual skills required to perform the job, and refrain from artificial or superfluous requirements unrelated to job performance, designed to discriminate against persons with disabilities. Pre-employment tests unrelated to job tasks are forbidden. The implementation of alternative testing procedures is required for persons with specific learning disabilities, dyslexia, visual impairment, or other conditions that interfere with reading, writing, and taking tests. Physical and medical examinations will be allowed only if they are related to job performance and are required of other non-disabled individuals. Employers are required to make reasonable accommodations to create a receptive work environment by modifying work schedules; revising job descriptions; restructuring jobs; modifying equipment, devices, and the environment; and removing attitudinal barriers. Employers must make reasonable accommodations for employees with physical or mental limitations, unless employers demonstrate that making such accommodations would cause "undue hardship" in conducting the business. In cases where employment is denied due to disability and the employer failed to make reasonable accommodations, affected persons can file complaints with the nearest office of the employment Standards Administration of the Department of Labor.[11]

In summary, Sections 501 through 504 provided civil rights and employment rights for people who have disabilities. The major thrusts of these provisions are integration, mainstreaming, and holistic participation at all levels in society. These sections of the Rehabilitation Act of 1973 provide four major tools for rehabilitation counselors and placement specialists to use in enhancing client employment potential and the education of persons with respect to their civil rights.

A major amendment to the Rehabilitation Act of 1973 was the Rehabilitation Comprehensive Services and Developmental Disabilities Amendments of 1978 (Public Law 95-602) that strengthened the existing provisions and expanded new services for persons with severe disabilities.[28] Section 130 of Title I and Part D of the act extended vocational rehabilitation services to include members of American Indian tribes who are disabled and residing on or around reservations and trust lands. It authorized the Rehabilitation Services Administration (RSA) to offer competitive grants to the governing bodies of federal and state recognized American Indian tribes for the establishment of vocational rehabilitation programs. These programs were designed to act as a supplement to the state-federal vocational rehabilitation agencies so that American Indian consumers can receive culturally appropriate services (e.g., ceremonial healing) on the reservation. The Navajo Vocational Rehabilitation Program was the first one to be funded.[16]

The act also established the National Institute of Handicapped Research (formerly, the National Institute on Disability and Rehabilitation Research and currently National Institute on Disability, Independent Living, and Rehabilitation Research) to promote and coordinate research activities that enhance the quality of life for persons with disabilities. It established an

Integrating Committee on Handicapped Research to avoid duplications and promote coordination and cooperation in Federal departments and agencies conducting rehabilitation research and established the National Council on the Handicapped (now, National Council on Disability) to increase consumer involvement in the rehabilitation movement. Consumer involvement was further strengthened by reconstituting and expanding the Architectural and Transportation Barriers Act.

Persons with disabilities have received attention from the federal government in over 200 pieces of legislation. Past legislation, however, tended to be of intent only and provided for minimal services, often in highly segregated settings. The 1970s, however, saw renewed attention focused on the rights of adults and children with disabilities. The principle that all persons, even if unequal in abilities, should be granted equal opportunities found implementation in another important piece of legislation, the Education for All Handicapped Children Act of 1975 (renamed Individuals with Disabilities Education Act in Public Law 94-142). This act, together with the Rehabilitation Act of 1973, provided the mechanism to assure that children and adults with disabilities are given a chance to be integrated into American society in the least restrictive manner possible. The right to a free and appropriate public education was mandated by this act.[18]

In 1979, for effective management, the Carter administration reorganized the U. S. Department of Health, Education, and Welfare (DHEW) into the Department of Health and Human Resources (DHHR) and the Department of Education (DOE). An Office of Special Education and Rehabilitative Services (OSERS) was created under the U. S. Department of Education. The Rehabilitation Services Administration (RSA) administers the Rehabilitation Acts, and the Office of Special Education Programs (OSEP) administers grants for special services and education for children with disability. Both agencies are now administered by an Assistant Secretary of OSERS, resulting in programs for persons with disabilities becoming more intricately linked.

THE 1980S AND BEYOND

The 1980s began with inflation and recession. While the fully functional worker had more than enough to do to keep up with double-digit inflation and was lucky to keep a job in those times of recession, the person with a disability was at a tremendous disadvantage when trying to work and make a decent living. Many rehabilitation professionals were concerned about the political conservatism that swept the United States, beginning with California's "Proposition 13," through the presidencies of Ronald Reagan and George H. W. Bush. At this time, researchers found disability to be more common in African American adults than it is among Caucasians and Hispanics; African Americans must confront discrimination on the basis of race as well as disability; and African American adults with work disabilities are much less likely to be employed as professional or managerial workers than are other individuals with disabilities.[6,35]

The Rehabilitation Amendments of 1984 (Public Law 98-221) reauthorized the earlier provisions through 1986, reemphasizing the activities of the National Institute of Handicapped Research (NIHR) and the National Council on the Handicapped (NCOH). The NIHR was authorized to establish a program of pediatric rehabilitation research; a research and training center in the Pacific Basin; and demonstration projects for persons with spinal cord injuries. NIHR was also authorized to conduct projects to provide job training, on-the-job training, job search assistance, job development, work site modification using the latest technology, and follow-up services for youth having disabilities entering the labor force.

The National Council on the Handicapped became an independent agency, and no longer an agency of the Department of Education. The Council was given added responsibility to promote full integration of individuals with disabilities in all walks of life and to study the process of eliminating disincentives in federal programs and increasing incentives, thus allowing persons with disabilities to become more productive members of society.

The 1984 amendment assured that consumers with disabilities would receive rehabilitation services from qualified rehabilitation professionals. The National Council on Rehabilitation Education defines the qualified rehabilitation professional as an individual who has received an academic degree from an accredited education program accepted by the rehabilitation profession as denoting professional status; is certified and/or licensed to practice in accordance with the rehabilitation profession's national certification board or commission and/or the state's licensing board; maintains her or his certification and/or licensure by completing continuing education units approved by the certification/licensure boards for renewal of certification/licensure; and has completed the amount of time on the job specified by the profession as denoting achievement of journeyman status.[15p.5-6]

The Rehabilitation Act Amendments of 1986 (Public Law 99-506) extended and improved the Rehabilitation Act of 1973 and authorized appropriations for 1986-1991. The amendment used gender-neutral terminology, changing the language to convey a positive attitude and the functional aspects of disability. For example, the phrase "handicapped individual" was replaced with "individual with handicaps," and "a handicapped individual" with "an individual with handicaps." The "National Institute of Handicapped Research" became the **National Institute on Disability and Rehabilitation Research** (NIDRR) and has since been renamed **National Institute on Disability, Independent Living, and Rehabilitation Research (NIDILRR)**. In 1988, the "National Council on the Handicapped" was renamed The **National Council on Disability** (NCD), and the "President's Committee on the Employment of the Handicapped" became the **President's Committee on the Employment of People with Disabilities** (PCPED). It is imperative that words reflect positive attitudes, convey functional aspects of the person, and create an image of ability and independence, which helps placement counselors facilitate placement of their clients.

The purpose statement of the National Council on Disability was amended to include "promot[ing] the full integration, independence, and productivity of handicapped individuals in the community, schools, the work place and all other aspects of American life."[p.1828] The duties of the Council were expanded to include review and evaluation of all statutes pertaining to Federal programs that assist individuals with disabilities and to assess the extent to which these policies, programs, and activities provide incentives or disincentives to the establishment of community-based services for individuals with disabilities promoting integration and independence in the community, in schools, and in the work place.

New provisions were added in the development of IWRP to include statements of determination of employability; long-range rehabilitation goals and intermediate objectives, based on an evaluation of rehabilitation potential; rehabilitation engineering services, when appropriate, to achieve rehabilitation goals and objectives; an evaluation procedure and schedule to determine whether such goals and objectives are met; an assessment of the need for post-employment services prior to case closure; annual review and revision as needed; and description of the availability of Client Assistance Programs.

The same Act added a number of responsibilities to NIDRR including disseminating information to Indian tribes and conducting studies of the rehabilitation needs of Indians. Other responsibilities included establishing a center for research and training concerning the delivery of rehabilitation services to rural areas; reporting to Congress on the development and distribution of cost-effective technological devices for persons with disabilities; studying health insurance practices and policies affecting persons with disabilities; authorizing grants for studies and analyses related to supported employment; demonstrating and disseminating innovative models for the delivery of cost-effective rehabilitation engineering services to assist in meeting the employment and independent living needs of individuals with severe handicaps in rural and urban areas; establishing two rehabilitation engineering centers, one in Connecticut and one in South Carolina, to demonstrate and disseminate innovative models to assist in meeting the needs of, and addressing the barriers confronted by, individuals with handicaps; and conducting research relating to children with disabilities and individuals 60 and over (55 for Indians) with disabilities.

NIDILRR became a part of the Administration for Community Living (ACL) under the Workforce Innovation and Opportunity Act of 2015.[1] This move broadens NIDILRR's focus on the major outcome domains of health and function, employment, and community living and participation. The impact of the products developed by NIDILRR's grantees are tracked and evaluated based on the capacity building and knowledge translation produced.

SERVICES FOR INDEPENDENT LIVING

The Rehabilitation Act Amendments of 1986 require each state to establish an Independent Living Council to provide guidance in developing and expanding independent living programs, including recreational services on a statewide basis through state agencies and local entities.[19] Members of the Council are appointed by the state agency director and include representatives of state and local agencies, groups, persons with disabilities, parents, and guardians of individuals with disabilities, directors of independent living centers, private businesses, and other appropriate individuals or organizations. The majority of each Council membership tends to be individuals with disabilities, including parents and guardians of persons with disabilities. Recreational services were added to the list of possible services that may be provided by the Centers for Independent Living.[19]

In summary, the changes in the Rehabilitation Act Amendments of 1986 have had significant impact on the delivery of services and outcomes in the rehabilitation of persons with severe handicaps. Previously, the functional aspects of severe handicapping conditions had been overemphasized in language and in the provision of services made for supported employment. Transitional employment and part-time employment are now considered viable outcomes of rehabilitation services.

THE AMERICANS WITH DISABILITIES ACT

The landmark legislation, the Americans With Disabilities Act (ADA), Public Law 101-336 signed by President George H. W. Bush on July 26, 1990, ushered in "another Independence Day" and "a bright new era of equality, independence, and freedom" for 43 million Americans with disabilities. The ADA is patterned after Section 504 of the 1973 Rehabilitation Act and the Civil Rights Act of 1964. The ADA is one of the most comprehensive civil rights laws ever enacted and has made sweeping changes in every sphere of life for persons both with and without disabilities.

The Act may be viewed as central to achieving equity and equal opportunity for African Americans with disabilities.[2] The five major provisions in the ADA prohibit discrimination against people with disabilities in Employment, Public Service and Transportation, Public Accommodations, Telecommunication Relay Services for the Deaf, and Activities of State and Local Governments.

TITLE I: EMPLOYMENT

Prohibits discrimination in hiring, employing, promoting, and training qualified workers with disabilities and requires reasonable accommodation, if it does not result in undue hardship to employers. The following terms in the statement require further explanations:

Qualified. An individual with a disability who, with or without reasonable accommodation, can perform the essential functions of the job held or sought. Consideration is given to the employer's judgment about which functions of a job are essential. The employer's written job description prior to advertising and recruiting applicants is considered evidence of the essential functions of the job.

Medical examination and inquiries. Pre-employment medical examinations can be required if they apply to all entering new employees to determine the ability to perform job-related functions, and only after an offer of employment has been made to the applicant. The employer should not conduct a medical examination or make inquiries about the type, nature, or severity of disability until after the offer of employment. Results of the medical examinations and disability information must be kept confidential and in separate medical files.

Reasonable accommodation. May include making existing facilities readily accessible; job restructuring; modifying work schedules; reassignment to a vacant position; acquiring or modifying equipment or devices; adjusting or modifying examinations, training materials, or policies; providing readers for persons who are visually impaired or interpreters for persons who are hearing impaired.

Undue hardship. Significant difficulty or expense to the employer in making reasonable accommodation. The following factors are considered in determining undue hardship to employers: the nature and cost of accommodation; the overall size, type, and financial resources of the facility; the overall size of the business, in terms of number of employees and number of facilities; and the employer's type of operation, including composition, structure, and function of its workforce, and geographic separations.

Employers are not obligated to hire employees who pose a direct threat to the health or safety of other individuals in the workplace. Drug testing is permitted and will not be considered a medical examination. The law does not protect current illegal drug users and alcoholics who cannot safely perform their job functions. Protection is provided to those who are, or have been, participating in a supervised rehabilitation program. People who are HIV-positive, have AIDS, or have other infectious and communicable diseases are protected. However, employers may transfer or reassign employees from food-handling jobs if the danger to possible health and safety cannot be eliminated by reasonable accommodation.[14] In 1991, the Secretary of Health and Human Services published a list of infectious diseases that are transmitted through handling foods.

TITLE II: PUBLIC SERVICES AND PUBLIC TRANSPORTATION

Prohibits discrimination from participation in services, programs, or activities of any public entity. The majority of the provisions of this title emphasize public transportation systems available to the general public, such as bus, train, taxi, and limousine. This excludes air travel, which is covered by the Air Carriers Act. New buses, rail cars, or other passenger-transporting vehicles purchased or leased by public entities, as well as remanufactured public transport vehicles, must be accessible and useable by people with disabilities, including wheelchair users. A public entity operating a fixed route system must provide para-transit or other special transportation services to individuals with disabilities that are comparable in service level and response time, without imposing an undue financial burden. Existing rail systems must have one accessible car per train. For wheelchair users, there must be space to park and secure wheelchair, transfer to seat, and fold wheelchair. Existing "key stations," and alterations to them, must be accessible. New bus and rail stations in intercity rail and commuter rail systems must be made accessible within two years of the date of enactment. Two-thirds of the key stations must be made accessible within 20 years. If expensive structural changes are required, then extension may be granted up to 30 years. Individuals may file complaints about violations with the Department of Transportation and bring private lawsuits.[25,36]

TITLE III: PUBLIC ACCOMMODATIONS AND SERVICES OPERATED BY PRIVATE ENTITIES

The major focus of this title is mainstreaming, integration, and fuller participation in all walks of life in the society. The title prohibits discrimination on the basis of disability in the full and equal enjoyment of the goods, services, facilities, privileges, advantages, or accommodations of any place of public accommodation and services operated by private entities. Goods, services, facilities, and privileges must be provided in the most integrated settings appropriate to the needs of the individual. Private clubs and religious organizations are exempted, however. Private entities providing transportation services (bus, rail, or any other conveyance excluded) must be accessible so that people with disabilities receive services equivalent to people without disabilities. All new vehicles purchased or leased must be accessible in fixed route system if they carry more than 16 passengers including the driver. Operators of public accommodation may not impose application of eligibility criteria that screen out, or tend to screen out, individuals with disabilities from full and equal enjoyment of goods, services, facilities, privileges, advantages, or accommodations. Auxiliary aids, such as readers, interpreters, taped texts, or similar services, must be provided to individuals who are vision or hearing impaired. Other individuals with disabilities must be given an equal opportunity to participate or benefit as do the non-disabled, unless such would result in an undue burden. All new construction and alterations in public accommodations and commercial facilities must be accessible. It is discriminatory to fail to remove architectural and communication barriers in existing facilities, or transportation barriers in existing vehicles and rail passenger cars, if the modification is readily achievable.

TITLE IV: TELECOMMUNICATIONS

This title amended Title II of the Communications Act of 1934 and added requirements that telephone companies must provide telecommunication relay services for hearing impaired and speech impaired individuals who use TDD (Telecommunication Device for the Deaf) or other non-voice terminal devices. Both interstate and intrastate telecommunication relay services must be available 24 hours and charges should not be greater than the charges paid for functionally equivalent voice communication services with regard to the day, time, duration, place, and distance called. The law prohibits the relay operators from keeping records and/or disclosing relayed conversations, altering, refusing, or limiting the length of calls. The title also requires that television public service announcements produced or funded by federal agencies be closed-captioned.

TITLE V: MISCELLANEOUS PROVISIONS

This title explains the relationship to other laws; prohibits state immunity; deals with insurance coverage; delineates implementation procedures and enforcement authorities; and provides congressional inclusion and dispute resolution. The ADA does not minimize the standard of the Rehabilitation Act of 1973 and its subsequent amendments or invalidate any state or local laws in providing equal protection to persons with disabilities. States are not immune from violation of this Act and are subjected to the same remedies as are available to any public or private entity. Insurers may not refuse, continue to underwrite, classify, and administer risks consistent with state laws. Retaliation is prohibited against an individual who has made a charge, testified, assisted, or participated in an investigation, proceeding or hearing under this Act. Interference, coercion, or intimidation against an individual's exercising his/her rights, or encouraging others to exercise his/her rights, is also prohibited. According to the ADA, homosexuality and bisexuality are not impairments, hence not disabilities. The definition of disability does not include transvestism, transsexualism, pedophilia, exhibitionism, voyeurism, gender identity disorders not resulting from physical impairments, or other sexual behavior disorders; compulsive gambling, kleptomania, or pyromania; or psychoactive substance use disorders resulting from current illegal use of drugs. The Senate, the House of Representatives, and the agencies of the legislative branch are prohibited from discrimination in hiring, discharging, promotion, compensation, or privileges of employment on the basis of age, color, race, national origin, sex, religion, or physical handicap. The ADA encourages voluntary/alternative means of dispute resolution, including settlement negotiations, conciliations, facilitation, mediation, fact finding, mini trials, and arbitration.

THE INDIVIDUALS WITH DISABILITIES EDUCATION ACT (IDEA)

Public Law (101-46) reauthorized and renamed the Education for All Handicapped Children Act of 1975 (previously discussed). Although revisions were made in both 1990 and 1991, the first significant changes to IDEA since its inception in 1975 occurred in 1997. Not only was IDEA reauthorized in 1997, but also changes were enacted to strengthen the bill. Parental involvement in eligibility and placement decisions and inclusion of children with disabilities into the general classroom and curriculum, which is to be emphasized in the IEP, were increased; local and state assessments were insured; transition planning for teenagers, starting at the age of 14, became a focus; the use of mediation over litigation for disputes between parents and educators was emphasized; and safety and learning environment conditions were emphasized.

IDEA was reauthorized in 2004 (Public Law 108-446). Under these most recent revisions, IDEA has been closely aligned with the No Child Left Behind Act (NCLB) and now includes new standards to ensure accountability and equity in education. The act addresses the need for clearly defined measurable goals for the IEP, and for progress reports on these goals to be made quarterly to parents; a greater need to focus on establishing educational practices that are based on peer-reviewed research; the manner in which learning disabilities are to be defined, releasing schools from earlier provisions in which the child must demonstrate a significant difference between intellectual ability and achievement in order for a learning disability to be diagnosed; parental rights to initiate requests for evaluation. It strengthened previous provisions that precluded educators from classifying a child as disabled if it was determined that the child's educational difficulties were a result of inappropriate instruction as identified in the NCLB act.

In addition to these changes, one of the most significant revisions to the 2004 IDEA, in terms of minorities, concerned the overrepresentation of minority students in special education classes. By the 2004 revisions, it had become clear that, in some cases, students were being inappropriately assigned to special education classes largely based upon racial or ethnic criteria.[5] Congress mandated that states and schools take positive action to ensure that this practice is eliminated. States are now required to develop specific policies that address this issue and collect and report data on the presence of minority students in special education classes. This revision went so far as to potentially require educators to use early intervention funds to address the overrepresentation of minorities.

Technology-Related Assistance for Individuals with Disabilities Act Amendments (Tech Act: Public Law 103-218) updated the 1988 Tech Act (Public Law 100-407), authorized the National Institute on Disability and Rehabilitation Research (NIDRR), currently renamed National Institute on

Disability, Independent Living, and Rehabilitation Research (NIDILRR), to fund initiatives in each of the 50 states and U.S. territories that would result in the delivery of assistive technology (AT) services and devices to individuals with disabilities. Toward this end, states and territories are provided federal grants to develop programs such as equipment loan libraries and information resources necessary to meet any of the primary goals of the Tech Act.[10] These goals include providing greater access to AT by individuals with disabilities, addressing AT funding, increasing consumer involvement, coordinating activities among the various state agencies, overcoming barriers for timely delivery of services, increasing advocacy for AT services and programs, and reaching out to underrepresented individuals.

In line with this last goal, the 1994 revisions of the Tech Act specifically address the funding and recruitment of minority service providers and institutions. Grant and contract agencies or organizations must now demonstrate that they have a specific strategy to recruit and train individuals with disabilities and/or minority group members who will then provide technology-related assistance. A portion of the grants provided under the Tech Act are reserved for historically Black colleges and other universities whose minority student enrollment is at least 50%. As a criterion for receiving federal grants, state "lead" agencies must demonstrate an ability to implement "effective strategies for capacity building, staff and consumer training, and enhancement of access to funding for assistive technology devices and assistive technology services across agencies" (Public Law 103-218, section 102).

The Rehabilitation Act Amendments of 1992 (Public Law 102-569) updated and revised the previous Rehabilitation Act of 1973 and made significant changes to the manner in which rehabilitative services are provided.[5] The impetus for such changes directly developed out of the ADA of 1990 and focused on providing a vehicle for helping individuals with disabilities gain more choice and assistance in finding and maintaining meaningful employment and full integration into the workforce and community.

In line with the ADA, the Rehabilitation Act Amendments of 1992 clearly articulate that disability is a "natural part of the human experience" and should in no way diminish the rights of disabled individuals in any aspect of their life.[5] Furthermore, the 1992 amendments highlighted the changing perception of disabilities, from that of un-abled to one of presumed ability. In other words, the bill is predicated on the idea that irrespective of the severity of disability, individuals can achieve meaningful employment and integration, provided the appropriate services and supports are supplied.

The overriding effect of such a change essentially switched the burden of proof from the individual to the rehabilitative system, so that in order to deny services, vocational rehabilitation services had to convincingly demonstrate that an individual is incapable of gaining any benefit from vocational services. In addition, the amendments placed considerable focus on rehabilitative technology and disability representation in the vocational rehabilitative process.

REHABILITATION CAPACITY BUILDING

In recognition of the disproportionate distribution of disabilities, pattern of inequitable treatment, and quality of vocational rehabilitation outcomes of culturally diverse groups reported by contemporary research,[3,9,32] Section 21 of the 1992 Amendments was promulgated as one of the most powerful pieces of legislation of the 1990s. This legislation represented the first concerted effort to address *the concept of cultural diversity in rehabilitation.* It set aside 1% of all the funds appropriated for programs authorized under titles II, III, VI, and VII, to conduct minority outreach programs and capacity enhancement. Section 21 provided several modalities for addressing the above exigency:

- ➤ funds were provided to minority entities and American Indian tribes for the conduct of research, training, technical assistance, or related activities geared to improve services to minorities,
- ➤ state-federal vocational rehabilitation must focus on recruiting professionals from diverse backgrounds,
- ➤ the Rehabilitation Services Administration (RSA) must provide scholarships to prepare students in vocational rehabilitation and related service careers at the bachelor's, master's, and doctoral levels at minority institutions of higher education, i.e., Historically Black Colleges and Universities (HBCUs), Hispanic Serving Institutions (HSIs), Tribal Colleges and Universities (TCUs), and other institutions with at least 50% minority enrollment, and
- ➤ the Commissioner of RSA shall develop a plan to provide capacity building and outreach services in order to increase the participation of minority entities in competition for grants, contracts, and cooperative agreements.

Section 21 paved the way for the preparation of qualified rehabilitation counselors of culturally diverse backgrounds, and the enhanced provision of quality services to minorities leading to long-term employment outcomes. As a direct result, the number of bachelor's and master's level programs in minority institutions increased from a mere 9 in the early 1990s to about 30 in 2006.[20,21] Despite significant improvements in the participation of culturally diverse groups in vocational rehabilitation, a study of 4,710 state-federal professionals found that 70% were Caucasians, 16% have documented disabilities, about 34% had degrees in rehabilitation, and only 10% were Certified Rehabilitation Counselors (CRCs).[21] It is imperative, therefore, that continued and intensive federal efforts are provided for introducing minorities in the mainstream of vocational rehabilitation.

National Institute on Disability, Independent Living, and Rehabilitation Research (NIDILRR), formerly known as The National Institute on Disability and Rehabilitation Research (NIDRR), has taken steps to implement multidimensional aspects of capacity building philosophy in incorporating its Long Range Plans (1999-2004 and 2005-2009) at individual and systems or organizational levels. The scope of its capacity building activities has been expanded to:

- provide advanced training in disability research (both qualitative and quantitative methodologies) for scientists, those with disabilities, and minorities;
- train at the pre-service, graduate, and in-service levels in application of research findings to improve the quality of lives for people with disabilities;
- develop capacity of researchers to conduct investigations focusing on the new paradigm as a contextual phenomenon, i.e., disability should be viewed as a function of the interaction between impairments and other personal characteristics and the larger physical, social, and policy environments;
- train the researchers to conduct holistic and interdisciplinary studies on cultural context of disability;
- develop capacity of the researchers to conduct studies at homes, work places, schools, recreational facilities, and community support programs;
- train consumers and family members to be involved in the Participatory Research and become advocate for review, evaluation, interpretation, and dissemination of research findings; and
- strengthen research portfolio by increasing the partnerships with federal and non-federal research and development agencies. The above objectives are being implemented through Rehabilitation Research and Training Centers (RRTCs), Advanced Rehabilitation Research Training Centers (ARRTCs), Mary Switzer Fellowships, New Scholars Program, Minority Enhancement Programs, and Disability Rehabilitation Research Projects (DRRPs).[12,13]

The School to Work Opportunities Act of 1994 (STWOA: Public Law 103-329) was created to assist students in making the transition from school to the workforce. In essence, the goal of STWOA is to increase education and career opportunities by promoting business and education collaboration. Federal venture capital grants are provided to state and local agencies to help restructure educational systems, and to establish school-to-work systems. Although there are a variety of grants available under STWOA, all school-to-work systems must include school-based learning that includes career counseling and career major exploration; work-based learning that includes job training, workplace mentoring, paid work experience, or instruction in workplace competencies; and connecting activities that incorporate both employers and educators, which not only can include matching students to job-based training, but also specialized training for those participating in the program (i.e. educators, counselors, work-place mentors).

The act makes explicit mention of students with disabilities, minority students, and women, with a focus on increasing work place opportunities that would be considered outside of those traditional for gender, race, or disability. STWOA also provides specific funding for technical assistance, capacity building, outreach, and research and evaluation.

The Health Insurance Portability and Accountability Act of 1996 (HIPAA: Public Law 104-191) was established to increase health care access and security. The most widely recognized components of HIPAA revolve around the privacy and security standards enacted by the bill. HIPAA's privacy rule created more stringent standards for the sharing and release of patient medical records. More specifically, HIPAA addressed the need for client consent before releasing information, the need for separate authorization for non-routine disclosures, the right of the patient to request a disclosure history, client access to their own medical records, limits of how information can be shared, standards that require the sharing of only the minimal amount of information necessary, and accountability and establishment of penalties for mishandling patient information.[37]

As important as its security and privacy aspects, HIPAA also focused on improving access to health care through its patient protection and portability standards. HIPAA set new rules governing pre-existing conditions, discrimination based on health-status related factors, the creation of special enrollment privileges, and the purchasing clout of individuals and small companies.[37] In an effort to reduce the rising administrative cost of medical care, HIPAA established national standards for electronic health care transactions to process claims and share information.[37] Combined, HIPAA's standards have been purported to increase the quality of patient care by ensuring increased security and accessibility, while at the same time lowering costs by establishing unified processing standards.

The Workforce Investment Act (WIA: Public Law 105-220) of 1998 consolidated a variety of employment and training programs into cooperative statewide systems. WIA supersedes the Job Training Partnership Act and subsumes the Rehabilitation Act. The ultimate aim of WIA is to promote employment, job retention, and increased earning potential (Employment Development Department, no date) by providing a wide range of workforce development activities and services. These services include, but are not limited to, basic skills assessments; advice, counseling, and support that includes access to labor market information, job search tools, and educational resources and guidance; literacy training; skills training; leadership development; job mentoring and workplace exposure; unemployment assistance; and on-the-job training programs.

In addition, WIA aims to connect the community, employers, and the workforce, and provides measures that allow local employers increased influence over local employment policies. In this manner, WIA serves job seekers, the unemployed, youth, incumbent workers, new entrants, veterans, individuals with disabilities, employers, and the community as a whole.

A significant portion of WIA is the Rehabilitation Act Amendments of 1998. These amendments focus on increasing consumer choice by mandating that consumers are provided with information and support services that allow them to make informed decisions throughout the VR process; linking services together under umbrella systems (such as staff training sessions, technical assistance, telephone hotlines), and forming cooperative arrangements between VR agencies and other public agencies to provide more efficient services; providing individuals with disabilities access to electronic and information technologies to the level of access afforded those without disabilities; and assisting educational institutions in identifying and implementing, including fiscal support, transitional programs and services for those with disabilities.

The Rehabilitation Act also renamed the State Rehabilitation Advisory Council to the State Rehabilitation Council, renamed the Individualized Written Rehabilitation Program to the Individual Plan for Employment, and relabeled individuals with the most severe disabilities.

An important part of WIA, and the subsumed Rehabilitation Act Amendments of 1998, is its focus on minority employees and groups. As outlined in the bill, WIA mandates specific funds for programs that address American Indian and migrant worker needs. In line with the basic tenets of WIA, programs for these minority populations focus on devolving academic, occupational, and literacy skills to make these populations more competitive. WIA established the Native American Employment and Training Council and set aside specific money for migrant worker services that provide for English language training, worker safety training, housing, support services, dropout prevention, and follow up services.

WIA also specially addressed the racial inequities found within the vocational rehabilitation system. The Rehabilitative Act Amendments of 1998 states: Patterns of inequitable treatment of minorities have been documented in all major junctures of the vocational rehabilitation process. As compared to Caucasians, a larger percentage of African American applicants to the vocational rehabilitation system are denied acceptance. Of applicants accepted for service, a larger percentage of African Americans' cases are closed without being rehabilitated. Racial/ethnic minorities are provided less training than their Caucasian counterparts. Consequently, less money is spent on minorities than on their Caucasian counterparts.

WIA provisions, therefore, highlight minority recruitment and outreach needs. Section 121 (changed from Section 130) of Title I and Part C re-authorized RSA to make grants for the establishment of American Indian

Vocational Rehabilitation Service projects for the provision of services to American Indians and Alaska Natives with disabilities. With assistance from RSA funded rehabilitation capacity building projects, the number of Section 121 projects has increased from 14 in 1991 to 76 in 2006, located in 23 states.[16] The states of Oklahoma and Alaska have the highest number of Section 121 programs at this time.

The Ticket to Work and Work Incentives Improvement Act (TWWIIA: Public Law 106-170) was signed into law by President Bill Clinton in 1999 as a means of removing Social Security and Medicare/Medicaid disincentives to employment.[7] Specifically, TWWIIA expanded Medicare and Medicaid coverage for those with disabilities by extending premium-free coverage for most disability beneficiaries who are employed, by permitting certain working individuals to purchase Medicaid coverage and facilitating the Medicaid and Medicare reinstatement process.

In addition, TWWIIA established the Ticket to Work and Self-Sufficiency Program. Under this program, individuals with a disability are provided with a "ticket," with which they can obtain vocational rehabilitation services and support services from an employment network of their choice. In this way, TWWIIA, as with previous legislation, focused on consumer empowerment by allowing the beneficiary more choice in the VR services that they obtain.

The ADA Amendments Act of 2008 (ADAAA: Public Law P.L. 110-325) was signed into law in 2008 by President George W. Bush and took effect on January 1, 2009. The ADAAA is not a revolutionary piece of legislation but rather a law reverted back to its original intent as decided by Congress when it was passed in 1990.[27] The Act accentuated the definition of disability and mandated that the definition should be interpreted broadly to the fullest extent permitted by the ADA. According to the ADAAA, the application of the term disability should not require microscopic scrutiny for determining disability or access to accommodations due to disability. This change was made in an effort to make it easier for an individual with a disability to seek protection under the ADA to establish that he or she has a disability.[27]

At the center of the controversy that led to the enactment of ADAAA was the emphasis on the criteria for determining if an individual had a disability rather than focus being placed on the lack of access or accommodations provided for an individual with a disability. The ADAAA retains the basic definition of a disability but rejects the meaning of the word disability as applied in various Supreme Court decisions. In essence, the ADAAA amends *how* the statutory terms should be interpreted.

Specifically, the ADAAA required that the EEOC revise its rules for determining if an individual has a disability in relation to the term "substantially limits" (which must be interpreted consistently with the ADAA). Additionally, due to the ADAAA, the definition of a disability must be interpreted broadly and in favor of an impairment that may substantially limit one major life activity even if the impairment does not limit other major life

CHAPTER 2 — LEGISLATIVE ASPECTS OF REHABILITATION

activities. The definitions of "major life activities" was expanded as a result of the passing of the ADAAA and now includes two non-exhaustive lists:

- List one: includes activities recognized by the EEOC (i.e., walking) as well as activities that are not specifically recognized by EEOC (i.e., reading, bending, communicating).
- List two: includes major bodily functions (e.g., "functions of the immune system, normal cell growth, digestive, bowel, bladder, respiratory, neurological, brain, circulatory, endocrine, and reproductive functions").

There are several other mandates passed down from the ADAAA. The Act specifies that only mitigating measures such as ordinary eyeglasses or contact lenses (that fully correct visual acuity or eliminate refractive error) can be considered when determining whether an impairment substantially limits major life activities during disability assessment. Moreover, any impairment that is episodic or in remission is a disability if that impairment would substantially limit a major life activity when active. Furthermore, if an individual with actual or perceived impairments are subject to an action prohibited by the ADA, they will meet the "regarded as" definition of disability unless the impairment is transitory and minor. If an individual is only covered under the "regarded as prong," he or she is not entitled to reasonable accommodations or modifications. The purpose for and the development of the ADAAA is rooted in case law. In 1990, when the ADA was passed, the definition of disability was based on the definition used in the Rehabilitation Act of 1973 which stated that "an individual with a disability has a physical or mental impairment that substantially limits one or more major life activities, a record of such an impairment, or is regarded as having such an impairment." This definition was used because it had worked well in the past. By 1999, the Supreme Court unexpectedly began to narrow the definition of disability through court proceedings. The first case, Sutton v. United Air Lines, was landmark in that the court decided when using the ADA definition for determining if an individual has a disability, the effects of mitigating measures must be considered (ex. corrective lenses, medications, hearing aids, and prosthetic devices) when deciding if the impairment is substantially limiting. This ruling also overturned the School Board of Nassau County v. Arline case which had broadly viewed the portion of the disability definition that emphasized a "record of" an impairment. Essentially, the Sutton case required a more restrictive definition of impairment be used when determining if an individual has a disability. Another shocking Supreme Court ruling was from the Toyota v. Williams case where focus was on the word "substantially" in the definition of disability. This word was interpreted to mean "considerably or to a large degree." The Court also decided that the scope of "major life activity" was too broad and the Court narrowed it to refer to an activity that was of central importance to daily living.[27]

These court rulings whittled down the definition of disability to such a degree that cases became more about the individual meeting the criteria of disability more so than the access or accommodations needed due to disability. Furthermore, EEOC regulations defined "substantially limits" as "significantly restricts," which was inconsistent with what Congress intended when the ADA was originally passed. These cases and the EEOC language led Congress to make the decision to amend the ADA. Congresses' findings, (the reasons why the new law is being written) for the ADAAA include:

- A need clear and comprehensive national mandate for the elimination of discrimination against individuals with disabilities and provide broad coverage,
- A need to address the inconsistent interpretation and application of the definition of a handicapped individual under the Rehabilitation Act of 1973,
- A need to rectify the statements from the Sutton and Toyota court proceeding that eliminated protection for many individuals that Congress intended to protect.

Workforce Innovation and Opportunity Act (WIOA: Public Law P.L. 113-128) is a historic expansion for individuals seeking employment and was signed into law on July 22, 2014 by President Barack Obama.[7] It was enacted to replace the Workforce Investment Act of 1998 and is considered vital primary federal workforce development legislation designed to fortify and advance the public workforce development system and increase coordination among key federal workforce development and related employment, education, and training programs.[35] WIOA helps Americans overcome barriers to employment, attain high quality careers, and ensure employers are able to select (and retain) workers from a skilled pool. In an effort to promote collaboration and coordination at the state and local levels among the core programs and other federal partner programs, WIOA is supported with extensive collaboration by the Department of Labor (DOL), the U.S. Department of Education (ED) and the U.S. Department of Health and Human Services (DHHS).[7]

WIOA incorporates a number of improvements to the workforce development system including:

- Assurance of coordinated workforce education and employment services by requiring a single, 4-year strategic State Plan for achieving the workforce goals of the state,

- ➢ A requirement that federal investments in education, employment, and training are evidence-based and data driven (to maintain accountability and transparency for participants and taxpayers),
- ➢ Establishment of partnerships with various federal programs to enhance services provided to individuals seeking employment through one-stop delivery systems, funds to assist with infrastructure and other shared costs, and an integrated intake, case management, and reporting system.

WIOA represents the first major legislative reform of the public workforce development system in more than 15 years. The Act increases economic prospects for individuals in the United States and specifically benefits youth and people with significant barriers to employment secure employment and take advantage of advancement opportunities. The goal of WIOA is to increase the skill and credential attainment, employment, retention, and earnings of these individuals thereby improving the quality of the workforce, reducing dependency on public benefits, increasing economic opportunity, and enhancing the productivity and competitiveness of the nation. WIOA recognizes the value of one-stop delivery systems where customer focus is emphasized. The regulations in WIOA were legislated to modernize the U.S. workforce system and to improve community support via integration of job-driven approaches and expansion of job growth. [35]

The WIOA supports innovative strategies to improve coordination and strengthen the alignment of the public workforce development system's six core programs and other Federal programs that support employment services, workforce development, adult education and literacy, and vocational rehabilitation (VR) activities. This task is accomplished via compelling unified strategic planning requirements, common performance accountability measures, and requirements governing the one-stop delivery system. Congress directs the Departments to issue regulations implementing statutory requirements to ensure that the public workforce system operates as a comprehensive, integrated, and streamlined system to provide pathways to prosperity and continuously improve the quality and performance of its services to job seekers and to employers.[35]

The WIOA rules include reforms for more than a dozen programs receiving $10 billion in annual training and education that serve approximately 20 million individuals annually.[35] A commendable level of engagement (2800 public comments) was noted from key stakeholders (including employers and community leaders) whose input and contributions informed the final regulations of the Act. The purpose of this Act is to spur local and regional economic growth and streamline the coordination of employment and training services across federal agencies. The final rules of the WIOA stipulate the provisions that directly affect the following programs:

- Adult, dislocated worker, and youth programs authorized under title I and administered by DOL,
- AEFLA program authorized under title II and administered by ED,
- Employment Service program authorized under the Wagner-Peyser Act, as amended by title III, and administered by DOL (Wagner-Peyser Act Employment Service program),
- VR program, authorized under title I of the Rehabilitation Act of 1973, as amended by title IV, and administered by ED.

One essential component to WIOA is the collection and reporting of accurate, timely information about the individuals who receive services from the associated programs under the law. This information is vital for informing public policy and analyzing effective strategies.

SUMMARY AND CONCLUSION

The essence of all rehabilitation efforts is to empower consumers to gain independence, improve quality of life, mainstream into the society, earn a full economic wage, and exercise their rights. Therefore, it is imperative that rehabilitation professionals be familiar with all legislation in rehabilitation and related fields. Besides federal laws and state-federal programs, each state may have special state and local laws, enactments, service provisions and facilities for citizens with disabilities. Familiarity with such local provisions will help immensely in the quest to become an effective counselor or placement specialist in directing, guiding, and efficient placing of clients in jobs in greater numbers.

Throughout this chapter, emphasis has been placed on civilian vocational rehabilitation acts and amendments over the last 100 years for individuals with physical and mental impairments in general. However, future rehabilitation counselors, placement specialists, and students need to become familiar with the laws, acts, and amendments related to specialized populations, such as persons who are blind and visually impaired, deaf and hearing impaired, who have developmental disabilities, veterans, and the aged.

The need to find jobs for individuals with disabilities in the future will increase rather than decrease in importance. Vocational rehabilitation, as has been pointed out, is not a social welfare program. It is a cost-effective program that places or returns people with disabilities to the world of work. When people work, their tax dollars return to the government coffers.

It is essential that each American do his/her share in contributing to the U.S. economy. This includes people with disabilities. Therefore, it is a greater necessity for rehabilitation counselors, placement specialists, and other professionals to assist people with disabilities, including youth, in obtaining the proper training and education so that are able to find jobs and become gainfully employed. Only in this way can individuals who have a disability do their share and become working Americans.

This chapter has attempted to identify some of the significant sociopolitical trends and legislative provisions impacting the quality outcomes for people with disabilities. The following chapters will investigate other relevant issues and provide a holistic overview and understanding of the unique field of rehabilitation.

REFERENCES

[1] Administration for Community Living. (2018). About the national institute on disability, independent living, and rehabilitation research (NIDILRR). Retrieved November 30, 2018, from https://acl.gov/about-acl/about-national-institute-disability-independent-living-and-rehabilitation-research.

[2] Alston, R. J., Russo, C. J., & Miles, A. S. (1994). Brown v. Board of Education and the Americans with Disabilities Act: Vistas of equal educational opportunities for African Americans. *The Journal of Negro Education, 63*(3), 349-357.

[3] Atkins, B. J., & Wright, G. N. (1980). Vocational rehabilitation of Blacks. *Journal of Rehabilitation, 46*, 42-46.

[4] Bitter, J. A. (1979). Introduction to rehabilitation. St. Louis: C. V. Mosby. Blackwell, H. (October 27, 1945). To NAACP Secretary of Veterans Affairs, NAACP Papers, Manuscript Division, Library of Congress, Washington, D.C.

[5] Boehner, J., & Castle, M. (2005). Individuals with Disabilities Education Act (IDEA): Guide to "Frequently asked questions." Committee on Education and the Workforce. Retrieved April 11, 2006, from http://www.house.gov/ed_workforce/issues/109th/education/idea/ideafaq.pdf

[6] Bowe, F. (1985). Black adults with disabilities: A statistical report drawn from Census Bureau data. President's Committee on Employment of the Handicapped.

[7] Bruyere, S.M., & Saleh, M.C. (2018). Disability policy and law. In V.M. Tarvydas & M.T. Hartley (Eds.), *The Professional Practice of Rehabilitation Counseling* (95-119). New York: Springer.

[8] Button, C. (1993). Reauthorized Rehabilitation Act increases access to assistive technology. A.T. Quarterly, 4. Retrieved April 11, 2006, from http://www.resna.org/taproject/library/atq/rehbact.htm

[9] Danek, M. M., & Lawrence, R. E. (1982). Client-counselor racial similarity and rehabilitation outcomes. *Journal of Rehabilitation, 48*(3), 54-58.

[10] Day, S. L., & Edwards, B. J. (1996). Assistive technology for postsecondary students with learning disabilities. *Journal of Learning Disabilities, 29*, 486-492.

[11]Department of Labor. (1975). Affirmative action obligations of contractors and subcontractors for handicapped workers. Employment Standards Administration. *Federal Register, 40*(169).

[12]Federal Register. (1998). National Institute on Disability and Rehabilitation Research; Notice of Proposed Long-Range Plan for Fiscal Years 1999-2004, *63*(206), 57215-57218. Washington, DC: US Government.

[13]Federal Register. (2006). National Institute on Disability and Rehabilitation Research; Notice of Proposed Long-Range Plan for Fiscal Years 2005-2009, *71*(31), 8192-8194. Washington, DC: US Government.

[14]Gamble, B. S. (1990). *Analysis and Reports*. Washington, DC: Bureau of National Affairs, 138(C1 through C4).

[15]Graves, W. H., Coffey, D. D., Habeck, R., & Stude, E. W. (1978). NCRE Position Paper: Definition of the Qualified Rehabilitation Professional. *Rehabilitation Education, 1*(1), 5-6.

[16]Guy, E. (1991). Vocational rehabilitation services for American Indians. *OSERS News in Print. 3*, 10-15.

[17]Jefferson, R. F. (2003). "Enabled courage:" Race, disability, and Black World War II veterans in postwar America. *Historian, 65*(5), 1102-1124.

[18]Jenkins, W. M. (1980). History and legislation of the rehabilitation movement. In R. Parker and C. Hansen (Eds.), *Rehabilitation Counseling*. Boston: Allyn and Bacon.

[19]Jones, A. (1986). *Detailed Survey of the Rehabilitation Amendments of 1986, Public Law 97-506*. Dunbar, WV: West Virginia Research and Training Center.

[20]Kundu, M. M., Dutta, A., & Walker, S. (2006). Participation of Ethnically Diverse Personnel in State-Federal Vocational Rehabilitation Agencies. *Journal of Applied Rehabilitation Counseling, 17*(1), 30-36.

[21]Kundu, M. M., & Dutta, A. (2000). Rehabilitation capacity building project Inclusion, empowerment, and integration. *Rehabilitation Education, 14*(4), 345-357.

[22]Kundu, M. M., & Dutta, A. (1995). Implementation of rehabilitation counselor training programs at Historically Black Colleges and Universities. *Disability and Diversity: New Leadership for a New Era* (pp. 45-52). Washington, D.C.: The President's Committee on Employment of People with Disabilities and Howard University Research and Training Center.

[23]Lee, J. C. (October 27, 1948). To NAACP Executive Secretary Walter White, Group II, Box G 18, VA Hospital Discrimination, 1945-1948, Veterans Affairs File, 1940-1950, NAACP Papers, Manuscript Division, Library of Congress, Washington, D.C.

[24]McGowan J., & Porter, T. (1967). *An introduction to the vocational rehabilitation process*. Washington, DC: U.S. Department of Health, Education and Welfare, Vocational Rehabilitation Archives.

[25]National Council on Disability. (1990). *The Americans with Disabilities Act*. Washington, DC: Author.
[26]Oberman, C. E. (1965). *A history of vocational rehabilitation in America*. Minneapolis: T. S. Deurson & Co., Inc.
[27]Parry, J. W., & Allbright, A. L. (2008). The ADA amendment act of 2008: Analysis and commentary. *Mental and Physical Disability Law Reporter 32*(5), 695-697.
[28]Rehabilitation Act of 1973, Public Law 93-112. (1973). Washington, DC: U. S. Government.
[29]Rehabilitation Act Amendments of 1984, Public Law 83-565. (1984). Washington, DC: U.S. Government.
[30]Rehabilitation Act Amendments of 1986, Public Law 99-506. (1986). Washington, DC: U. S. Government.
[31]Rehabilitation Comprehensive Services and Developmental Disabilities Act Amendments of 1978, Public Law 95-602. (1978). Washington, DC: U.S. Government.
[32]Rehabilitation Services Administration. (1993). *Training on 1992 Amendments to the Rehabilitation Act*. Washington, DC: U.S. Department of Education.
[33]Rivera, O. A. (1974). Vocational rehabilitation of disabled Hispanics (Doctoral dissertation, University of Utah). *Dissertation Abstracts International, 35*(4-A), 2059-2060A.
[32]The Americans With Disabilities Act of 1990, Public Law 101-336. Washington, DC: U. S. Government.
[34]Thoben, P. J. (1975). Civil rights and employment of the severely handicapped. *Rehabilitation Counseling Bulletin, 18(4),* 240-244.
[35] U.S. Department of Education. (2014). *RSA:Workforce Innovation and Opportunity Act*. Retrieved from: https://www2.ed.gov/about/offices/list/osers/rsa/wioa-reauthorization.html
[36]U.S. Department of Justice. (no date). *Americans with Disabilities Act, Requirements in Public Accommodations Fact Sheet*. Washington, DC: Author.
[37]U.S. Department of Health and Human Services. (2003). *Administrative simplification under HIPAA: National standards for transactions, privacy, and security*. Retrieved April 12, 2006, from http://www.hhs.gov/news/press/2002pres/hipaa.html
[38]U.S. Department of Labor. (December 2004). *The Health and Insurance Portability and Accountability Act (HIPAA)*. Retrieved April 12, 2006, from http://www.dol.gov/ebsa/newsroom/fshipaa.html
[39]Wilkerson, D. A., & Penn, L. A. (1938). The participation of Negroes in the federally-aided program of civilian vocational rehabilitation. *The Journal of Negro Education, 7*(3), 319-330.

CHAPTER 3

ETHICAL ISSUES IN REHABILITATION COUNSELING

PAIGE N. DUNLAP
QUINTIN BOSTON
KAYE COLE

CHAPTER TOPICS

- Ethical Decision Making
- Personal Virtual Relationships
- Ethics in Private Rehabilitation
- Ethics and Technology in Rehabilitation Counseling
- Case Studies

ETHICAL ISSUES IN REHABILITATION COUNSELING

All rehabilitation counselors should strive to attain an in-depth understanding of ethical issues within the rehabilitation counseling field. The diversification of the ethical standards of the profession has historically been a topic of discussion. For example, McGinn, Flowers, and Rubin[23] showcased a need for additional areas related to diversity and ethics. Furthermore, areas of concern were noted by both Harley, et al.,[18] and Middleton, et al.,[24] As such, changes and updates have been made within the *Code of Professional Ethics for Rehabilitation Counselors* (hereafter referred to as *Code of Ethics*) (Commission on Rehabilitation Counselor Certification (*CRCC*).[10] The goal of this chapter is to feature some of the newest updates to the 2017 *Code of Ethics* and showcase the applicability of diversity to specific areas by using case studies as examples.

ETHICAL DECISION MAKING

The 2016 Standards from the Council for Accreditation of Counseling and Related Educational Programs (CACREP) requires that clinical rehabilitation counselors meet preparation standards related to ethics. In preparing students to become professional counselors, programs must cover content relative to "ethical standards of professional counseling organizations and credentialing bodies, and applications of ethical and legal considerations in professional counseling."[9] Specifically, "legal and ethical considerations unique to clinical rehabilitation counseling" must be covered in Clinical Rehabilitation Counseling programs.[9] This gives support to the understanding that counselors should be qualified to review a problem, interpret the situation, identify concerns and pertinent information, and allow an outline to help guide them to an appropriate solution.

As in any field, the body of knowledge changes as the profession grows and expands within an ever-evolving society. Prominent changes in the 2017 *Code of Ethics* showcase a need for greater understanding of some of the more traditional categories showcased in the standards.[10] Of particular interest in this chapter are Personal Virtual Relationships, Role Changes in Forensic Settings, and Technology. In general, a rehabilitation counselor's conduct for professional practice is outlined by the *Code of Ethics*. The *Code of Ethics* speaks to both the counselors' and the clients' rights and welfare. Therefore, it is critical to have an understanding of decision-making skills when discourse surrounds ethics in rehabilitation counseling.

History showcases a number of decision-making models from which a counselor can choose to aid them; examples include Kitchener,[21] and Rest.[27] Other, more recent models of decision-making provide an outline that rehabilitation professionals may find useful. These include Tarvydas;[33]

Cottone;[13] Garcia, et al.;[17] Corey, et al.;[11] Herlihy & Watson;[20] and Ling and Hauck.[22] Each of these ethical decision-making models contain some similar features, but many can be adapted to more thoroughly discern the situation and make appropriate decisions.

Using the Ling and Hauck[22] and the Corey, et al.,[11] models as examples, rehabilitation counselors may choose to adapt and integrate the models. The following steps demonstrate what the two integrated models might look like together. Rehabilitation counselors may find it helpful to interpret their ethical dilemma and evaluate courses of action when ethical decision-making models are combined:

- **E** – Evaluate the Dilemma
  (Recognize the problem)
- **T** – Think Ahead
  (Develop solutions)
- **H** – Help
  (Seek assistance from a colleague/consultant)
- **I** – Information
  (Gather relevant codes and legal documents)
- **C** – Calculate Risk
  (Determine the consequences)
- **S** – Select an Action
  (Choose the best course of action)

Utilizing ethical decision-making models allows counselors to have flexibility, while offering them a more inclusive way of assessing each ethical dilemma and its respective diversity issues.[35] This, in turn, aids in the creation of an ethical orientation. According to Dufrene and Glosoff,[15] counselors' ethical decisions are influenced by their current state on an ethical orientation continuum consisting of five levels:

- punishment,
- institutional,
- societal,
- individual, and
- principle.

As rehabilitation counselors develop a greater level of comfort with utilizing ethical decision-making models and employing them with the 2017 *Code of Ethics*, their personal ethical orientation will be developed and/or enhanced.[8]

Keeping the ethical decision-making models and the idea of an ethical orientation in mind throughout this chapter will assist the reader to have a better understanding of how situations can be handled. Utilizing the tools of an ethical decision-making model as a framework will help the counselor work through various dilemmas. Subsequently, it will also prove beneficial in showcasing competency and professionalism, while decreasing bias throughout the process of helping a client.

PERSONAL VIRTUAL RELATIONSHIPS

A new standard specific to roles and relationships with clients was an important addition to the 2017 *Code of Ethics*.[8] In Section A: The Counseling Relationship, Standard A.4.f. Personal Virtual Relationships states:

> Rehabilitation counselors are prohibited from engaging in personal virtual relationships with current clients (e.g., through social media).

Furthermore, the *Code of Ethics* goes on to define social media as:

> Forms of electronic communication through which users create online communities to share information, ideas, personal messages, and other content.

The CRCC standard echoes that of the American Counseling Association's *Code of Ethics*[1] standard A.5.e which states:

> Personal Virtual Relationships With Current Clients: Counselors are prohibited from engaging in a personal virtual relationship with individuals with whom they have a current counseling relationship (e.g., through social and other media).

The National Board for Certified Counselors[25] Standard 19 expounds on the idea within their ethics code for National Certified Counselors (NCC) by stating:

> NCCs shall recognize the potential harm of informal uses of social media and other related technology with clients, former clients, and their families and personal friends. After carefully considering all of the ethical implications, including confidentiality, privacy, and multiple relationships, NCCs shall develop written practice procedures in regard to social media and digital technology, and these shall be incorporated with the information provided to clients before or during the initial

session. At a minimum, these social media procedures shall specify that personal accounts will be separate and isolated from any used for professional counseling purposes including those used with prospective or current clients. These procedures shall also address "friending" and responding to material posted.

With more than 1 billion active daily users on Facebook, social media is one of the most common forms of communication within society.[16] The *Code of Ethics* standard is due in part to the growing amounts of digital citizenship that have become customary in the lives of many counselors. Ribble[28] stated "Digital citizenship can be described as the norms of appropriate, responsible behavior with regard to technology use."[p.10]

While specifics of the standard within the *Code of Ethics* are open to interpretation by the subscriber, the standard suggests that counselors treat personal and professional means of social media as separate entities. Specifically, CRCC[8] makes a distinction regarding a Professional Electronic Presence stating: In cases where rehabilitation counselors maintain both professional and personal presences for social media use, separate professional and personal pages and profiles are created to clearly distinguish between the two kinds of electronic presence.[Standard J.4.a] For example, many professional counselors will have social media accounts that are strictly for professional use to engage clients and colleagues and another account for personal use to engage family, friends, etc. Using a personal account to "friend" or "follow" a client on social media would be inappropriate. Utilizing privacy settings that restrict who can access and "post" material to each page is critical in not crossing the professional/personal boundary line on social media.

There are a number of benefits to having a professional social network. For example, many potential clients are likely to search for professional websites or through social media platforms before making an appointment with a counselor.[2,36] Having a social media account can provide the client with more access to information about a counselor's practice and personal style of counseling, thereby helping the client to better determine if a specific counselor would be a good fit for them. However, caution should be taken by the counselor to ensure that they understand the legal and ethical issues involved in engaging clients on a social networking platform.[2]

Rehabilitation Counselors who adhere to the *Code of Ethics* are required to have an informed consent that speaks to the benefits, limitations, and boundaries of social media in the provision of services.[8] To assist with this task, CRCC[7] created a technology, social media, and distance counseling considerations list which offers suggestions for navigating social media. Specifically, considerations include:

➢ Online interactions and boundaries,
➢ Online consultation,

- Confidentiality and privacy,
- Posting and moderating content,
- Addressing non-compliance.

Each area contains additional considerations specific to the provision of rehabilitation counseling services. Employing this consideration list in determining how to structure an informed consent or social media policy would benefit rehabilitation counselors who choose to engage clients and/or potential clients via social media. It is important to note that the list is not exhaustive and would need to be tailored to one's own usage, but it does provide a starting point for counselors who wish to have a professional electronic presence.

Every rehabilitation counselor's level of comfort varies when it comes to both personal and professional relationships in an online environment. In an era when technology and forms of communication are evolving daily, there is no specific or clear method for rehabilitation counselors to engage clients via social media. Each counselor who chooses to engage clients in this format is cautioned to ensure that they are following the guidelines for confidentiality and informed consent. However, it is clear that personal virtual relationships should not be established with current clients. If counselors find themselves in a situation that is ethically challenging, they are encouraged to utilize an ethical decision-making model to help them arrive at the best choice.

ETHICS IN PRIVATE REHABILITATION

The newly revised *Code of Ethics* for the Rehabilitation Counseling (RC) profession offered from CRCC has provided an update to the standards regarding working in the private sector of rehabilitation counseling.[8] The information is particularly important as several rehabilitation counselors are beginning to explore different alternatives to work in the field. The traditional workplaces such as Vocational Rehabilitation (VR) and or the Department of Veteran Affairs (VA) are still reliable options. However, there are other places for counselors to provide services to persons with disabilities (PWD). In addition, with the influx of RC's entering the private workforce, enforcing and having an understanding of the *Code of Ethics* becomes even more paramount.[32]

REHABILITATION COUNSELING PROGRAMS TRAINING

The shift in employment has forced several RC training programs to offer more courses, or even change their curriculum as it applies to private rehabilitation. Currently, there are only a handful or RC programs that either offer a certificate in Forensic Rehabilitation Counseling or offer courses centered around private rehabilitation.[10] However, with the new additions to the standards, it is imperative that rehabilitation counseling programs provide these courses. Furthermore, from an ethical standpoint, it at least ensures that the students graduating from the programs will have more knowledge as it pertains to private rehabilitation.

Rehabilitation counselors working in forensic settings provide unbiased reviews of findings associated with persons of disability.[8] Therefore, it is important for the RC training programs to be able to provide evidence-based practice situations for students to be able to hone these skills and have opportunities to build upon their case management competencies.[32] In addition, programs will have to become more cognizant of their students' understanding of informed consent regarding the purposes of certain evaluations.[8] The new *Code of Ethics* has revamped situations centered around informed consent and the importance of the RC providing the nature of the evaluation. This information for RC's in training builds upon the information being taught in the traditional rehabilitation counseling ethics courses. As a result, counselor educators must become more familiar with content centered around the forensic setting. As portrayed in the new *Code of Ethics*, the role of the RC in the forensic setting has clearly been expanded upon.[8]

FORENSIC SETTING

As mentioned earlier in the chapter, RC's work in a variety of settings.[31] As a result, it is important to understand the forensic setting and the opportunities provided to rehabilitation counselors working in such settings. Rehabilitation counselors working in forensic settings can provide expert testimony, perform vocational evaluations for legal experts, and can also serve as advocates.[34] In many of these settings, RC's are charged with providing systematic caseload management, job development, and placement to persons with disabilities. Depending on the agency or place of employment, the RC's consistently must monitor and remember the importance of the *Code of Ethics* while providing effective guidance and counseling to Persons with disabilities (PWD).[34]

In addition, the forensic setting offers the rehabilitation counselor the opportunity to work within numerous roles while providing services to clients. This change in the *Code of Ethics* specifically highlights the importance of the RC to understand their changing roles while providing services to clients.[8] The *Code of Ethics* further explains that the counselor is to provide the client with new and updated professional disclosure statements when roles change within the counseling relationship.[8] This information is important as it provides the clients with the ability to understand and be an active part of their rehabilitation plan. Also, the RC is responsible for informing the client of risk and benefits of the changing roles in the counseling relationship.[34]

While providing services in expert testimony work, the *Code of Ethics* is clear that the RC has an obligation to present findings based on the facts.[8, 34, 32] This portion of the *Code of Ethics* is clear, as it provides guidance to the RC to help prevent areas of other ethical dilemmas from arising. In addition, the counselor is to clearly acknowledge their qualifications for all parties to understand their ability to provide testimony of their work. When a rehabilitation counselor is providing expert testimony, they work on behalf of the United Social Security Administration, and the RC is to offer an unbiased testimony.[34] The *Code of Ethics* is also clear that the RC is to form their opinions based on data, in addition to providing a sound methodology as they come to their conclusions.[8]

COMPETENCY AND CONDUCT

Section F. 2 of the new *Code of Ethics* speaks to the RC's ability to be competent in their line of work, and conduct themselves in an ethical manner.[8] As a result, and as stated earlier in the chapter, the *Code of Ethics* is very specific in how a RC is to conduct themselves in an ethical manner within a forensic setting. Due to the nature of the RC providing and working with many other allied professionals in a private rehabilitation setting, the counselor is to clearly differentiate the client in their roles and responsibilities from the other allied professionals working with the client.[32] Therefore, as conflicts arise in the private work setting, it is important for the counselor to adhere to the *Code of Ethics* and make their commitment to the CRCC *Code of Ethics* known to the parties involved, as those conflicts are being resolved.[34] The code also explicitly reaffirms that the RC will use their clinical judgment regarding entering potentially harmful relationships with clients in a forensic setting. Hence, the RC must continuously keep in mind the *Code of Ethics* as they decide which cases are feasible for them to provide effective services.

Regarding the RC's competency, there is also a need for them to recognize apparent conflict of interest and handle the situation in an appropriate manner. The revised standards are clear regarding what actions a RC should take in the event they find themselves in a conflict of interest. As pointed out in many counseling ethics text books, there is an ethical discussion making model for counselors to use, should they find themselves in a conflict.[12] However, as stated in the *Code of Ethics*[F.2] "the counselor is to under such circumstances decline participation or limit their assistance in a manner consistent with professional obligations."[8 p.22] The RC's duty is not only to the client, but also to the public by reaffirming that the RC is acting both in the best interest of the client as well in the best interest of the public. As highlighted by Rubin and Rosselor,[31] the RC has an ethical obligation to the public as well. Accountability to the public also ensures that the RC will not enter into a financial obligation, so as to not jeopardize the quality of services that the RC provides.[8] As a result, according to the standards, the RC is not to receive commission, rebates, or referral fees when referring cases to other professionals. In addition, it is also unethical for RC's to make it explicit that their services are not contingent on outcomes of specific cases.

DIVERSITY CONSIDERATIONS

Understanding the new *Code of Ethics* for RC's working in a private setting is ethical practice. As with the latest updates in Section F, the RC cannot forget to maintain competency centered around issues of diversity, when working in the private sector. As mentioned earlier in the chapter, as more RC's enter the private workforce, being aware of one's biases continues to be of upmost importance. The multicultural counseling competencies (MCC) is a constant reminder for RC's to work within the framework of providing services to clients in an impartial manner.[3] Therefore, regardless of the private employment setting, working with the client from an unbiased perception can help facilitate ethical practices in the forensic setting.

CONCLUSION

The new *Code of Ethics* revisions to Section F provides a good operating structure for rehabilitation counselors to conduct themselves in an ethical manner in a forensic setting. The latest updates will also help with the implementation of curriculum changes to RC counseling programs. With such a small number of programs offering certificates in forensic rehabilitation counseling, the new standards can help RC educators add new and innovate information to their curriculum. Furthermore, the new addition also provides practicing forensic rehabilitation counselors with the information and tools needed to provide effective and ethical practices in such settings.

ETHICS AND TECHNOLOGY IN REHABILITATION COUNSELING

The newly revised *Code of Ethics* in RC has provided an update to the emergence of technology in the field of RC. Rehabilitation counselors are no longer limited to working and seeing clients face-to-face.[8] With the new advancements in technology, understanding ethics and how it relates to RC is paramount.[19] The use of technology when working with PWD may possibly serve as an enhancement for the RC's ability to provide services.[19] Therefore, the revamping of the *Code of Ethics* in Section J regarding technology has provided RC's with a roadmap if ethical situations pertaining to the use of technology arise.[8]

CONFIDENTIALITY

Over the last few years, social media and the use of technology have become the primary means of communication within the US.[30] Given these findings, RC's must have an awareness of how this impacts their ability to provide services to PWD. For example, issues pertaining to confidentiality can easily arise with the use of accessibility. Confidentiality is a critical piece of any counseling relationship.[12] With the use of technology and the ability for cyber-attacks and viruses, RC's must be sure to use the most updated technology to lessen their chances of cyber-attacks. In addition, because RC's work in a variety of settings (e.g. traveling case managers, traveling vocational evaluators) using cell phones or tablets may not provide the most up-to-date software, depending on the data plan.

There is also a growing expectation that the counselor, as well as the clients are equipped with the understanding of using social media as a form of communication.[30] It would behoove the rehabilitation counselor to have a conversation with the client prior to assessing their competency with the usage of technology.[29] This will allow the counselor to decide the appropriateness of certain types of technology when communicating with the client. According to the new revisions in the *Code of Ethics*, the RC has an ethical obligation to communicate to the client the risks associated with using technology in the counseling relationship.[8] Furthermore, the RC must use their clinical judgement if the transmission of communication (e.g. text messages, email) are beneficial methods of communication with the client.

The RC must make reasonable efforts to ensure that the technology they are using is being transmitted over a secure server.[8] In addition, the client also should be aware of the risk and potential harms of sending and receiving transmitted data over servers.[19] RC's have a standard that they must meet regarding the information shared in emails, and the counselor should take extra steps to ensure that the communication is not harmful to his or her clients. Furthermore, when sending information to another party who is involved in the rehabilitation process for the PWD, the RC also has an ethical obligation to ensure that information is related to and has a benefit to the rehabilitation of the client.[4]

ACCESSIBILITY

The client can decide whether they want to use technology in the counseling relationship.[14] However, accessibility can present an issue when using technology in the counseling relationship. Traditionally, PWD have been underserved individuals in society.[26] Therefore, the RC should understand the issues centered around accessibility for clients. The *Code of Ethics* is explicit regarding informing the client of the turnaround time for the RC to respond to the client.[8] This allows for and presents an open layer of communication to the client regarding the key issue of communication. In addition, the *Code of Ethics* mentions time zone differences when using technology with clients. The cost of the software depending on what the client needs should also be considered if technology is going to be used with the client.

Ethically, the cost of the technology should not present an undue hardship on the client. As a result, the RC must consider such factors when working with the client on their plan. As PWD still earn well below the national income average compared to other populations,[26] it is important to consider the fact that the cost of video conferencing and other methods of live, face-to-face communication may be inaccessible and unaffordable to clients.[5] Therefore, it is in the best business practices of RC's using technology to consider the ethical issues centered around the client's ability to access such technology.

DIVERSITY CONSIDERATIONS

Highlighted throughout the *Code of Ethics* is the rehabilitation counselor's ability to work and maintain a good ethical stance in the profession. Having an unbiased mindset as it pertains to who has access to technology is critical. For instance, if working with individuals from underserved populations, the RC should maintain the same level of commitment to working with those clients as clients from other populations.[8] In addition, access to technology in some instances can be looked upon as a privilege. Therefore, the RC must have an understanding that access for clients from diverse backgrounds can possibly present an issue. The Code of Ethics clearly reminds the practicing RC to remember that the client can either want to use technology or not.[8] As a result, if the RC wants to use technology and the client does not have adequate access to such technology, the RC can always advocate on behalf of the client's lack of technology.[19]

CONCLUSION

Using technology as a RC can present several ethical issues. Having an awareness of the new standards centered around technology will help enhance the relationship with consumers who prefer those methods of communication. Since society has moved towards a more social media driven age, the RC's competency using technology is paramount. Like other advances in society, the use of technology can present both enhanced services, as well as certain disadvantages. As pointed out earlier in the chapter, the RC must understand that not all clients present with the same level of competency when it comes to using social media. In addition, the RC must also be willing to keep themselves abreast of changes and advances to technology.

According to the *Code of Ethics*, the RC's effort to ensure confidentiality in the counseling relationship is critical to the development of the counseling relationship. As a result, the RC must make efforts to reasonably ensure those standards are being met. As with other forms of counseling, counselors using social media must also continue to maintain an active continuing education regimen centered around ethical issues in technology-driven counseling.

CASE STUDIES

After reading the chapter, readers are encouraged to showcase their skills of ethical practice by completing the case studies found below. This exercise allows the reader to engage in the reading material from a practical stance. The following case studies each have an element of diversity, which allows for a deeper and more natural engagement of the material while mirroring the uniqueness of our society. This section of the document serves as a roadmap to help guide the reader to an ethical solution while also allowing flexibility and personal counseling styles to flourish.

CASE ONE
Robert

BIODATA: Robert is a 46-year old, married, White American Southern Baptist minister who has sought counseling for his continued pornography addiction. He has a history of alcohol abuse but has managed to kick the habit.

BACKGROUND: Robert was raised in a small town in South Carolina. He grew up in a strict home with both parents and his three siblings. Both parents made it a point to attend church every Sunday, including bible study during the week. While his siblings scoffed at the idea of having to attend church so regularly, Robert enjoyed it. After high school, he enrolled and graduated from seminary school. During the summer months, he went on mission trips and acted as visiting pastor to many churches in his area. He married his high school sweetheart upon graduating from high school and the two had children shortly thereafter. The pressures of fatherhood and his career began to take a toll on Robert, so he turned to alcohol to "take the edge off". After many years of drinking, Robert sought help with an addictions counselor and made enormous progress. However, once the drinking stopped, he turned to pornography to deal with marital stress.

ISSUE: Robert is struggling with his religious beliefs and the constant need to watch pornography. He is ashamed and guilt-ridden about his urges and believes he should be punished. He has left the church and has isolated himself from everyone, including his wife. Robert's therapist knows Robert personally, as they both live in the same small town, and he is a member of Robert's congregation. He's the only addiction counselor in town.

Respond to each question from your worldview. Address any ethical codes which are pertinent to the case study.

   1. What are some of the challenges associated with providing counseling services to Robert?
   2. How might your worldview affect how you address Robert's presenting problem?

3. What are the obvious ethical considerations, if any?

4. What steps might you take to minimize any dual relationships?

CASE TWO
Jackie

BIODATA: Jackie is a 15-year-old African-American girl who suffered a horrific spinal cord injury that left her paralyzed from the waist down due to a car accident. Since the accident, she has chronic depression and fantasizes about suicide.

BACKGROUND: Jackie is an only child and lives at home with her mother. Prior to the accident, she was physically active and participated in high school sports. She was an honor student who had big dreams of running track in college. It has been two years since her injury and Jackie has given up any hope of ever walking again. At the urging of her mother, Jackie has been seeing a mental health therapist for the past year. Her suicidal ideation continues to increase, and her mother has grown more and more concerned about her mental state.

ISSUE: Jackie has disclosed numerous times that she would like to end her life. Her therapist has insisted that Jackie come to church with her. She has also informed Jackie that if she commits suicide, she will not go to heaven.

Respond to each question from your worldview. Address any ethical codes which are pertinent to the case study.

1. What are the multicultural implications of this case?

2. What are some clinical and ethical issues associated with working with Jackie?

3. Discuss boundary crossings and boundary violations. Has either occurred? Please elaborate.

4. Explain why one might breech confidentiality in Jackie's case.

CASE 3
Malcolm

BIODATA: Malcolm is an 18-year old Hispanic male who has a documented learning disability. He recently completed high school and would like to pursue a trade. He is shy and lacks self-confidence.

BACKGROUND: Malcolm lives in a mid-sized city. He has always attended mixed schools and lived in diverse neighborhoods. Malcolm lives with both parents and three siblings. Both parents work outside of the home. As a student, Malcolm struggled through elementary and middle school, and was later diagnosed with a learning disability during his eight-grade year. Once the appropriate accommodations were in place, Malcolm matriculated through high school without any problems. Malcolm is a likeable student, however, because of his disability he lacks self-confidence and the ability to communicate effectively. To address his lack of self-confidence, the school counselor suggested that Malcolm receive counseling services from a rehabilitation counselor upon graduation.

ISSUE: Malcolm lacks transportation and doesn't have the ability to meet with his counselor face-to-face each week. Since Malcolm has shown interest in receiving counseling, the rehabilitation counselor has offered to provide counseling services using technology.

Respond to each question from your worldview. Address any ethical codes which are pertinent to the case study.

1. Discuss the dimensions of confidentiality in your relationship with Malcolm.
2. What does the process of informed consent involve?
3. What might be some limitations of confidentiality associated with working with Malcolm?

CASE 4
Tara

BIODATA: Your colleague, Tara is a 36-year-old rehabilitation counselor in a mental health facility. She has been a counselor for five years in a large metropolitan city.

BACKGROUND: Tara enjoys working as a rehabilitation counselor. Her clients are from all walks of life with varying disabilities. She works very closely with the other counselors in the office and feels comfortable asking for assistance when necessary. Tara is highly motivated and is always seeking ways to provide her clients with the best care possible.

ISSUE: Tara has noticed a shift in her client demographics. Her new clients consist of millennials and those who are technologically advanced. Many of them have requested that Tara communicate with them via text, social media, and other electronic modalities.

Respond to each question from your worldview. Address any ethical codes which are pertinent to the case study.

1. What might be some ethical implications of communicating with clients via texting and social media platforms?
2. As her colleague, how might you help her address any ethical considerations?
3. What can Tara do to establish boundaries with her clients, should she decide to move forward using social media platforms and communicating via text messaging?
4. Do you believe that is it ethical to communicate with clients outside of a "traditional" setting? Please elaborate.

REFERENCES

[1] American Counseling Association (2014). ACA Code of Ethics. Alexandria, VA: Author.

[2] Barnett, J. E. (2010). Psychology's Brave New World: Psychotherapy in the Digital Age. *The Independent Practitioner*, 30/3, 149-152

[3] Boston, Q., Vaughn, S., Robertson, S. L., Fuerth, K., & Baldwin, B. (2011). Multicultural counseling and cultural beliefs in rehabilitation counseling: Implications for practice and advocacy. *Rehabilitation Counselors' and Educators' Association Journal, 4(2), 33-41.*

[4] Chapin, M. H., & Byrne, A. M. (2013). Ethical decision making applied to social networking. *Journal of Rehabilitation, 79(3),* 11-16.

[5] Chester, A., & Glass, C. A. (2006). Online counselling: A descriptive analysis of therapy services on the internet. *British Journal of Guidance & Counselling, 34(2),* 145–160.

[6] Commission on Rehabilitation Counselor Certification. (2001). Code of professional ethics for rehabilitation counselors. Schaumburg, IL: Author.

[7] Commission on Rehabilitation Counselor Certification. (2016). *Technology, Social Media, and Distance Counseling Considerations.* Retrieved from, www.crcccertification.com/filebin/pdf/CRCC_TechSMDCConsiderations.pdf

[8] Commission on Rehabilitation Counselor Certification. (2017). Code of professional ethics for rehabilitation counselors. Schaumburg, IL: Author.

[9] Council for Accreditation of Counseling and Related Educational Programs. (2016). 2016 standards for accreditation. Alexandria, VA: Author

[10] Council on Rehabilitation Education. (2017). CORE accredited rehabilitation counseling program. Retrieved http://www.core-rehab.org/AccreditedPrograms

[11] Corey, G., Corey, M. S., & Callanan, P. (2015). *Issues and ethics in the helping professions* (8th ed.). Belmont, CA: Thomson Learning, Inc.

[12] Cory, G. (2015). *Theory and practice of counseling and psychotherapy.* Belmont CA: Thompson Brooks/Cole.

[13] Cottone, R. R. (2001). A social constructivism model of ethical decision-making in counseling. *Journal of Counseling Development, 79,* 39-45.

[14] Crtalic, K. A., Gibbs, L. R., Sprong, E. M., & Dell, F. T. (2014). Boundaries with social media: Ethical considerations for rehabilitation professionals. *Journal of Applied Rehabilitation Counseling, 46 (3),* 44-50.

[15] Dufrene, R. L., & Glosoff, H. L. (2004). The ethical decision-making scale-revised. Measurement and Evaluation in Counseling and Development, 37, 1-13.

[16] Facebook (2017). Press Room. Retrieved from www.facebook.com/press/info.php?statistics

[17] Garcia, J., Cartwright, B., Winston, S., & Borchukowska, B. (2003). A transcultural integrative ethical decision-making model in counseling. *Journal of Counseling and Development, 81,* 268-276.

[18] Harley, D. A., Feist-Price, S., & Alston, R. J. (1996). Cultural diversity and ethics: Expanding the definition to be inclusive. *Rehabilitation Education, 10,* 201-210.

[19] Hartley, M., Tarvydas, V., & Johnston, P. S. (2015). The ethics and practice of social media advocacy in rehabilitation counseling. *Journal of Rehabilitation, 81 (1),* 42-51.

[20] Herlihy, B. & Watson, Z. E. (2007). Social justice and counseling ethics. In C.C. Lee (Ed.), *Counseling for social justice* (2nd ed., pp. 181-199). Alexandria, VA: American Counseling Association.

[21] Kitchener, K. S. (1984). Intuition, critical evaluation and ethical principles: The foundation for ethical decision in counseling psychology. The Counseling Psychologist, 12, 43-55.

[22] Ling, T. J., & Hauck, J. M. (2017). The ethics model: Comprehensive, ethical decision making. Vistas Online.

[23]McGinn, F., Flowers, C. R., & Rubin, S. E. (1994). In quest of an explicit multicultural emphasis in ethical standards for rehabilitation counselors. *Rehabilitation Education, 7*, 261-268.

[24]Middleton, R. A., Rollins, C. W., Sanderson, P. L., Leung, P., Harley, D. A., Ebener, D., & Leal-Idrogo, A. (2000). Endorsement of professional multicultural rehabilitation competencies and standards. *Rehabilitation Counseling Bulletin, 43*, 219-240.

[25]National Board for Certified Counselors. (2016). National Board for Certified Counselors Code of Ethics. Retrieved from http://www.nbcc.org/Assets/Ethics/NBCCCodeofEthics.pdf

[26]Power, W. P. (2013). *A guide to vocational assessment. (5th ed).* Austin, TX: Pro-Ed.

[27]Rest, J. R. (1984). Research on moral development: Implications for training counseling psychologists. The Counseling Psychologist, 12, 19-29. doi:10.1177/0011000084123003

[28]Ribble, M. (2011). Digital citizenship in schools (2nd ed.). Eugene, OR: International Society for Technology in Education.

[29]Richards, D., & Richardson, T. (2012). Computer-based psychological treatments for depression: A systematic review and meta-analysis. *Clinical Psychology Review, 32(4)*, 329–342.

[30]Richards, D., & Vigan'o, N. (2012). *Online Counseling. In Y. Zheng (Ed.), Encyclopedia of Cyber Behavior (Vol. 1, pp. 699–713).* New York, NY: IGI Global.

[31]Rubin, S. E., & Roessler, R. T. (2008). *Foundations of the vocational rehabilitation process.* Austin, TX: Pro-Ed.

[32]Stahl, C., MacEachen, E., & Lippel E. (2014). Ethical perspectives in work disability prevention and return to work: Toward a common vocabulary for analyzing stakeholders' actions and interactions. *Journal of Business Ethics, 120*, 237-250.

[33]Tarvydas, V.M. (1998). Ethical decision-making processes. In R.R. Cottone & V.M. Tarvydas (Eds.), *Ethical and Professional Issues in Counseling* (pp. 144-154). Upper Saddle River, NJ: Prentice Hall.

[34]Upton, T.D. (2011). *Private rehabilitation: Evolving opportunities.* Osage Beach, MO: Aspen Professional Services.

[35]Welfel, E. R. (2015). *Ethics in counseling & psychotherapy.* Cengage Learning.

[36]Zur, O. (2009). Psychotherapist Self-Disclosure and Transparency in the Internet Age. (Invited lead article to "Focus on Ethics" section) *Professional Psychology: Research and Practice*, 40, 22-26.

CHAPTER 4

HEALTH DISPARITIES IN RACIAL-ETHNIC MINORITY GROUPS:
IMPLICATIONS FOR REHABILITATION AND ALLIED HEALTH PROFESSIONALS

VALERIE E. D. RUSSELL
ALLEN N. LEWIS, JR.
LAWANDA FORD-JOHNSON

CHAPTER TOPICS

- Significance of Racial-Ethnic Health Disparities
- Sources of Disparities in Health Care
- System-level Context for Health Care Services
- Disparity Models
- Strategies for Service Providers

Racial-ethnic disparities in health care exist and remain a growing public health concern. Research has shown disease and premature deaths that affects minorities can be linked to poor health status, disease risk factors, and limited access to health care. Furthermore, racial and ethnic disparities in health care are pervasive despite comparability in insurance status, income, age, and severity of conditions. As the United States becomes increasingly diverse, it is imperative to support efforts focused on addressing health disparities and the wide range of factors that contribute to disparities, including social and environmental factors extending beyond the health care system. This chapter will examine pertinent areas of racial-ethnic disparities in health care as well as various issues and future considerations for multicultural clients, and both rehabilitation and allied health professionals. The subjects that will be covered are the significance of racial-ethnic health disparities, sources of disparities in healthcare, system-level context for healthcare services, disparity models and strategies for service providers.

SIGNIFICANCE OF RACIAL-ETHNIC HEALTH DISPARITIES

Racial-ethnic minority groups now constitute 28 percent of the United States (U.S.) population, while Non-Hispanic Whites remain the "majority" group, accounting for greater than 50 percent of the nation's total population.[8] By 2060, racial-ethnic minority groups are projected to increase substantially. It is expected that the African American group will comprise 60 million persons—approximately 14 percent of the US population, while 29 percent of the United States is estimated to be Hispanic—more than one-quarter of the total population. Between 2014 to 2060, Asian Americans are expected to nearly double from 5.4 percent to represent 9.3 percent, while American Indian/Alaska Native will be comprised of 5.6 million persons—approximately one percent of the total US population.[8] Even though non-Hispanic Whites are considered both the largest racial and ethnic group, by 2060, this group is projected to become the "minority,"[8] magnifying the importance of addressing racial-ethnic disparities in health and health care.

DEFINING RACE AND ETHNICITY

Racial and ethnic health disparities occur around the world, but the conglomerate of different race and ethnic groups and the disparities in health associated with these minority groups have been an important issue in the U.S.[40] The concepts of race and ethnicity are complex and relatively difficult to define, as the definition of race originally denotes physical and biological characteristics. However, this definition has been refined to incorporate social characteristics and their interactions.[47,19] Likewise, the concept of ethnicity has been proposed as a replacement category for race since ethnic groups share common ancestry, history, or culture but highlight cultural and social characteristics rather than biological ones.[15] Further, the assignment to a racial or ethnic category in census data or clinical studies is usually self-reported information.

The racial and ethnic categories currently in use relate to those defined by the federal government. At present, the race categories recognized by the government include, White: a person having origins in any of the original peoples of Europe, North Africa, or the Middle East; black or African American: a person having origins in any of the black racial groups of Africa; American Indian or Alaskan Native: a person having origins in any of the original peoples of North and South America, including Central America, who maintains cultural identification through tribal affiliations or community attachment; Asian: a person having origins in any of the original peoples of the Far East, Southeast Asia, or the Indian Subcontinent, including Cambodia, China, India, Japan, Korea, Malaysia, Pakistan, Philippine Islands, Thailand; Hispanic or Latino: a person of Cuban, Mexican, Puerto Rican, South or Central American, or other Spanish culture or origin, regardless of race.[29,31]

DEFINING HEALTH DISPARITIES

Disparities exist when differences in health outcomes or health determinants are observed between populations. Disparities in "health" and "health care" are interconnected concepts, but they are not one and the same. A "health disparity" refers to a higher burden of illness, injury, disability, or mortality experienced by one population group comparative to another group.[7] A "health care disparity" describes differences between groups in health insurance coverage, access to and use of care, and quality of care.[7] More specifically, health and health care disparities often refer to differences that cannot be explained by variations in health care needs, patient preferences, or treatment recommendations. Addressing disparities in health is not only important from a social justice standpoint, but also for improving the health of all Americans by achieving improvements in overall quality of care and population health.

Moreover, health disparities are costly, resulting in added health care costs, lost work productivity, and premature death. Recent analysis estimates that 30% of direct medical costs for African-Americans, Hispanics, and Asian Americans are excess costs due to health inequities and that overall, the economy loses an estimated $309 billion per year due to the direct and indirect costs of disparities.[2]

EVIDENCE OF HEALTH DISPARITIES

There is a preponderance of evidence indicative of health disparities in racial-ethnic minority groups in the U.S.[40] Moreover, the Institute of Medicine report[18] confirmed that disparities are pervasive. Racial-ethnic minority disparities in health care occur even when clinical factors, such as stage of disease presentation, comorbidities, age, and severity of disease, are considered.[46] For example, African Americans and Hispanics receive a lower quality of health care for a variety of conditions, including cancer, cardiovascular disease, HIV/AIDS, diabetes, mental health, and other chronic and infectious diseases, according to the Institute of Medicine report.[18] Further, African Americans and American Indians/Alaska Natives have higher overall premature mortality rates than any other population group.[43]

MORTALITY

While the average life expectancy has increased, these gains have not been evenly distributed among all racial-ethnic groups. Disparities occur in life expectancy and mortality. Infant mortality rates are significantly higher for African American and American Indians/Alaska Native babies compared to other groups. African Americans males of all ages have the shortest life expectancy compared to all other groups.[2] In the 2010 census, African Americans endured a disproportionate burden of disease, injury, death, and disability for many health conditions.

Although the top three causes and seven of the 10 leading causes of death are the same for blacks and non-Hispanic whites, the risk factors and incidence, morbidity, and mortality rates for these diseases and injuries are often greater among blacks than whites. A 2010 study revealed striking disparities in life spans between different racial-ethnic groups in the U.S., where life expectancy ranged from 86.7 years for Asian American women to 61.7 years for black or African American men. The study also found that Asian Americans had an average life expectancy of 84.9 years; whites living in the rural northern plains/Dakotas, 79 years; mostly white "middle Americans," 77.9 years; low income whites in Appalachia and the Mississippi Valley, 75years; black or African American "middle Americans," 72.9 years; American Indians in the West, 72.7 years; blacks or African Americans in the South, 71.2 years; and high-risk urban-dwelling blacks or African Americans, 71.1 years.[34]

CARDIOVASCULAR DISEASE

Coronary heart disease (CHD) is the dominant cause of death in the United States among non-Hispanic whites and blacks or African Americans.[10] However, race and ethnic minorities are disproportionately impacted by heart disease and experience higher mortality rates and re-hospitalization rates than non-Hispanic whites.[10] Heart disease prevalence is highest among blacks, Hispanics, and American Indian/Alaskan Natives, and lower among whites and Asians or Pacific Islanders.[10] It is well established that hypertension and high blood pressure rates are higher among blacks compared with whites, and diabetes mellitus is more common among several race/ethnic minority groups than in whites.[12,22]

A comprehensive review of the literature extrapolated several factors associated with differential outcomes by race and ethnicity among patients with heart disease,[10] including differences in distribution of socioeconomic and clinical resources.[3,34] Likewise, differences in distribution of comorbid illnesses, heart disease risk factors, and preventive lifestyle behaviors are key factors that are also implicated in contributing to racial and ethnic disparities in heart disease outcomes.[13,22]

CANCER

Cancer is the second leading cause of death for non-Hispanic whites and the leading cause of death for Hispanics, African Americans, Asians, and Native Americans.[7] In fact, the incidence of cancer is expected to increase by 45% between 2010 and 2030, with the greatest increase occurring in older adults and minorities. By 2030, approximately 28% of all cancers will be diagnosed in racial-ethnic minority groups.[2] The increase in minorities is also likely to impact cancer care, particularly as prior evidence suggests that certain minorities have higher cancer incidence rates and lower cancer survival rates as compared with non-Hispanic whites.[36] Further, minorities have continued to experience a disproportionate burden of both cancer incidence and mortality, and clinical trials have failed to accrue sufficient numbers of minorities.[5,17]

Likewise, research suggests disparities in cancer treatment with minorities who are still more likely to receive substandard care for breast, lung, prostate, and colorectal cancers.[7] Socioeconomic factors may explain much about the poor outcomes for Hispanics, blacks, and Native Americans, but racial and ethnic differences in susceptibility and tumor biology may also be contributing factors. Without focused national attention, gaps in cancer care experienced by diverse populations in the U.S. will widen.[17]

CEREBROVASCULAR DISEASE

Stroke is the third leading cause of death for African-Americans, Asians, and non-Hispanic whites. However, the greater risk factor burden is in racial-ethnic minorities rather than in whites, and accounts for a significant proportion of the higher stroke incidence and mortality[10] observed —especially among African Americans. For example, African Americans have a higher prevalence of hypertension, diabetes mellitus, and left ventricular hypertrophy than whites. Hispanics have a higher prevalence of metabolic syndrome and diabetes mellitus than whites and African Americans. The prevalence of at least two risk factors for stroke is also higher in American Indians/Alaskan Natives than in whites.[10]

DIABETES

Racial and ethnic minorities have a higher prevalence and greater burden of diabetes compared to non-Hispanic whites.[7,2] Specifically, African Americans, Hispanics, and American Indians experience a 50–100% higher burden of illness, complications, and mortality from diabetes than white Americans.[13] Of note, African Americans with diabetes are 1.5 times more likely to be hospitalized and 2.3 times more likely to die from diabetes than non-Hispanic whites.[7] Although Asian Americans tend to have lower BMIs in some subgroups, they are 30% more likely to have type 2 diabetes than their white counterparts.[13] The rate of diabetes-related kidney failure is 3.5 times higher in American Indians than in the general U.S. population.[7]

MENTAL HEALTH

Racial/ethnic disparities in mental health care exceed disparities in many other areas of health care services,[2] with blacks and Hispanics accessing mental health care at only half the rate of non-Hispanic whites.[2,45] Members of racial and ethnic minority groups have less access to mental health services than their white counterparts, are less likely to receive needed care, and are more likely to receive poor quality care when treated.[32] In a study, Wells, et al.,[45] found that African Americans were more likely to have no access to drug and alcohol abuse treatment or mental health care and Hispanics were more likely to have less care than needed or delayed care.

ACCESS AND QUALITY OF CARE

Access to care is a complex concept that incorporates availability, accommodation, affordability, and acceptability[33] Minorities are less likely to receive cardiovascular care, cancer diagnostic tests, and many other important interventions and care.[11] A 2005 study revealed that Asians, Hispanics, and African Americans were less likely than non-Hispanic Whites to have a usual source of care, a healthcare visit, or a dental visit in the previous year.[39] Further, African Americans and possibly Hispanics have longer waiting times in the emergency room, which may contribute to the likelihood of exacerbating symptoms.[10]

Disparities in quality of care are like disparities in access to care. Overall, African American, Hispanics, Asians, and American Indians /Alaska Natives have less access to care than non-Hispanic Whites. African Americans and possibly Hispanics experience poorer health resulting from substantial obstacles to receiving care, including lower access to state-of-the-art care and lack of health insurance.[28]

Consequently, individuals without health insurance tend to: (a) be more likely to forgo routine physical examinations; (b) be unaware of a personal diagnosis of hypertension, diabetes mellitus, or hyperlipidemia; (c) have higher levels of neurological impairment; (d) have longer lengths of hospital stay; (e) have higher rates of stroke; and (f) be at higher risk of death.[11,38] Additionally, uninsured Americans are less likely to receive preventive care or obtain prescription drugs.[9]

CHAPTER 4   HEALTH DISPARITIES IN RACIAL-ETHNIC MINORITY GROUPS

SOURCES OF RACIAL-ETHNIC DISPARITIES IN HEALTH CARE

SYSTEM LEVEL FACTORS

Disparities are not attributable to biologically related factors, but a confluence of systemic, structural, interpersonal, and intrapersonal factors. When policies promote and uphold health disparities between racial-ethnic groups, their structural factors lead to denial of access, thereby affecting utilization rates of services. For example, the cost of health care has been a barrier to accessing care for racial-ethnic minorities.[37] Rowan, et al.,[37] stated that even after one year of being insured, persons with health and mental health concerns reported that the cost of care was still a barrier to receiving healthcare services. This was especially true for persons in lower income strata. For these persons, deductibles, co-payments, and other indirect costs were still out of range and impacted affordability of care.

Also, location of health care services is a structural barrier affecting differential utilization and creating racial-ethnic disparity. As with cost of care, multiple economic factors have been found to underly this issue. Persons who cannot afford the time, private transportation, fuel, or vehicle maintenance will find services located outside of their normal routes prohibitive. Even for those who are skilled in utilizing public transportation, travel time is often a major concern. Many appointments would require one to miss a full day of work, which often is not feasible for lower income clients. Location of services is especially a barrier for racial/ethnic minorities in rural areas, on reservations, or in remote locations.[37]

These systemic barriers denote what literature views as institutional racism. According to Jones,[19] *institutionalized racism* is the "structures, policies, practices, and norms resulting in differential access to the goods, services, and opportunities of society by race."[p.8] Institutionalized racism is normative and results in differential access to quality education, secure housing, gainful employment, appropriate medical and mental health treatment.[19]
Policies addressing costs of care must be implemented at the systemic level to impact this barrier, especially for persons with physical and mental health needs with lower family income.

PROVIDER FACTORS (INTERPERSONAL)

In addition to systemic and structural factors, many interpersonal factors lead to racial-ethnic disparity in health care as well. For instance, the ability to communicate effectively with clients is vitally important to health care engagement and continuity. However, there is a scarcity of bilingual or multilingual health professionals, which can serve as a barrier for seeking help.

Recent immigrants may be especially challenged by language barriers. Often these barriers result in lack of understanding, which may prevent entering and staying in treatment.[23] Other interpersonal factors may involve beliefs, decisions, and related practices of any person in positions of decision-making, power, or influence. Such persons including clinical supervisors, medical professionals, therapists, and counselors are powerful agents of change who must first assess their own personally-mediated biases reflected in recruitment, training, hiring, teaching, and supervising policies and practices. Moreover, training and supervision of students who are preparing to provide services in allied health and related fields must address the need for culturally competent professionals.

CLIENT FACTORS (INTRAPERSONAL)

Cultural values shape our attitudes and behaviors regarding health and wellness, help-seeking behavior, and both physical and mental disorders. Additionally, emotional expressions and communication styles are influenced by cultural values.[23] Some racial and ethnic groups are oriented more toward collectivistic values, like African-Americans, Latinos and Asians. For these groups, the process of counseling may seem foreign with its emphasis on thoughts, feelings and its requirement to be openly transparent about intimate issues with a person who is not a family member.[23]

Value differences lead to mistrust of the system, which often leads to treatment refusal and lack of compliance with treatment protocols. Additionally, negative cultural views pertaining to the use of medication—particularly for preventive or mental health reasons may play into non-compliance. Many Latino and African-American clients rely on faith in a higher power, prayer, saints, and miracles for healing. On the other hand, the majority culture views many modalities as "medicine" including those that occur naturally, including counseling, spirituality, and psychotropics.[12]

When considering race and ethnicity among persons with physical disabilities, the issues are even more complicated. Historically the disability rights movement has modeled itself on the civil rights movement of the 1960s. Ironically, literature and disability research have traditionally focused on the "white" experience and neglected the specific issues of minorities with disabilities, including unique needs such as access to health insurance, personal assistance services, and assistive technology within the racial-ethnic disability community.[49]

The interconnected nature of systemic, structural, interpersonal, and intrapersonal factors often operates concurrently to widen the disparity gap. Therefore, as allied health professionals, we must support policies that increase access to health care for all people, create a more diverse health care workforce, and increase support for research that investigates both causes and solutions regarding racial-ethnic health disparities.[14]

CURRENT SYSTEM-LEVEL CONTEXT FOR HEALTH AND DISABILITY SERVICES

The health system, including the disability system, in the United States today faces an economic, social, and policy context that is characterized by austerity and accountability. The lean fiscal environment has existed since the 1980s,[1,4] continued into the 1990s,[6] and has continued today in this new century.[25] The tight fiscal realities of health and human service budgets, including disability system budgets over the last three-plus decades have resulted in heightened accountability demands. These demands can perhaps be best understood through the Multiple Demands model.[26]

This model posits four types of countervailing demands that most health and human services, inclusive of disability, face these days. The first demand is monetary resources that fund the system. Rarely, if ever, do these resources increase, and if they do, they typically do not increase at a rate that is commensurate with the increase in demands for services. Additionally, such resources are never guaranteed. They are subject to changes in the legislature if they are public funds, and changes in health care financing priorities and approaches if they are private sector funds. This demand can be best thought of as limited and uncertain funding.

Immediately opposite the demand of limited and uncertain funding is the demand of increasing needs for more services. Demands for health and disability services are always on the upswing. This is due to several reasons. First, the population in the United States is increasing rapidly, as per 2010 United States Census population projections. According to census projections, the United States' population is expected to exceed 500 million by the year 2100. Secondly, the population is becoming more diverse, which means providers must attain expertise in cultural matters to effectively serve an increasingly diverse customer base. Another factor is that new developments improving the delivery of services and outcomes are usually expensive at market inception. These first two demands—limited and uncertain funding, along with increasing demands for services directly oppose each other. As if these were not enough, there are two other accountability demands to be considered.

The first accountability demand comes from service recipients, families, and advocacy groups. Accountability derives from these stakeholders being fully empowered and informed about their rights, service providers' obligations, and the full nature of the dynamics of the service delivery and service recipient relationship. Stakeholders these days know what is supposed to happen, how it is to happen, their rights at every point in the service delivery process, and avenues of redress if there are problems or improprieties in the process. No longer are stakeholder's captive to the whims of service providers. They have expertise on the content of service delivery from online sources via the Internet as well as the nature of how services are supposed to be delivered. Having fully empowered and self-determining stakeholders is a positive development in the service delivery system. This accountability demand manifests in the fact that providers of services no longer have free reign in what they do or in how they do it and must now deliver services that conform to the full expectations of customers.

The second accountability demand is similar, yet different. It is similar in that it originates from stakeholders, but from a broader segment of the stakeholder group (i.e., the general population). This demand relates to the power of the citizenry that ultimately pays for all health and disability services through tax dollars or insurance premiums. The accountability here derives from the fact that rarely, if ever, do the payers in the United States system (i.e., citizens) want to pay more for health and disability services. Rather, they want systems to become more efficient in using existing funding and resources to increase the reach of such resources. Therefore, this accountability demand takes on the form of forcing providers to provide services within the constraints of existing funding amounts and in alignment with the parameters of the rules and requirements of the mechanisms through which the funds flow (e.g., state general revenue, Medicaid, private insurance, etc.).

A final aspect of this fourth demand related to accountability is an expectation the general populace has that service delivery systems be effective in keeping the challenges that are commonplace with health and disability out of sight of the daily lives of the lay public. The average citizen does not want to witness the brutal reality of severe health and disability challenges that health and disability systems address daily. In this way, the lay public and citizenry are operating from a "not in my backyard" (NIMBY)-like perspective, and this too holds health and disability service providers accountable. See Figure 1 that depicts visually the four countervailing demands of (a) limited and uncertain funding, (b) increasing demands for services, and the two types of accountability that come from, (c) service recipients, families, and advocacy groups on the one hand, and that come from, (d) citizens and funding entities on the other hand.

Figure 1: Multiple Demands on Disability and Allied Health Professionals in the 21st Century

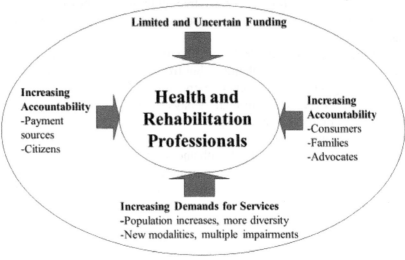

{Lewis, 1990}

Legislation and health care systems are two other aspects worth noting that are significant factors in today's health and disability service context. In the disability system, especially as it relates to vocational rehabilitation, legislation has served a significant role in the development of the current system of services. Since the dawning of the 20th century and over the ensuing century, there have been approximately two dozen significant pieces of legislation to shape the current profile, personality, and array of services and rights that are now afforded to individuals with disabilities in the state-federal vocational rehabilitation system.

The role of legislation in building a system of services for persons with disabilities with full policy support could not be discussed without also mentioning the role of advocacy. Much of the beginning activity that resulted in legislation was borne out of the grass roots advocacy of a few well-intentioned individuals who had a vision of how things could be better for individuals with disabilities. These cadres of individuals also had the tenacity to vigorously ask for what they believed would improve the lives of persons with disabilities. They also had the organizational acumen to pull together the needed critical mass of persons to gain the support to begin the needed system change.

For the health system, there are two seminal aspects that have influenced the system of services over the last 50 years in a major way. The first is the advent of managed care in the 1970s that brought into focus the need for health service systems to do a better job of balancing cost, access, and quality outcomes. Efforts to balance the iron triangle of managed care (cost, access, and quality outcomes) continue today. The other important aspect is the passage of the Patient Protection and Affordable Care Act of 2010 (Affordable Care Act/ACA). This new act empowers service recipients and places them in control of their healthcare.[43] (Specifically, it offers several key advantages in terms of health care costs (e.g., eliminates lifetime coverage limits), coverage (e.g., no more arbitrary insurance coverage withdrawals), and care (e.g., covers preventive care at no cost).

DISPARITY MODELS

CULTURE INFLUENCES, THE SERVICE RECIPIENT EXPERIENCE

Disparity models explain why the cultural orientation of the service recipient can lead to a less-than-optimal experience in the formal service delivery system—be it the health or disability system. Therefore, disparity models offer some heuristic value in fully understanding the system-level context for health and disability services.

The model propagated by the Institute of Medicine (IOM) is arguably the most well-known health disparities model. The text *Unequal Treatment: Confronting Racial and Ethnic Disparities in Healthcare*[40] (is the seminal discussion of the IOM health disparities model). This model purports that a health disparity is an uneven outcome of health services based primarily on cultural orientation (i.e., race or ethnicity) when factors related to access and affluence are held constant. In the text, Smedley, et al.,[40] offer several hundred empirical studies between 1992 and 2002 as evidence that when access and affluence are controlled, there are differences in health outcomes based on race and ethnicity. Such disparities are attributed primarily to bias that is inherent in health systems and bias that stems from individual providers, both subconsciously and consciously. In the IOM model, preferences of service recipients can also play a role.

Kilbourne, et al.,[21] offer a three-phase conceptual model that categorizes health disparities research. These phases are detection, understanding, and reduction/elimination. The overarching point is that research on health disparities falls into one of these categories that intuitively speaks to the need for research to proceed in a stepwise development manner to first identify disparities, then to understand them, and finally, to devote attention toward mitigation and removal. The Kilbourne, et al.,[21] model groups factors that contribute to disparities into the four categories of:

➢ health system factors (e.g., organizational culture, financing, and delivery),

➢ service recipient factors (e.g., beliefs and preferences),

➢ provider factors (e.g., knowledge and bias), and

> clinical encounter factors (e.g., communication and cultural competence).

The visual portrayal of the Kilbourne, et al.,[21] model follows a modified Venn diagram format with a series of circles. Health system factors are the large, all-encompassing circle that encapsulates the other three factors. Both service recipient and provider factors are separate circles, and where they overlap constitute the clinical encounter factors.

The Lewis[24] Disability Disparities model was developed specifically to address disability disparities. Prior to this model's development, there was no explicit disparities model designed specifically to address the concept of disability. The health disparities models have applicability to the disability phenomenon, but there is a subtle, but important distinction to be made between the concepts of a health condition and a disability. While it could easily be argued that all disabilities involve a health condition or an aspect of health, conversely, it cannot be argued that all health conditions are disabilities. Health conditions are the existence of some abnormality, disease, or illness that is not considered normal. Disabilities, on the other hand, involve some health-related abnormality that are permanent, (i.e., not curable), and they pose a functional limitation in some area of major life functioning (which not all health conditions do). Some health conditions rise to the level of being a disability, and pretty much all disabilities comprise of a health or health related component.

Most viable definitions of disability contain some aspect that addresses the health abnormality—an aspect that speaks to the chronicity or permanence of the health concern, and an aspect that addresses the resulting functional limitation in a major life area. In the United States, the Americans with Disabilities Act defines disability as pervasive, especially as it relates to allegations of employment discrimination due to disability. The best definition of disability is the one offered by the World Health Organization in the International Classification of Function, Disability and Health. This definition posits that disability is best understood on an individualized basis because a full understanding requires knowing the complex interplay among the factors of health condition, impairment, level of participation, environment, and personal characteristics.[48]

The Lewis[24] model offers the following definition of a disability disparity:

> *A disability disparity exists when an underserved or ethnic minority cultural group's goal is to receive services within the formal rehabilitation and disability system (public or private), but there is a differential experience based primarily on cultural orientation that results in more incidence of disability, and/or lower participation levels in the formal helping system, and/or fewer successful individual outcomes when compared to majority culture groups.*[p.1140]

This model is based on understanding the concept of disparity from the point of occurrence of disability (incidence) to outcomes of services. It is a continuum that represents a five-point progression. This progression matches the natural flow of an individual who realizes s/he has a disability and enters the formal system to receive services, and eventually has an outcome of services. The continuum encompasses:

➢ Domain 1 - incidence of disability,

➢ Domain 2 - contemplation about participation in the formal system,

➢ Domain 3 - accessing the formal system once a decision is made to do so,

➢ Domain 4 - level of participation once in the formal system, and

➢ Domain 5 - the individual level outcomes achieved as facilitated by the formal system.

Visually portrayed at the top of the model is a set of five factors that represent a hypothesized view of the components believed to account for the different experiences of culturally diverse and underserved populations along the five-point continuum. The five factors represent intuitive and logical explanations to explain and offer rationale for why disability disparities exist (see Figure 2). The Lewis[24] model is also comprised of both macro- and micro-level components that match the five-point continuum. On the macro level, there are factors that account for each of the five points on the continuum. The same is true on the micro level. A key distinction between the macro and micro levels is that the macro level attempts to offer a conceptual understanding of Domains 1 through 5. Alternatively, the micro level lays out aspects that clinicians can explore if it is believed that a disability disparity exists at this point on the continuum, and if further exploration is desired with a particular service recipient to confirm the existence of the disparity.

CHAPTER 4   HEALTH DISPARITIES IN RACIAL-ETHNIC MINORITY GROUPS

Figure 2

Lewis Disability Disparities Model

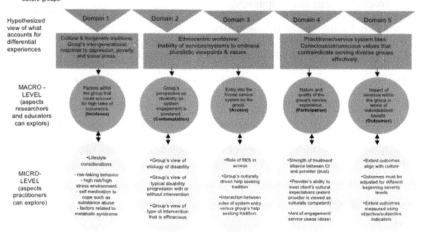

CHANGE STRATEGIES FOR INDIVIDUAL SERVICE PROVIDERS

MANAGING BIAS

Managing bias is a key strategy for individuals who strive to be a part of positive change in addressing health and disability disparities based on race and ethnicity. Rarely in a discussion of bias within the counseling professions is a definition included. A bias is a preference for one's own perspective that is manifested consciously or unconsciously even in situations when such a preference goes against proper clinical practice or service delivery.[27] Considering this definition, at some point all service providers possess bias since, in some instances, the cultural orientation of the service recipient is not obvious. Therefore, it is best if bias can be managed proactively.

There are four suggested steps for service providers to proactively manage bias.

1. Understand the true nature of the bias. Offer a reason why this is a bias. Determine if the bias is permanent or amenable to change. If the bias can be changed, begin to identify possible modifications, and if it cannot, begin thinking about management strategies.

2. Understand the potential negative impact of the bias. Assess how the bias impacts service provision. Acknowledge the type of person that may invoke this bias along with the specific negative impact.

3. Identify strategies for effectively managing the bias. Determine what strategies will contain the bias. Think about how to proactively monitor the status of the bias over time.

4. Recognize the personal learning that having this bias facilitates.

Understand the personal lessons learned and the implications of those lessons going forward. Plan to revisit this four-step process routinely. This four-step process is an intentional approach for managing bias. With regular use, it can help to minimize the negative impact of service providers' held biases on service recipients.

CULTURAL COMPETENCY, HUMILITY, AND EFFICACY

Cultural competency is a key strategy for the success of service providers working cross culturally in disability and allied health settings. The literature on cultural competency spans several decades. According to Sue, et al,[41] cultural competency comprises the three skills of:

- being aware of one's own assumptions about human behavior, values, preconceived notions, limitations and biases,

- understanding the worldview of service recipients who are culturally different without imposing negative judgments, and

- practicing appropriately with culturally different service recipients.

Beyond cultural competency, there are two related, but newer generation concepts. They are cultural efficacy and cultural humility. Cultural efficacy, as coined by Nunez,[30] is an evolved concept based on the perspective of ethnorelativism, which means that neither the provider's nor service recipient's cultural orientation is preferred. Both orientations are comparable perspectives among many equally important points of view. Cultural efficacy also discourages the view that cultural competency is an end state (proficiency in a defined content area) to be reached as the word competency implies.

Cultural humility[42] is a concept that is remarkably similar to cultural efficacy. It requires service providers to exhibit humility toward culturally diverse and underserved populations. This humility entails self-awareness, self-critique, and active reflection. These three processes aim to modify the traditional service provider-service recipient power imbalance toward improved communication, full collaboration, and respect. Ultimately, cultural humility strives to improve alliances with culturally diverse groups and their communities, as well as service provider self-congruence and efficacy.

REFERENCES

[1] Adams, C. T., Perlmutter, F. D. (1995). Leadership in hard times: Are nonprofits well-served? Nonprofit and Voluntary Sector Quarterly, 24, 253–263.

[2] Agency for Healthcare Research and Quality (AHRQ). (2010). *National Healthcare Quality Report.* Rockville, MD: U.S. Department of Health and Human Services.

[3] Arnold, S. V., Chan, P. S., Jones, P. G., Decker, C., Buchanan, D.M., Krumholz, H. M., et al. (2011). Cardiovascular outcomes research consortium. Translational research investigating underlying disparities in acute myocardial infarction Patients' health status (TRIUMPH): Design and rationale of a prospective multicenter registry. *Circulation: Cardiovascular Quality and Outcomes,* 4, 467–76.

[4] Bargal, D., Schmid, H. (1989). Recent themes in theory and research on leadership and their implications for management of the human services. Administration in Social Work, 13, 37-51.

[5] Bouchardy, C., Rapiti, E., Blagojevic, S., et al. (2007). Older female cancer patients:Importance, causes, and consequences of undertreatment. *Journal of Clinical Oncology,* 25, 1858–1869.

[6] Burchard, J. D., & Schaefer, M. C. (1992). Improving accountability in a service delivery system in children's mental health. *Clinical Psychology Review, 12,* 867–882.

[7] Centers for Disease Control and Prevention (CDC). (2011). Prevalence of coronary heart disease—United States, 2006–2010. *Morbidity and Mortality Weekly Report,* 60, 1377–81.

[8] Colby, S, L. & Ortman, J. M. (2014). Projections of the Size and Composition of the U.S. Population:2014 to 2060, Current Population Reports, P25-1143, U.S. Census Bureau, Washington, DC.

[9] Collins, S. R., Davis, K., Doty, M. M., Kriss, J. L, Holmgren, A. L. et al. (2006). *Gaps in health insurance: An all-American problem.* New York, NY: The Commonwealth Fund.

[10] Cruz, S., Rabinstein, A., Biller, J., Elkind, M. S. V., Griffith, P., Philip, B., Gorelick, et al. (2011). Racial-ethnic disparities in stroke care: The American experience. American Heart Association/American Stroke Association, Stroke, 42, 2091-2116.

[11] Fowler-Brown, A., Corbie-Smith, G., Garrett, J., & Lurie, N. (2007). Risk of cardiovascular events and death: Does insurance matter? *Journal of General Internal Medicine,* 22,502–507.

[12] Garrett, M. T. (2007). Hear the eagle's cry: Native American spiritual traditions. In O. J. Morgan (Ed.), *Counseling and spirituality: Views from the profession* (pp. 139-164). Boston: Lahaska.

[13] Go, A. S., Mozaffarian, D., Roger, V. L., Benjamin, E. J., Berry, J. D., Blaha, M. J., et al. (2014). On behalf of the American heart association statistics committee and stroke statistics subcommittee. Heart disease and stroke statistics—2014 update: a report from the American heart association. *Circulation*, 129, 28–292.

[14] Goin, D., & Long, S. K. (2014). Health care access and cost barriers for adults with physicalor mental health issues. Health, 4, 12-8.

[15] Gorelick, P. B. (1998). Cerebrovascular disease in African Americans. *Stroke*, 29, 2656 – 2664.

[16] Graham, L., Brown-Jeffy, S., Aronson, R., & Stephens, C. (2011). Critical race theory as theoretical framework and analysis tool for population health research. *Critical Public Health*, 21(1), 81-93.

[17] Gross, C. P., Smith, B. D., Wolf, E., et al. (2008). Racial disparities in cancer therapy: Did the gap narrow between 1992 and 2002? *Cancer*, 112, 900–908.

[18] Institute of Medicine. (2003). *Unequal Treatment: Confronting Racial and Ethnic Disparities in Health Care*. Washington, DC: National Academies Press.

[19] Jones, C. P. (2000). Levels of racism: A theoretic framework and a gardener's tale. *American Journal of Public Health*, 90, 1212–1215.

[20] Jones, C. P. (2002). Confronting institutionalized racism. *Phylon (1960-)* 7-22.

[21] Kilbourne, A. M., Switzer, G., Hyman, K., Crowley-Matoka, M. & Fine, M. J. (2006). Advancing health disparities research within the health care system: a conceptual framework. *American Journal of Public Health*, 96(12), 2113-2121.

[22] Koch, C. G., Li, L., Kaplan, G. A., Wachterman, J., Shishehbor, M. H., Sabik, J., et al. (2010). Socioeconomic position, not race, is linked to death after cardiac surgery. *Circulation: Cardiovascular Quality and Outcomes*, 3, 267–76.

[23] Leong F. T. L., Kalibatseva, Z. (2011). Cross-cultural barriers to mental health services in the United States. *Cerebrum*, http://www.ncbi.nlm.nih.gov/pmc/articles/PMC3574791/.

[24] Lewis, A. (2009). Disability disparities: A beginning model. *Disability and Rehabilitation*, 31(14), 1136–1143.

[25] Lewis, A. N., Armstrong, A. J., & Karpf, A. (2005). Using data to improve outcomes in rehabilitation practice. *Journal of Rehabilitation Administration*, 29(1), 43-56.

[26] Lewis, A. N. (2014). Program evaluation for rehabilitation and allied health administrators (in C. Flowers, J. Soldner, & S. Robertson, Eds.), *Counseling supervision and administrative practices in allied health professions*. Aspen Professional Services: Linn Creek, MO.

[27] Lewis, A. N. (2011). The anatomy of cultural bias and strategies to overcome it. *Journal of Minority Disability Research and Practice*, 1(4), 10-41.

[28]Mead, H., Cartwright-Smith, L., Jones, K., et al. (2008). Racial and ethnic disparities in US healthcare: A Chartbook. *The Commonwealth Fund, New York, NY.*

[29]National Forum on Education Statistics, Race/Ethnicity Data Implementation Task Force. (2008). *Managing an identity crisis: Forum Guide to implementing new federal race and ethnicity categories.* Washington, DC: National Center for Education Statistics, Institute of Education Sciences, US Department of Education.

[30]Nunez, A. (2000). Transforming cultural competency into cross-cultural efficacy in women's health education. *Academic Medicine, 75,* 1071–1080.

[31]Office of Management and Budget. (2001). Provisional guidance on the implementation of the 1997 standards for federal data on race and ethnicity.

[32]Ojeda, V., & McGuire, T. (2006). Gender and racial/ethnic differences in use of outpatient mental health and substance use services by depressed adults. *Psychiatric Quarterly, 77,* 211–222.

[33]Penchansky, R., & Thomas, J. W. (1981). The concept of access: Definition and relationship to consumer satisfaction. *Medical Care, 19,* 127–140.

[34]Phelan, J. C., Link, B. G., & Tehranifar, P. (2010). Social conditions as fundamental causes of health inequalities: Theory, evidence, and policy implications. *Journal Health of Social Behavior,* 51(2), 28–40.

[35]Rehabilitation Act of 1973, 29 U.S.C. Section 701-744, as amended in 1992; Title I, Section 21, Pub. L. 102-569.

[36]Ries, L. A. G., Melbert, D., Krapcho, M., Stinchcomb, D. G., Howlader, N., Horner, M.J. et al. (2008). *SEER Cancer Statistics Review, 1975-2005.* Bethesda, MD: National Cancer Institute.

[37]Rowan, K., McAlpine, D. D., & Blewett, L. A. (2013). Access and cost barriers to mental health care, by insurance status, 1999–2010. Health affairs, 32(10), 1723-1730.

[38]Shen, J. J. & Washington, E. L. (2007). Disparities in outcomes among patients with stroke associated with insurance status. *Stroke,* 38,1010 – 1016.

[39]Shi, L. & Stevens, G. D. (2005). Disparities in access to care and satisfaction among U.S. children: The roles of race/ethnicity and poverty status. *Public Health Reports,120,* 431–441.

[40]Smedley, B. D., Stith, A. Y., & Nelson, A. R. (2003). *Unequal treatment: Confronting racial and ethnic disparities in health care.* Washington, DC: National Academies Press.

[41]Sue, D. W., Arredondo, P., & McDavis, R. (1992). Multicultural counseling competencies and standards: A call to the profession. *Journal of Multicultural Counseling and Development,* 20(2), 64-88.

[42]Tervalon, M., & Murray-Garcia, J. (1998). Cultural humility versus cultural competency: A critical distinction in defining physician training outcomes in multicultural education. *Journal of Healthcare for the Poor and Underserved,* 9(2), 117-125.

[43] United States Department of Health and Human Services, HHS.gov/HealthCare. Retrieved from http://www.hhs.gov/healthcare/rights/.

[44] United States Census Bureau. *Twenty third census of the inhabitants of the United States 2010*, Washington DC: United States Congress and Secretary of State.

[45] Wells, K., Klap, R., Koike, A., & Sherbourne, C. (2001). Ethnic disparities in unmet need for alcoholism, drug abuse, and mental health care. *American Journal of Psychiatry, 158,* 2027–2032.

[46] Whitehead, M. (1991). The Concepts and Principles of Equity and Health. *Health Promotion International.* 6 (3), 217–228.

[47] Williams, D. R. (1997). Race and health: Basic questions, emerging directions. *Annual Epidemiology*, 7, 322–333.

[48] World Health Organization. (2011). International Classification of Functioning, Disability and Health. Retrieved from http://who.int/classifications/icf/en/

[49] Wright, T. J., & Leung, P. (1993). *Meeting the unique needs of minorities with disabilities.* Report to the President and the Congress.

CHAPTER 5

RELIGION, SPIRITUALITY, AND SECULARISM:
THE RELEVANCE TO CULTURE AND PREPARING COMPETENT HEALTH CARE PROFESSIONALS

WILLIAM TALLEY
JOYCE BELL

CHAPTER TOPICS

- Terms and definitions pertinent to spirituality
- The relevance of spiritual orientation to the counselor
- A journey toward cultural awareness
- Cultural encapsulation and spirituality
- Spiritual competencies
- Dimensions of spirituality
- Considering ones degree of spirituality
- Assessing religiosity

PREFACE

As you consider a serious discussion of issues that influence the provision of services to individuals with disabilities and their families, a topic that should immediately surface relates to that individual's orientation toward religion and/or spirituality. That is to say, what are that person's thoughts, feelings, and dispositions regarding their religious and spiritual beliefs. By some accounts, 90% (ninety percent) of the clients seen in the United States (US), either belong to a religious group or have some defined set of spiritual beliefs.[31] It seems clear then to these authors that in order to take a holistic approach to working with individuals with disabilities, and to effectively serve those that we work with, we must have a working knowledge of and appreciation for our clients' orientation toward religion and spirituality.

INTRODUCTION

As the field of counseling evolves, authors have increasingly stressed the significance of exposing those who aspire to become competent and complete counseling professionals to the various issues that relate to working with individuals who are culturally different.[30,38,8] This is a concept that, over time, has become a generally accepted and guiding principle in the field of counseling. As this notion has evolved, authors[20,1,8,30,36,8] have increasingly drawn attention to the role that spiritual and religious beliefs play in the helping process. Therefore, whether the topic is an emphasis on indigenous forms of mental health interventions[22] or on modern spiritual and religious practices in general,[8] authors seem to be increasingly aware of the relevance that spiritual and religious matters play in the counseling relationship and process. From the perspectives of the authors of this chapter, there is little doubt that one's OTS should be seen as a critical concern for the aspiring counseling professional. However, as noted in a study by Walker, et al.,[46] most therapists from other professions rarely engage in spiritual practices or participate in organized religion, with the exception of marriage and family therapy.

The following chapter reflects the authors attempt to expose the reader to the basic concepts related to spiritual and religious matters in an effort to allow them to develop a useful framework from which to understand how these matters relate to concerns faced by counseling professionals. As you review the literature on culture, there are a number of issues that stand out. When you explore religions and the issue of spirituality, what seems apparent is that unique societies and or cultures seem to develop around those religions and the individuals involved in them. While the degree to which this happens varies from one setting to the next, it is hard to argue against the fact that unique customs, develop in association with these groups. Views of the afterlife, family structure, marriage, funeral and wedding customs, diet, consumption of intoxicants, dress and more are examples of decisions that are typically influenced by and at times dictated by religious and spiritual principles.

As you will read later in this chapter, in the world at large, the majority of individuals that counseling professionals are likely to serve will have some sort of spiritual or religious beliefs. In as much as that is fact, it seems clear that well trained counselors should be prepared to address the needs of their clients with this in mind. To be clear, counseling professionals should strive to comprehend how spiritual and religious beliefs influence both the practitioner, the client, and when appropriate those who make up the clients' circle of influencers. As Corey[9] suggests, the practitioner who ignores basic and critical differences in people, such as their spiritual and religious beliefs, are in all probability not doing what is in the best interest of that individual.

TERMS AND DEFINITIONS

Orientation toward Spirituality, (OTS): refers to ones' orientation toward spiritual matters to include religious, spiritual, secular, agnostic, and atheistic thought. In other words, in this chapter we refer to individuals from all five categories.

The authors have chosen to use the term Orientation toward Spirituality (OTS), to refer to the individual's belief system as it relates to any spiritual orientation, including individuals who consider themselves religious, spiritual, secular, agnostic, or atheistic. If we wish to refer to a specific orientation or mindset related to religion or spirituality, we will use Spiritual Thought, (ST): Religious Thought, (RT): Secular Thought, (SCT): Agnostic Thought, (AGT): or Atheistic Thought, (ATT). If on the other hand, a specific set of religious or spiritual beliefs are relevant, then we will refer to that specific orientation (i.e... Hinduism, Taoism, Shintoism, etc.) It should also be noted, that while some authors consider matters pertaining to secular thought to include agnostic and atheistic thought, we clearly distinguish the boundaries between these categories. We have found that there is ample evidence in the literature to demonstrate the clear distinctions between these categories.

Ones' orientation toward spirituality can be described in a number of ways and as you might well suspect, because individuals in many cases, hold strongly to their respective beliefs, there is a great deal of disagreement over how any discussion of the matter should be presented. As we begin the discussion of secular thought, the reader will get a small taste of the complex nature of the discussion that lies ahead.

SECULAR THOUGHT

Secular thought pertains to those things that are non-religious, non-spiritual and not related to things that are sacred. Secularism is the school of thought promoted by individuals who believe that religion is a matter that should be the private affair of the individual. The separation of church and state which is a key part of Jeffersonian thought, and which is codified in the US Constitution, is a very practical manifestation of secular thought. Here is the basic principle espoused. The government should not be guided by or developed according to the standards of religion. Therefore, when Jefferson describes government "without religion" he is describing governmental practices that are secular. It supports the notion that the individual must be free to have whatever orientation toward religion that they choose. That also means that they can choose to have no religious beliefs at all.

Strictly speaking, an individual can hold secular beliefs and still be either religious or spiritual. That is to say, they can believe in a secular government, which is government without religion and still be religious or spiritual in their private lives.

AGNOSTIC THOUGHT

The agnostic holds the belief that one cannot know if God or the gods exist. The agnostic does not deny the existence of a higher being or deity, they simply profess not to know if one exists. To be clear, the agnostic does not deny the existence of a deity or deities, but instead, they adopt the position that one cannot know of the existence of god and therefore, they do not know if a God exists. To complicate the discussion further, there are agnostic theists, who profess not to know if God exist and yet choose to believe in God and there are agnostic atheists who profess that they cannot know if God exists and choose not to believe in God.

ATHEISTIC THOUGHT

Atheism refers to those who do not believe in any deity at all or in other words, it is the absence of belief in god, the gods, or any form of deity. The atheist rejects the notion that any deity or higher being exists at all. Atheistic thought is therefore much simpler and definitive in that it rejects the possibility that god, the Gods or any other sort of deities exist.

SPIRITUAL THOUGHT

Spirituality pertains to one's relationship with the transcendent and involves one's effort to be connected with something greater than themselves. Spirituality shares many of the same elements of religion and yet it is more ambiguous, fluid, and organic. The act of being spiritual involves engaging in doing spiritual things such as praying, meditating, and finding ways to move closer to the transcendent. You might well say that these are components of religion and you would be correct. Religion, however, involves the act of believing, while spirituality is mostly about being. One can be spiritual without being religious; however, it is difficult to imagine someone who is religious without being spiritual. For some, spirituality is defined as an internal process, which may or may not include a belief in a supreme being while others may connect their sense of spirituality to some being, as in the Buddha, or a higher being or beings. Taylor[44] defined spirituality as the underlying dimension of consciousness that strives for meaning, union with the universe, and with all things; it extends to the experience of the transcendent or a power beyond the individual.[p.14] According to Bullis,[5] spirituality is that inward part of a person that enables the individual to see good in others and to develop meaningful relationships. Spirituality is the aspect of humankind that enables and motivates the individual to search for meaning and purpose in life and to find one's place in the universe. Spirituality concerns ideas and beliefs and concepts that give meaning and direction to a person's life.[40]

RELIGIOUS THOUGHT

Taylor,[44] defined religion as an organized set of beliefs and practices of a particular faith community. The religious system of beliefs, rituals, and practices generally has an institutional structure of ritualistic style worship. This type of worship includes congregations, parishes, and temples, in which people become members and take on religious roles, identities, and relationships with others. Religion is the external expression of one's faith and is comprised of beliefs, ethical codes, and worship practices that unite an individual with a moral community.[44] It is a visual sign to the person as well as to others that the person is part of a particular belief system. Religion usually connotes a belief in a higher or Supreme Being. In some people's belief system, this Supreme Being is God; in other systems, it is Buddha or the Ultimate. Faiver, et al.,[12] describe religion as "the social vehicle to nurture and express spirituality."[p.2]

Since we now have a working definition of religion, it is only natural to offer some discussion of the separate groups that fall under that description. Numerous religions can be categorized in various ways, however most often when people speak of the organized religions they begin with Christianity, Judaism, Islam, and the Eastern Religions. Then they will engage in a discussion of the major denominations in Christianity, the major divisions in Islam and Judaism and the major Eastern Religions.

Conversely, when discussing spirituality there are a number of terms and phrases that are important to include in the discussion. One phrase that is currently popular, especially in the United States is Spiritual but not Religious (SBNR), which is used to describe an orientation to life that rejects the utilization of traditional religions as the method of describing ones orientation to the spiritual. There are a number of similar terms, which include freethinkers, the unchurched, the religiously unaffiliated, the spiritually eclectic, and the spiritually independent.

Those who desire to be counselors should know something about their OTS, the OTS of those they plan to serve and how spirituality impacts individuals as counselors. A good first step is to ask the question, are their ethical reasons that would cause us to explore these issues. The simple answer to that question is found in the ethical codes that counselors are expected to adhere to. If you examine the ethical codes for the American Counseling

Association, (ACA) or the American Psychological Association, (APA) you will discover that they both address the issue in detail. These codes indicate that spirituality or religion is rather significant to both client and practitioner, and the details are clearly outlined by the Association for Spiritual, Ethical, and Religious Values in Counseling (ASERVIC) in the new ASERVIC Competencies for Addressing Spiritual and Religious Issues in Counseling.[10,6] Secondly, a simple review of today's literature will demonstrate that leading authors such as Corey,[7] indicate that all counseling is multicultural in nature and that religion is a critical component of culture. Thirdly, as we explore the impact of spiritual beliefs on the individuals whom we serve, we should ask ourselves does this issue affect a significant number of those that we serve.

According to Newport,[29] approximately ninety one percent (91%) of those who live in the United States report that they believe in God or some universal spirit. Which makes the US one of the most religious countries in the industrialized world. Of course, it also means that if you are seeing clients, chances are that nine in ten individuals have some sort of spiritual belief. Spirituality is one of those topics that becomes more complex and difficult to discuss with the more thought that you give it.

The range of views on religion vary as widely as the definitions that apply to religion and spirituality. You can find those who are devoutly religious, those who reject religion but consider themselves spiritual, those who do not know if there is a God and those who are sincerely convinced that there is no God. The perspective that you adopt as a rehabilitation professional is a personal matter and we can find no justification for demanding that you adopt one position on spirituality over another. It is the author's view that we must learn to respect divergent perspectives.

THE ORIGINS OF SPIRITUAL AND RELIGIOUS THOUGHT IN HISTORY

From a historical context, religion and spirituality have often been used interchangeably and frequently seen as terms that were synonymous. Gradually, over time, religious thought came to be perceived as the public expression of belief in one of the doctrines affiliated with a particular religion. Spiritual thought on the other hand, became affiliated with the internal process of thinking, feeling, or seeing oneself as it pertains to ones orientation to non-worldly beliefs.

There is evidence[28] of artifacts which appear to be religious in nature, that have been observed by scientists dating back over 5000 years. The origins of religion, however, are lost somewhere in our distant past. Determining when someone first wondered if there was a higher authority or deity that influenced human behavior is impossible to isolate. There is evidence that people began to practice some sort of burial ritual hundreds of thousands of years ago which implies that they thought that the spirit of their loved ones should be cared for.

The Existence of Religion Today

When we look at the people who live in the United States,[31] we find that approximately 70% are Christians, 9% are Muslims, 7% are Hindus, 7% are Buddhist while 3% belong to other religions. In the world at large however the figures are somewhat different and breakdown as 33% Christians, 21% Muslims, 13% Hindus, 6% Buddhist, 12% other religions and 14% non-religious. So, it seems that the majority of people who live on earth believe in some sort of deity. In total over eighty percent (80%) of the world's population identifies with one of the world's many religious or spiritual groups.

Religion is one of several variables such as race, ethnicity, age, and socioeconomic status that can have a significant impact on the counseling relationship. It is the nature of religion, however, and the significance that it has to the lives of those who choose to adhere to it, that foster its potential to play a very crucial role in defining who an individual is and how they may react to counseling. Even in its absence, the sensitivity of clients to religious issues can play a role. Individuals who are having doubts about their religious beliefs may find it difficult to address this issue, especially if they come from a community that holds religious matters in high regard.

When considering client's OTS the counselor should bear in mind that those with strong beliefs may be similar in many ways to those with marginal beliefs. It is always important to consider how religion affects the client both culturally and individually. Knowledge of the client's religious identity can be used as an additional means of support for the client. It is also important for the counselor to be keenly aware of how their religious values affect the counseling relationship. As Gladding[15] notes, being aware of religious orientation is especially important if the counselor's religious beliefs differ from those of the client. Bullis[5] suggested that religious or spiritual applications to practice, involve a recognition of one's own religious and spiritual issues in order to provide effective service delivery.

The first implication for practitioners is "to know thyself" as it pertains to one's orientation toward spirituality. This self-knowledge should involve an on-going process of openness and reflection on one's personal beliefs, values, and attitudes concerning the religious or spiritual dimensions of human existence.

UNDERSTANDING OUR OWN ORIENTATION TO SPIRITUALITY

Making the effort to move toward self-awareness is a critical component of becoming a good counselor. Corey[9] suggests that if we are to promote discovery in others, we need to first understand who we are and how our view of life impacts us. When we are in the process of getting to know our new clients, we should take the time to develop a clear picture of them, and to fully grasp their orientation toward things religious and spiritual. Understanding who they are as religious and spiritual beings could give the practitioner additional insight into who the client is as a person and what the nature of some of their problems might be. To better grasp the matter of their own OTS, the counselor should consider the points listed below and give some thought to how they may impact them as an individual, as a counselor, and in their relationships with others:

- How relative spirituality is to the client's lifestyle.
- Understanding if the client is moved to have concerns about spiritual matters in their life and if so why?
- The client's level of commitment to spiritual mattes relative to where they feel they are or should be.
- Whether or not the clients spiritual beliefs tend to influence their interactions with others (do they connect significant feelings such as distrust, worthiness, anger, fear, repulsion with people) based on the perception of that persons orientation toward spirituality.
- If the client ties their past mistakes or current problems to decisions they have made relative to some spiritual condition, action, position, or lack thereof.
- Whether or not the client is experiencing conflict because of their spiritual beliefs or their ability to conform to those beliefs?

As the counselor develops a keener understanding of their own OTS, they may find themselves better equipped to consider how these same issues may affect those that they serve.

TABLE 1

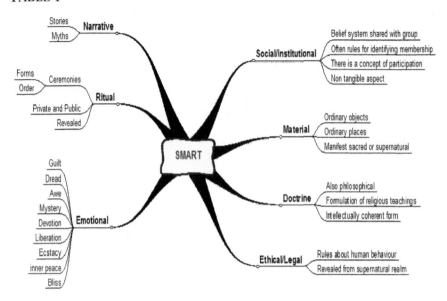

THE EVOLUTION OF PRACTITIONERS THOUGHT ON SPIRITUALITY

While early authors such as Freud virtually ignored the existence of culture and expressed disdain toward the mere existence of religion, the current literature and numerous ethical codes relevant to counseling clearly indicate that being culturally competent with regard and respect for the importance of a client's religion and spirituality is necessary.

Freud did not believe that religion was pertinent to psychology and in fact often referred to himself as a Godless Jew. Freud reported that it was his belief that "Religion is an illusion, and it derives its strength from the fact that it falls in with our instinctual desires."[14]

As the discipline of psychology and counseling evolved, so did the views of the leading authors of the day. A progression of authors[22,30,31,9] have noted the significance that religion and spirituality play in the lives of individuals.

The practice of being a counselor is necessarily bound up in being aware of who we are as individuals. While we cannot be certain that our counseling efforts will always be successful, we can increase the likelihood of success by becoming aware of how our actions are influenced by our cultural values, such as religion. As Corey[7] notes, "knowing how your own culture influences your decisions and daily behavior, provides a frame of reference for understanding the worldview of those who differ from you."[p.30] Corey[7] further notes that self-awareness is a "central characteristic for any therapeutic person."[pg.32]

CULTURAL ENCAPSULATION

Cultural encapsulation is a term that was developed by Wrenn and is first noted in the publication *"The Culturally Encapsulated Counselor."*[47] The term refers to the individual who approaches interactions from a distinctly ethnocentric perspective. That is to say, that the culturally encapsulated individual would engage someone from another culture from a posture that is distinctly biased toward their own culture and against that of the person they engage. The assumption of the individual is in essence that theirs is the perspective that has merit. Their approach to interactions with those from other cultures could be described as one that is either ignorant of other cultures or one where they discount the value of the others culture.

In our efforts to address issues that influence counseling it is useful to consider the relevance of cultural encapsulation since it may significantly affect the counselor, the client, those significant to the counseling process such as family members or all of the above. Corey[8] suggests that the phenomena of cultural encapsulation stems from the idea or belief that "certain cultural values are supreme."[p.57] As it pertains to religion or spirituality, it would involve an individual assuming that one set of religious beliefs are necessarily superior or correct and the only acceptable point of view to hold. Further, it would allow the individual in question to discount the value or relevance of another religious perspective, thus relegating that perspective unimportant. In such an event, by denying the relevance of the others point of view, the individual disallows the possibility of gaining understanding of behavior through the eyes or from the perspective of the other person.

It should not be difficult to grasp how this attitude might negatively affect the clinical relationship. The problem in holding such a position is that if you assume that one set of beliefs, for example your specific religious or spiritual beliefs, are exclusively correct, then you must also conclude that holding any other perspective is equally wrong or inferior. This could be quite problematic for both client and clinician since it will seem quite difficult to assume a posture of unconditional positive regard for someone if you conclude that a perspective that is critical to them is inferior to your own. The concept of cultural encapsulation speaks to the importance of a counselor's sense of self-awareness as well as a relative sense of who they are as a practitioner. Covey, et al.,[10] defined self-awareness as "our capacity to stand apart from ourselves and examine our thinking, our motives, our history, our scripts, our actions, and our habits and tendencies. It enables us to take off our "glasses" and look at them as well as through them. Self-awareness makes it possible for the practitioner to become aware of the social and psychic history of the programs that are in us and to enlarge the separation between stimulus and response."[p.1] An examination of ones' own values, motivations, beliefs and attitudes toward religion and spirituality and its place in their practice is imperative to developing a culturally and spiritually sensitive practice.

ASSUMED HOMOGENEITY

There is often a tendency for individuals to assume that all the members of a particular spiritual group (Southern Baptist, Buddhist, and Muslim) are like all the other members of that group in thought and behavior. There are several pitfalls with such assumptions that the practitioner should be careful to avoid. First, as noted elsewhere in this chapter, spiritual and religious groups may be divided into numerous subgroups. Christians (see Table 2) are subdivided into the major categories of Catholic and Protestant and are then further subdivided into numerous denominations. Likewise, Muslims are divided into numerous sects and subsects.

Members of these spiritual groups may also find that their practices are further refined by the region of the world that they practice their faith. Some individuals consider themselves very devout believers and make a conscious effort to live their lives according to the edicts of their beliefs or the rules of their respective religious document. However, you may also find those who belong to the same religion, on the other end of the spectrum, who barely adhere to the major tenets of what they identify as their belief.

Then there is the issue of spiritual fluidity, which simply refers to the fact that religious beliefs may evolve or change overtime. While there are many individuals who strongly object to those who would leave their faith, a person's spiritual beliefs may not be immutable.

THE RELEVANCE OF SPIRITUALITY TO CLIENT COUNSELOR INTERACTIONS

Developing an understanding of the religiosity of a client is an important step in the counseling process. It is widely accepted in counseling today[16,9] that counselors interested in effectively servicing individuals with specific religious or spiritual beliefs should make themselves familiar with and when appropriate, use related language and imagery as part of the healing process that is consistent with the belief system of the client.

As rehabilitation professionals, counselors, and allied health professionals, we are obliged to work to develop an understanding of the numerous and interactive ways that religious, spiritual, and secular beliefs influence our clients. Secondly, we should also work to develop a clear understanding of how the factors influence our perception and development as professionals. In addition, we should give considerable thought to how the interactions of these variables may influence the client/counselor relationship.

In order to practice our profession in a manner that is considered culturally competent, the health care professional should give due consideration to how their respective beliefs influence their professional behavior.

TOWARD CULTURAL AWARENESS

Lowman,[26] suggests that health care professionals are "subject to the same implicit and explicit biases about religious difference as anyone else."[p.151] As rehabilitation professionals seeking to practice in a manner that is both ethical and demonstrative of cultural competence we are obligated to make ourselves aware of the myriad problems that may impact the effectiveness of the relationship between the clients we serve and ourselves.

To effectively serve the diverse clients that we will encounter as practitioners today, we should all strive to attain cultural competence. This process is grounded in being a lifelong learner. In current literature[8] when the issue of cultural competence is addressed, authors are generally speaking of the "knowledge and skills required to work effectively in any cross-cultural encounter."[p.34] Becoming or moving toward being a culturally competent counselor requires that one develop a thorough understanding of one's own unique cultural assumptions and beliefs. As this pertains to religiosity, the process entails becoming aware of how one is oriented toward religion, how this orientation impacts us personally and how it impacts our relationships with others such as clients and colleagues.

There are several factors to consider when contemplating how the religious and spiritual beliefs of the practitioner affects their lives and the services provided to others. The clinician who has specific religious and or spiritual beliefs, that guide their personal behavior during the course of their day-to-day lives, may at times inadvertently impact the behavior of their clients by;

➢ Misinterpreting the actions of someone who holds a different set of beliefs.

➢ Developing an unrealistic set of expectations based on their beliefs that may not be shared by the client.

➢ Acting in a way that is off putting or offensive to the client .

➢ Acting in a way that is confusing to the client who does not share the same or similar beliefs.

As service providers, we should remember that our clients have the right to expect us to practice our profession in a manner that does not impose our particular set of beliefs on the counseling relationship. If we work in a setting that is religious by nature (i.e. Catholic Charities Counseling Service), and we identify ourselves as religious counselors, then it is reasonable for us to practice from that perspective. It is reasonable to conclude that someone who comes to a religious facility and seeks out a religious counselor should be comfortable with getting counseling services, which bear that in mind. It should, however, be our duty to identify ourselves as such. This will give them an opportunity to make an informed decision regarding their desire to take advantage of the service in question. Regardless of where we practice, we should not insist on imposing our religious beliefs on a client.

As clinicians that are trained to be culturally competent, we should always attempt to understand and respect the values of our clients without expecting them to alter their beliefs to fit our own. As clinicians, we hold positions of authority and influence and we should not use that power to reshape our clients' beliefs to suit our own belief system. As a guide, it is useful to keep the following in mind. We should practice such that:

- As clinicians we purposefully spend the time to fully comprehend our orientation toward religious and spiritual matters.
- We give careful consideration to how our orientation to things spiritual and religious impacts our behavior.
- We consider how our orientation to religious and spiritual matters may impact our interactions with others.
- There is a need for us to be aware of the possible differences in the religious and spiritual beliefs of the clients that we serve and ourselves and that this could potentially impact the client counselor relationship.
- That we are aware of the possibility that client values may influence how they perceive certain life activities (business, marriage, dating, diet etc.).
- That we should be aware of the potential for spiritual values to impact the value that a client holds for others.

RELIGION, SPIRITUALITY, SECULARISM, AND CULTURAL COMPETENCE

If we are to be effective counselors, we should be prepared to address issues such as religion. How we as professionals choose to handle such matters can have a significant impact on our relationship with clients and our response in these situations can serve as either an aid or a hindrance to the client's growth.

Due to the increased attention being given to religious issues in counseling, rehabilitation and related areas, the ACA (American Counseling Association) put forth fourteen religious and spiritual competencies that the Association for Spiritual, Ethical and Religious Values in Counseling outlined. These competencies address the areas of culture and worldview, counselor self-awareness, human and spiritual development, communication, assessment, and diagnosis and treatment and can be found on the ACA web site. (ACA Code of Ethics; https://www.counseling.org/resources/aca-code-of-ethics.pdf).

While the authors clearly feel that being aware of these competencies is a necessary component for moving toward being a spiritually and religiously competent practitioner, in and of itself it is not sufficient to automatically make one a religiously competent practitioner. There are thousands of religions in the world today and it is not practical to assume that any one person could be well versed in all of them. Sue & Sue,[43] suggest that the ethical practitioner is compelled to make every effort to ensure that our cultural values and biases do not take precedence over those of our clients.

If we are to apply these values to religion and spirituality, it simply means that we must begin by becoming aware of our own unique religious, spiritual, and/or secular orientation and that we understand how those circumstances impact our work as clinicians.

THE DIMENSIONS OF SPIRITUAL VALUES

A tool that might assist us to explore our personal spiritual or religious values is a framework that helps us put religious and spiritual beliefs in context. While a number of authors have discussed the dimensions of religion, for the purpose of our discussion we will refer to the seven dimensions of religion described by Ninian Smart.[42] Smart describes seven dimensions, which include the practical, experiential, narrative, doctrinal, ethical, social, and material. The practical or ritualistic dimension of religion describe what people do as a part of that religion. Christians have one set of rituals which are tied to their religious document (the Bible) while Muslims have another set of rituals which are also tied to their religious document (the Koran). Of course, as you may have already suspected it is not quite that simple. There are often differences in traditions based on sub traditions. In the Christian faiths, one often describes these sub traditions as denominations (Catholic, Episcopalian, Baptist, Jehovah's Witness, Mormon, etc.). While in the Islam belief system, one often refers to the difference as Sect' (Sunni, Shia, Kharijite, Sufism, etc.). For the sake of brevity, four of the major sects that are followed in the Muslim faith are listed. As in other faiths, there are a number of sub sects that exist. In the Islam belief system, if you are Sunni for example you may belong to the Hanafi, either Maliki or Zahiri sub sects. There are at least seventy-three sects in Islam. Because of the fluid and ever-changing nature of religion, you may find that over time numerous new divisions evolve. The authors do not maintain that this list is exhaustive or complete.

Religious traditions can also be further defined by region or country of origin, (Greek Orthodox, Ethiopian Orthodox, Egyptian Orthodox, Southern Baptist etc.). While Christians tend to follow the same basic practices, understanding which denomination a person hails from can tell you a lot about what their specific traditions are and what they may believe. Someone who is Roman Catholic for example would have been exposed to the concept of confession with a priest and would be comfortable with the idea of having a solitary leader, the Pope, with a lifetime appointment serving as the head of their church. Someone who grew up as an Orthodox Jew on the other hand would be accustomed to an entirely different set of traditions such as not leaving one's community on the Sabbath.

These traditions might differ in a number of other ways as well which could include prayer, asceticism (self-discipline), pilgrimage, spiritual possession, modes of dress and how one approaches rituals associated with life and death.

The act of prayer or praying, can also take many forms, depending on which religion one adheres to and how you were taught to pray. For some, prayer may represent a quiet opportunity to reflect or commune with God, while for others prayer may be noisy, involve a large group, singing, chanting, and incense, music and more. The particular religion that one follows, may require that you chant a prayer directly from your holy book, while kneeling to the east toward Mecca or it may involve the act of singing and dancing while casting your eyes toward heaven.

Some religious traditions require that its followers observe strict self-discipline. This could involve refraining from strong drink, dancing, and renouncing other pleasures. It could also dictate what they must or must not wear or require the act of flagellation. There are also religions that strongly believe in demonic or godly possession. There are many and varied rituals associated with the numerous religions that exist. Rituals affiliated with some religions may require male circumcision while others may require the use of a sacrificial animal. There are many different rites of passage affiliated with the life cycle and there are others that address the joining (marriage) of one person to another. It is not within the scope of this text to enumerate these rituals.

Experiential

When we talk about the experiential component of religion, we refer to the feelings that are aroused within those who practice that religion. It is the emotion that followers attach to religion that makes it such a potent force. Today, for example, being "born again," describes both a spiritual and emotional transition that a person goes through when they commit to make a significant change in their lives and to walk in the path of Jesus.

Narrative

What is pertinent here is the story that communicates the message that is pertinent to the particular religious belief. With each religion, some sacred narrative or myth communicates a story about the religion that serves as a guide to its followers. In most instances, this comes in the form of a sacred text. For Christians, that text is the Bible, which offers guidance for how its followers should live in the present based on its telling of the sacred story found in the Old and New Testament of the Bible. In Islam, the text is the Quran, which interestingly enough, shares its origins with Christians but changes with the introduction of the Prophet Mohamed and his writings. You can find similar examples in Judaism and Buddhism.

Doctrinal

One of the best examples to turn to in this case is the Buddha and Buddhism. From the beginning, the Buddha presented a philosophical set of ideals that laid down a doctrine for the lives of his converts to follow. He set down a path that one must follow to reach enlightenment.

Ethical

The Ethical dimension of spirituality can be summed up as follows; as you believe then so you behave. In other words, the values communicated to you via your spiritual belief system guide the way that you behave in life. The teachings of various religions provide its followers with a set of values and traditions, which are based on the behavior that the religion in question finds to be acceptable. Conforming to those beliefs indicates to the believer that their behavior is leading them to a desirable goal. For example, if one is to find salvation, one behaves in a way that will lead one to salvation (in the case of Christians). On the other hand, one's beliefs might dictate that one seek enlightenment (for Buddhist) and therefore one sets off in pursuit of enlightenment by following the path of the Buda. It is incumbent upon the follower to adhere to the ethics dictated by their respective religion if they are to see themselves as a faithful adherent to that religion. Hence, in the case of Catholics, that might mean that they go to confession, or in the case of Muslims, it might mean that they pray five times a day.

Social

The social aspect of spiritual belief is usually attached to some group of people. Most religious movements are promoted by groups which eventually organize themselves formally into an entity which itself becomes a part of the belief system. The act of sharing one's beliefs with a larger group invests one in the act of belonging to that group. Rules for identifying who can be a member of the group and how they must behave are formed by and shared among the members dictating who gets to belong and who does not. As often as not the existing cultural values of the group forming a spiritual or religious group make their way into the fabric of that religion.

Material

While some forms of spiritual belief promote the belief that its followers should divorce themselves from material belongings, spiritual groups, particularly religions, usually find some way to attach some aspect of their belief system to objects. For some that might mean forming an attachment to the building, (church, temple, synagogue, or mosque) where one goes to worship. Others may find that the symbols of one's belief is vested in a sacred object, such as a cross, or a particular star, or a replica of a pudgy man. These material symbols of one's spiritual belief can have great significance to a believer.

There are numerous distinct religions, spiritual, and secular perspectives existing in the United States today. As noted above, the largest of these perspectives or groups are the individuals classifying themselves as Christian (approximately 70%). There are also significant numbers of Muslims, Jews, Hindus, and Buddhists and a significant group that self identifies as non-religious. If we consider the worldwide population, the figures change somewhat intermittently.

THE COUNSELOR

Serving as a counselor is necessarily bound up in being aware of who we are as individuals. While we cannot be certain that our counseling efforts will always be successful, we can increase the likelihood of success by becoming aware of how our actions, as influenced by our cultural values, such as religion, affects those we serve. As Corey,[7] notes "knowing how your own culture influences your decisions and daily behavior, provide a frame of reference for understanding the worldview of those who differ from you."[pg. 30]

THE CLIENT

Developing an understanding of the spirituality of a client is an important step in the counseling process. Not knowing about a client's spiritual beliefs are analogous to working through an old minefield. You could inadvertently set off an undesirable chain of events by simply stepping in the wrong area.

A client's belief system are often a means of garnering additional support to help them navigate whatever circumstances they find themselves in. If, for example, this client desires to engage in social activities and they want to have more exposure to religious events then connecting them with an appropriate religious institution could prove to be quite beneficial. Therefore, when it is possible to tap into a client's religious or spiritual beliefs as an additional source of support, the counselor should consider doing so as long as it is viable to do so. Therefore, when this seems like a feasible approach, counselors should make themselves familiar with the client's belief system and as appropriate, incorporate the language and imagery of those beliefs to support the healing process of their clients.

THE EXTENT OF RELIGIOUS BELIEFS

We should also remember that religious beliefs can be fluid. That is to say, that people can go through conversion events.

- From no religion to a religion,
- From one religion to another,
- From one religion to plural religions,
- From one level of commitment to a religion to another level (for example from being religious but not deeply committed to being very deeply committed).

With religion, it may also be helpful to consider the depth of one's religious beliefs. There are those who put religious values above all else and there are those for whom religion is simply one of many other issues that they take into consideration. In other words, as counselors we must be careful to remind ourselves that our client's religious beliefs are uniquely their own.

ASSESSING RELIGIOSITY

When most counselors think of assessment, they focus in on the bio-psycho-social aspect of the individual. Information is gathered regarding the individual's health, mental health, stability, and their social environment. The goal is to uncover any deficiencies in either of those areas, look for patterns of behavior and to be able to relate this information back to the individual's behavior or current situation in order to create a plan of action. The counselor is looking, attempting to discover the "scope and magnitude of the problem."[40]

Of equal importance to many clients is their religious or spiritual health. For many clients being disharmonious with their spirituality makes dealing with life issues even more difficult. Faiver, et al.,[12] suggest that counselors should maintain a concurrent awareness of religious/spiritual factors that may contribute to their client problems and their potential resolution. The authors suggest considering questions like, "How much does the client have invested in this area" (religion/spirituality), or "What would be different in your life if you didn't have this religion or spirituality?"

There are several brief tools, which can be used to assess spirituality, such as the FICA, (see table below).

TABLE 2
FICA SPIRITUAL HISTORY TOOL

CATEGORY
 Faith and belief
 	
 SAMPLE QUESTIONS
 Do you have spiritual beliefs that help you cope with stress? If the patient responds "no," consider asking: What gives your life meaning?
 	
 Importance Have your beliefs influenced how you take care of yourself in this illness?
 Community Are you part of a spiritual or religious community?
               Is this of support to you and how?
 Address in care
               How would you like me to address these issues in your care?
 	
 Adapted with permission from the George Washington Institute for Spiritually and Health. FICA spiritual history tool.
 http://www.gwumc.edu/gwish/clinical/fica.cfm. Accessed March 10, 2011.

The HOPE questions are another example of a guideline that can approach this topic. These questions lead the physician through general concepts by asking about patients' sources of hope and meaning whether they belong to an organized religion, their personal spirituality and practices, and what effect their spiritually may have on medical care and end-of-life decisions. A third tool, the Open Invite, is a patient-focused approach to encouraging a spiritual dialogue, structured to allow patients who are spiritual to speak further, and to allow those who are not to easily opt out. First, it reminds physicians that their role is to open the door to conversation and invite (never require) patients to discuss their needs.[39] Preaching or prescribing spiritual practices generally is beyond the proper bounds of physician-patient relationship. Second, Open Invite provides a mnemonic for the general types of questions a physician may use. The tool provides questions that allow the physician to broach the topic of spirituality. Questions may be similar to those used in the FICA and HOPE mnemonics, or may be customized, Examples include, "May I ask your faith background?" or "Do you have a spiritual or faith preference?"[39] The "invite" questions encourage patients to discuss their needs as their comfort allows. Sample questions include, "Does your spiritually impact the health decisions you make?" or "Is there a way in which you would like for me to account for your spirituality in your health care?"[39] The key to this approach is to use questions that are natural and conversational while being respectful and nonthreatening.

CONCERNS RELATED TO COUNSELING.

The literature[15,45,27,] identified several types of religious and spiritual problems that the counselor may encounter in their work with clients. Topics that a counselor who works with persons with disabilities may encounter, include the following:

SPIRITUAL OR RELIGIOUSLY BASED ISSUES:

- ➢ A change in denomination or conversion to a new faith
- ➢ A change in the way the individual practices their faith or religious or spiritual belief (such as Intensification of practices or adherence to beliefs)
- ➢ Loss of faith or questioning of faith
- ➢ Salvation by works
- ➢ The belief that faith will protect you or keep you from pain.
- ➢ Near-death experiences
- ➢ Spiritual or religious emergence (when the individual has either a gradual or sudden religious or spiritual development)
- ➢ The religious upbringings of children

SOCIAL OR DAILY LIVING ISSUES:

- ➢ The client's death and dying issues
- ➢ Family, friends, or significant others dealing with terminal illness issues
- ➢ Family, friends, or significant others dealing with ongoing illness issues
- ➢ Marriage
- ➢ The birth of children

PROCESS RELATED ISSUES:

- ➢ Relationship concerns tied to religious or spiritual beliefs
- ➢ Ethical Decision-making issues

> Circumstances that may lead the counselor to believe that work with the individual is contraindicated.

The specific issues faced by the various individuals will vary and are linked to the unique concerns faced by that person. We must also note that at times, our fellow clinicians and perhaps even we as practitioners will need to recognize that we are impacted by these issues as well.

THE IMPACT ON THE COUNSELING RELATIONSHIP

As clinicians, we must always consider how variables influence our relationship with the client we serve, and vice versa. Religious and spiritual issues simply represent one set of variables that need to be addressed as a part of that process. It should come as no surprise by now to learn that the counseling process can be impacted by issues surrounding religion or spirituality. A full understanding of ones beliefs can serve as an asset to the counselor and understanding the beliefs of the client can also provide the counselor with a tool, which can enhance the counseling process. Knowledge of the client's beliefs can more fully inform the counselor about the client and provide them with additional insight into their behavior and how they see the world and their circumstances.

When the counselor fully understands a client's beliefs then it may be possible to incorporate them into the counseling process in a way that is meaningful and helpful to the client. Conversely, a lack of appreciation for and understanding of the client's spiritual beliefs can be problematic.

LISTENING ACROSS CULTURES/RELIGIONS

When we encounter someone from a spiritual perspective that differs from our own, we need to be aware of the potential for misunderstanding that the person may be experiencing and how it affects them. A colleague was relating the difficulty she was having working with a client of Lebanese descent who happened to be Muslim. The client was a mother of two and a stay at home mom. She had been married since she and her husband met during her teens back home. She had never worked and since they settled in the United States, she had not had an opportunity to complete her education. She had few friends and at times felt isolated. Listening to the client, the counselor concluded that the client's problem was centered on the restrictions placed on her by her husband's rigid religious beliefs. This of course turned out not to be the case and her conclusions seemed more related to her attempt to define the clients situation from her own liberal protestant experience.

The counselor in this case was listening to her client, who by the way had a vastly different worldview, from a perspective (worldview) that was based on an entirely different set of life experiences. What she heard the client saying was tainted by her view of what was accepted as dictated by the worldview that she knew and understood. As it turned out, the husband was not as devoted to

Islam as the client was and this lack of devotion deprived the client of the many chances she would have had to socialize with other women of her faith. This was something that she missed and something that left a void in her life.

When we try to understand those from different spiritual backgrounds, it can often be difficult. As clinicians, we have to learn to listen to the client's story within the proper context. This means that we may have to work harder at understanding the client's story within the proper context. In other words, we often have to work hard to keep from judging them from our standards or from being dismissive of their beliefs or values.

Having knowledge of the client's spiritual beliefs is a critical part of being able to work with that client in a way that is accepting of and effective for that client. So, if we try to look at client concerns or behavior within the context of their respective spiritual beliefs, we are quite likely to gain additional insight into their circumstances and concerns.

CONCLUSION

If we wish to practice in ethical, competent, and indeed a practical manner then there are issues that relate to religion, spirituality, and related cultural issues that we, as professionals, need to be knowledgeable of. Knowing how to define one of the many categories that clients and practitioners place themselves in is a beginning. While we cannot expect ourselves to be experts in each of the many religions that exist around the world, we should at least have a basic working knowledge of them. Walker, et al.,[46] suggest that "one danger in providing religious and spiritual interventions is that the lack of formal training to supplement therapists' imposing their own values or applying religious and spiritual interventions inappropriately. Given that therapists do use their own personal religious and spiritual experience in integrating religion and spirituality into counseling, additional training, when offered, should address how to make appropriate use of one's own religious and spiritual experience as well as training regarding clients' religious backgrounds."[p.77]

More importantly, however, should be our concern that we develop a clear working picture of each client's orientation toward these matters. As we do so, we should endeavor to determine the relevance these matters have to their daily lives and the sort of significance they attach to them. Being aware of the competencies associated with religion and spirituality is a good first step for those entering the field of counseling. Having knowledge of this information, however, does not automatically make one a religiously competent practitioner. In light of the fact that there are thousands of religions in the world today, it is impractical to assume that any one person could be well versed in all of them. Sue,[43] suggests that the ethical practitioner is compelled to make every effort to ensure that our cultural values and biases do not take precedence over those of our clients. It is as much as we can do to be aware of our orientation to these matters and to be sensitive to the orientation others have chosen for themselves.

As psychology itself evolved, notable and respected authors such as Eric Erikson, Abraham Maslow, Erich Fromm, and Victor Frankl each, in their own way, acknowledged the impact of religion and spirituality and discussed the importance of including it in the therapeutic process. As health care professionals, we acknowledge that understanding the role of religion and spirituality is an important part of being a competent professional. Understanding an individual's orientation to religion and spirituality gives us a more detailed perspective on that person and it gives us another tool with which we might assist them to flourish within their current environment.

TABLE 2
BRIEF SUMMARY OF THE MAJOR RELIGIONS IN THE US

Religion	% of US pop	Deity	Holly text	Major division/ sects
Agnostic	2.4	Nome	None	None
Atheist	1.6	None	None	None
Buddhism	0.7	Dharma, which is not a god in the traditional sense. It means the ultimate truth. It is a principle that transcends everything.	Tipitaka	• Mahayana Buddhism Niehiren • Pure Land Buddhism • Tendai Buddhism • Tibetan Buddhism • Vajrayana (Tantric) • Zen
Christianity	78.4	God and the son of God, Jesus Christ	The Christian Bible Old Testament New Testament	• Anglicanism • Cathari • Catholicism • Christian Science • Donatism • Easter Orthodox • Jehovah's Witnesses • Protestantism
Hinduism	0.4	One Supreme Reality (Brahman) manifest in many gods and goddesses.	The Vedas The Upanishads	• Eckankar • Har Krishna • Shaivism • Vaishnavism

			Reincarnation based on karma.		• Vedanta
Humanist		0.6	None	None	None
Judaism		1.7	God	The Tanakh: related to the Christian Bible. The Talmid: Rabinic teachiings.	• Conservative Judaism • Hasidism • Kabbalah • Orthodox Judaism • Reform Judaism • Zionism
Islam		0.6	Allah	The Quran The Hadiths	• Ahmadiyya • Shi'a Islam • Sufism • Sunni Islam
Native American		0.3	Mother Earth and various spirits.	None	Peyotism
No religion		12.1	None	None	None
Pagan		1.2	Gods and Goddesses	None	Asphode.
Sidhism		1.2	One God: Ik Onkar	Guru Granth Sahib	• Orthodox • Nirankaris • Nam-Dharis • Kuka
Spiritualist		1.2	Generally based in a Christian worldview. Main focus is spirits of deceased humans.	None	None
Unitanian/ Universalist		1.2	Nome	The seven principles.	• Zen Buddhist meditation. • Listening for truth with Christian lectio divina. • Praying for the spirit of life. • Chanting in a circle at winter solstice.
Wiccan		1.2	Polytheism, centered on the Goddess and God, each in various forms; also a belief in a	The Book of Shadows	• Dianic Wicca • Tylwyth Teg • Feri Tradition • Alexandrian Wicca

		Supreme Being over all.		• Gardnerian Wicca

World Religions Chart

Religion/ Symbol	Followers/ Numbers	Principal Figure(s)	Sacred Writings	Beliefs	Where Begun	Place/Day of Worship	Other
Judaism ✡	Jews About 13 million followers	Abraham Moses	Torah Hebrew Bible	• One God • Observe 10 commandments • Keep the Sabbath • Messiah will come	Middle East	Synagogue, Temple or Shul Saturday (begins sundown on Friday)	Hebrew Language Bar/Bat Mitzvah Fasting Candles in service Jerusalem important city
Christianity ✝	Christians About 2 billion followers	Jesus Christ Also recognizes Abraham & Moses	Bible Old & New Testaments	• One God • Jesus is the Son of God • Observe 10 commandments • Jesus is the Messiah	Middle East	Church Sunday	Latin Language Fasting Candles in service Baptism Communion Jerusalem important city

Islam ☪	Muslims Over 1 billion followers	Muhammad Also recognizes Abraham, Moses, and Jesus	Quran	• One God
				• Five Pillars
				  -declare belief in 1 God
				  -pray 5x daily
				  -give alms to the poor
				  -fast during Ramadan
				  -Hajj or pilgrimage to Mecca
					Middle East	Mosque Friday	Arabic Language Religious attire for women Men & women worship separately at Mosque Mecca important city

Hinduism ॐ	Hindus About 900 million followers	The Aryans	The Vedas	• One God – many forms
				  -Brahma
				  -Vishnu
				  -Shiva
				• Reincarnation
				• Karma & Dharma
					India Indus River Valley	Temple (Mandir) Daily	Sanskrit Language Fasting Oil Lamps Statues Varanasi important city Ganges River

Buddhism ☸	Buddhists About 330 million followers	Siddhartha Guatama (aka Buddha)	Tripitaka	• Four Noble Truths • Eightfold Path • Karma • Rebirth • Dharma • Enlightenment	North-East India	Temple (Stupa) Daily	Candles Prayer wheels Prayer flags Statues Mandala or sand painting
Sikhism	Sikhs About 25 million followers	Guru Nanak	Guru Granth Sahib	The Five Virtues (Truth, Compassion, Contentment, Humility, & Love)	North-West India	Gurdwara (means gateway to the guru) Daily	-Three Pillars (Meditation, self-actualization, community living) Avoid the Five Thieves (lust, wrath, greed, attachment, & ego)

A CLOSING THOUGHT

In closing, we would like to share a personal matter that has affected us and speaks directly to our topic. As we finished this chapter, one of the authors experienced the loss of her loved one. Her husband of 30 years was the Reverend Ronald Bell Sr. He passed from this life this past December, after a long struggle with illness. As he did so, per his wish prior to passing, he shared the following sentiment with his family and friends. He said "I've spent my life preaching about this moment: Entering the Kingdom of God. Now I get to see it firsthand. I am blessed. I've had grace on top of Grace."[3] If you understood this aspect of the man, the nature of his belief and the significance that these things had in his life then you would have had a keen insight into who he was as an individual. You would know that as he passed, he did so with a measure of peace and that it was perhaps his greatest desire to share that peace with others.

REFERENCES

[1]Allport, G. W. (1950). Indigenous models of mental health interventions. In J. C. Ponterroto, J. M. Casas, L. A. Suzuki, & C. M. Alexander (Eds.), *Handbook of multicultural counseling (pp. 441-456)*. Thousand Oaks, CA: Sage

[2]Ambalu, S., Coogan, M. D., Feinstein, E. L., Freedman, P., Philip, N., Stobart, A., Weeks, M. (2013). *The religions book: Big ideas simply explained*. NY, NY: DK Publishing.

[3]Bell, Ronald Obituary - Visitation & Funeral Information. (n.d.). Retrieved November 23, 2020, from https://www.benniesmithfuneralhome.com/memorials/Bell-Ronald/3678224/obit.php

[4]Buse, N. A., Burker, E. J., & Bernacchio, C. (2013). *Cultural variation in resilience as a response to traumatic experience*. Journal of Rehabilitation, 79(2), 15-23.

[5]Bullis, R. R., (1996). *Spirituality In Social Work Practice*. Taylor and Francis Washington D.C.

[6]Cashwell, C. S., Watts, R. E. (2011). The New ASERVC Competencies for Addressing Spiritual and Religious Issues in *Counseling, Counseling and Values:* 55, (1), pages 2-5. onlinelibrary.wiley.com/doi/10.1002/j.2161-007X.2010.tb00018.x/...

[7]Corey, G., & Corey M. S. (2002). Groups: Process and Practice. Cengage

[8]Corey, G. (2015), *Theory and practice of counseling and psychotherapy (10th Ed)*, 560 pages.

[9]Corey, G. (2016), *Theory and Practice of Group Counseling*, (9th Ed), 544 pages.

[10]Covey, S. R., Merrill, A. R., Merrill R. R. (1994) First *things first Simon & Schuster*, New York, 373 pages.

[11]Dailey, S. F., (2016), *Counseling and values. Presidents' welcome*. 61.2 page 131-132. http://dx.doi.org/10.1002/cvj.12031

[12]Faiver C., Ingersoll, R. E., O'Brien, E., & McNally, C. (2001). *Exploration in counseling and spirituality: Philosophical, practical, and personal reflections,* Belmont CA:Wadsworth/Thomson Learning

[13] Frendreis, J. R. (2013). *Secularization, modernization, or population change: Explaining the decline of prohibition in the United States secularization, modernization, or population change.* Social Science Quarterly. (Wiley-Blackwell), 94(2), 379-394.

[14] Freud, Sigmund, Ferenczi, Sandor, & Brabant, Eva. The Correspondence of and Sandor Ferenczi: Volume 3, 1920-1933. Edited by Ernest Falzeder and Eva Brabant. The Belknap Press of Harvard University Press. Cambridge, Massachusetts
https://www.biography.com/scholar/sigmund-freud

[15] Fukuyama, M. A., Sevig, T. D., (2002) Spirituality in Counseling Across Cultures in Pedersen, P. B., Draguns, J. G. Lonner, W. J., Trimble, J. E. (2002) Counseling Across Cultures 5th Edition. Thousand Oaks, Sage

[16] Gladding, S. T. (2000). *Counseling: A comprehensive profession.* Upper Saddle River, NJ: Merrill.

[17] Grof, S., & Grof, C., (EDs.). (1989). Spiritual emergency: When personal transformation becomes a crisis, Gateway, Los Angeles, CA

[18] Gutting, G. (2013). *Religious Agnosticism. Midwest studies in philosophy,* 37(1), 51-67. doi:10.1111/misp.2002

[19] Hall, W., Chapman, M., Lee, K., Merino, Y., Thomas, T., Payne, B., Eng, E., Day, S. & Coyne-Beasley, T. (2015). *Implicit Racial/Ethnic Bias Among Health Care Professionals and Its Influence on Health Care Outcomes: A Systematic Review. American Journal of Public Health.* 105. e1-e17. 10.2105/AJPH.2015.302903.

[20] Hill, P. C., & Dik, B. J. (2012). *Psychology of religion and workplace spirituality.* Charlotte, NC: Information Age Pub.

[21] Hodge, D. R. (2011*). Using spiritual interventions in practice: Developing some guidelines from evidence-based practice.* Social Work, 56(2), 149-158

[22] Jung (1933) *Indigenous models of mental health interventions.* In J. C. Ponterroto, J. M. Casas, L. A. Suzuki, & C. M. Alexander (Eds.), *Handbook of multicultural counseling (pp. 441-456).* Thousand Oaks, CA: Sage

[23] Lee, C. C., & Armstrong, K. L. (1995). *Indigenous models of mental health interventions.* In J. C. Ponterroto, J. M. Casas, L. A. Suzuki, & C. M. Alexander (Eds.), *Handbook of multicultural counseling (pp. 441-456).* Thousand Oaks, CA: Sage

[24] LeDrew, S. A. (2013). *Discovering Atheism: Heterogeneity in trajectories to Atheist identity and activism.* Sociology of Religion, 431.

[25] Limberg, B. (2013*). Religion, spirituality, and secularism in multicultural and international contexts.* In R. L. Lowman, R. L. Lowman (Eds.), Internationalizing multiculturalism: Expanding professional competencies in a globalized world (pp. 143-170). Washington, DC, US: American Psychological Association. doi:10.1037/14044-006

[26]Lowman, R. L. (2013). *Internationalizing multiculturalism: Expanding professional competencies in a globalized world.* Washington, D.C.: American Psychological Association.

[27]Lukoff, D., Turner, R. (1996). *Diagnosis: A transpersonal clinical approach to religious and spiritual problems.* New York: Basic Books.

[28]Marcie. "World Religions Chart." *SlideServe,* 25 July 2014, www.slideserve.com/marcie/world-religions-chart.

[29] Marini, I., Marini, I., & Stebnicki, M. A. (2012). *The psychological and social impact of illness and physical ability.* New York: Springer Pub.

[30]Maslow, A. (1964). *Indigenous models of mental health interventions.* In J. C. Ponterroto, J. M. Casas, L. A. Suzuki, & C. M. Alexander (Eds.), Handbook of multicultural counseling (pp. 441-456). Thousand Oaks, CA: Sage

[31]May, R. (1969). *Indigenous models of mental health interventions.* In J. C. Ponterroto, J. M. Casas, L. A. Suzuki, & C. M. Alexander (Eds.), Handbook of multicultural counseling (pp. 441-456). Thousand Oaks, CA: Sage

[32]Melton, J Gordon, (2014). Faiths Across Time: 5,000 years of religious history. Santa Barbara, California, ABC-CLIO

[33]Newport, Frank (2012). The Future of Religion In America: God is Alive and Well. Gallup Press. New York New York: ISBN 978-1-59562-062-0

[34]Ottavi, T. M., Pope-Davis, D. B., & Dings, J. G. (1994). *Relationship between white racial identity attitudes and self-reported multicultural counseling competencies.* Journal of Counseling Psychology, 41, 149-154

[35]PEW Research Center. 2018. The Future of World Religions: Population Growth Projections, 2010–2050. At: http://assets.pewresearch.org/wp-content/uploads/sites/ 11/2015/03/PF_15.04.02_ProjectionsFullReport.pdf. Accessed 28/5/2018

[36]Paniagua, F. A. (2005). *Assessing and treating culturally diverse clients: A practical guide.* Thousand Oaks, CA: Sage Publications

[37]Pedersen, P. (2002). *Counseling across cultures.* Thousand Oaks, CA: Sage Publications.

[38]Pigliucci, M. (2013*). New Atheism and the scientific turn in the Atheism Movement.* Midwest Studies In Philosophy, (1), 142.

[39]Saguil, A., & Phelps, K. (2012, September 15). *The Spiritual Assessment.* Retrieved November 23, 2020, from https://www.aafp.org/afp/2012/0915/p546.html

[40]Saleebey, D. (1997). The strengths perspective in social work practice, 2nd edition. New York: Longman Publishers

[41]Sellner, E. C. 1990. *Indigenous models of mental health interventions.* In J. C. Ponterroto, J. M. Casas, L. A. Suzuki, & C. M. Alexander (Eds.), Handbook of multicultural counseling (pp. 441-456). Thousand Oaks, CA: Sage

[42]Smart N. (1996) *Dimensions of the sacred,* London HarperCollins.

[43]Sue, D. W., & Sue, D. (1999). *Counseling the culturally different: Theory and practice (2nd ed.)*. Oxford, England: John Wiley & Sons

[44]Taylor, R., J., Chatters, L., M., (1988). Church Members as a Source of Informal Social Support. Review of Religious Research. Vol. 30. No 2 (Dec 1988). 193-203

[45]Turner, R. P., Lukoff, D., Barnhouse, R. T., & Lu, F. G. (1995). Religious or spiritual problem: A culturally sensitive diagnostic category in the DSM-IV. *Journal of Nervous and Mental Disease, 183*(7), 435-444.

[46]Walker, D. F.; Gorsuch, R. L. & Siang-Yan T. (2004). *Therapists' integration of religion and spirituality in counseling: A meta-analysis.* Counseling and Values, 49(1), 69-80. http://doi.org/10.1002/j.2161-007X.2004.tb00254.x

[47]Wrenn, C. G. (1962). *The Culturally Encapsulated Counselor. Harvard Educational Review, 32(4). 444-449.*

CHAPTER 6

POWER AND PRIVILEGE

ALLEN N. LEWIS, JR.
BRIGITTE DESPORT
MARGARET KAPLAN
LORAINE ANTOINE
SHUSHAWNA DEOLIVEIRA
JOANNE KATZ

CHAPTER TOPICS

- Power in the United States Context
- Privilege in the United States Context
- Power, Privilege, and Cultural Diversity
- Power and Privilege: Ethical Considerations
- Multi-level Framework to Address Power and Privilege Challenges

At this point in the 21st century, a textbook on multicultural issues in rehabilitation and allied health would not be complete without some discussion of the concepts of power and privilege. The reality is that power and privilege (to be fully defined later) are arguably part of the fabric of all societies and the United States' society is no exception. These two concepts are integral components in the landscape of this nation and having a basic understanding of them helps to provide a context to fully comprehend the interaction between cultural, rehabilitation and health care matters. As a nation, the United States has some unique attributes that render an understanding of power and privilege especially relevant.

The United States prides itself on being the land of opportunity and free enterprise. These two attributes support capitalism, and the notion of competition as well as the Darwinian concept of natural selection are alive and well and have been since the country's inception. Capitalistic societies typically have a capitalist class that controls goods, services, means for production and distribution. This class tends to have wealth. Conversely, a working class strives to produce goods and services in exchange for a wage and tends to not have wealth.[35] This characteristic in conjunction with America's 250+ year dark history of slavery makes for an interesting dynamic. America's pluralistic nature also adds a unique dimension to the power and privilege discussion.

Pluralism in the United States results primarily from the steady flow of immigrants that have come to this nation since before its inception. This heavy immigrant composition of the population was a fundamental aspect of the founding of America. In addition, this nation has been experiencing a rapid diversification of its population over the last several decades. The U.S. Census Bureau projects the population to be 50% non-White by 2050, if not sooner, compared to a 20% non-White population proportion in 1999.

The increasingly diverse populace in the United States has prompted many rehabilitation and health professions to issue a mandate for culturally competent services. Much of the attention to culture, legislative and within discipline-specific curricula, peaked in the final few decades of the 20th century. Today, the focus on providing culturally appropriate services is still strong, and primarily targeted to mitigate disparities in rehabilitation and health care service system access, participation, experiences, and outcomes based on the cultural orientation of the client. There are several disability[15] and health disparities models[31] in the literature that provide a conceptual understanding of the phenomenon of disparities in services and outcomes due primarily to cultural affiliation. The push for a keen understanding of disability and health disparities today comes with an acknowledgement that serving culturally diverse populations effectively makes good business sense.

In today's multicultural landscape of rehabilitation and health system service recipients, the business argument for providing effective services, culture notwithstanding, is compelling. On the one hand, we have a rapidly growing and increasingly culturally diverse population of citizens in the nation, and thus, potential service recipients.[17] On the other hand, resources that support the delivery of rehabilitation and health care services are not growing at a rate commensurate with the increasing demand.[17] Accountability pressures to deliver quality services are growing as well—both from sources internal to the system (i.e., rules and regulations about how services can be provided) as well as sources external to the system (from empowered service recipients, families and advocacy groups).[17] The sum of these demands (increasing population, more diversity, resources not growing to keep pace with demands, and accountability all around) provides a critically important system imperative.[17] That imperative is to "do more with less." Given this, systems can no longer afford to provide ineffective services to any segment(s) of the service recipient population without wasting precious resources. Therefore, it behooves rehabilitation and health service providers to learn how to serve culturally diverse service recipients effectively, even amid the power and privilege dynamics that are pervasive in this country.

The interrelated nature of culture and the concepts of power and privilege cannot be overstated. To fully understand how culture impacts service access, participation and outcomes, one must also have a working knowledge of power and privilege. Culture, power, and privilege share an inextricable relationship. Herein is the importance of this chapter on power and privilege in a textbook on multicultural issues in rehabilitation and allied health professions.

POWER IN THE UNITED STATES CONTEXT

Power has different forms in American history, including Colonial power, political power, and social power. Power is defined as the possession of control, authority, or influence over others.[27] Power, like privilege, cannot be separated from race. The history of Colonial power was constructed on race. White Europeans colonized people of color for centuries upon arriving here in America, as well as in Africa, India, Cuba, Puerto Rico, Japan and countless other countries. Colonization involved brutalizing and raping people of color, taking away their land, and stripping them of the power over their culture and lives. Today, the balance of power in the nation continues to fall on the side of White Americans.

One historical example is the United States Constitution, which purposefully made Black people the property of their masters (i.e., chattel slavery). The Constitution prohibited Congress from banning the slave trade and required that fugitive slaves be returned to their masters. Another example was prohibiting Blacks from becoming literate, thereby preventing them from reproducing their culture and changing their social and economic status. South Carolina's Slave Code of 1740 prohibited enslaved Blacks from learning to read and write and growing their own food. Forcibly removing Native Americans from their land, and later sending their children to the infamous government Indian schools where they were punished if they spoke in their own language are other historical instances where White privilege was pervasive.[14]

The influence of the health care professional over the public is one that is debated. Health care analysts might argue that we see the balance of power falling on White Americans in the health care industry. This is because the majority of medical professionals are White and male, which is not reflective of the sick patient population that primarily consists of people of color. This imbalance of power—White, educated males treating a person of color who is often less educated—precipitates disempowerment that becomes almost hardwired. Many people find themselves relinquishing their authority to decide what is best for their own health to the professionals who have taken an oath to ethically serve the public at all times. In contrast, the role of the health care professional is to empower the individual (client/patient) to make informed decisions.[12] The dynamics of the health care system may lead many to feel a loss of power and vulnerability when dealing with the professionals providing the care as well as the bureaucratic health insurance companies. This imbalance of power can have a range of negative effects on a person's experience in health care.[8]

Traditionally, power has been maintained by the health care professional based on the idea that the client lacks the knowledge required to determine own best treatment(s) for one's medical condition and be included in the decision-making process.[8] Patients have not been typically encouraged or allowed to question the medical expertise of their health care providers. Subtle factors such as the one's vulnerability when ill and the desire to comply can affect the patient's/client's ability to gain autonomy and make decisions regarding care.[36]

Increasing service recipient autonomy in health care can help decrease opportunities for abuse in health care. Individuals should be offered options and allowed to make voluntary choices about potentially life altering health care interventions.[9] Improved clinical interactions between the provider and service recipient can bolster the patient's autonomy (despite challenging diagnoses, symptoms and/or treatments) and promote one's ability to deal with the emotions related to their vulnerability when ill. The ability of the health care provider to facilitate client/patient autonomy by allowing individuals to make informed decisions will ultimately factor into the provider's influence and effectiveness in treatment.

PRIVILEGE IN THE UNITED STATES CONTEXT

The Preamble to the United States Constitution declares that one of the originating purposes of the United States is to promote the general welfare of its people. The Constitution was drafted in 1787 and has served as the framework of the American governmental system. The document has since served to protect the fundamental rights of the United States' citizen. However, many argue that the basic rights that were once justified for all may now be considered privileged and as such, available and afforded only to a portion of the population.

Privilege is recognized as a right, advantage, or immunity granted that is available to a particular person or group of people[28] In defining the term privilege, it is contradictory to explain it as a concept that is separate from the socially constructed term of "race." Race is the primary, and some would argue, the only determinant for having privilege. Being born White usually grants people access to power and resources in the United States. Throughout history, American institutions, laws, and customs have consistently granted White people privileges. This has not been by accident or happenstance. Plessy v. Ferguson in 1896 is an example of how the passing of laws preserved the legal separation and inequalities between Whites and Blacks (de jure discrimination). Another example of White privilege is the use of affirmative action to advance opportunities for White men and women rather than for people of color. A final example is determining how historical characters and events are remembered by presenting only the White parts of a story.[14]

These few examples in American history underscore White privilege, and deem it impossible to separate race or racism from privilege. The historical patterns determine what people of color experience today. This includes ongoing systemic discrimination (de facto discrimination) that impacts their access to equal education, housing, health care, and judicial outcomes. People of color are acutely aware of the obvious ways they are excluded. They do not have the "privilege" of removing such experiences from their day-to-day consciousness.

Jesse Benn, a White journalist, argues that the term "White privilege" does not accurately illustrate the racial hierarchy that exists. He prefers to use the term White supremacy, referring to "a racial hierarchy in which Whiteness sits atop of." Benn further asserts that the United States was founded on White supremacist, classist, legal, economic, cultural, and political systems that still exist in 2017. White supremacy should not be associated only with the Ku Klux Klan, Nazis, neo-Nazis, or other White terrorist hate groups because those associations allow White people not affiliated with those particular groups to identify themselves as different and not recognize their participation in the racial hierarchy.

Benn defines White privilege as "a reference to the myriad of benefits on White people stemming from White supremacy." Benn's distinction of the two terms, with "White privilege" being used more often than "White supremacy," is an example of the definition of privilege and the way privilege works.[2] That is, White privilege is a term used euphemistically to dampen the vicious reality of White supremacy under which inequalities are maintained and perpetuated by White people depicting themselves and behaving as if they are better or more deserving than others. The existence and use of the term "White privilege" works to further illustrate the power of a group to separate itself from the negative impact of its history that led to the oppression of others and the taking of their rights.

Privilege also encompasses defining equity. Equity means fairness, or social justice and is seen as an ethical concept.[5] Equity is the lack of systemic disparities regardless of social hierarchy. This can be applied across American social and institutional life, including health care (both physical and mental well-being). Social hierarchy can be determined by wealth or power and can lead to individuals or groups within the system becoming privileged, thus increasing the presence of inequities. Educational level, income, occupational class, and economic assets are all ways that the population may be divided into socioeconomic groups, defining the social hierarchy.

The lack of economic resources has been adversely linked to health in America.[5] Health care has been treated as a commodity in the United States, such that those who are able to pay higher premiums for health insurance or out of pocket may receive not only medical care due to pathology, but also preventative health care.[32] The concept of privilege in the United States as it relates to health care is highly debated and forces both the government and health care institutions to determine whether health care is a fundamental right.[1,24]

Privilege in the United States has been linked to wealth, social class, gender, ethnicity, race, religion, marital status and many other facets. Each dimension uses different standards to determine the advantageous gain of being considered an elite or preferred group. Defining privilege and assessing its effect on the daily decisions made by individuals and groups, including the government, can lead to the decrease in inequities throughout society, and furthermore, can increase the promotion of the general welfare of all American people.

Many conversations on the topic of power and privilege have a negative tone. And while one can argue that power and privilege generally reinforce the norm, it is important to note that both concepts can also be used to disrupt the status quo and create improved practice of the rehabilitation and health care professional. Alliances and collaborations can be formed to change the philosophy of oppression or at the very least transform the health care delivery models that would otherwise favor certain traditional differences. Committing to this change effort could enable the helping professional to explore not only how we each might embrace cultural dimensions, but how to contribute in the nurturing of the well-being of individuals, community, and the larger health system which is essential to the practice of health care.

POWER, PRIVILEGE, AND CULTURAL DIVERSITY

The concepts of power and privilege intersect with our own individual characteristics as providers along with those of service recipients. As clinicians and educators, we must be culturally competent and aware of those we educate and treat, as well as ourselves. Self-awareness within our community will, at the very least, result in rehabilitation and health professionals' ability to improve how they interact with patients cross culturally, as they continue to encounter a diverse student and patient population. This includes being knowledgeable about an individual's background, race, ethnicity, class, gender, sexual orientation, religion, socioeconomic status, age, language, physical, and mental ability, along with the power and privilege implications for each dimension. While cultural diversity dimensions span the continuum comprised by power and privilege, the key to understanding the essence of the relationship between power and privilege is awareness. In this way, health care providers may begin to understand how power and privilege as well as dimensions of cultural diversity connect, and potentially interact. Figure 1, as pictured below, depicts relationships among power, privilege, and cultural diversity.

FIGURE 1

POWER AND PRIVILEGE AND THE RELATIONSHIP WITH CULTURAL DIVERSITY

Figure 1: Power and Privilege and the Relationship with Cultural Diversity

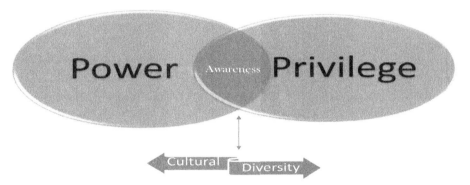

Often, discussions about power and privilege begin with social difference (race, gender, class, etc.). While addressing these differences is of critical importance, we must begin to explore some indirect approaches such as engaging in self-reflection about both individual internal differences along with external power and privilege differences. In doing so, rehabilitation and health care providers can begin to recognize systemic symptoms of power and privilege and develop strategies to engage with the pressures around cultural, power, and privilege differences of those whom they treat. Health care professionals who practice engaging differently in this way may begin to recognize patterns associated with differences that may be targets for healthy change. Ultimately, helping professionals could use power and privilege to identify points in systems where change can be leveraged to improve the delivery of health care.

Health care providers frequently assume that their knowledge makes them better judges of what is best for service recipients. They are often not aware that they are privileged to have superior knowledge compared to their patients, and as such, they tend to overlook the negative impact of this inherent power and how it diminishes patient autonomy to exert undue control.[13] In other words, health care providers often use their power to dominate their patients' preferences under the guise of benefitting the individual when recommending treatment, typically without being aware of it. This common practice in health care leads to an increase of potential abuse and a decrease in patient autonomy and empowerment.

The power and privilege of rehabilitation and health care providers can be viewed as a threat to the service recipient's independence. Treatment options accessible to both patients and providers are often limited by governmental policies and third party payers. With more stringent restrictions on access to treatment options, providers find themselves as gatekeepers between cost and treatment and between needs and preferences.[30] The privilege of autonomy is unjustly given to those who have the ability and power to use their economic resources to access the nation's most desirable rehabilitation and health care providers and treatments.

Power and privilege are highly related concepts for both the health care provider and the service recipient. Providers are privileged to have access to constantly evolving medical information via research, journals, textbooks, continuing education, and classes. The expectation is that the provider will use the information gained to empower the individual seeking rehabilitation, treatment, or preventative care. The provider has power of knowledge in the relationship, and therefore, can greatly influence the decision-making process. The provider informs the patient about a menu of options regarding his/her care and has the power to state and determine which options are available or unavailable, and why.[33] The determination of what information to divulge may vary significantly based on the privileges assigned to the patient by the health care provider. The patient has power to determine which professionals will ultimately provide care. However, this power is frequently limited to those who are privileged with favorable income, economic assets, educational level, and occupational class.

Since we are all interlocked in a huge and complicated network of health affiliations, our very existence in those relationships is contingent on the behavior of many others. The achievement of the whole is contingent on the success of each individual, while the achievement of each individual hinges upon the accomplishment of the community as a whole. Understanding the relationship between power and privilege (such as social dimensions, cultural competency, etc.) will enhance and expand the health professional's practice of engaging with different individuals while contributing to their ability to practice a more integrative and inclusive approach to the delivery of services.

Our environment within the United States is constantly changing and increasing in diversity. Rehabilitation and health care providers should increase self-awareness and cultural sensitivity to ensure service recipients will be provided with adequate information to improve basic understanding of their health. This will ultimately lead to increased patient autonomy and allow patients the privilege and power to provide informed consent regarding the services they receive.

POWER, PRIVILEGE, AND CULTURAL DIMENSIONS

At a glance, it would be easy to think that race and ethnicity are the only cultural dimensions in the United States that are salient. The nation has a preoccupation with race and ethnicity for two reasons.[18] First, race and ethnicity are visible and many individuals feel they can make a judgment about a person's racial or ethnic identity based on sight. Secondly, the distinction between who was and was not enslaved in the slavery experience in United States' history was based on race. However, culture includes much more than race and ethnicity. Most definitions of culture make clear that the concept is an attribute that defines both group membership and non-membership based on lifestyles, traditions, values, assumptions, beliefs, and ways of seeing the world.[16]

Essentially, a cultural dimension is anything that provides a specific worldview or subjective reality for the group.[18] Given this concept of a cultural dimension, there are other dimensions that divide groups' experiences based on worldview or subjective reality. For example, spirituality or religion, gender, sexual orientation, profession, disability, political affiliation, social economic status, and many other factors are dimensions of culture. Edwin Nichols[23] maintains that culture varies based on what he calls the philosophical aspects of cultural difference (i.e., axiology, epistemology, pedagogy, logic, and others).

Each and every cultural dimension interfaces with the concepts of power and privilege in this country. Groups defined by any one of the cultural dimensions in the United States could make the argument that power, and privilege manifest ways based on the specific cultural dimension. The degree to which an individual or a group has power and privilege in this country is the extent to which that individual/group has access to the American dream.

POWER AND PRIVILEGE IMPACT ON THE TRUST DYNAMIC

Trust is important in rehabilitation and health care in many ways. One crucial aspect is that people who mistrust the health system may not seek care when they need it or may delay care until a condition is advanced. A legacy of racial discrimination in medical research and care has been linked to a low level of trust in health care research, the medical system, and care among Blacks. Trust in health care providers has been shown to vary by race, with lowest trust in health care providers resident among Black adults.[3] Trust is essential to the health care provider/client relationship. Clients with high trust in their provider have been found to have improved outcomes, increased use of preventive services, and satisfaction with care.[22] Trust affects a service recipient's willingness to disclose the full extent of their medically relevant history, expose themselves to physical examinations, or act on recommendations for tests, treatments, and interventions.[10]

Rehabilitation and health care providers need to understand and remain aware of the fact that there is an imbalance of knowledge and power in rehabilitation and health care relationships. The importance of health to achieve life goals and fully participate in activities makes vulnerability greater. People seeking health care are vulnerable emotionally, physically, spiritually, and often, financially. The rehabilitation or health care professional has knowledge that the client needs, and this creates an imbalance of power and the necessity for trust in the provider to receive the best care. A provider's sensitivity to this imbalance of power will help the provider to be cautious when stating recommendations. Moreover, the provider must carefully discuss how the client understands their health challenge(s) and the interventions that may be feasible and realistic for implementation. Too often, a provider tells a client what they should do to alleviate symptoms or progress toward attaining goals and the client may not agree but does not want to offend the provider. Therefore, the client agrees to all recommendations, regardless of whether they are able or wish to carry through on them or not.

How do we engender trust in our clients, particularly those with mistrust of the system in general? We can begin by adopting a conscious, non-judgmental attitude in our words and our non-verbal reactions to what our clients/patients tell us. We can explicitly ask about things that our clients may be reluctant to share, feeling that they risk our disapproval. For example, this may include such things as alternative supplements and treatments that the client uses or has used and may be important for us to know, especially if the client has received relief of symptoms from these methods. By respecting our clients' opinions and experience with their own medical issues, we begin the process of building trust. We continue to build trust by being honest with clients about the evidence base of the recommendations we give. We can often give choices to our clients among several recommendations with explanations and respect their choices as to which will be most feasible and beneficial to them. As trust improves, so will follow-up with future appointments, with recommendations, and with sharing the results of the interventions we have suggested.

Another important aspect to gaining trust on individual and group levels is to make the clients' experience in seeking care welcoming and comfortable. If a person cannot understand the complex system they are entering or the words being used, they are less likely to trust the provider. Providers can practice expressing medical terminology in "lay English" or in other languages, as necessary. Signage and people who greet and register the clients/patients can be encouraged to be a helpful and welcoming as well.

An understanding of each person's health literacy is also important. A client/patient may be literate and may have finished various levels of education but have poor health literacy. They may not understand the terminology and the importance of health maintenance and preventive recommendations in the same way as the provider or other clients. A determination of health literacy can inform the provider how to best communicate important information to each service recipient. The Agency for Healthcare Research and Quality (AHRQ) has researched and published free health literacy assessments. These can be found at ahrq.gov (retrieved 3-20-17).

Awareness of the code of ethics to which rehabilitation and health care professionals subscribe will help providers remember the importance of honesty and autonomy of the service recipient in helping to select options that will be best for them and their families. Further, the importance of respect for each client will improve trust and full participation in the provider/service recipient relationship and improve outcomes.

POWER AND PRIVILEGE: ETHICAL CONSIDERATIONS

Rehabilitation and health care providers may not give much consideration to their own training as a privilege since it has been earned. Though there has been much emphasis on the power of the helping professional, far less discussion has been dedicated to the privilege aspect. As a result, this section examines how both power and privilege can be understood between the helping professional and the service recipient. By bringing students to the clinical/program services sites, we are teaching them to apply skills they have learned (in a privilege-based, professional program). However, at the same time, they are not full professionals yet, and therefore, may interact with clients from less of a power perspective.

Most rehabilitation and health care professionals/providers follow a common code of ethics described by the following principles: beneficence (taking action to help others), nonmaleficence (doing no harm), autonomy (respecting the rights of self-determination, privacy, and consent), justice (fairness, objectivity, and resource allocation to offset disadvantage), veracity (truthfulness), and fidelity (treating all with respect, fairness, and integrity). The wording may be unique to each profession, but the concepts are similar across professions.

A health professional is in a position of power in relation to a person seeking help. The professional has information and ideas that the person seeking services needs to feel better, participate more fully in their life activities, gain employment, etc. In addition, most health professionals are White, and therefore, belong to a group of privilege. As Peggy McIntosh[19] states, Whites are carefully taught not to recognize White privilege, so this awareness remains largely unarticulated. If a helping professional does not fully understand their position of power and privilege in relation to the client/patient, there is possibility for unintentional lapses in ethical conduct. In addition, the current state of rehabilitation and health care and reliance on reimbursement requires each of us to "do more with less." We are asked to see more people, do more paperwork for the same pay and in the same number of work hours. Can we help others in a fair and objective way in less time and still provide the same quality service to all?

In the United States, health, medical, and rehabilitation services are often restricted by what is covered under a client's insurance policy. Does this collide with the professional's ethical duty to provide the most helpful service in a fair and equitable manner? For instance, many insurance policies do not cover or provide only very limited counseling or mental health treatment, even though studies have shown these interventions to be advantageous to those we treat.[7,34] People receiving services in rehabilitation facilities or as outpatients are often limited to a short amount of time for those services, whether they are ready to be home and independent or not. Professionals are confronted daily with ethical situations when a client needs services, but does not receive them or receives less than they need due to insurance coverage. People with limited coverage or no coverage often belong to segments of society that are viewed as underserved, disempowered, and do not have the privilege of receiving the rehabilitation and health care services they need.

Helping professionals/providers are sometimes forced to turn patients away because the service recipient cannot afford the treatment and because of the clinician's own financial obligations to themselves and the medical institution for which they work.[25] As helping professionals, we must work together to impart change and to help incorporate ethical deliberation around the very power we possess. To do so, helping professions must adopt an approach to working across cultures and be able to apply practice to certain social groups. Specifically, helping professionals must embrace cultural diversity and recognize the significance of culture in their practice. It is important to also apply cultural competence when rendering services and advice to those treated. Furthermore, helping professionals must remember to be aware of their own cultural perspectives, ethical beliefs and values.

Providers are also overwhelmed with regulations regarding patients' treatment and monetary penalties for out-of-network services. Providers are expected to see more clients in less time, which can encourage practitioners to neglect consideration of the full picture of complex clients with multiple needs and challenges. Behavioral health challenges that require more extensive counseling or other intensive rehabilitation/interventions may be neglected.[4] Another ethical consideration around power for helping professionals is reimbursement that encourages interventional procedures and diminishes the use or recommendation for counseling.

MULTI-LEVEL FRAMEWORK TO ADDRESS POWER AND PRIVILEGE CHALLENGES

The key to any discussion that highlights concepts that can influence the delivery and outcomes of rehabilitation and health services to multicultural populations, like power and privilege, is to offer strategies for addressing the challenges. Strategies structured systematically and comprehensively tend to be beneficial. The Social Ecological Model (SEM)[21] from the health promotion literature offers a useful framework for organizing the strategies at multiple levels. This model posits that sustained change is most probable when strategies are targeted at five levels of influence: individual, interpersonal (individuals in their immediate context), organization, community, and policy. So, in the case of power and privilege, it would make sense for rehabilitation and health service providers serving multicultural populations to think systematically about power and privilege dynamics across all five of the SEM levels. The goal would be to mitigate the natural imbalance that exists in power and privilege in underserved, non-White, and disenfranchised groups versus White, majority groups.

Power and privilege can obviously impact services delivered and outcomes at the level of the individual service recipient. Assuming the direction of the power and privilege dynamic is one that disadvantages non-White, under-resourced groups, one strategy that could be deployed by providers is empowerment of the client to be more self-determining. If the power and privilege dynamics also come into play at the second level that includes the person receiving services in his or her interpersonal context (most often a family context), then an appropriate strategy to level the playing field for the non-White, disadvantaged client might be to engage natural supports and strengthen resources for the family to bolster its power and privilege status.

Similarly, at the organization level, power and privilege might be a factor in the organizational milieus the person has routine contact with (e.g., work, school, or church), so targeted strategies might also be warranted. A viable strategy to address power and privilege discrepancies might be targeted advocacy to bring about meaningful change within the organizational context where the disparity occurs. More broadly, the same might be true for needing strategies to address power and privilege imbalanced dynamics at the community level of the SEM. Individuals who have power and privilege deficits in this realm tend to reside in communities that match this attribute. Strategies to address community-based power and privilege imbalances tend to be more challenging due to their inherent macro-level application, but could be worthwhile if interventions at that magnitude could be developed, adequately scaled, and appropriately implemented. For example, one such strategy might be mobilization efforts, particularly grassroots that involve bringing together multiple key stakeholder groups into a coalition that can exert pressure to rectify power and privilege imbalances at the community level.

At the policy level, typically there are efforts already underway to alter the power and privilege dynamics through legislation and regulations. Whether these are bona fide efforts that are genuinely deployed for real change may be debatable. If they are authentic, such efforts will have varying success because they are frequently paralleled with social engineering, which is a tall order since the locus of change is attitudes. Nevertheless, more concerted energy toward lobbying to leverage the legislative process might be indicated.

CONCLUSION

When we think of individuals with power and privilege, we often think about persons with advantages and benefits deriving from being members of a dominant social group in the United States, such as being White, able-bodied, heterosexual, male, Christian, middle-class, middle-aged, and English-speaking. Individuals in these groups may not fully realize their extent of possessing power and privilege. When this lack of recognition occurs in the group of individuals who are rehabilitation and health care providers, it can be especially challenging.

Still today, arguably most of rehabilitation and health care providers in this country come from this privileged group. How do these providers learn to deliver services to service recipients who are poor and/or non-White in a culturally respectful manner? This is a formidable task, yet one that must be done. The diversification trend in this nation is clear. The Pew Research Center indicates that the United States will have no racial or ethnic group as its majority within the next few decades, and has announced that minority babies are now the majority among infants born in the nation.[26]

In most rehabilitation and health care professions today (e.g., physical therapy, rehabilitation counseling, occupational therapy, medicine, speech and language pathology, dietetics, athletic training, health administration, public health, midwifery, physician assistant, medical informatics, diagnostic medical imaging, and others), the majority of students enrolled in programs across the nation are White. They are the next generation of the workforce.

Promotion of the change to bring about less power and privilege imbalance will require several strategies. First, the current mostly majority population workforce must increase its awareness of its powerful and privileged status. Because most providers are White, immediate recognition of this fact can be elusive unless one has exceptional insight, usually resulting from special training. Therefore, more attention in this area (i.e., enhanced awareness and insight among majority providers of this dynamic) will be an initial step.

Secondly, the rehabilitation and health care workforce must become more culturally diversified. This will require several strategies such as, for example, developing more awareness of these disciplines in Black communities. The key here will be developing more pathways in such communities that meet individuals with potential where they are currently, in addition to leading and nurturing them along toward the level of professional development needed to become a rehabilitation or health profession provider. The stark reality is that we have just begun to identify the need for this work to be done as it relates to the rehabilitation and health professions, so we have much to do.

REFERENCES

[1] Bauchner, H. (2017). Health care in the United States: A right or privilege. *Journal of American Medical Association,* 317(1), 29.

[2] Benn, J. (2015). The White anti-racism tome police: White supremacy vs. white privilege. *The Huffington Post.* Retrieved from: http://www.huffingtonpost.com/jesse-benn/the-white-antiracism-tone_b_7861740.html.

[3] Boulware, L. E., Cooper, L. A., Ratner, L. E., LaVeist, T. A. & Powe, N.R. (2003). Race and trust in the health care system. *Public Health Reports,* 118, 358-365.

[4] Braddock, C. H., Edwards, K. A., Hasenberg, N. M., Laidley, T. L., Levinson, W. (1999). Informed decision making in outpatient practice: Time to get back to basics. *Journal of the American Medical Association,* 282, 2313-2320.

[5] Braveman, P. & Guskin, S. (2003). Defining equity in health. *Journal of Epidemiology Community Health,* 57, 254–258.

[6] Braveman, P. & Guskin, S. (2003). Poverty, equity, human rights and health. *Bull World Health Organ,* 81, 539-545.

[7] Coffield, A. B., Maciosek, M.V., McGinnis, M. (2001). Priorities among recommended clinical preventive services. *American Journal of Preventive Medicine,* 21, 1-9.

[8] Corless, L., Buckley, A., & Mee, S. (2016). Power inequality between patients and nurses. *Nursing Times,* 112(12-13), 20-21.

[9] Entwistle, V. A., Carter, S. M., Cribb, A., & McCaffery, K. (2010). Supporting patient autonomy: The importance of clinician-patient relationships. *Journal of General Internal Medicine,* 25(7), 741–745.

[10] Goold, S. D. (2002). Trust, Distrust and Trustworthiness. *Journal of General Internal Medicine,* 17(1), 79–81. doi: 10.1046/j.1525-1497.2002.11132.x.

[11] Health Literacy Measurement Tools (Revised). Agency for Healthcare Research and Quality, Rockville, MD.Retrieved from: http://www.ahrq.gov/professionals/quality-patient-safety/quality-resources/tools/literacy/index.html.

[12] Henderson, S. (2003). Power imbalance between nurses and patients: A potential inhibitor of partnership in care. *Journal of Clinical Nursing,* 12(4), 501-508.

[13]Ingel, L. H., Lerner, B. H. (2016). Moving past individual and "pure" autonomy: The rise of family-centered patient care. *American Medical Association Journal of Ethics*, 18(1), 56-62.
[14]Kendall, F. E. (2002). *Understanding white privilege*. Retrieved from: http://www.cpt.org/files/Undoing%20Racism%20-%20Understanding%20White%20Privilege%20-%20Kendall.pdf.
[15]Lewis, A. N. (2009). Disability disparities: A beginning model. *Disability and Rehabilitation*, 31(14), 1136-1143.
[16]Lewis, A. N. (2011). The anatomy of cultural bias and strategies to overcome it, *Journal of Minority Disability Research and Practice*, 1(4), 10-41.
[17]Lewis, A. N. (2008). Vocational rehabilitation in the 21st century: Skills professionals need for systems success. *WORK: A Journal of Prevention, Assessment, and Rehabilitation (special issue)*, 31(3), 345-356.
[18]Lewis, A. N. (2014). *We are all racists: The truth about cultural bias*. Tate Publishing, LLC: Oklahoma City, OK.
[19]McIntosh, P. (1988). White Privilege and Male Privilege: A personal account of coming to see correspondences through work in women's studies. *Working Paper 189*, Wellesley Centers for Women, Wellesley, MA.
[20]McIntosh, P. (1989). White Privilege: Unpacking the Invisible Knapsack. *Peace and Freedom Magazine*, July/August, pp. 10-12, a publication of the Women's International League for Peace and Freedom, Philadelphia, PA.
[21]McLeroy, K. R., Bibeau, D., Steckler, A. & Glanz, K. (1988). An ecological perspective on health promotion programs, *Health Education and Behavior* 15(4), 351–377.
[22]Murray, B. & McCrone, S. (2015). An integrative review of promoting trust in the patient-primary care provider relationship. *Journal of Advanced Nursing*, 71(1), 3-23. doi: 10.1111/jan.12502.
[23]Nichols, E. J. (1989). *The philosophical aspects of cultural difference*. Unpublished paper delivered at The Evergreen State College, Tacoma, Washington.
[24]Papadimos, T. (2007). Healthcare access as a right, not privilege: A construct of western thought. *Philosophy, Ethics, and Humanities in Medicine*, 28, 2:2.
[25]Pellegrino, E. D. (1990). The Medical Profession as a Moral Community. *Bulletin of the New York Academy of Medicine*, 66.3, 221-32. Retrieved from: https://www.ncbi.nlm.nih.gov/pmc/articles/PMC1809760/pdf/bullnyacadmed00014-0025.pdf.
[26]Pew Research Center (2016). It's official: Minority babies are the majority among the nation's infants, but only just. Retrieved from: http://www.pewresearch.org/fact-tank/2016/06/23/.
[27]Power. (n.d.). In *Merriam-Webster Dictionary online*. Retrieved from: https://www.merriam-webster.com/dictionary/power.

[28] Privilege. (n.d.). In *Merriam-Webster Dictionary online*. Retrieved from: https://www.merriam-webster.com/dictionary/privilege.

[29] Schout, G., de Jong, G. & Zeelen, J. (2010). Establishing contact and gaining trust: an exploratory study of care avoidance. *Journal of Advanced Nursing*, 66(2), 324-333. http://dx.doi.org/10.1111/j.1365-2648.2009.05171.x.

[30] Sherwin, S. (1998). A relational approach to autonomy in health care. Sherwin S; eds. In: *The Politics of Women's Health: Exploring Agency and Autonomy*. Philadelphia, PA: Temple University Press, 19-47.

[31] Smedley, B. D., Stith, A. Y., & Nelson, A. R. (2003). Unequal treatment: *Confronting racial and ethnic disparities in health care*. Washington, DC: National Academy Press.

[32] Susser, M. (1993). Health as a human right: An epidemiologist's perspective on the public health. *American Journal of Public Health*, 83(3), 418-426.

[33] Wirtz, V., Cribb, A., & Barber, N. (2006). Patient-doctor decision-making about treatment within the consultation: A critical analysis of models. *Social Science and Medicine*, 62, 116–24.

[34] Woolf, S. H. (1999). The need for perspective in evidence-based medicine. *Journal of American Medical Association*, 282, 2358-2365.

[35] World Socialist Movement. Retrieved from: http://www.worldsocialism.org/english/what-capitalism.

[36] Zbikowski, A., Brüggemann, A. J., Wijma, B., Zeiler, K., & Swahnberg, K. (2012). Ethical guidelines and the prevention of abuse in healthcare. *European Journal of Obstetrics and Gynecology and Reproductive Biology*, 165(1), 18-28.

CHAPTER 7

COUNSELOR CULTURAL COMPETENCE:
FACILITATING SERVICES FOR PEOPLE WITH DISABILITIES IN THE UNITED STATES

KEITH B. WILSON
ABDOULAYE DIALLO
ALLEN LEWIS

CHAPTER TOPICS

- Learning Objectives
- Study Questions
- Demographic Transformation
- Multicultural Counseling Competencies
- The Need for Cultural Competence and Advocacy
- Challenges Associated with the Application of Multicultural Counseling Competencies
- Summary and Conclusion

INTRODUCTION

The changing demographics is a wake-up call for the counseling profession in several ways. As the changing demographics increase, there will be a need for personnel in the human services to become more culturally competent in one-on-one interactions with people who are part of racial and ethnic minorities and other underrepresented groups. Since many employed in the human services are not as culturally competent as would be expected, training to increase awareness and accountability is rising in the rehabilitation education/counseling communities. The increased awareness coupled with behavior and application changes will hopefully facilitate a surge of more human service professionals who are part of underrepresented groups. Given this backdrop, this chapter will explore issues surrounding the preparation and potential barriers to becoming a culturally competent counselor in the context of living in North America. This chapter will conclude with a discussion of the need for advocacy.

LEARNING OBJECTIVES

At the conclusion of this chapter, the reader should be:

1. Aware of the changing demographic profile of the United States population and the increased cultural diversification that will exist going forward,

2. aware of the landscape of outcome studies that exist illustrating the need for improved multicultural counseling competencies among providers who deliver rehabilitation services to persons with disabilities,

3. familiar with the concept of multicultural counseling competencies and why they are needed,

4. familiar with the need for advocacy as it relates to multicultural counseling competencies,

5. familiar with some of the challenges associated with the application of multicultural counseling competencies, and

6. familiar with reasons why we should advocate for people who are part of underrepresented groups and possible barriers that might prevent advocacy.

DEMOGRAPHIC TRANSFORMATION

It is undeniable that the demographic transformation is well underway in the United States. The nation is seeing an increase of women and people who are part of racial and ethnic minorities and other underrepresented groups, and in some parts of the country, being the majority population. For example, the United States Census[59] reported that the U.S. population grew about 5 percent between April 1 and July 2005. However, the European American population decreased about 10 percent during this period. In comparison, American Indian and Alaskan Natives, Asians, African Americans, Native Naïve Hawaiians and other Pacific Islanders, and Latinos increased during this same period. Wilson, et al.,[70] and Wilson and Senices[73] reported that the increased demographic changes will likely result in a higher level of discrimination based on phenotype (i.e., color of skin) in the U.S. Thus, as we see more people who are part of underrepresented groups use our human services and educational systems, there will be a need to ensure that all people receive fair and equal treatment when professional services are delivered, including people with disabilities. Wilson [65,66] and Wilson and Gines[68] reported that people with disabilities and people of color have clear barriers to accessing services in the United States.

DISABILITY OUTCOMES AND RACIAL AND ETHNIC MINORITIES

The idea that race impacts vocational rehabilitation (VR) outcomes in the public rehabilitation system in the United States was first highlighted in the seminal work of Atkins and Wright[7] when they found that African Americans had lower VR acceptance rates. Beyond this early work, the literature has been generally consistent with several studies confirming the early conclusions of Atkins and Wright,[7] Dziekan & Okocha,[21] Jones,[45] Wilson,[66] Wilson, Harley, & Alston,[71] and some demonstrating that VR acceptance rates are not lower for African Americans.[24,43,62,67] It is clear that racial and ethnic minorities tend to be accepted less for VR services than European Americans with disabilities in this country.

Since the early work of Atkins and Wright,[7] a litany of studies have reinforced the point that cultural factors, e.g. race, influence all aspects of the experience of being disabled in this country, and especially service outcomes. Rehabilitation data frequently shows that persons with racial and ethnic minority status exhibit outcomes that fall below those of non-minority group members.[27] The variable of race, as it pertains to both the counselor and the service recipient, is a key factor in disparate rehabilitation service outcomes.[2,9,16,37,39,50,51,63] While there are many variables of discrimination that may influence outcomes in the VR systems, race and ethnicity are not only the most studied but tend to be linked to negative outcomes in the VR system.

In 1992, Section 21 of the reauthorization of the Rehabilitation Act of 1973 made it clear that individuals with disabilities who are part of racial and ethnic minorities typically have higher incidence of disability, lower participation rates in the public VR system, and achieve less favorable outcomes when compared to majority populations of persons with disabilities. This legislation pointed to the need for public VR services to be more culturally competent. Disparities in outcomes related to cultural orientation, namely race, are not unique to the field of rehabilitation or the disability world. We have observed outcomes studies in education and medical fields as well.

Differential outcomes of services delivery based on race or ethnicity have been widely discussed as the concept of health disparities. It can be argued that the Institute of Medicine (IOM) offers the most pervasive concept of health disparities in the United States. To this point, the IOM[54] maintains that health disparities are disproportionately negative outcomes of health services in racial and ethnic minority populations when access and socioeconomic factors are controlled. While there have been similar studies that have controlled many variables of discrimination to inch closer to a higher connection between race, ethnicity and VR outcomes, it is undeniable that socioeconomics is linked to many VR and related conclusions. Race and ethnicity are primary factors that determine why certain groups might not have comparable outcomes in the VR and other systems in this country.

It has been consistently purported that improved cultural competency or multicultural counseling competencies are the solution to disparate rehabilitation outcomes based on cultural orientation, primarily race or ethnicity.[11,17,26,40,60] Most of the extant conceptual literature supports this point of view. After all, it is intuitive that improved competency when it comes to cultural considerations should improve rehabilitation outcomes among culturally diverse groups.

THE NEED FOR MULTICULTURAL COMPETENCY

In general counseling literature, the importance of cultural competency has been stressed for well over 20 years. As early as 1982, Sue, et al.,[55] put forward a three-part multicultural counseling model that consisted of cultural beliefs and attitudes, knowledge, and skills. Later, Pedersen[42] offered that multiculturalism is the fourth force in counseling. In 1992, Sue, et al.,[55] identified three core aspects of cultural competency and offered 31 specific multicultural competencies. Subsequent to the three core aspects of competency noted by Sue, et al.,[55] Arrendondo, et al.,[6] offered an operationalized view of the multicultural competencies. However, despite the several decades push for improved multicultural counseling competencies within both the rehabilitation and the general counseling arenas along with the substantial literature that extols the virtues of possessing such competencies, it is ironic that there is still a need for a stronger evidence base to empirically justify outcomes related to multicultural counseling competencies in the human services. We have come a long way but still have a long way to go with the application of the competencies by both practitioners and educators. Next, we will briefly highlight the Multicultural Counseling Competencies (MCC) as a foundation from which this chapter is based.

MULTICULTURAL COUNSELING COMPETENCIES

Several authors have commented that there is a gap between what we know as MCCs and the follow through with the application of the said competencies[1,64,72] The foundation of the MCC was based on the observation that many underserved and underrepresented populations were not being served and treated fairly in the human service system.[55] Additionally, Sue, et al.,[55] also noticed the number of human service workers being overwhelmingly European American who did not necessarily have the MCCs to facilitate services for underrepresented populations. To this end, the MCCs were generally developed to hopefully facilitate services for all clients interacting with the human services, recognizing that people who are part of underrepresented groups are likely to receive inadequate services when compared to their European American counterparts. A concise description of the competencies will be presented with what we consider is the order of development for most.

AWARENESS

As delineated by Sue, et al.,[55] the awareness level of the MCCs is understanding one's own morals and attitudes and the morals and attitudes of others. We believe that this level is the most challenging because of the enculturation process that is connected to the majority culture. Secondly, because the consequences of the enculturation process are so intense, many tend to belong only to groups that are considered part of "their" identity group(s). Thus, it is problematic to facilitate services for groups who are considered underrepresented when human service workers have no idea of their own internal conscious or unconscious biases when interacting with those who may be considered different on a host of demographic variables of discrimination. Wilson, et al.,[69] reported that while is it important to understand one's own values, it is more critical to understand how one's values may not facilitate services for groups who are underserved and underrepresented in the U.S.

KNOWLEDGE

While context has a lot to do with acquiring knowledge,[55] it may be the easiest of the three levels to obtain. Again, context is important whether a person is willing to pursue "understanding" about groups that might be different than oneself. Although not all exhaustive, knowledge can be gained by:

- personal interactions with diverse groups in a variety of settings,
- attending workshops where information is presented about different underrepresented groups (e.g., classroom, workshops, and other professional development opportunities), and
- taking the initiative to study and or educate oneself on diverse groups.

However, having the knowledge about certain groups of clients and acquiring skills to facilitate services for such clients is a long bridge to cross. There is an argument to be made that skills can be acquired on the way to getting knowledge about certain groups. However, these two concepts are distinct, which we will now discuss.

SKILLS

It is hoped that the acquisition of awareness and knowledge will lead to the attainment of skills. Sue, et al.,[55] reported that skills are the tools one will employ to facilitate services for groups who are considered underrepresented. It must be noted, however, that the acquisition of awareness, knowledge, and skills will more likely not lead to application of the aforementioned knowledge and skills. Wilson,[69] reported that the level of awareness and knowledge are cognitive and both might involve *thinking* and *behavior* (e.g., the act of moving). Wilson, et al.,[69] goes on to adduce that skills and application are different. We agree!

Because behavior/action seems to be viewed as application, we have decided to define and operationalize and give an example to further clarify what we mean by these two terms. Although this may seem like we are splitting hairs, the denotation of the following words is obvious.

Behavior. Behavior is any physical activity or movement that is observed in a human being or animal.[8]

Application. On the other hand, application[5] is putting your behavior to use in a particular context or purpose. Context may be people, location, time of day, for example. There are several stories about people with the awareness, knowledge, and skills of the multicultural counseling competencies who might use these particular tools in the wrong context. Using these tools without the proper context will equate to what we call behavior or action, not application. For example, applying a firm handshake to many people who might be from the

African continent would be behavior/action. Why? Because we know that many from the African continent do not have firm handshakes because the context (i.e., the way many from the African continent were acculturated and enculturated) communicates to us that firm handshakes show aggression. However, applying a firm handshake to many who were born, acculturated, and enculturated in the United States would be considered applying the tools (i.e., handshake) in the appropriate context (i.e., geographically). We understand that many in the North American continent view a firm handshake as appropriate with the understanding that many assumptions are made about a handshake (e.g., none trust worthy, not assertive).

THE NEED FOR ADVOCACY

DEMOGRAPHIC CONTEXT

The racial and ethnic minority population in the United States is on the rise, and it is expected to constitute a numerical majority by 2050.[29] Given this context, racial and ethnic minorities are also overrepresented as a percentage of those suffering from chronic illnesses and disabilities.[12] The disproportion of illness and disability is due partly to environmental factors such as social stigma, sexism, heterosexism, racism, and classism,[13] factors that can be addressed through social justice advocacy. It appears the barriers that racial and ethnic minorities with disabilities must overcome is observed in social, political, and economic conditions.[46] These and other factors may affect the counseling or therapeutic encounter for racial and ethnic minority clients encountering the vocational rehabilitation (VR) systems or other human services provided in the United States. Biases, discrimination, and oppression, for example, are often embedded in how clients are diagnosed and treated by service providers who may come from different ethnic or socioeconomic groups.[70] Rather than helping underrepresented racial and ethnic minority clients, diagnosis and treatment may disempower them through paternalism, stigmatization, and deficit-oriented labels.[22] It is clear that advocacy is an appropriate general intervention to facilitate the growing population of racial and ethnic minorities who face tremendous challenges that are due partly to environmental factors.

ENVIRONMENTAL FACTORS

Looking at environmental factors and outcomes, Lee and Park[29] recently documented various outcomes of environmental factors on racial and ethnic minorities. Given this backdrop, counselors and counseling frameworks are still minimizing the vital link between environmental forces and their clients' psychological problems.[46] It stands to reason that if environmental factors (e.g., social stigma, sexism) are not considered in counseling or psychotherapy practice, the results can negatively affect psychological well-being of racial and ethnic minorities and any group interacting with the human service system.

Thus, environmental factors can result in depression, suicide, and delayed growth and development, and may hinder a client's ability to achieve their full vocational potential.[4,23] Counseling and psychotherapy are important because these particular interventions may address internal issues, such as affect and cognition, at the expense of the environmental barriers.[34] While multicultural counseling competencies typically focus on the counselor's awareness, knowledge, and skills in understanding the impact of cultural bias and oppression on the client and on the counseling process itself, bias, discrimination, and other environmental issues cannot easily be resolved by one-on-one counseling.[34] Therefore, common office-based interventions, which use a counselor's micro skills, are crucial, but they are rarely effective in helping the client deal with systemic problems.[58] The detrimental effects of systemic barriers, which are created at least in part by sociopolitical factors, cannot be resolved by common direct counseling alone.[32] Social advocacy, in which these environmental factors are addressed, is needed, as it provides the means to turn the client's awareness and knowledge into action.[46] Given the connection between mental health and environmental factors on both physical and behavioral health concerns, it is really important that human service providers become better advocates to address environmental issues to facilitate better outcomes for all who seek human services.

We know that advocacy as part of the counseling process benefits all clients. In addition to providing one-on-one services in the office, counselors may also observe the settings in which their clients experience bias, discrimination, and oppression by involving themselves in the community. Counselors' involvement in the community can help their client's understand and become more empathic to their clients' problems and concerns.[44] Additionally, community involvement can also shift the counselor's focus from viewing their clients' problems solely as internal phenomena. As a result, the counselor may be more helpful because of empathy and understanding that the client is not responsible for the many barriers they encounter both inside and outside of the office setting.[57] While the following list is not exhaustive, advocacy can address several concerns: 1. systemic problems at the institutional level; 2. biased values rooted in communities; and 3. local, state, and federal policies/laws that are adversarial to minorities. Through the application of advocacy, the counselor and/or client may meet with counseling and educational programs leaders, community leaders, and legislators to help resolve individual, social/cultural, and institutional forms of injustice. The application of advocacy can be empowering and liberating for clients,[15] as they come to see certain problems as environmental, and as they and/or others take actions to break through structural and attitudinal barriers to achieve their goals. Accordingly, the delivery and progress of the client's therapy may take a new direction. Counselors may now be able to articulate and deal with issues once masked or worsened by environmental factors with the openness of the human service professional. Furthermore, clients may be in a better position to attain their highest potential via advocacy support from their counselor. As Maslow[38] noted, for one to attain one's highest potential, basic needs such as security and safety, both of which can be disrupted by racism and discrimination, must first be addressed. By first assisting clients to deal with environmental barriers, counselors can facilitate clients to achieve their full potential during their interactions with the human service organization. Advocacy, as Lewis, et al.,[33] pointed out, is an effective way to clear solvable environmental problems for effective counseling to begin. Advocacy deals with issues that affect client wellbeing and present barriers to therapy, though they are not generally considered in common practice.

STANDARDS OF CARE

Advocacy not only benefits clients, but it is in line with the philosophy of many governing bodies that credential human service professionals like the Commission on Rehabilitation Counseling Certification and the World Health Organization's International Classification of Functioning, Disability and Health (ICF) frame, for example. The ICF frame and the social model of disability both emphasize the worth of personal characteristics (P), environmental factors (E), and the value of their interaction (P × E), in the integration of individuals with chronic illnesses and disabilities into their communities.[13,31] Social justice advocacy is in line with this frame in acknowledging the interplay between clients and their environments. As part of our identity and philosophy as counselors, we should focus on the environmental factors that act as barriers to minority individuals' progress, rather than on the idea that the problem resides solely within the individual or group of individuals. More importantly, the link between multiculturalism and social justice advocacy and its application is reflected in the counseling profession's Codes of Ethics (e.g., ACA Code: E. 5.a.; CRCC Code: C1/C2), which obligates counselors to advocate ethically with and on behalf of clients at the individual, group, institutional, and societal levels.[3,14] Omitting advocacy for clients may result in those clients seeing us solely as part of an entity that stigmatizes them, and this may ultimately jeopardize the credibility of our profession. Our advocacy efforts represent our identity as counselors and therapists, and our environmental interventions embody equality for all who may seek our services.

CHALLENGES ASSOCIATED WITH THE APPLICATION OF MULTICULTURAL COUNSELING COMPETENCIES

HISTORICAL LEGACIES OF PREJUDICE AND DISCRIMINATION

Agencies, whose duty it is to provide resources to facilitate the implementation of multicultural counseling competencies via counselors, are actually part of the problem. Counselors and the agencies/institutions they serve have historically been biased toward racial and ethnic minorities, often denying them access to resources.[41,67] Counselors have been seen by racial and ethnic minority clients as adversarial and not having their best interests in mind.[52] In part, this view is held by many racial and ethnic minorities of human services workers because of the sociopolitical nature of therapy and vocational rehabilitation, in which clients are asked to take a subordinate position, their cases interpreted by counselors that may be racist, sexist, ageist, heterosexist, ablest, and classist.[29] For example, an application of outcomes based on views of the service provider can be observed in the research on people who may have substance dependency. Persons with drug dependency are seen as responsible for their drug problem and accordingly, service providers provide inadequate services for them.[52,53] In order to provide better services to all, there is a need for human service providers to become more aware of how their perceptions are impacting the bottom line for many of their clients who are part of racial and ethnic minority groups in the United States. Being aware of counterproductive attitudes is the first step in the process to providing good services to all clients.

TRAINING PROGRAMS

Another obstacle to the application of multicultural counseling competencies comes from the emphasis and approach of counselor training programs. Many of these programs are based on European-American values and traditions, which can be major barriers in multicultural counseling.[19] These particular programs focus on individualism, on insight as cure, on brief, time-limited therapy, on psychological distance between the counselor and client, on English-centered verbal communication, and on openness between counselors and clients.[28,35] Sensitivity to diversity is barely addressed in many forms of psychotherapy.[10] European-American values and traditions, as well as the intake procedures, objectives, goal-setting, and printed documents associated with conventional treatment may all conflict with or be antithetical to racial and ethnic minorities' world views and may also conflict with multicultural counseling competencies standards. This particular focus on psychotherapy and other parts of the training process leaves little room to accommodate cultural values of populations that may be underrepresented. For example, in some cultures, the family is involved in every aspect of life.[18,19] Yet in some counseling settings, such as the state-federal VR arena, treating a large group of people (e.g., an entire family) may be impossible, given that the system is designed to focus on individuals.[36] Likewise, minorities from non-English backgrounds may not understand the counselor, let alone understand complicated therapy lingo. Thus, the adverse attitudes of counselors and their agencies and European-American based approaches that ignore non-European American cultural values and world views can be barriers to the implementation of multicultural counseling competencies in a significant way. It is the responsibility of educators/mentors/allies to understand and transform these systems of oppression that go unchallenged and effect many in unproductive ways.

In addition to the negative attitudes of service providers and European-American based approaches used in counseling and educational training programs, these programs generally focus on imparting knowledge useful for treating internal issues in traditional office settings, minimizing the client's link to environmental factors.[20] Such an autoplastic view—at the expense of an alloplastic conceptualization that would consider environmental factors—does not foster development of counselors' macro level (policy- and legislation-related) interventions and advocacy interventions skills.[58] There will certainly be a gap between counseling theory and practice, in spite of the increase in the literature on advocacy and counselor multicultural counseling competence. As Ratts, et al.,[45] noted, social justice advocacy has not been infused throughout the counseling profession. Many counselors still view advocacy as taking place in a world of politics and social action, best suited to activists.[35] While we have made significant strides, it is clear we have a long way to go in viewing advocacy in a way that will truly facilitate services for our clients.

TRAINING PROGRAMS KEEPING PACE WITH REAL ISSUES

Counseling training programs have failed to keep pace with racial minority clients' issues and needs. While multicultural competency acknowledges the emic perspective, knowledge of the literature and of multicultural competency as it relates to specific cultural groups is still incomplete. For example, the African nation of Guinea is home to more than 20 ethnic groups, each with a unique culture and unique world view. However, American counselors who treat Guinean immigrants and refugees typically regard Guinea as one nation with one culture and they recommend interventions designed for that one, essentially invented culture. The same is true for immigrant groups with varying acculturation levels (e.g., Some immigrants have replaced their cultural values with European American values, while others have only partially embraced such values), yet counselors lack detailed knowledge about differences between these levels. Knowledge is also lacking with regard to non-Western interventions—such as folk or spiritual healing interventions—which may involve trancelike states and direct communication with a deity. Western counselor training programs generally do not incorporate such approaches in their curricula, and evidence-based research on these approaches is lacking as well.[49] The lack of knowledge of specific ethnic groups (e.g., among Guineans, the Susu, or Fulani) makes it difficult to design multicompetent, evidence-based interventions for these groups.

Finally, counseling training programs draw most of their graduates from the majority culture. As a result, the counseling dyad usually involves a counselor from the majority culture, who is generally uninformed about minority clients' issues, such as spirituality, the role of the community in making decisions, discrimination and other factors in the client's new environment, etc. A client from a minority culture may thus find U.S. counseling approaches foreign and may distrust the counselors from the majority culture.[61] It has been found that minority clients stay longest in therapy with counselors of their same racial/ethnic background.[49] Increasing the number of minority counselors and better preparing both minority and majority counselors, would create an atmosphere in which clients and their cultural values would be understood. This would make it easier for counselors to implement competent multicultural counseling.

CONCLUSION

The MCCs were created to guide counseling professionals to provide better services for populations that are considered underrepresented. It is our belief that the MCCs will continue to be a worthwhile framework to benefit the human services for some time to come. While the MCCs are well established, there are observations that lead many to believe that the application of the aforementioned competencies lacks follow-through by researchers and practitioners. Counseling training programs have yet to gear their practices towards multiculturally competent counseling, including competences related to environmental factors, an especially egregious omission, given that all counseling encounters are in one way or another multicultural. Many scholars have noted that counselors are generally not specifically trained to counsel non-whites, immigrants, indigenous cultures, the elderly, and sexual and other minorities, and they lack the knowledge and the desire to advocate regarding environmental barriers for minorities. Given the current importance of multicultural competence, including its advocacy aspect, application of multiculturally competent counseling should be of utmost importance in the profession. As Robbins[48] noted, practice without theory is dead.

OTHER ACTIVITIES

How Diverse is Your World? from Lewis[30]

Because we live in a pluralistic nation, many individuals assume they are diverse in their lifestyles. This short exercise is designed to determine how diverse one's world is in terms of those aspects of living where one has total control over to whom they interface. Please candidly answer the ten questions that follow, indicating a primary diversity for each response (specify the dominant or numerical majority of the race or ethnicity that fits the answer, adhering to instructions after the ten questions.

1. Who are you married to or who do you date mostly?

2. Who are your best friends?

3. Who are you likely to invite to your home for dinner or on a holiday?
4. Who do you socialize with on a regular basis?
5. Who do you worship with? (If you do not worship, answer as if you did.)
6. Who are you likely to eat lunch with on a regular basis at work or school?
7. If your family took a vacation with another family, how would you describe the other family?
8. Who is the ideal person for your son or daughter to marry? (If you do not have children, answer as if you did.)
9. Describe who you are least likely to fear in a dark alley.
10. If you had to sit with a group of complete strangers while dining in a new restaurant, describe the group with whom you would be most comfortable sitting?

What are the themes related to race or ethnicity that are dominant in the responses? If the descriptions in a majority of questions (at least six questions) match who you are in terms of race or ethnicity, your world is not truly diverse. If the descriptions in six or more questions do not match your race or ethnicity, your world is pretty diverse. Individuals with diverse worlds are likely to exhibit less cultural bias related to race or ethnicity.

One of the key ingredients to exhibiting multicultural counseling competencies is to understand that we are all cultural beings. Being a cultural being in a pluralistic society like America means we all have biases that contraindicate our ability to deliver quality rehabilitation services to some individuals. Part of our responsibility as helpers is to be aware of our personal biases. The extent to which we can be aware of them gives us a chance to devise strategies that can control them and mitigate their potential negative impact in a counseling situation.[30]

Biases in the context of multicultural counseling competencies are those values, beliefs, stereotypes, and ways of thinking that are comfortable to us, but that are not universally shared by all persons, and that may compromise our effectiveness as a helper if they surface in certain clinical situations as we seek to provide optimal services to specific individuals. I am suggesting a four-step process of self-exploration that allows one to identify their own biases and have a proactive game plan for ensuring they do not have a deleterious effect on the customers we serve. Please see the four-step process below.

1. Become aware of the nature of the specific bias – evaluate why it is a bias, how long it has existed, and if it is subject to change, what

could change it. If the bias is modifiable, then seek those modifying experiences.

2. Realize the probable negative impact of the bias – assess how this bias could interfere with the provision of effective services and who specifically might cause this bias to surface.

3. Devise strategies to manage the bias – develop strategies to minimize the harm this bias could produce and continue to update strategies over time.

4. Understand the implication of having this bias – learn what this bias means about you as a helper and embrace whatever lessons it reveals about you professionally.

The aforementioned four-step process should be engaged in with each new bias that one becomes aware of. It should also be a lifelong process that rehabilitation professionals use in an ongoing manner to identify and keep biases in check as we grow and mature. The natural human maturation process means that biases will come and go throughout one's professional career.

INTERNET RESOURCES

- American Counseling Association – Division: Association of Multicultural Counseling and Development: https://www.counseling.org/docs/competencies/multcultural_competencies.pdf?sfvrsn=5

- National Rehabilitation Association – Division: National Association of Multicultural Rehabilitation Concerns: http://www.namrc.org/resources.htm

- United States Health Resources and Services Administration: http://www.hrsa.gov/culturalcompetence/index.html

- United States Department of Health and Human Services: https://www.thinkculturalhealth.hhs.gov/

- National Institutes of Health: http://www.nih.gov/clearcommunication/culturalcompetency.htm

STUDY QUESTIONS

1. Describe the current trends in the changing population demographics in the United States as they pertain to culturally diverse individuals and people with disabilities.

2. Based on the outcomes literature, discuss the types of disparities that individuals with disabilities who are culturally diverse experience when receiving services in the public rehabilitation system.

3. Discuss your current readiness to function in a manner that is culturally competent in the delivery of rehabilitation services. Specify the steps you could take to improve your readiness.

4. What role(s) could you play as an advocate for more widespread adoption and use of multicultural counseling strategies?

5. What ideas do you have to enhance the application of multicultural counseling competencies in the profession of rehabilitation counseling?

REFERENCES

[1]Ahmed, S. Wilson, K. B., Henriksen, R. C., & Jones, J, W. (2011). What does it mean to be a culturally-competent counselor? *Journal for Social Action in Counseling Psychology*, 3(1)17-28.

[2]Alston, R. J., Gayles, T., Rucker, R., & Hobson, M. (2007). The centrality of race in rehabilitation: Views of former service recipients who are African American. *Journal of Applied Rehabilitation Counseling*, 38(1), 12-19.

[3]American Counseling Association (2014). ACA code of ethics. Alexandria, VA: Author.

[4]American Public Health Association (2009). Promoting public health research, policy, practice, and education. Retrieved from http://www.counseling.org/knowledge-center/ethics/code-of-ethics-resources.

[5]Application (2016). Dictionary.com unabridged. Retrieved April 18, 2016, from http://dictionary.reference.com/browse/application

[6]Arrendondo, P., Toporek, R., Brown, S. P., Jones, J., Locke, D. C., Sanchez, J., & Stadler, H. (1996). Operationalization of the multicultural counseling competencies. *Journal of Multicultural Counseling and Development*, 24, 42–78.

[7]Atkins, B. J., & Wright, G. N. (1980). Three views: Vocational rehabilitation of Blacks: The statement. *Journal of Rehabilitation*, 46(2), 40, 42–46.

[8]Behavior (2016). Dictionary.com unabridged. Retrieved April 18, 2016, from http://www.dictionary.com/browse/behavior?s=t

[9]Bellini, J. (2003). Counselors' multicultural competencies and vocational rehabilitation outcomes in the context of counselor-client racial similarity and difference. *Rehabilitation Counseling Bulletin*, 46(3), 164-173.

[10] Bishop, M., & Fleming, A. R. (2015). Rational emotive behavior therapy. In F. Chan, N. L. Berven, & K. R. Thomas (Eds), *Counseling theories and techniques for rehabilitation and mental health professionals* (pp. 109-133). New York, USA: Springers.

[11] Cartwright, B. Y., Daniels, J., & Zhang, S. (2008). Assessing multicultural competency: perceived versus demonstrated performance. *Journal of Counseling and Development*, Development, 86, 318–322.

[12] Center for Disease Control and Prevention (2015). Racial and ethnic approaches to community health: The finding solution to health disparities at a glance. Retrieved from http://www.cdc.gov/chronicdisease/resources/publications/aag/reach.htm

[13] Chan, F., Bezyak, J., Romero-Ramirez, M., Chiu, C. Y., Sung, C. & Fujikawa, M. (2010). Concepts, challenges, barriers, and opportunities related to evidence-based practice in rehabilitation counseling. *Rehabilitation Education*, 24(3/4), 179-190.

[14] Commission on Rehabilitation Counselors Certification (2010). Code of ethics for rehabilitation counselors. Retrieved from https://www.crccertification.com/code-of-ethics-4

[15] Crethar, H. C., Torres Rivera, E., & Nash, S. (2008). In search of common threads. *Journal of Counseling and Development*, 86, 269-278.

[16] Cumming-McCann, A., & Accordino, M. P. (2005). An investigation of rehabilitation counselor characteristics, European American racial attitudes, and self-reported multicultural counseling competencies. *Rehabilitation Counseling Bulletin*, 48(3), 167-176.

[17] Davis E. L., & Rubin S. E. (1996). Multicultural instructional goals and strategies for rehabilitation counselor education. *Rehabilitation Education*, 10, 105–114.

[18] Diallo, A., (2014). A silver lining in the dark clouds of treatment for minorities. *Austin Journal of Psychiatry and Behavioral Science, 1(5)*, 1.2.

[19] Diller, J. V. (2001). Cultural diversity: A primer for the human services. Brooks/Cole: United States.

[20] Durham, J. C., & Glosoff, H. L. (2010). From passion to action. In M. J. Ratts, R. L. Toporek, & J. A. Lewis (Eds), *ACA advocacy competencies* (pp. 139-148). Alexandria, VA: American Counseling Association.

[21] Dziekan, K. I., & Okocha, A. G. (1993). Accessibility of rehabilitation services: Comparison by racial-ethnic status. *Rehabilitation Counseling Bulletin, 36,* 183–189.

[22] Follette, W. C., & Houts, A. C. (1996). Models of scientific progress and the role of theory in taxonomy development: A case study of the DSM. *Journal of Consulting and Clinical Psychology, 64,* 1120–1132.

[23] Gee, G. C., Ryan, A., Laflamme, D. J., & Holt, J. (2006). Self-reported discrimination and mental Health Status among African descendants, Mexican Americans, and other Latinos in the New Hampshire. *American Journal of Public Health, 96(10),* 1821-1828.

[24]Giesen, J. M., Cavenaugh, B. S., & Sansing, W. K. (2004). Access to vocational rehabilitation: The impact of race and ethnicity. *Journal of Visual Impairment & Blindness, 98,* 410-19.
[25]Jones N. A. (2008). Acceptance Rates Research and Program Evaluation. *International Journal of Psychosocial Rehabilitation,* 13(1), 5-9.
[26]Leal-Idrogo, A. (1997). Multicultural rehabilitation counseling. *Rehabilitation Education,* 11, 231-240.
[27]LeBlanc, S. & Smart, J. F. (2007). Outcome discrepancies among racially/ethnically diverse service recipients of vocational rehabilitation services: Summary and critique of the literature. *Journal of Applied Rehabilitation Counseling ,* 38(1), 3-11.
[28]Lee, C. C (2013). The cross cultural encounter. In C. C. Lee (Ed), *Multicultural issues in counseling* (pp. 13-23). Alexandria, VA: American Counseling Association.
[29]Lee, C. C., & Park, D. (2013). A conceptual framework for counseling across culture. In C. C. Lee (Ed), *Multicultural issues in counseling* (pp. 3-13). Alexandria, VA: American Counseling Association.
[30]Lewis, A. N. (2014). *We are all racists: The truth about cultural bias.* Tate Publishing, LLC: Oklahoma City, OK.
[31]Lewis, A. N. (2006). Three-factor model of multicultural counseling for consumers with disabilities. *Journal of Vocational rehabilitation, 24,* 151.
[32]Lewis, J. A., & Arnold, M. S. (1998). From multiculturalism to social action. In C. C. Lee & G. R. Walz (Eds), *Social action* (pp. 51-65). Alexandria, VA: American Counseling Association.
[33]Lewis, J. A., Cheek, J. R., & Hendricks, C. B. (2001). Advocacy in supervision. In L. J. Bradley & N. Ladany (Eds), Counseling supervision (pp. 330-341).
[34]Lewis, J. A., Ratts, M. J., Paladino, D. A., & Toporek, R. L. (2011). Social Justice Counseling and Advocacy: Developing New Leadership Roles and Competencies. *Journal for Social Action in Counseling and Psychology, 3(1),* 5 – 16.
[35]Liu, W. M., & Toporek, R. L. (2004). Advocacy. In T. F. Riggar & D. R. Maki (Eds), *Handbook of rehabilitation counseling* (pp. 188-19). USA: Springer.
[36]Manthey, T. J., Brooks, J., Chan, F., Hedenblad, L. E., & Ditchman, N. (2015). Motivational interview. In In F. Chan, N. L. Berven, & K. R. Thomas (Eds), *Counseling theories and techniques for rehabilitation and mental health professionals* (pp. 247-279). New York, USA: Springers.
[37]Martin, F. H. (2010). Racial variation in vocational rehabilitation outcomes: A structural equation modeling approach. *Rehabilitation Counseling Bulletin,* 54(1), 26-35.
[38]Maslow, A. H. (1943). A theory of human motivation. *Psychological Review, 50(4),* 370-396.

[39]Matrone, K. F. & Leahy, M. J. (2005). The relationship between vocational rehabilitation client outcomes and rehabilitation counselor multicultural counseling competencies. *Rehabilitation Counseling Bulletin*, 48(4), 233-244.

[40]Middleton, R. A., Rollins, C. W., Sanderson, P. L., Leung, P., Harley, D. A., Ebener D, Leal-drogo A. (2000). Endorsement of professional multicultural rehabilitation competencies and standards: a call to action. *Rehabilitation Counseling Bulletin*, 43, 219–240.

[41]Mpofu, E., & Harley, D. A. (2015). Multicultural rehabilitation counseling: Optimizing success with diversity. In F. Chan, N. L. Berven, & K. R. Thomas (Eds), *Counseling theories and techniques for rehabilitation and mental health professionals* (pp. 417-443). New York, USA: Springers.

[42]Pedersen, P. B. (1991). Multiculturalism as a fourth force in counseling [special issue]. *Journal of Counseling and Development*, 70, 6–12.

[43]Peterson, G. E. (1996). *An analysis of participation, progress, and outcome of individuals from diverse racial and ethnic backgrounds in the public vocational rehabilitation program in Nevada*. Unpublished doctoral dissertation, University of Northern Colorado, Greeley. Rehabilitation Act Amendments of 1992, Pub. L. No. 102-569, 106 Stat. 4344–4488 (1992).

[44]Ratts, M. J., Singh, A. A., Nassar-McMillan, S., Butler, S. K., McCullough, J. R. (2015). Multicultural and social justice counseling competencies. Journal of Multicultural Counseling and Development, 44, 28-48.

[45]*Ratts, M. J., Toporek, R. L., & Lewis, J. A. (Eds.). (2010). ACA Advocacy Competencies: A social justice framework for counselors. Alexandria, VA: American Counseling Association.

[46]Ratts, M. J. & Wood, C. (2011). The fierce urgency of now: Diffusion of innovation as a mechanism to integrate social justice in counselor education. *Counselor Education and Supervision,* 50(3), 207-223.

[47]Rehabilitation Act of 1973, 29 U.S.C. § 701–744, as amended in 1992; Title I, Section 21, Public Law 102–569.

[48]Robbins, J. W. (1972)"The Crisis of our Time." In G. H. Clark (Ed). *The Johnnine Logos*. Jefferson, MD: The Trinity Foundation. Retrieved from http://www.dtl.org/ethics/article/theory.htm

[49]Rosenthal, H. (2008). Encyclopedia of counseling. New York, USA: Routledge.

[50]Rosenthal, D.A. (2004). Effects of client race on clinical judgment of practicing European. American vocational rehabiitation counselors. *Rehabilitation Counseling Bulletin* , 47(3), 131-141.

[51]Rosenthal, D. A., Wong, D., Blalock, K. M., & Delambo, D. A. (2004). Effects of counsellor race on racial stereotypes of rehabilitaiton counselling service recipients. *Disability and Rehabilitation*, 26(20), 1214-1220.

[52]Scheppers, E., Dongen, E. V., Dekker, J., Geertzen, J. & Dekker, J. (2005). Potential barriers to the use of health services among ethnic minorities: a review. Family Practice, 23 (3), 325 – 348. Retrieved from Nation Institute of Health: http://www.ncbi.nlm.nih.gov/pubmed/16476700

[53]Smart, J. (2001). Disability, society, and the individual. Gaithersburg, MD: Aspen.

[54]Smedley, B. D., Stith, A. Y., & Nelson, A. R. (2003). *Unequal treatment: Confronting racial and ethnic disparities in health care.* Washington, DC: National Academy Press.

[55]Sue, D. W., Arredondo, P., & McDavis, R. (1992). Multicultural counseling competencies and standards: A call to the profession. *Journal of Multicultural Counseling and Development,* 20, 64–88.

[56]Sue, D. W., Bernier, Y., Durran, A., Feinberg, L., Pedersen, P. B., Smith, E. J., & Vasquez-Nuttal, E. (1982). Position paper: Cross-cultural counseling competencies. *The Counseling Psychologist,* 10, 45-52.

[57]Sue, D. W., & Sue, D. (2008). Counseling the cultural diverse: Theory and practice (5th ed.). New York, NY: Wiley.

[58]Toporek, R. L., Gerstein, L. H., Fouad, N. A., Roysircar, G., Isreal, T. (2006). Handbook for social justice in counseling psychology. Thousand, Oaks, CA; Sage.

[59]United State Census (2005). Race and Hispanic origin in 2005. Retrieved from http://www.census.gov/population/www/poprofile/files Dynamic/RACEHO.pdf

[60]Watson, A. L. (1988). Importance of cross-cultural counseling in rehabilitation counseling curricula. *Journal of Applied Rehabilitation Counseling,* 19, 55–61.

[61]Whaley, A. L. (2001). Cultural Mistrust and mental health services for African American: A meta-analysis. *The Counseling Psychology,* 29, 513-521.

[62]Wheaton, J., (1995). Vocational rehabilitation acceptance rates for European Americans and African Americans: Another look. *Rehabilitation Counseling Bulletin,* 38, 224-231.

[63]Whitfield, H. W., Venable, R., & Brousard, S. (2010). Are client-counselor ethnic/racial matches associated with successful rehabilitation outcomes? *Rehabilitation Counseling Bulletin,* 53(2), 96-105.

[64]Wilson, K. B. (March 2010). *What does it mean to be a culturally-competent counselor?* Paper presented at the meeting of the American Counseling Association, Multicultural Social Justice Leadership Academy, Pittsburgh, PA.

[65]Wilson, K. B. (2000). Predicting vocational rehabilitation eligibility based on race, education, work status, and source of support at application. *Rehabilitation Counseling Bulletin, 43,* 97-105.

[66]Wilson, K. B. (2002). The exploration of vocational rehabilitation acceptance and ethnicity: A national investigation. *Rehabilitation Counseling Bulletin, 45*, 168-176.

[67]Wilson, K. B., Alston, R. J., Harley, D. A., Mitchell, N. A., (2002). Predicting VR acceptance based on race, gender, education, work, status at application, and primary source of support at application. *Rehabilitation Counseling Bulletin, 45(3)*, 132 – 142.

[68]Wilson, K. B. & Gines, J. E. (2009). A national reassessment: Exploring variable that predispose people with disabilities to vocational rehabilitation acceptance. *Rehabilitation Education, 2*, 159-170.

[69]Wilson, K. B., Gines, J. E., & Caldwell, T. (2014). Counselor advocacy for access: Addressing the challenges of people with disabilities. Manuscript Submitted for Publication.

[70]Wilson, K. B., Gines, J. E., & Glassett, K. F. (2013). Vocational rehabilitation acceptance: Rationale for Bias [Monograph]. In Wehman, P., Gray, K. W., & Bourdon, J. L. (Eds.), *Race, ethnicity, and disability research: Modern Advancement and future endeavors in the field (pp. 111-118)*. Richmond, Virginia: Virginia Commonwealth University.

[71]Wilson, K., Harley, D., & Alston, R. (2001). Race as a correlate of vocational rehabilitation acceptance and explaining bias in the rehabilitation process: Revisited. *The Journal of Rehabilitation, 67(3)*, 35-41.

[72]Wilson, K. B., Pitt, J. S., Raheem, M. A., Acklin, C. L., & Wilson, J. M. (2017). Multicultural counseling competencies: Why is it difficult to apply what we know…? In L. Leavitt, S. Wisdom, & K. Leavitt (Eds.), *Cultural awareness and competency development in higher education* (pp. 237-254). Hershey, Pennsylvania. IGI Global.

[73]Wilson, K. B. & Senices, J. (2010). Access to vocational Rehabilitation services for Black Latinos with disabilities: Colorism in the 21st century. In Balcazar, F. B., Suarez-Blcazar, Y., Taylor-Ritzler, T. & Keys, C. B. (Eds.) *Culture, Race and Disability: Issues in Rehabilitation Research and Practice* (pp. 81-96). Sudbury, MA: Jones and Bartlett.

CHAPTER 8

PREPARING CULTURALLY COMPETENT PRACTITIONERS FOR REHABILITATION AND ALLIED HEALTH

WILLIAM TALLEY
CHANDRA DONNELL CAREY
BENSON COOKE
NGOZI CHIMA

CHAPTER TOPICS

- Culture and the Counseling Process
- Evidence of a paradigm shift
- The language of cultural competence: The nature of culture
- Cultural identity development and intersectionality
- Multiculturalism and diversity
- Power, privilege, and oppression
- Context and cultural counseling
- Counseling models designed to work with diverse populations

CULTURE AND THE COUNSELING PROCESS

Rehabilitation counseling, counseling psychology, and related helping professions are always evolving. Research often fosters changes, brings about new discoveries, and changes perceptions. Some changes are more dramatic. A discovery or series of discoveries can result in a significant change in the way that people think. Such changes are known as paradigm shifts.

The field of human behavior has experienced a paradigm shift, beginning with Freud's introduction of psychoanalysis to his colleagues in 1895. For the next eight decades, psychotherapists, psychologists, counselors, rehabilitation counselors, and other helping professionals embraced the paradigm posited by Freud, which inherently ignored the role that culture plays in shaping human behavior. As counseling theories have evolved, however, helping professionals have seen evidence of a gradual move toward recognition of the significance of role that culture plays in shaping human behavior. This counseling evolution has also hastened the implementation of cultural competencies, while simultaneously emphasizing the value of being aware of key historical events impacting diverse populations. Additionally, the influencing life events associated with the philosophical aspect of cultural differences among ethnic/racial groups,[53] helps minimize the establishment of a one-size-fits-all approach to helping. "The route to becoming a culturally competent organization can be quite daunting given the enormous population diversity and the socio-political and economic baggage that is associated with the racial and ethnic history of the United States."[p157] The intersectionality[21] of multiple identities and the resulting convergence of race, economics, gender, etc. further complicates the cultural responsiveness to an individual's diverse needs.

Indeed, even over the past two decades, there continues to emerge a shift in how the counseling profession understands, discusses, and conceptualizes the impact of culture in the counseling relationship.[11,31,71] The advent of concepts such as *social justice, intersectionality, and cultural humility,* have created a burgeoning era where the complexities of culture have been examined once again to shift the dialogue on how culture intersects with the counseling process.

As recent as 2014, Ratts ,et al.,[74] updated the Multicultural Competencies standards previously operationalized in 1996 to reflect multicultural competence and social justice praxis, quadrants, domains, and competencies. Since the initial development, the focus on broader social justice issues surrounding gender identity, disability status, and sexual identity, has catapulting the discipline into a wholehearted embrace to examine and enhance understanding of multiple identities and their impact on the counseling relationship as they intersect. This new focus encompasses both the lived experiences of historically marginalized groups, but also the institutions in the United States that have been complicit in maintaining them.

Cultural diversity in the United States represents an idea of observing people's differences as having value in so far as how they define themselves as much as they are defined by the majority population. Consequently, Wrenn[87] initially described the culturally encapsulated counselor and laid the framework for what has come to be one of the most discussed issues of the day. This latest paradigm shift notes the critical importance that other cultural variables, such as disability status, ethnicity, gender identity, religion, sexual orientation, and age, play in the counseling process. Today, given the impact of this critical paradigm shift, it would be thought nearly implausible to ignore the relevance of culture to the process of counseling. Sue and Sue,[84] fittingly report that cultural competence requires three key strategies. First, practitioners must become self-aware of their own culture; Second, they must be open to cultural differences exhibited by those whom they seek to treat; and Third, they must be in a constant state of acquiring relevant knowledge, skills, strategies, and techniques intended to better understand and optimally support clients who present with a diverse set of needs. It is within this context that how we define culture can provide a proper context for understanding cultural sensitivity within the health care field. Nobles[61] describes the role of culture as follows:

> Culture rightfully should be viewed as a scientific construct representing the vase structure of language, behavior, customs, knowledge, symbols, ideas, and values which provide a people with a general design for living and patterns for interpreting reality.[61, p.71]

Some authors[56] feel "there is considerable reason to believe that a new paradigm shift is, in fact, currently taking place in counseling."[p.5] Counseling may be taking the next step up the evolutionary ladder, so to speak, by shifting from seeing culture as one of many variables which should be incorporated into existing theoretical approaches, to recognizing the need to develop counseling approaches which address culture as the core issue behind their design. These changes continue to highlight the importance of cultural competence to the counseling profession.

EVIDENCE OF A PARADIGM SHIFT

The importance and necessity of training rehabilitation professionals, counselors, psychologists, and others, who are sensitive to culture, as well as competent to work with today's changing client populations, has been highlighted within the fields of rehabilitation, psychology, and counseling for the past several decades. So significant has this been to counseling, that Pederson[65] hailed it to be the "fourth force in counseling." In 1992, Sue, et al.,[81] identified thirty-one proficiencies that were necessary for counselors to work with a culturally diverse clientele. Three broad categories or domains were identified: cultural self-awareness and other awareness, knowledge, and skills.

A comprehensive definition proposed by Pope-Davis and Dings,[70] further explains that Multicultural counseling competencies are centered on:

- understanding the different experiences of members of various cultural groups,
- understanding the barriers to communication across cultures that exist as a result of these differences, and
- possessing a specific set of abilities that can potentially make a counselor culturally skilled.[p.288]

The generally accepted understanding of cultural competence refers to a counselor's preparedness to effectively serve the needs of clients from differing cultural backgrounds by illustrating sensitivity and respect for the cultural norms, values, and mores upheld by the client. The literature in the fields of rehabilitation, psychology, counseling, and related helping professions increasingly refers to the need for counselors to pursue and maintain cultural competence. In recent years, the literature has illustrated the enhanced interest and more concerted efforts to address the issue of cultural competence.[16,14,18,78,58,69,6,34,54,63,21,85] As the discourse on culture, multiculturalism, diversity, and related issues propels forward, the discussion of cultural competence and the need for counselors to pursue it has also been fused into the literature. Most practitioners today would consider it unethical for counselors who lack cultural competence and the characteristics inherent therein to attempt to provide counseling for those clients who are culturally different from themselves. This is a clear departure from practices of the past and an indication of the growth that has occurred in the helping professions.

Diller[27] notes, "in its broadest context, cultural competence is the ability to effectively provide services cross culturally."[p.10] Lum,[58] on the other hand, suggests that cultural competence "is a measurable professional standard that evaluates the incorporation of the differential historical, political, socioeconomic, psychophysical, spiritual, and ecological realities, their interaction, and its impact on individuals or groups."[p.8] Definitions of cultural competence have taken very different approaches, as different researchers and practitioners define culture, multiculturalism, transculturalism, and diversity differently.

As this process has evolved, what appears to have emerged as the most viable standard is the definition proposed by Sue, et al.,[85] that was accepted by the American Psychological Association, the American Counseling Association, and the Association for Multicultural Counseling and Development. According to Sue,[85] attaining multicultural counseling competence means that the individual must work to minimize the far-reaching influence which results from the socialization we experience in our personal and professional development. To do so effectively, we are encouraged to address what they have described as the three Dimensions of Cultural competence, which are:

➢ Counselors' need to be aware of their culture, values, assumptions, and biases,

➢ The ability to understand the worldview of culturally different clients, and

➢ Developing appropriate intervention strategies and techniques for use with different cultural populations.

While the language surrounding cultural competence dominates within counseling and other counseling related disciplines, there is an expansion of that terminology in the literature that is also shifting the conversation surrounding the complexity of understanding culture. Researchers[32] have recently investigated the concept of moving beyond a framework for mastery, to a culture of accountability. This acknowledges the on-going nature of the work of building culture responsiveness, while also highlighting the 'transformative social justice agenda'[p.169] required to holistically facilitate successful outcomes for clients. This shifts the counselor narrative from a singular focus on self and the clients' cultural identity to an acknowledgement of the social injustices that perpetuate inequities in quality of life for historically marginalized populations.

Even with these recent developments, it's important to understand that whether you are focused on competence, responsiveness or humility; your interactions with individuals with historically marginalized identities should be guided by your willingness to examine not only yourself, but the people you will work with in relation to their lived experiences and the impact of institutionalized social injustices as they impact each individual.

THE LANGUAGE OF CULTURAL COMPETENCE THE NATURE OF CULTURE

Developing a framework for a dialogue regarding cultural competence requires that we first understand the language of cultural competence. Terms such as culture, multiculturalism, bias, prejudice, discrimination, oppression, acculturation, and diversity are commonly used, and yet there is substantial debate regarding the meaning of these terms.

CULTURE

Culture impacts all aspects of our lives from the way we perceive ourselves, others, and our environment, to the way that we assess and choose to respond to the situations and individuals that we encounter. Despite the fact that culture permeates every aspect of our daily lives, satisfactorily explaining "what culture means" from a counseling perspective is a unique challenge. The root of that challenge is the fact that culture means different things to different people. Historically, race and ethnicity have been used as virtually synonymous terms for *culture*. Okun,[63] however clearly states that:

> Race and ethnicity are both social constructs. Social constructs are categories created by a culture or a society to serve the needs of that society. What this means, for the purpose of our discussion, is that we should recognize that often, who belongs to, or who does not belong to a category is determined by society. For example, in the United States, anyone with African ancestry is labeled African American, and in Brazil, anyone with white ancestry is labeled white.[p.3]

Despite the artificial nature of its origins, as the discussion of culture evolved in the fields of rehabilitation, counseling, and psychology, race is often seen as a critical variable. Membership in one of the racial groups defined by America was viewed as the determining factor for one's values, beliefs, and perceptions. In contrast to race, Diller[27] defines ethnicity as "any distinguishable people whose members share a common culture and see themselves as separate and different."[p.4] As the discussion of culture has evolved, so has our understanding of race and ethnicity and their relevance to culture. While still seen as a critical component of culture, it is now more practical to include race and ethnicity as variables that should and have been joined by a number of other variables. To accurately reflect the way that culture is treated in the field today, Sue, et al.,[85] appropriately point out that "culture is not synonymous with 'race' or 'ethnic group.'" [p.7]

Most importantly, race is an artificial construct that has been used to classify or lump individuals into groups that they may or may not share much in common. Recent developments in genetics suggest that there is as much within-group difference as there is between-group difference among members of various racial groups. As aforementioned, this "artificial construct" has had, and continues to have, major implications in regard to social justice and equity.

Culture, broadly defined, includes variables such as race, disability status, social class, gender, age, spirituality, and sexual preference. Slattery[78] includes race, ethnicity, class, gender, age, religion, affectional orientation, and ability in his definition of culture, while Ivey[51] includes age, ethnicity/race, gender, geographical location or community, language, sexual orientation, spiritual/religious beliefs, socioeconomic situation, and trauma.

As Sue[85] stated, "there are many definitions of culture,"[p.7] many of which seem quite viable. As you examine the various definitions available in the literature, the process of considering which definition fits best with your worldview can, in itself, provide a perspective toward greater cultural awareness.

Even those who devote considerable time to the discussion of the subject disagree over whether it should be defined narrowly or from a broader perspective. A historical and somewhat narrow definition of culture promotes a view of race and ethnicity as the key variables to be considered. The argument for defining culture in this manner is that "doing so helps the term maintain integrity and meaning."[77,p.5] When culture is defined more broadly, race and ethnicity are still considered, but in conjunction with variables such as gender, disability status, age, social class, spirituality, and sexual orientation. The latter, broader definition tends to complicate our ability to understand culture and its impact at the individual level, but it also allows for a more comprehensive reflection of culture. Additionally, the broader definition, in a sense, allows for a multi-level examination of the societal and psychological impact of diversity when considering both social and policy-related ramifications. This broader definition is discussed frequently in the fields of rehabilitation, psychology, counseling, and other helping professions. For the purpose of our discussions, the broader definition will be applied.

CHARACTERISTICS OF CULTURE

We should recognize that, as a matter of course, some aspects of our culture is passed on to us from the moment we are born. It is instilled in us through the first human interactions that we have, and it is imprinted on us through countless repetitive exposure. Gollnick[39] describes culture as the "natural and only way to learn and to interact with others."[p.6] While Erickson[30] notes "culture is in us and all around us, just as the air we breathe."[p.33] Culture is not to be considered as a part of our biological makeup. Culture is neither fused into our genetic makeup nor somehow mysteriously passed on to us at the moment of conception. It is the very nature of culture, that it is *learned*. Culture is passed on to us as a part of an ongoing process or more accurately, two similar processes known as socialization and enculturation. Socialization is defined as "the process through which a child learns the rules and norms of a society."[38,p.112] One example might occur within the realm of religious identity. Children born to parents who are perhaps devout Catholics, are typically taught at a young age the values, mores, and social norms of the religion. Throughout their childhood development, they practice rituals, attend events, and engage in other practices that support these beliefs. They are socialized in the way of being a Catholic.

As part of this process, we learn how a member of our group is expected to behave. So, as we encounter situations that require us to assume different roles such as son, daughter, brother, sister, husband, partner, wife, we have a frame of reference on which we might rely. As we interact with others, our behavior towards them may be influenced by our interpretation of how well they fit with our cultural notion of how someone should behave as a spiritual leader, friend, teacher, politician, or lover.

Enculturation describes the process through which we internalize the characteristics of a culture. Through exposure to that culture, we learn its language, its behaviors, and its nuance. While we are typically born into a culture, what we are at birth grows in relevance when you also consider socialization and enculturation. It is the combined impact of socialization and enculturation that shapes us into members of our respective cultures.

CULTURAL IDENTITY DEVELOPMENT

As you may have suspected, just as there are various ways of explaining culture there are also a number of models to explain how cultural identities develop.

TABLE I
CULTURAL IDENTITIES MODELS

Authors		Model
Downing and Roush[29]	1985	Feminist Identity Development for Women
Troiden[86]	1989	Model of Homosexual Identity Formation
Helms[45]	1990	White Racial Identity
Cross[25]	1991	Nigresance Theory
Sellers, et al.,[76]	1998	The Multidimensional Model of Racial Identity
Sue and Sue[84]	2003	Racial Cultural Identity

Skouhold and Rivers[77] explain that identity development models attempt to offer a plausible explanation of how individuals "grow, see the world, develop and change attitudes, and relate to other people and groups."[p. 367] As we attempt to understand ourselves, our clients, and the world that we live in, identity development models can serve as useful tools. Because they recognize the disparate variables that influence our development, they can help us see and understand how our cultural experiences with power, privilege, oppression, and other variables influence our behavior and shape our identities as unique cultural individuals.

MULTICULTURALISM AND DIVERSITY

In general, the term multicultural relates to the idea that there is more than one viable cultural group and that all cultures have value to their respective members. Multiculturalism also recognizes that race, gender identity, disability status, sexual orientation, religion, and social class are categories that can be used to define and understand the cultural perspectives of individuals. As suggested by Sommers-Flanagan and Sommers-Flanagan,[19] the discussion of culture and the meaning of the term may take on a slightly different meaning depending upon who is framing the discussion.

Currently, multicultural counseling is considered the phrase of choice when describing counseling scenarios that involve individuals from differing cultural backgrounds. There is, of course, no universally accepted definition for multicultural counseling, but there are a number of definitions that are commonly accepted. Consider, for example, the following definition offered by Sue.[84]

> Multicultural counseling refers to a helping role and process that uses approaches and defines goals consistent with the life experiences and cultural values of clients, balancing the importance of individualism versus collectivism in assessment, diagnosis, and treatment.

According to Corey,[16] "Multicultural counseling focuses on understanding not only racial and ethnic minority groups (African Americans, Asian Americans, Latinos, Native Americans, and white ethnics) but also women, gay men and lesbians, people with physical disabilities, elderly people, and a variety of special needs populations."[p.15] As we define multicultural counseling and consider its relevance to our work, we must bear in mind that it refers to both the helping role and the process that we choose, as well as the various modalities that we employ. It is also shaped by the cultural values of consumers, and it should promote the application of strategies that are designed to be compatible with those we serve.

Multicultural counseling may be alternately described as cross-cultural, intercultural, culturally sensitive, culturally competent, or culturally aware counseling. Given the diverse nature of the world today, when the categories gender, race, disability status, sexual orientation, religion, and social class are considered to be elements of an individual's culture, it is difficult to imagine any counseling session that would not involve multicultural counseling.

While *Trans culturalism* is a term that appears less frequently in the literature, it is useful to mention it, even though its meaning differs slightly from that of multiculturalism. While multicultural approaches give equal consideration to both the differences and the similarities that exist between cultures, the term Trans culturalism has as its sole focus, the discovery of those elements that are common to all cultures. Unlike multicultural approaches and related research, the focus of transcultural approaches and research is on exploring those variables which all cultures share in common.

INTERSECTIONALITY

As briefly mentioned earlier in the chapter, intersectionality of clients introduces complexity when interacting with individuals with diverse needs. Intersectionality is a term that has been a major paradigm of research over the past few decades[21,40,52] and has recently garnered renewed attention since it was first promoted as relevant terminology in the study of multiculturalism. The term portrays man as a combination of more than one or more social status positions namely gender, race, sexual orientation, and class. For the purpose of illustration, a typical example in a counseling session would be a Black Lesbian Woman. Although there seems to be a lot of mixed reactions towards use of intersectionality, it was initially meant to address the issue of inequality and social injustice.[21] Being in the helping profession, demands having more than just a knowledge of an ailment or condition that a client presents with, it also requires an ability to effectively manage other possible layers of Identity that they might have. As we consider the additional cultural identities and group belongings individuals' claim, it is also critical to understand that the potential for individuals to walk within a framework of privilege and oppression simultaneously exists.[10] The onus therefore lies on Rehabilitation Counselors, Psychologists, and other Allied health Professionals to consciously acquaint themselves with skills to improve their cultural responsiveness to the multiple diversities which exist to enhance their professional cultural competence and humility.

ASSIMILATION AND ACCULTURATION

Assimilation and acculturation are terms that have been used to provide an explanation of the changes that individuals experience as cultures collide. Brammer[8] suggests that as the fields of counseling and psychology discovered the relevance of culture to the practice of counseling, they sought ways to explain it. Initial suppositions relied heavily on the assumption that indigenous cultures were inferior to the dominant culture. Since the dominant culture was superior by definition, it was only natural to assume that those from inferior cultures would either simply be overwhelmed by it or willingly give into it. Assimilation and acculturation offer slightly different explanations of what takes place when cultures come into contact with each other. The underlying assumption behind assimilation is that when two separate and distinct cultures come together, the dominant culture would, and from the counselors' perspective, should absorb the members of the non-dominant culture. In that process, members of the non-dominant culture would be transformed to fit into the dominant cultural structure. Here again, the assumption is that this process would be healthier for the client.

There are, of course, several problems with this concept; starting with the flawed assumption that one culture is superior to another. What seems unlikely is that the members of any culture would willingly give up their values for those of another culture. The implication that members of the culture that by definition must be seen as lesser will give up their cultural identity in preference for becoming a member of the dominant culture, seems unlikely. Even if the members of the lesser culture intended to divest themselves completely of their old culture, it seems impractical, to think that they could. A third assumption, which seems unlikely, is that the members of the dominant culture would remain relatively unchanged by this interaction.

Assimilation soon proved to be a flawed and ineffective means of describing what happens when cultures collide. Brammer[8] and Jackson[52] noted the even if it were possible for individuals to "assimilate," the harmful effects that they would experience far outweighed any potential benefit that they would derive through the counselor's efforts to facilitate their assimilation. Acculturation was thus proposed as an alternative means of explaining what should take place when members of different cultures encounter one other.

Acculturation is similar in nature to assimilation in that it too infers the existence of lesser and greater cultures. Unlike assimilation, acculturation implies that members of the presumed lesser cultures can be merged and integrated into the greater culture. As the two cultures come into contact, the members of the lesser culture find a means of grafting themselves onto the second (dominant) culture. This adaptation to the dominant culture, supported by the counseling professional, is supposed to assist clients to make a healthy transition from their inferior culture, to the dominant culture. It should be noted that assimilation and acculturation are concepts that were developed and practiced in the US as conceptualized by practitioners that, for the most part, thought of themselves as members of this superior culture. While acculturation is a well-known and commonly used term, its application, much like other terms used to frame discussions concerning culture, is still being debated. Diller,[27] notes,

> Researchers have long argued over how best to conceptualize the process of acculturation. Is it one-dimensional or multidimensional? That is, does acculturation, exist on a single continuum ranging from identification with the indigenous culture at one end to identification with the dominant culture at the other? Or does it make more sense to conceive of an individual's attachment to the two groups as independent of each other, with the possibility of simultaneously retaining an allegiance to one's traditional culture as well as to the dominant American culture? [p.96]

The debate regarding the conceptualization of acculturation, like the debate over culture, multiculturalism, and diversity is quite likely to linger for some time.

Assimilation and acculturation are useful concepts in that they offer some insight into the thinking that was historically prevalent in the field of counseling. Assimilation and acculturation, however, share a common flaw.

They are based on the premise that members of non-dominant or indigenous cultural groups would be agreeable to supplanting portions of their cultural underpinnings, in part or wholly, in favor of elements that would be derived from the culturally dominant group. While plausible under some circumstances, it would not seem that such an assumption would be viable or healthy for most people. Brammer[8] suggested, "there is a growing awareness that people remain distinct and maintain primary friendships within various cultural groups. Rather than form a single shared culture, multifarious societies seem to exist as a collective of distinct components."[p.4] Recently, the model of acculturation has given way to that of cultural pluralism. Cultural pluralism is an approach that recognizes that cultures tend to maintain their integrity even as they are mixed together in what Pope-Davis[70] refers to as the salad bowl effect. While assimilation and acculturation suggest the existence of a dominant culture which might absorb or convert those from other, inferior cultures, cultural pluralism suggest that all cultures tend to maintain their identities even when exposed to other cultures. Cultural pluralism is built on the assumption that the world is comprised of a number of separate and distinct cultural groups that for practical reasons maintain a degree of separation from other cultures. It is also built on the assumption that while differences may exist between cultures, all cultures are, relatively speaking, equal, and valued by the individuals who belong to them. As cultures come together, they simply add their unique flavor to the existing group.

The fact remains, however, that when cultures interface, people change. How they change, what factors influence the ability and extent to which an individual may change, and how those changes impact the individuals who change is still a matter of some debate, but that they change seems evident. When the interface between cultures is sudden and the individuals involved do not have adequate time to prepare for the interface or the interface is too prolonged or intense, the phenomena known as culture shock takes place. Culture shock describes the anxiety, disorientation, and fear that occur when an individual from one culture is abruptly immersed in a second, unfamiliar culture.[58] Take for example how an individual from an agrarian based, technologically unsophisticated, rural culture might respond if some disaster forced them to relocate to a country where a different language is spoken, and they find themselves in a large, modern, technologically advanced, urban setting. The cultural mechanisms that they have employed to survive and prosper in their old environment would no longer apply, and they would, in all probability, find it difficult to adapt to the new environment.

POWER, PRIVILEGE, AND OPPRESSION

As we attempt to understand oppression from a counseling perspective, it is important to place it in its proper context. People often struggle to explain the cause of oppression, and of course, we can explain it from various theoretical perspectives. Using a behavioral model, for example, we could say that the behavior *oppression* exists because the individual or group exhibiting the behavior receives a reward or positive reinforcement that perpetuates the behavior. Those who are rewarded by increased access to jobs, educational opportunities, membership in social groups or organizations, or simply peer approval, will tend to persist in that behavior as long as the reinforcement carries sufficient weight.

There seems to be no simple answer to the question: Why do people discriminate? One plausible explanation is that people in power, the privileged, tend to want to stay in power, and simply take those actions needed to keep themselves and their group in power, thus retaining their privilege. Another explanation could be that people simply discriminate against those that their peers and other situational pressures place outside of their group. When Muslims in Saudi Arabia discriminate against Christians, it could be because their peers drive them to do so. The discrimination could also be rooted in the perceived inferiority of the group being discriminated against. You may find that people without disabilities, or those temporarily able-bodied, will discriminate against persons with disabilities because of a perception of the person with the disability being "less than" or "beneath" the person who is able bodied. This treatment could also be attributed to our society's values of strength, the body beautiful and perfection; variables that some perceive persons with disabilities to not have.

For the purpose of our discussions, the criteria for determining oppression rest in the consequences of that behavior, and not the cause. After all, as health care professionals, we must find a means of addressing, and when possible, *ameliorating* the consequences regardless of the cause. Ridley[75] agrees that the criteria for determining racism, lie in the consequences of behavior, not the causes. Racism is not determined by the causes of behavior, because good intentions often lead to bad interventions. As culturally competent practitioners, the question we need to respond to, is not whether someone intends to oppress, but whether the consequences of their behavior have the effect of oppressing.

Most people like to think of themselves as fair and unbiased, and yet they are generally not. Bias is simply another part of the human condition that exists in everyone. Consider what it means to be biased. According to Gladding,[38] it means, "To have a negative attitude toward an individual, an idea or a group." p.18 Each time we express a preference or dislike for something or someone, we flirt with bias, because if we prefer something do not we also prefer something else less? Bias, however, is not the problem. We can like or dislike a person, group, or thing, or be prejudiced in our opinions because we hold some stereotype of a group. If we do not act or if we cannot act on those feelings; if we fail to discriminate against or in favor of someone or some group, then what harm has been done? As rehabilitation professionals, we should at the very least, endeavor to make ourselves aware of any bias or preconceived attitude that we may hold.

Consider for a moment what it is like to be a member of a privileged group or, for that matter, its polar opposite, an oppressed group. Can you be a member of an oppressed group and not be harmed by it? Can you be a member of a privileged group and not benefit from it? As you consider your answers, consider this. Those who have privilege and choose to act to ensure that they retain that privilege obviously do so to their advantage, and if it is to their advantage, does that not also imply that it is to the injury of someone else? Of course, there are those who, in their estimation, do nothing to discriminate against others, but simply choose not to give up their privilege. If they do not actively participate in the effort to bar the door for some racial, ethical, religious, disability, or gender group, are they still acting in an oppressive manner? The same simple question would seem to apply in this situation as well. Do those with privilege benefit from the situation?

We should also acknowledge that systemic oppression or discrimination continues to exist today. It too is the legacy of decades of racial, gender, ability, and age bias that existed, unchecked in our society. As a consequence of these years of oppression, today's systems are often set up in ways that continue to discriminate against many of these same groups. Even though the discrimination may be unintentional, it is harmful, nonetheless. A system that is set up from a monoculture perspective is unlikely to be responsive to the needs of those who fall outside of that culture.

Notwithstanding the fact that we live in one of the most enlightened democracies on the planet, privilege, much like oppression, continues to permeate the fabric of our daily lives. It is our legacy from the racist, sexist, ability biased, age biased, society that serves as the foundation of what exists today.

Having a meaningful discussion about privilege and who is or is not the beneficiary of privileged status can be challenging, to say the least. One of the most difficult aspects of having an equitable dialogue about privilege is related to the deep feelings many people have on the matter. Many African Americans, for example, feel that they continue to be victimized because of the privileges enjoyed by whites in the United States. On the other side of the issue, many whites feel that America is no longer a racist society, and they, in turn, feel victimized by affirmative action. Race, of course, is not the only factor to be considered where privilege is concerned. Individuals with disabilities are often bothered by the privileges they see afforded to the able, and women express frustration with a system that offers so much privilege to men.

The underlying problem in discussing privilege was aptly pointed out by Slattery[78] as he states, "Becoming aware of privilege, is often difficult because it requires that we give up the Just World Hypothesis."[p.71] The central belief in the Just World Hypothesis is that we have all that we have because we have earned it, and of course, we deserve it. To acknowledge that we are members of a privileged class means that we must acknowledge that we have, at times, benefited from that privilege. If we have benefited, then others have been victimized. It brings us face to face with the issue of discrimination, and more importantly, the fact that we may have discriminated against others, or at the very least, allowed surrogates to discriminate against them on our behalf.

If the privileged exist, then so do the oppressed. Hays[42] viewed oppression in terms of the actions taken by the privileged that excluded or marginalized groups of people. Those who had their ability to participate in any of the daily acts of living negatively impacted by their group membership were then, by definition, oppressed. Unless it is an extremely obvious example of discrimination, it is often difficult to see and understand oppression. Slattery[78] notes that "Most of us would recognize lynching as a racist act; however, most oppression is much more difficult to see."[p.67] Because privileges attributed to gender, race, class, ability, et cetera have evolved as integral parts of our respective cultures; they are often so subtle that they are simply taken for granted. The interplay of several dimensions, race and class or gender and disability, also present challenges for understanding the impact of oppression and limits one's ability to decipher the roots of any subtle or overt experiences of discrimination.

BIAS OR PREJUDICE

The discussion of bias, and its impact on the counseling process has become a critical component of understanding the counseling process and preparing to become an effective counselor. Allport[2] defined prejudice as "feeling, favorable or unfavorable, toward a person or thing, prior to, or not based on actual experience."[p.6] The author further defines bias as a "human trait resulting from our tendency and need to classify individuals into categories as individuals strive to quickly process information and make sense of the world."[p.7] Bias is defined by Gladding[38] as "prejudice or a negative attitude toward an individual, idea or group."[p.18] Prejudice, on the other hand, is defined as "Preconceived opinions or judgments about someone or something formed without just grounds or sufficient knowledge."[p.94] A male may be prejudice, for example, if he judges all women to be too emotional to participate in a debate. A heterosexual who assumes all homosexuals are sexually promiscuous also shows prejudice. The existence of prejudice or bias does not necessarily lead to discrimination nor does it always do harm to the person toward whom the bias is directed. While difficult, it is possible that a person with a bias or prejudice could refrain from acting on said bias and, therefore, avoid harming the party toward which the prejudice is directed. Of course, if you are unaware that you have a bias, it seems unlikely that you could avoid acting on it.

Unlike prejudice, stereotypes can be either positive or negative. Allport[1] defined stereotypes as "exaggerated beliefs associated with a social category."[p.191] Gladding[38] describes a stereotype as "a fixed image or thought of people, things, and places that is oversimplified, rigid, and often prejudice.[p.115] Some common stereotypes might be "all persons with disabilities are mild mannered;" "all African American men are naturally good athletes;" "all Asians are good in math;" and "all those of Jewish decent are good managers of money." Bias, prejudice, and stereotypes do exist where discrimination is found, but the existence of bias does not always result in discrimination. For discrimination to exist, people must not only have a prejudice, but also act in a discriminatory manner. People will usually act in their self-interest, so if social edicts indicate that acting in a discriminatory manner will produce results they do not desire, they will tend to refrain from discriminating. Of course, when a society provides rewards for acting in a discriminatory manner, people will tend to discriminate.

There are people who will simply choose not to discriminate because they feel it is the right thing to do. People do not always realize or acknowledge that they have a bias, or that they themselves are members of some privileged group. Knowingly or not, people are likely to act on their prejudices, and such action by definition is discrimination and does cause harm.

CONTEXT AND CULTURAL COUNSELING

It is a simple matter to recognize that behavior does not occur in a vacuum. That people differ in the way that they perceive, assess, and react to others is obvious: the question is, why? What shapes the behavior of a client, or the way that the client responds to a given situation? For that matter, what shapes the way that the client perceives an individual or a situation in the first place? To understand why people perceive others and circumstances as they do, we must understand the context in which their perceptions and behaviors take place. As we learn to understand the cultural context within which behavior takes place, we move closer to understanding the individual. Understanding who people are and why they behave the way they do, requires that we consider them and their behavior from a cultural context. The individual's behavior can then be understood by considering how the various elements of their culture, language, race, disability status, gender preference, spirituality, et cetera contribute to their perception of their environment, and subsequently, their response to that environment. We must learn to look at others and ourselves from a cultural context. As we noted, culture shapes our perceptions, views, and behaviors across a number of dimensions such as spirituality, gender preference, locus of control, individuation, gender roles and much more. To the extent that we understand how these variables impact us, we develop a keener self-awareness and we develop a broader framework from which to consider the behavior of others.

Consider the relative value you assign to your independence. This is represented by a cultural dimension referred to as individuation. Individuation is one of the cultural variables that are frequently used to differentiate one cultural group from another. Cultures that are highly individualistic place a high value on personal independence, and on having autonomy. On the other end of the spectrum, you have cultures that are collectivist in nature. These cultures place a high value on the needs and desires of the group. Cultures that are considered more collectivist include African Americans, Asian Americans, First Nation Peoples, and Latino Americans. European Americans, on the other hand, are considered to be relatively more individualistic in nature. If you understand how this impacts individuals from their respective cultures, it may help you place the behavior of a client in its proper context, giving you greater insight into the person. Take a moment to consider your own orientation toward individuation. If you are a European American (white), chances are that you are relatively individualistic in nature. Consider this bit of information as a piece of a larger puzzle. The more pieces you fill in, the more of the puzzle you get to see. To better understand clients from a cultural context, you must understand how they are impacted from a cultural context.

PUTTING CULTURE IN CONTEXT

Knowing that a person is Hispanic American or African American may tell you something about their culture, but their disability status, gender, sexual preference, social status, country of origin, or religion might tell you just as much. Where you begin your discussion of culture often influences where you end up. Worldview is a concept that is used to encompass individuals' understanding and perception of their world based on their upbringing, disability status, gender, parental relationships, spiritual beliefs, education, sexual orientation, socioeconomic status, heritage, and ethnic group membership, to name a few.

According to the literature,[63,49,84] the term worldview refers to "one's basic perceptions and understandings of the world."[63,p.12] An individual's worldview develops as a consequence of their life experiences. Individuals have a worldview that is shaped by these variables as well as many others that can impact persons during their lives. It is the very nature of culture that ensures that it touches virtually every aspect of our lives. It is a complex multifaceted construct, which shapes the way we view and interact with our environment, while it in turn is shaped by that environment.

For the purpose of our discussions, let us consider the definition of culture provided by Gladding,[38] who describes culture as the "shared values, belief, expectations, world views, symbols, and appropriate behaviors of a group that provides its members with norms, plans, and rules for social living.[p.34] As the definition implies, culture shapes individuals' perceptions of the world they live in and the way they interact with the various elements of that world. "The philosophy underlying the MCCs is as follows: All counseling is multicultural in nature; sociopolitical and historical forces influence the culture of counseling beliefs, values, and practices, and the worldview of clients and counselors; and ethnicity, culture, race, language, and other dimensions of diversity need to be factored into counselor preparation and practice."[4,p.266]

PREPARING CULTURALLY SENSITIVE/ COMPETENT COUNSELORS

Achieving some degree of cultural competency is a process. One that, to be effective, must be preceded by the struggle to understand one's personal cultural beliefs, values, and attitudes. A counselor seeking to develop culturally sensitive and competent counseling skills will need the ability to both acknowledge and accept the similarities and differences that exist between themselves and their clients. Bellini,[6] asserts that skilled multicultural counselors understand that helping styles and intervention strategies may be culture bound, and they seek to adjust their counseling approaches to the culture, values, and needs of the individual. In rehabilitation counseling, it can be argued that historical indifference to the significance of racial/ethnic diversity on issues affecting clients with disabilities may be attributed not only to the low numbers of racially/ethnically diverse populations participating in rehabilitation, but also the documented differential treatment they encounter in the system.[60] The process of striving toward cultural competence is pertinent to the process of effective counseling and service provision.

Corey[19] states, "first, effective counselors have moved from being culturally unaware to ensuring that their personal biases, values, or problems will not interfere with their ability to work with clients who are culturally different from them."[pg.26] Counselors are faced with the challenge of finding a means of moving toward this state of cultural awareness in a way that is consistent with their needs. Because we are the unique beings with cultures, personalities, and theoretical orientations that are our own, our routes to obtaining cultural competence will also be uniquely our own. A Detailed discussion of this topic can be found in Chapter 7.

TRADITIONAL COUNSELING THEORIES

Historically, the traditional counseling theories were validated on and practiced from a mono-cultural perspective. The culturally competent practitioner should consider how specific critiques relate to their application to diverse client populations. Many theories have been revised to acknowledge and address the impact of culture in the counseling relationship. In the chart that follows, we have attempted to provide a brief overview of widely used traditional models that are thought to have some potential for use with multicultural populations. This overview includes reference to key characteristics that each theory/model may offer, which may make them suitable for utilization with specific populations.

TABLE 2
TRADITIONAL COUNSELING THERAPIES AND CHARACTERISTICS OF CULTURAL STRENGTHS AND LIMITATIONS

Theoretical System	Founder/Major Contributors	Key Characteristics	Multicultural Focus
Psychoanalytic	Sigmund Freud	Deterministic, historical, insightful, unconscious	Importance placed on family history is appealing to various cultural groups. Symbolic work alleviates reluctance some diverse clients feel about sharing/ talking in therapy.

STRENGTHS AND LIMITATIONS OF CULTURAL INFLUENCES

Focus on interpersonal issues shaped by family, societal influences, and environmental factors may be strength. However, limitations of Psychoanalytic approach occurs due to emphasis on a euro-centric paradigm in problem solving developmental issues without giving contrasting considerations to impact of ethnic/racial differences affecting the immediate concerns of the client in the here-and-now often resulting in cultural deficit modeling.

Theoretical System	Founder/Major Contributors	Key Characteristics	Multicultural Focus
Adlerian	Alfred Adler	Holistic, Phenomalogical, Socially Oriented	Historically focused on equality and sensitivity. Driving force is social involvement and equitable participation of everyone.

STRENGTHS AND LIMITATIONS OF CULTURAL INFLUENCES

Focus on family constellation can be strength given the importance of social relationships across diverse multicultural groups. However, the legacy of cultural mistrust may minimize therapeutic disclosure. Additionally, Adlerian approaches methodically, employing a post-Freudian counseling Dynamic in which the Counselor is the authority figure which may result in the client believing that they do not process the answers to facilitate their healing.

Theoretical System	Founder/Major Contributors	Key Characteristics	Multicultural Focus
Trait-Factor	E. Griffin Williamson U. of Minnesota	Rational problem-solving, non-pathological maladjustment, unique traits	Person X environment fit. Focus on choice vs. change and approach appears less threatening. May have intrinsic appeal due to time-limited and goal-oriented attributes.

STRENGTHS AND LIMITATIONS OF CULTURAL INFLUENCES

Focus on Trait-Factor issues that are time-limited with clear goals can be one way to increase social transformation and support interpersonal growth and development. However, the focus of trait-based approaches on a broad range of standardized assessments to determine personality characteristics and their influence on maladaptive/adaptive behaviors in a counseling setting is a challenge. While research has examined racial/ethnic/cultural bias in standardized and norm-referenced assessments. The outcome these efforts suggest is that considerable caution be used and special attention be give especially to non-white populations in which acculturation has not occurred. Additionally, when Trait-factor assessments are applied to diverse Populations in counseling, cultural sensitivity is particularly important to Minimize potential hidden and/or overt bias.

Theoretical System	Founder/Major Contributors	Key Characteristics	Multicultural Focus
Existentialism	Karl Jaspers J. P. Satre	Philosophical orientation toward human existence and decision.	Promotes individuals' unique set of choices. Moves away from deterministic and genetically bound outcomes.

STRENGTHS AND LIMITATIONS OF CULTURAL INFLUENCES

Focus on positive aspect of the Client's world-view can provide a sense of personal empowerment. However, cultural sensitivity to diversity will require an understanding that while not all ethnic/racial groups are homogeneous, that their does exist an historical sociological context for recognizing (common), ethnic world-views which can provide effective (diverse), problem solving strategies.

]

CHAPTER 8   PREPARING CULTURALLY COMPETENT PRACTITIONERS

Theoretical System	Founder/Major Contributors	Key Characteristics	Multicultural Focus
Person Centered	Carl Rogers	Humanistic self-theoretical, unconditional	Promote understanding, accepting and valuing diversity. Promotes cross-cultural empathy.

STRENGTHS AND LIMITATIONS OF CULTURAL INFLUENCES

Focus on developing a genuine caring for client in counseling which is Centered on valuing the client (and their world-view), as a whole person. Additionally, there is a de-emphasis on traditional assessments, which help to reduce cultural mistrust, while increasing a client's by-in (when appropriate), to clinical treatment interventions with a belief that this added intervention may offer genuine therapeutic support to address their most predominant issues and concerns. However, limitations may be seen via the less structured intervention approach used in Person-Centered counseling and how it may minimize a client's expectations that one goal of counseling is to provide more direct structured responses and assistance.

Theoretical System	Founder/Major Contributors	Key Characteristics	Multicultural Focus
Gestalt	Frederick Pearls	Existential, here-and-now oriented, confrontational	The primary focus on **what** (process) is happening to client vs. content is an advantage to diverse clients. Can be empowering to those with gender issues by focusing on self-awareness.

STRENGTHS AND LIMITATIONS OF CULTURAL INFLUENCES

Focus empathizes the value of client's metacommunication (i.e., non-verbal and verbal communication pathways), as well as the diversity of multi-linguistic language meanings and interpretations related to expressing client issues and concerns. However, limitations could come into play in the session if the client is asked to become responsive to ethnic/cultural situations which increases memory of a post-traumatic experience, without the opportunity to understand prominent problems.

Theoretical System	Founder/Major Contributors	Key Characteristics	Multicultural Focus
Behavioral	B. F. Skinner	Behavioristic, pragmatic, learning theoretical, goal-oriented	Focus on modification of behavior is appealing to diverse clients. Straightforward steps and application make sense to people from various walks of life.

STRENGTHS AND LIMITATIONS OF CULTURAL INFLUENCES

Focus emphasizes client learning behavioral conditions which impact effective or ineffective interpersonal/adaptive outcomes. Consequently, the therapeutic/counseling relationship may be perceived as more direct structurally and objectively responsive to influencing behavior. This strength is further demonstrated when the client is encouraged to take on the personal management of behavioral change with the active and direct involvement of the counselor. However, therapeutic limitations may occur if the new behavioral changes inhibit the client's ability to sustain like-group support systems by directly disparaging the client's ethnic/cultural identity as a result of their newly acquired therapeutic behavioral change.

Theoretical System	Founder/Major Contributors	Key Characteristics	Multicultural Focus
Cognitive Behavioral	A. Beck, D. Meichenbaum	Cognitive, rational, mental and emotive, perceptual	Initiates a relationship of mutual trust and promotes appreciation of the client's point of view.

STRENGTHS AND LIMITATIONS OF CULTURAL INFLUENCES

Focus emphasizes the counselor/therapist understanding of the client belief system by establishing both empathy and forming a recognition of their worldView. Additionally, the client is invited to disclose their thoughts which are believed to influence their feelings and actions especially when they are comprised of contradictory or incorrect conjectures, beliefs, or ideas. However, therapeutic limitations may occur if the counselor/therapist is not sensitive to the cultural beliefs of the client and how interpersonal change affecting longstanding cultural values and belief systems may need to be effectively managed to ensure the client's ability to sustain healthy interpersonal change outcomes.

Theoretical System	Founder/Major Contributors	Key Characteristics	Multicultural Focus
Reality	William Glasser	Present focused, strong counselor-client working alliance	Supports strong, trusting relationship between counselor-client to promote allegiance and adherence to counseling treatment plan.

STRENGTHS AND LIMITATIONS OF CULTURAL INFLUENCES

Focus highlights the client's personal choices and the impact on behaviors and thoughts, which may enhance or constrain their quality of life. Cultural Competence requires accepting redirection of attention being focused on client making social, political, environmental, and associated external changes as a way of impacting their life.

Theoretical System	Founder/Major Contributors	Key Characteristics	Multicultural Focus
REBT	Albert Ellis	Action-oriented, cognitive, emotive, philosophical	Promotes potential to understand emotional relationship to behavior and need for balance.

STRENGTHS AND LIMITATIONS OF CULTURAL INFLUENCES

Focus on Rational Emotive Behavioral Therapy (REBT) emphasizes the counselor/therapist understanding of the client belief system so that the client can better understand the behavioral impact of what they believe. By the client becoming knowledgeable of their though processes, it is believed that the client May dispute irrational beliefs, thereby changing their disturbance-creating beliefs and attitudes. However, therapeutic limitations may occur if the counselor/therapist is not sensitive to the cultural beliefs of the client and how interpersonal change affecting longstanding cultural values and belief systems may need to be effectively managed to ensure the client's ability to sustain healthy interpersonal change outcomes.

System	Contributors	Characteristics	Focus
Solution Focused Brief Therapy	S. de Shazar Insoo Kim Berg	Positivistic, focuses on client strengths, here-and-now	Focus on client strengths is appealing to some diverse clients. Construction of

solutions also resonate with some diverse clients who are goal oriented.

STRENGTHS AND LIMITATIONS OF CULTURAL INFLUENCES

Focus of Solution Focused Brief Therapy (SFBT), is considered one of the Post-Modern Approaches to counseling or therapy. The emphasis of SFBT is as the name implies; a goal or solution oriented counseling approach, with an emphasis on a brief intervention. The intervention would look at present issues and focus treatment on creating future positive/healthy change. Little focus is on how the issue occurred. Instead, solutions are pursued, which will be optimal for the client presenting the concerns. SFBT presumes that the client entering treatment has the capacity to benefit from this approach which emphasizes what is working vs. what may not work and within a reasonable timetable focuses on instruction and applying what can therapeutically work best. Culturally, this approach is empowering. However, one limitation may be working with a client who chooses to believe that the counselor/therapist shall take a greater role in managing the solutions available to the client.

Many of the other modern models of psychotherapy have been updated to address multicultural issues. Although these models have been updated to address some aspects of culture, their beginnings were not predicated on the consideration of cross-cultural interactions. They were not designed with counseling persons from diverse backgrounds in mind. Due to this oversight, there were movements to develop models that focused on working with diverse populations.

COUNSELING MODELS DESIGNED TO WORK WITH DIVERSE POPULATIONS

There are literally hundreds of counseling models in existence today, many of which can be used effectively with diverse cultural populations. It is not our intent to tell the reader what theory is "the best" approach to use; that is a personal decision that should rest with the reader. Instead, we provide a summary of key counseling models with observations regarding their relative strengths and weaknesses when applied to selected cultural groups.

Unlike our predecessors, today's counselors and psychotherapists have access to a wide variety of counseling models, and many of these more effectively address the issue of diversity in counseling. Counseling models, such as Multicultural Counseling and Therapy (MCT), Respectful, and Addressing have been developed with the understanding that culture is a critical element of counseling. Below, we briefly discuss these models that have been designed to effectively serve culturally diverse client populations.

Multicultural Counseling and Therapy

Multicultural Counseling and Therapy (MCT) is considered to be the first counseling model to use culture as a core concept.[62,82] MCT is based on six basic assumptions:

> - MCT can be used to provide an organizational framework for understanding Western and non-Western theories and methods of helping.

> - Counselors' and clients' identities are reflected in various levels of human experience (individual, group, system, and universal). Contextual issues in treatment must, therefore, be addressed as necessary.

> - Cultural identity development affects how the counselor and the client view themselves and others and how they formulate counseling goals and interventions. It is, therefore, important to be cognizant of how cultural identity development is impacting the counseling process, including an awareness of the different socio-cultural forces that influence its development.

> - The efficacy of MCT is enhanced when counselors use procedures congruent with the values and experiences of the client. Counselors are encouraged to broaden their helping responses so that they demonstrate multicultural sensitivity throughout the counseling process.

> - MCT encourages counselors to expand their helping roles to include conventional and alternative methods of helping necessary to meet the cultural needs of clients.

> - A fundamental goal of MCT theory is the liberation of consciousness from a relation-contextual perspective. In this regard, MCT attempts to provide opportunities to promote an awareness of how cultural and relationship issues impact present concerns.

A detailed account of this theory can be found in "*Introduction to Counseling: An Art and Science Perspective.*"[62]

Respectful Counseling Model

The *respectful* counseling model, which shares some points in common with MCT, was developed by D'Andrea and Daniels in the late 1990's. The authors[56] describe the model as follows: "The RESPECTFUL counseling framework (a) recognizes the multidimensional nature of human development and (b) addresses the need for a comprehensive model of human diversity that has practical utility for the work of mental health professionals."[p.8] The model is comprised of 10 factors, which D'Andrea and Daniels selected in an effort to comprehensively list those factors which impact "psychological development and personal wellbeing."[p.9]

The specific factors that the RESPECTFUL counseling framework directs attention to include:

R religious/spiritual identity
E economic class background
S sexual identity
P level of psychological maturity
E ethnic/racial identity
C chronological/developmental challenges
T various forms of trauma and other threats to one's sense of well-being
F family background and history
U unique physical characteristics
L location of residence and language differences

ADDRESSING MODEL

Another culturally based approach to counseling is the Addressing model developed by P. A. Hayes. This model was designed to systematically consider the influence that culture has in counseling. In the Addressing model, each letter represents a different cultural factor to be considered during the counseling process. The factors included in this model include:

A age and generational influences
D disability related issues
R religious and spiritual issues
E ethnicity and race
S social status
S sexual orientation
I indigenous heritage
N national origin
G gender

The Addressing counseling model is considered trans-cultural in nature and "places a high value on culture-specific expertise."[43,p.334]

These models rest on the foundation of multicultural counseling and multicultural counseling competency. They assert that you must comprehensively consider the diverse aspects of your individual clients. By doing so, you must have a basic knowledge of the diverse variables, an awareness that this diversity exists, and a skill base to address these variables as they mediate the clients' experience.

CHAPTER 8   PREPARING CULTURALLY COMPETENT PRACTITIONERS

OTHER CULTURALLY SENSITIVE APPROACHES

Counselor Wisdom Paradigm	Hanna, Bemak & Chung[41]	(1999)
Multicultural Model of Psychotherapy	Ramirez[73]	(1999)
Model of Multicultural Understanding	Locke[57]	(1998)
Coping with Diversity Counseling Model	Coleman[13]	(1997)
Perspectives in Internalized Culture	Ho[47]	(1995)
Cross Cultural Specific Model	Herring & Walker[46]	(1993)
Multicontextual Model	Steenbargers[80]	(1993)

OUTLINING A PROCESS OF BECOMING

Becoming a culturally competent counselor is a process, not an event. There are several steps that individuals may take to move themselves forward from a state of being less culturally competent toward a process to seek becoming more culturally responsive. Those who wish to enhance their cultural competence should begin that process by taking actions that will allow them to facilitate that process. Those who wish to be culturally competent counselors should:

➢ Seek to become culturally aware,

➢ Avoid the temptation to supplant the client's cultural values with their own,

➢ Accept the impact that culture has had on the development of their life related behaviors,

➢ Recognize how little they may actually know about other cultures and work to improve their knowledge of cultures other than their own, especially those of the clients they serve,

➢ Recognize stereotypes when they exist and avoid them,

➢ Consider whether their approach to counseling is culturally sensitive,

➢ Acknowledge the historical, systemic barriers that impact marginalized groups.

➢ Be aware of the culturally valid or invalid assumptions that exist within counseling theories,

➢ Commit to taking active steps to continue learning about and interacting with diverse cultures,

➢ Select interventions that are culturally appropriate.

Becoming aware of your culture does not suggest that you are free of negative attitudes or bias. It does, however, make it more likely that you will be cognizant of whatever culturally based biases or prejudices that you do have. Culturally aware counselors should be sensitive to the culturally based concerns of others. The experience of exploring your culture, what it is, what it means to you, and how it has shaped you, should provide you with a framework from which to explore the culture of those with whom you come into contact. A benefit of exploring your culture is that it also has the potential of providing you with insight into the process that clients go through as they attempt to explore their own. You should also learn to acknowledge any negative or overly positive reactions that you experience toward individuals from cultures other than your own. Once counselors develop sensitivity to cultural variables, they are better equipped to monitor their reactions to certain clients and behaviors which may be generated as a result of their culturally influenced view of the world.

Becoming a culturally competent practitioner is a process and one must understand that the process may take considerable time, thought, and energy. To minimize the potential for encountering problems, counselors should develop a planned approach to assist their efforts to become culturally competent.

There is no one route that we or anyone else have discovered that can direct you as you continually seek cultural competence. It does seem logical and practical to suggest that if you intend to pursue becoming a culturally responsive practitioner, you do so as a part of a structured, and diverse experiential effort. Your results will be dependent on how you strategize, the diversity of resources you include in the process, and the creativity you build into the process. Varied online educational and competence-focused social media outlets that focus on equity and marginalized voices that are more heterogeneous than your typical daily interactions should enhance your chances of having a successful experience. It is important before you start to consider what may happen, and to not confuse the degree of comfort you have with any given group identity with your potential of improving cultural competence. You should also seek to expand your experiences by locating diverse cultural experiences that will require in-depth interactions with representatives from those identity groups. Look for activities that give you the opportunity to have new experiences with those who differ from yourself. If you are uncomfortable around those who differ from yourself, consider what this means, both to you and for anyone you might counsel that could also be different.

This can be a meaningful experience that will continually enhance your skills throughout your professional career and beyond. The steps we recommend that you consider as a part of your group process are:

- ➤ Start by participating in a process designed to facilitate self-analysis.
- ➤ Complete a cultural biography for yourself.

- Develop a cultural ethnography.
- Develop a community ethnography.
- Review the major assumptions, values, and attitudes affiliated with your cultural group.
- Discuss how your culture impacts your view of the world and your interactions with it.
- Using the information that you have collected so far, begin to research from educational sources, group identities that are different from yours.
- Discuss the treatment of culture in counseling theory, both historically and currently.
- Review the literature and discuss which theories (both traditional and culturally sensitive) most effectively address the needs of diverse client populations.
- If you have not already done so, consider and select the theory that will guide your approach to counseling, and consider its strengths and weaknesses.
- Study the issues involved in working with special populations.
- Pay special attention to barriers to effective cultural counseling.
- Develop a working definition of culture, and the related terms.
- Put what you have learned into practice. Developing responsiveness is work – constantly immerse yourself with others unlike you. You will learn a lot about yourself as well as the individuals you are interacting with.
- Refine your practice base of experience and research.

An important part of this process centers on your choice of a theoretical foundation for your practice. When selecting a counseling theory to serve as the underpinning for your practice as a counselor, you should take the time to answer several critical questions about the theories that you consider. Is it a system that is compatible with your personal beliefs? Does it offer a satisfactory explanation of human behavior and personality? Is the approach advocated one that you can comfortably and consistently apply? Is it a good personal fit? Will it (as it is or could it be with the addition of other techniques) meet the needs of the client populations that you plan to work with?

To effectively serve you, the theory that you select should be one that you can live by. It should be a comfortable fit and give you clear guidance in your interpersonal interactions. It should also allow some flexibility with appropriate application of techniques from other theoretical approaches that may be better suited to individual clients' needs. Counselors should take great care when selecting the theory of counseling that will serve as the foundation for your orientation to human behavior.

BARRIERS TO CULTURALLY COMPETENT COUNSELING.
Despite the emphasis that has been placed on meeting the needs of culturally diverse clients,[26,81] there still exists a gap from that point of knowledge to service delivery. Subsequently, one might assume the following barriers still exist:

- Counselor ability to thoroughly assess themselves.
- Counselor educator receptiveness to the concept of multicultural counseling competencies.
- Lack of effective training programs.
- Varying definitions of "multicultural" and the terms that surround it.
- The entrenched nature of monocultural values that remain in some systems.

The ability of counselors to see clients for who and what they are, to objectively assess the client's situation and to realistically interpret how he/she may assist the client are all critical aspects of counseling. Acknowledging and appreciating the worldview of the client is imperative to any counseling relationship. Counselors, who are hampered by the inability to accurately understand clients from a cultural perspective, will be impeded in their efforts to assist their clients.

CULTURE AND THE COUNSELING PROCESS
Some authors[16,20,66,68] have suggested that clients may fair better if the counseling process employed is more suitable to their cultural makeup. Rehabilitation counselors must employ multicultural understanding to effectively provide appropriate services to culturally diverse clients, and to begin to combat the inequities that have been previously noted in rehabilitation counselor literature.

Culture tends to shape the way we perceive our environment and it often impacts us in ways too subtle for us to understand. Our collective experiences have reinforced some negative observations our parents, friends, and peers offered over the years. This is why we are seldom surprised when African American clients act in a similar manner. In fairness, other studies,[33] have noted that they failed to substantiate differences in the preference of clients for one counseling process over another.

Dinkmeyer and Sperry[28] suggest that people tend to view things a particular way because their culture provides them with a unique way of looking at the issue. Alston and Bell[3] also purport that historical treatment by government institutions of African Americans and other underrepresented groups in the country, has festered into a huge snowball of cultural distrust for modern-day governmental programs and services.

Working with individuals who have disabilities, their families, and significant others, presents the aspiring rehabilitation professional with an additional set of cultural concerns. The well-trained rehabilitation professional must be aware of culture in its traditional sense, and as it is uniquely impacted by the existence of disabilities. Hearing impaired individuals who identify with the Deaf culture, for example, will have little difficulty in explaining that their culture is unique and one in which they have great pride. There are many ways of considering the nature of the impact that culture has on work that includes individuals who have disabilities. There are cultural influences associated with selected groups of individuals, the impact of and acceptance of the use of technology, and the nature of the relationships to family members and significant others. Belgrave and Jarma[7] offer some insight when they state that "Culture influences disability prevalence, the experience of disability, participation in rehabilitation, and one's overall level of functioning and adaptation to a disability."[p.585]

In the sixties, Wrenns'[87] suggestion that culture significantly impacted counseling was nothing short of radical. Gradually, a number of scholars[67,27] have highlighted the importance of considering how culture impacts the client, the counselor, and indeed the counseling process. Today it is difficult to imagine that there was ever a time when culture was not seen as an issue that must be considered as a critical element of the counseling process.

Despite the tremendous progress made in this area, multicultural counseling is still an emerging field. This should come as no surprise, however, in view of the huge task at hand. Freud and his peers, in the psychoanalytic congress of Vienna, struggled for decades to build a model of psychotherapy, which began to describe the psychology of man. Considerable research utilizing empirical, qualitative, and narrative story methodologies are examining multicultural competencies, their impact in the field, on counseling outcomes, client satisfaction, and counselor efficacy in serving diverse clients.[68] Continued examination and validation of competency scales also promises to further promote the need and true worth of multiculturally competent counselors to the overall mental health of *all* the individuals we serve.

CULTURE IS THE LENS THROUGH WHICH WE VIEW LIFE

It may help if you remember that culture tends to act as a lens or filter that colors our perception of life. The lens has always been there, so we view life through it without considering how it impacts our perception of it. Consider then, the impact cultural values have on the way you view families, religion, good food, property, and the gendered social roles of people in society, even something as mundane as what you find acceptable to wear to work. As you do so, remember that your client has cultural values that are just as relevant to them. If you can manage to accomplish this small step, then congratulations, you have taken one of the many steps you will need to complete, to move toward becoming a culturally competent practitioner.

REFERENCES

[1] Allport, G. W. (1979). *The nature of prejudice* (25th anniversary ed.). Cambridge, MA: Perseus Books.
[2] Allport, G. W. (1954). *The nature of prejudice*. Cambridge, MA: Addison-Wesley Publishing Co., pp. 6-7.
[3] Alston, R. J., & Bell, T. J. (1996). Cultural mistrust and the rehabilitation enigma for African Americans. *Journal of Rehabilitation, 62(2), 16-20.*
[4] Arredondo, P., & Arciniega, G. M. (2001). Strategies and techniques for counselor training based on the multicultural counseling competencies. *Journal of Multicultural Counseling and Development, 29,* 263-273.
[5] Atkinson, D. R., Morten G., & Sue, D. W. (1997). *Counseling American Minorities: A cross-cultural perspective* (5th ed.). New York: McGraw-Hill.
[6] Bellini, J. (2002). Correlates of multicultural counseling competencies and vocational rehabilitation counselors. *Rehabilitation Counseling Bulletin, 45*(2), 66-75.
[7] Belgrave, F. Z. and Jarama, S. L. (2000). Culture and the disability and rehabilitation experience: An African American example. In R. G. Frank and T. R. Elliott (Eds.) *Handbook of Rehabilitation Psychology.* Washington, DC: American Psychology Association, pp. 585-600.
[8] Brammer, R. (2004). *Diversity in Counseling*. Belmont CA: Thompson/ Brooks/Cole.
[9] Capuzzi, D., and Gross, D. R. (1999). *Counseling & Psychotherapy: Theories and interventions.* Upper Saddle River, New Jersey: Merrill/Prentice Hall. *Children's Ethnic Socialization: Pluralism and development.* Nebburing Park, CA: Sage Publications.
[10] Chan, C. D., Cor, D. N., & Band, M. P. (2018). Privilege and oppression in counselor education: An intersectionality framework. *Journal of Multicultural Counseling and Development, 46*(1), 58-73. doi:10.1002/jmcd.12092
[11] Chao, R., Wei, M., Good, G., & Flores, L. (2011). Race/Ethnicity, color-blind racial attitudes, and multicultural counseling competence: The moderating effects of multicultural counseling training. *Journal of Counseling Psychology, 58*(1), 72-82. doi:10.1037/a0022091Link
[12] Chao, R. (2012). Racial/Ethnic identity, gender-role attitudes, and multicultural counseling competence: The role of multicultural counseling training. *Journal of Counseling and Development, 90*(1), 35-44. doi:10.1111/j.1556-6676.2012.00005.x

[13]Coleman, H. L .K. (1997). Conflict in Multicultural Counseling Relationships: sources and resolution. *Journal of Multicultural Counseling and Development, 25*, 195-200.

[14]Coma-Diaz, L. (2014). Multicultural theories of psychotherapy. In Wedding & R.J. Corsini (Eds.), Current psychotherapies (10th ed., pp. 533-567). Belmont, CA: Brooks/Cole, Cengage Learning.

[15]Corey, G. (2018). *Groups – Process and Practice* (10th ed.). Pacific Grove, CA: Brooks/Cole.

[16]Corey, G. (2016). *Theory and Practice of Counseling and Psychotherapy* (9th ed.). Pacific Grove, CA: Cengage Learning.

[17]Corey, G. (2013). *Theory and Practice of Counseling and Psychotherapy* (9th ed.). Boston, MA: Brooks/Cole.

[18]Corey, G. (2012). *Theory & Practice of Group Counseling* (8th ed.). Pacific Grove, CA: Brooks/Cole.

[19]Corey, G. (2001). *Theory and Practice of Counseling and Psychotherapy* (6th ed.). Brooks/Cole.

[20]Corey, M. S. & Corey, G. (2003). *Becoming a Helper* (4th ed.). Pacific Grove, CA: Brooks/Cole.

[21]Crenshaw, K. (1989). Demarginalizing the intersection of race and sex: A black feminist critique of antidiscrimination doctrine, feminist theory and antiracist politics. *U. Chi. Legal F.*, 139.

[22]Cross, T. L., Bazron, B. J., Dennis, K. W. and Isaacs, M. R. (1989). *Toward a Culturally Competent System of Care*. Washington, D.C.: Georgetown University Child Development Center.

[23]Cross, W. E. (1987). A Two-Factor Theory of Black Identity: implications for the study of identity development in minority children. In J. S. Phennay and M. J. Rotheram (Eds.)

[24]Cross, W. E., Jr. (1971). The Negro-to-Black Conversion Experience: Toward a psychology of black liberation. *Black World, 20* (9), 13-27.

[25]Cross, W. E., Jr. (1991). *Shades of Black: diversity in African American identity*. Philadelphia, PA. Temple University Press

[26]D'Andrea, M., Daniels, J., & Heck, R. (1991). Evaluating the impact of multicultural counseling training. *Journal of Counseling and Development*.

[27]Diller, J. V. (1999). *Cultural Diversity: a primer for the human services*. Toronto, Canada. Brooks/Cole. Wadsworth.

[28]Dinkmeyer, D. & Sherry, L. (2000). *Counseling and Psychotherapy: An integrated, individual psychology approach* (3rd ed.). Upper Saddle River, NJ. Merrill, Prentice Hall

[29]Downing, N. E. & Roush, K. L. (1985). From Passive Acceptance to Active Commitment: a model of feminist identity development for women. *The Counseling Psychologist, 13*, 695-709.

[30]Erickson, F. (1997). Culture in Society and in Educational Practices. In J.A. Banks and C. A. M. Banks (Eds.), *Multicultural Education: classes and perspectives* (3rd ed., pp 32-60). Needham Heights, MA: Allyn & Bacon.

[31]Fietzer, A. W., Mitchell, E., & Ponterotto, J. G. (2018). Multicultural personality and multicultural counseling competency in counselor trainees. *Counselor Education and Supervision, 57*(2), 82-97. doi:10.1002/ceas.12095

[32]Fisher-Borne, M., Cain, J. M., & Martin, S. L. (2015). From Mastery to Accountability: Cultural Humility as an Alternative to Cultural Competence. *Social Work Education, 34(2), 165-181.* http://dx.doi.org/10.1080/02615479.2014.977244

[33]Folensbee, R. W., Draguns, J. G., & Danish, S. J. (1986). Impact of two types of counselor intervention on Black American, Puerto Rican, and Anglo-American analogue clients. *Journal of Counseling Psychology, 33 (4), 446-453.*

[34]Fuertes, J. N., Bartholomeo, M., & Nichols, M. (2001). Future research directions in the study of counselor multicultural competency. *Journal of Multicultural Counseling and Development, 29,* 3-12.

[35]Gay, G. (2000). *Culturally Responsive Teaching: Theory, research, & practice.* New York: Teachers College Press.

[36]Gillard, B. E., James, R. R. and Bowman, J. T. (1994). *Theories and Strategies in Counseling and Psychotherapy* (3rd ed.) Needham Heights, MA. Allyn & Bacon.

[37]Gladding, S. T. (1999). *Counseling: A comprehensive profession* (4th ed.). New York: Merrill Gladding, S. T. (2001). *Counseling: A comprehensive profession* (5th ed.). New York: Merrill.

[38]Gladding, S. T. (2001). *The Counseling Dictionary: Concise definitions of frequently used terms.* Upper Saddle River, NJ. Merrill, Prentice Hall.

[39]Gollnick, D. M. & Chinn, P. C. (2004). *Multicultural Education in a Pluralistic Society* (6th ed.) Upper Saddle River, New Jersey Pearson, Merrill, Prentice Hall.

[40]Hancock, A. M. (2007). When multiplication doesn't equal quick addition: Examining intersectionality as a research paradigm. *Perspectives on politics, 5*(1), 63-79.

[41]Hanna, F. J. and Bemak, F. (1999). Toward a new paradigm for multicultural counseling. *Journal of Counseling & Development, 134.*

[42]Hays, P. A, (1995). Multicultural applications of cognitive-behavior therapy. *Professional Psychology: Research and Practice,* 26(3), 309-315. http://dx.doi.org/10.1080/02625479.2014.977244

[43]Hayes, J. R. (1996). *A new framework for understanding cognition and affect in writing.* In C. M. Levy & S. Randell (Eds.), *The science of writing: Theories, methods, individual differences, and applications* (p. 1-27). Lawrence Erlbaum Associates, Inc.

[44]Helms, J. E. (1984). Toward a Theoretical Explanation of the Effects of Race on Counseling: a black and white model. *The Counseling Psychologist, 12*(4), 153-165.

[45]Helms, J. E. (Ed.) (1990). *Black and White Racial Identity: theory research and practice.* West Point CT: Greenwood.

[46]Herring, R. D., & Walker, S. S. (1993). Synergetic Counseling: toward a more holistic model with a cross-cultural specific approach. *TCA Journal. 22*(2), 28-53.

[47]Ho, D. Y. F. (1995). Internalized Culture Culturocentrism and Transcendence. *The Counseling Psychologist, 23*, 4-24.

[48]Hook, J. N., Farrell, J. E., Davis, D. E., DeBlaere, C., Van Tongeren, D. R., & Utsey, S. O. (2016). Cultural humility and racial microaggressions in counseling. *Journal of Counseling Psychology, 63*(3), 269.

[49]Ibrahim, F. A. (1985). Effective cross-cultural counseling and psychotherapy: A framework. *The Counseling Psychologist, 13*, 625-638.

[50]Ivey, A. E., & Ivey, M. B. (2003). *Intentional Interviewing and Counseling: Facilitating client development in a multicultural society* (5th ed.). Pacific Grove, CA: Brooks/Cole.

[51]Ivey, A. F., Ivey M. B. & Simck-Morgan. (1997). *Counseling and Psychotherapy: a multicultural perspective* (4th ed.) Boston, MA: Allyn & Bacon.

[52]Jackson, J. W. (2017). Explaining intersectionality through description, counterfactual thinking, and mediation analysis. *Social psychiatry and psychiatric epidemiology, 52*(7), 785-793.

[53]Jones, B. A. & Nichols, E. J. (2013). *Cultural Competence in America's Schools: Leadership, Engagement and Understanding* (Educational Policy in the 21st century; Opportunities, Challenges, and Solutions) (Illustrated ed.). Information Age Publishing.

[54]Leal-Idrogo, A. (1997). Multicultural rehabilitation counseling. *Rehabilitation Education, 11*(3), 231-240.

[55]Lee, C. C., & Richardson, B. L. (1996). *Multicultural issues in counseling* (2nd ed.). Alexandria, VA: AACD.

[56]Lewis, J. A., Lewis, D. L., Daniels, J. A., & D'Andrea, M. J. (2003). *Community Counseling: Empowerment Strategies for a Diverse Society* (3rd ed.). Pacific Grove, CA: Brooks/Cole.

[57]Locke, D. C. (1998). *Increasing Multicultural Understanding (2nd ed.).* Newbury Park, CA: Sage.

[58]Lum, D. (2003). *Culturally Competent Practice: a framework for understanding diverse groups and justice issues.* Toronto, Canada. Thompson. Brooks/Cole.

[59]Meir, S. T. (1989). *The elements of counseling.* Pacific Grove, CA: Brooks/Cole.

[60]Middleton, R. A., Rollins, C. W., Sanderson, P. L., Leung, P., Harley, D. A., Ebener, D., & Leal-Idrogo, A. (2000). Endorsement of professional multicultural rehabilitation competencies and standards: A call to action. *Rehabilitation Counseling Bulletin, 43*(4), 219-245. doi:10.1177/003435520004300407

[61]Nobles, W. (1876). *Seeking the Sakhu: Foundational Writing for an African Psychology* by Wade W, Nobles (2006-09-01). Third World Press.
[62]Nystul, M. S. (1999). *Introduction to Counseling: An art and science perspective.* Needham Heights, MA: Allyn and Bacon.
[63]Okun, B. F., Fried, J., & Okun, M. L. (1999). *Understanding Diversity: A learning-as-practice primer.* Pacific Grove, CA: Brooks/Cole.
[64]Parrott, L. (2003). *Counseling and Psychotherapy* (2nd ed.). Pacific Grove, CA: Thompson, Brooks/Cole.
[65]Pederson, P. B. (1990). The Multicultural Perspective of a Fourth Force in Counseling. *Journal of Mental Health Counseling, 12*, 93-95.
[66]Pedersen, P. B., Draguns, J. G., Lonner, W. J., & Trimble J. E. (Eds.), (2002). *Counseling Across Cultures* (5th ed.). Thousand Oaks CA: Sage
[67]Pedersen, P. B., Lonner, W. J., & Draguns, J. G. (eds.), (1976). *Counseling Across Cultures.* Honolulu: University of Hawaii Press.
[68]Ponterotto, J. G. Casas, J. M. Suzuki, L. A. & Alexander, C. M. (Eds.), (2001) *Handbook of Multicultural Counseling.* Thousand Oaks, CA: Sage.
[69]Pope-Davis, D. B., Coleman, H. L. K., Liu, W. M., & Toporek, R. L. (2003). *Handbook of multicultural competencies in counseling and psychology.* Thousand Oaks, CA: Sage Publications.
[70]Pope-Davis, D. B., & Dings, J. G. (1995). The Assessment of Multicultural Counseling Competencies. In J. G. Ponterotto, J. M. Casas, L. A. Suzaki, & C. M. Alexander (Eds.) *Handbook of Multicultural Counseling* (pp 287-311). Thousand Oaks, CA. Sage Publishing.
[71]Presseau, C., Luu, L. P., Inman, A. G., & DeBlacre, C. (2018). Trainee social justice advocacy: Investigating the roles of training factors and multicultural competence. *Counselling Psychology Quarterly,* , 1-15. doi:10.1080/09515070.2018.1476837
[72]Rahimi, M., Rosenthal, D. A., & Chan, F. (2003). Effects of Client Race on Clinical Judgment of African American Undergraduate Students in Rehabilitation. *Rehabilitation Counseling Bulletin, 46*(3), 157-163.
[73]Ramirez, M., III (1999). *Multicultural Psychotherapy: an approach to individual and cultural differences* (2nd ed.). Boston: Allyn & Bacon.
[74]Ratts, M. J., Singh, A. A., Nassar-McMillan, S., Butler, S. K., & McCullough, J. R. (2016). Multicultural and social justice counseling competencies: Guidelines for the counseling profession. Journal of Multicultural Counseling and Development, 44(1), 28-48. doi:10.1002/jmcd.12035
[75]Ridley, C. R. (2005). Overcoming Unintentional Racism in *Counseling and Therapy: a practitioner's guide to intentional intervention* (2nd ed). Thousand Oaks, California. Sage Publications.
[76]Sellers, R. M., Shelton, N., Cooke, D., Chavous, T., Rowley, S. J., & Smith, M. (1998). A Multidimensional Model of Racial Identity: assumptions, findings, and future directions. In R. L. Jones (Ed.) *African American identity development* (pp 275-302). Hampton, VA: Cobbs & Henry.

[77]Skouhold, T. M.,& Rivers, D. A. (2004). *Skills and Strategies for the Helping Professions*. Denver Colorado: Love Publishing Company.

[78]Slattery, J. M. (2004). *Counseling Diverse Clients: bringing context into therapy*. Nelson Caradu. Thompson, Brooks/Cole.

[79]Sommers-Flanagan, J. & Sommers-Flanagan, R. (2004). *Counseling and Psychotherapy Theories in Context and Practice: Skills, strategies, and techniques*. Hoboken, New Jersey.

[80]Steenbarger, B. N. (1993). A Multicultural Model of Counseling: bridging brevity and diversity. *Journal of Counseling and Development, 72*, 8-15.

[81]Sue, D. W., Arrendondo, P., & McDavis, R. J. (1992). Multicultural Competencies/Standards: a pressing need. *Journal of Counseling and Development, 70*, 477-486.

[82]Sue, D. W., Ivey, A., & Pederson, P. (Eds.). (1996). *A Theory of Multicultural Counseling and Therapy*. Pacific Grove, CA: Brooks/Cole.

[83]Sue, D. W., & Sue, D. (1999). *Counseling the Culturally Different: Theory and practice* (3rd ed.). New York: Wiley.

[84]Sue, D.W., & Sue, D. (2013). Counseling the Culturally Diverse: Theory and Practice (6th Edition). New York: Wiley.

[85]Sue, D. W. et al (1998). *Multicultural Counseling Competencies: individual and organizational development*. Thousand Oaks, California. Sage Publications.

[86]Traden, R. R. (1989). The Formation of Homosexual Identifies. *Journal of Homosexuality, 17*, 43-73.

[87]Wrenn, C. Gilbert (1962). *The Counselor in a Changing World*. Personnel and Guidance Association, Washington DC.

CHAPTER 9

CASE MANAGEMENT AND VOCATIONAL REHABILITATION COUNSELING

KEITH B. WILSON
TYRA N. TURNER WHITTAKER
VIRGINIA BLACK

CHAPTER TOPICS

- Introduction
- Demographics of people of color with disabilities in the United States
- Multicultural counseling techniques
- An overview of case management
- Models in case management
- Case management strategies to assist consumers who are racially diverse
- Conclusion

CHAPTER 9   CASE MANAGEMENT AND VOCATIONAL REHABILITATION COUNSELING

In the United States, minority is a term usually applied to individuals who are persons of color who belong to the four major racial and/or ethnic groups, Black (African American) Asian (Asian American), American Indian (Native American), and Latino/Hispanic.[1,47] The authors will refer to the aforementioned groups as "people of color" and/or racial and ethnic minority groups. Speaking of people of color, most Hispanics in the VR systems (over 90 %) classify themselves as White/European American, not people of color. This distinction is important because Hispanics are included under the "people of color" category in most demographic studies.[55] The racial flexibility of Hispanics/Latinos is made more interesting because Hispanics/Latinos will become the largest ethnic minority group in the United States, passing people who classify themselves as African Americans.[35] Rawlings and Saluter[29] reported that "Hispanics constitute an ethnic group rather than a racial category, and their members may classify themselves as White, Black, or some other race."[p.xii] As reported by Wilson and Senices, among the four major racial and ethnic groups in the United States, many Hispanics/Latinos may not have as many negative experiences because of their phenotype (i.e., white skin color/hue).

The word *race* includes biological and physical traits used to depict certain people, mainly hue or skin color.[55] In contrast, ethnicity tends to deal with things like shared cultures, values, and language of a particular population.[8] Not withstanding how people who are Hispanic/Latino classify themselves racially, many people who are part of racial minority groups can be characterized by three different qualities: identifiably, differential power, and pejorative treatment.[10] We will use the terms minority and people of color interchangeably in this chapter.

INTRODUCTION

Case management has been a core function of the rehabilitation professional since the inception of the profession. The concept of case management has evolved greatly in the health and human service profession in general, and the rehabilitation profession in particular. In the beginning, case management was birthed during World War II to outline the extensive services needed for those with psychiatric disabilities.[14] In the 1960's, case management was viewed as a systematic method to organize and deliver services without duplicating such services[12] In the 1970's, as a result of escalating costs for worker's compensation and the passage of the 1973 Rehabilitation Act, the development of a more comprehensive service delivery system in the private rehabilitation sector began to emerge.[36] In the 80's, we observed a fundamental change in the direction of case management. In particular, case management began to be viewed as case or care coordination where the focus was on client empowerment.[57] Today, case management is considered a multidimensional role in the rehabilitation counseling process that provides case coordination, monitoring, and follow-up services to persons with disabilities. This chapter provides the reader with an overview of effective case management practices, and culturally sensitive service delivery for racial and ethnic minorities.

DEMOGRAPHICS OF PEOPLE OF COLOR WITH DISABILITIES IN THE UNITED STATES

Evidence suggests that access to Vocational Rehabilitation (VR) services is more difficult for racial minorities than for non-minorities/White Americans in the United States.[48,49,55] While access to VR services have been studied for several years,[51,52] the impact of certain processes has received less attention, such as case management relative to racial and ethnic minorities in the VR system. Given that the process of case management is a primary function of VR counselors, variables affecting case management outcomes, such as the race and ethnicity of a consumer, are not only worthy of examining but also necessary when looking at the changing complexion of consumers in many human service organizations.

With the aforementioned demographic backdrop in motion, Organista, et al.[24] reported that racial and ethnic minorities are approximately 25% of the population in the United States and are projected to become the majority of the United States population by the year 2050.[45] The Census also projects that racial and ethnic minorities will become a numerical majority by 2050. According to some private polls, however, White Americans may become the numerical minority by the year 2030. This demographic milieu is helping not only VR agencies, but also human service agencies focus their attention on issues of multicultural concerns that have arisen concerning the lack of diversity issues in many organizations in the United States. Although it is important to acknowledge the increasing numbers of diverse consumers in human service organizations, it is more problematic to address these concerns in the context of how case management services are delivered to diverse populations in the VR system in the United States. In California and Texas, the demographic transformation can be readily observed. It is evident that the complexion of the United States already reflects more racial and cultural diversity than in prior years. In order to successfully serve a more diverse population, human service organizations in general, and VR agencies in particular, must continue to seek new ways of facilitating services to our expanding clientele. If not, these populations will continue to feel isolated and disconnected from many human service organizations.

MULTICULTURAL COUNSELING TECHNIQUES

Because much of case management deals with the VR counselor interacting with both people who are consumers and VR personnel, it is important to advocate for VR counselors to use Multicultural Counseling Techniques (MCT) in their strategies to facilitate services for not only people of color, but for all people with disabilities in the state-federal system. Wilson, et al.,[50] reported:

> The study of multicultural counseling [techniques] (MCT) has continued to grow and become influential in the human services. Early advocates of MCT pointed out that there was little understanding about the history, experiences, lifestyles, and worldviews of culturally different populations. Furthermore, counseling professionals did not take into consideration the sociopolitical realities of the clients they served. Hence, counselors are less likely to include a systematic approach to address sociopolitical issues when dealing with racial and ethnic minority clients.[p. 8]

Utilizing MCT in case management with non-White Americans will allow counselors to determine the efficacy of services. Although not recognized earlier by many counselors, MCT continues to gain acceptance within the counseling community to access the history, experiences, life styles, and worldviews of racially and culturally diverse populations.[50]

While an exhaustive list of variables need not be addressed when using MCT, it is vital to pay close attention to the consumers' worldview, social class, gender, sexual orientation, and disability status when delivering case management services. For example, let us explore worldview. Because much of what we know about counseling and case management tends to be from a White American perspective (e.g. abstract ideas and linear analytic thinking), many VR counselors may inadvertently harm people of color because they are imposing a worldview on people of color that may be different in many respects (i.e., holistic and none linear thinking). Because many White Americans tend to value decisiveness when making decisions during the case management (intake) process, consumers who delay making a decision to consult with elder family members may be viewed as non-assertive and passive aggressive. When in fact, consulting with family members by some African Americans, for example, may be viewed within the family as a protocol of respect and inclusion. A good MCT would be for the White American VR counselor to allow the African American consumer enough time to consult with family members, if necessary, to facilitate the planning process and goals for the consumer. Locke[15] states that a holistic approach is valued and Blacks tend to respond to things in sum as opposed to focusing on the parts. In addition, reciprocity and altruism are valued and one's worth is found in what one contributes to the family and/or community.[41] As viewed in the aforementioned example, tension can exist when worldviews are in direct opposition to one another. Not only do human services professionals risk diagnosing undue pathology in racial minorities when worldviews collide, but it is likely that racial minorities will not return to VR or to other human service organizations.

CULTURAL VALUES

Though common cultural values have been reported for each of the four major racial minority groups (e.g., African Americans, Asian Americans, Native Americans, & Hispanics/Latinos) in the United States, it is vital to note that cultural variation exists within each of these groups.[1,15,26] Because a discussion of intra-group cultural differences is beyond the scope of this book chapter, the reader is referred to other chapters in the text for further explanation of how cultural values impact various racial groups during and after the initial interview process.

INEQUITY OF SERVICE DELIVERY TO PEOPLE OF COLOR

Historically, there has been a discrepancy in services received between people of color and their White American counterparts during the rehabilitation process. People of color have been disproportionately rejected for vocational rehabilitation services and prematurely terminated at a higher rate than their Caucasian counterparts.[9,51,52,53] Further, research conducted by Wilson, et al,[56] concluded that there were differences in the types of services received by African-Americans and White Americans upon successful closure. They discovered that African-Americans were more likely to receive maintenance, transportation, and adjustment training, whereas their White American counterparts were more likely to receive diagnostic, college training, and physical/mental restoration services.[56] Several research teams have deduced that racial and ethnic biases within the VR systems is a primary reason why many disparities appear not only in the VR system regarding racial and ethnic minority outcomes, but in the human services as well.[52,54] In part, these disparities revealed a lack of cultural sensitivity on behalf of the rehabilitation counselor. The lack of cultural sensitivity is a common theme in both the VR and psychology literature. To address the cultural sensitivity issues, or the lack thereof, is constantly under debate.

The authors recognize that increasing one's level of cultural sensitivity can enhance the rehabilitation process and assist the rehabilitation counselor in providing equitable services with noted outcomes for the consumer of color. Because over 93 percent of VR counselors and approximately 92 percent of VR administrators classify themselves as White American in the United States,[46] the need for cultural sensitivity is not only warranted, but necessary, to begin to address the needs of racial and ethnic minorities in the VR system. How one is perceived when seeking VR services has been and remains an issue in the state-federal system. For example, evidence suggests that people of color may have a more difficult time in the VR system when compared to people who classify themselves as White Americans. More importantly, not all people who classify themselves as racial and ethnic minorities have similar experiences with discrimination. As Wilson and Senices[55] recently adduced regarding VR outcomes, many forms of discrimination in the VR systems are based on ones color (hue). Vocational rehabilitation consumers with darker hues (e.g., Black, Hispanics/Latinos) are more prone to be discriminated against inside and outside of the VR agency than consumers who classify themselves as White Americans.

AN OVERVIEW OF CASE MANAGEMENT

Within a single lifetime, how many adaptations does an individual make? Individuals change and adapt to their own growth and developmental patterns as well as to the environmental pressures and social situations of a given milieu, such as the VR agency. Persons with physical, intellectual, or emotional disabilities have their own unique way of adapting to the demands of their surrounding environment. The role of case managers and vocational counselors is to help each individual adapt to one's own particular situation through the use of case management models.[4]

If we think of case management as an umbrella, then we are able to tease out the various components involved in this creative and collaborative process, which involves organizing, consulting, counseling, assessing, teaching, monitoring, and advocating.[21] Case management is generally defined as "a creative and collaborative process, involving skills in assessment, consulting, teaching, modeling, and advocacy that aim to enhance the optimal functioning of the consumer's served."[21, p.4] Roessler and Rubin[31] describe case management in rehabilitation counseling as the counselor's capability to guide the consumer through the rehabilitation process from intake to case closure. Because case management is a process that involves individuals making decisions for VR consumers, VR counselors and administrators must remember to address possible stereotypes that may lead some VR consumers, like African-Americans with disabilities, to not receive the services they need and deserve. To support the stereotype assertion,[34,35,19] all reported that racial and ethnic group stereotypes could lead practitioners to hasty conclusions and unsound postulations about consumers. More specifically, Rosenthal and Berven reported that counselors in training bring their stereotypes into the counseling session. They also reported that African American consumers might not receive the services they are eligible for because of negative prejudices held against them. Our point is that one must look at both the process of case management and the people who police the process, who are VR counselors, staff, and administrators, to name a few.

Case management is obviously a complex service that is constantly evolving to meet the increasing diversity of consumers and job opportunities. As a case manager, how do all of the various components (e.g., consulting, counseling, assessing, teaching) get addressed, considering the uniqueness of each individual? Case management is viewed as a process for assessing the client's total situation and addressing the needs and problems found in that assessment.[42, p.37] To meet the needs of each individual, various models of case management have been introduced over the years. Several models of case management are available, because services need to be delivered in a variety of ways. Case management remains a flexible process in order to meet the unique needs and goals of each individual.[57] While the process of case management is dynamic, people operating as "gate keepers" may not be flexible enough to adjust to different clientele. Thus, the following models are provided as guides to not only facilitate the case management process for racial and ethnic minorities, but the human service profession in the United States.

MODELS IN CASE MANAGEMENT

Several models of case management exist to enhance the method in which services are delivered in the VR system. We view the following model as salient to facilitating the case management for all VR populations, not just for people of color. Five models of case management will be introduced: The Crux Model, the Broker Model, the Rehabilitation Model, the Assertive Community Treatment (ACT) Model, and the Strengths Model. Information on the advantages and disadvantages and the utility of each model for persons of color is provided to assist human service personnel to achieve productive outcomes for their particular clientele.

THE CRUX MODEL

The rehabilitation counselor's main goal is to promote the quality of life (QOL) of persons with disabilities. One central supporting element of QOL is obtaining and maintaining employment. Rehabilitation counselors prepare individuals to obtain employment by first helping them progress toward personal independence, adjustment, and health. As these three basic requirements gain momentum, rehabilitation counselors can begin assisting persons with disabilities in meeting specific educational standards that conform to the prerequisites of their specified employment interests.[30] Matching the individual to a job is one of the core concerns in vocational counseling. With all the extraneous variables, where does the counselor begin? Roessler and Rubin[30] reported back in 1979 that the Crux Model is structured towards bringing in all the relevant variables of the vocational counseling process and organizing them into vocational possibilities.

The Crux Model is divided into an evaluation phase and a planning phase. Within the evaluation phase, the counselor collects information on "the consumer's past, current, and potential capacities in physical functioning, psychosocial functioning, and educational and vocational skill development."[30, p.31] Roessler and Rubin[30] also asserted that assessing the consumer's current economic situation is an important part of the evaluation phase of the Crux Model. They outline a series of factors that might assist in the evaluation phase of the model (physical factors, psychosocial factors, educational and vocational factors, and economic factors), in order to get a broad picture of the consumer.

A culturally sensitive rehabilitation counselor should also obtain information about the consumer's cultural background, including issues with race, ethnicity, and nationality. Information can be obtained through a dialogue with the consumer as rapport is being established and also through personal research of the consumer's particular culture. In fact, it is useful to do additional research on any culture that one is unfamiliar with. While gaining additional information about a particular clientele might be time-consuming, the potential gains, advantages, and positive outcomes will clearly outweigh any possible inconveniences. Collecting culturally sensitive information is also useful in evaluating the material gathered in a cultural context (e.g., To what extent do the family and friends support the rehabilitation process? Does the family have unrealistic expectations of the individual with the disability? Is the community involved in economically supporting the individual?). Many VR counselors and other human services professionals fail to address culture during the case management process.

The evaluation phase of the Crux Model is completed once the rehabilitation counselor obtains adequate information in the four aforementioned areas outlined by Roessler and Rubin.[30] Rehabilitation counselors need to fully utilize all the available information from intake interviews, vocational tests and evaluations, medical evaluations, psychological evaluations, and any other relevant sources. Using a range of information allows the VR counselor to fill in any gaps in the evaluation phase and move smoothly into the second phase of the Crux Model, the planning phase. In the initial steps of the planning phase, the counselor analyzes all the evaluation information. Upon consideration of possible vocational positions, the counselor must remain aware of the consumer's strengths and limitations. Depending on the demands of the potential jobs, the consumer's mental and physical abilities, their socio-cultural background, and their goals and interests, a range of vocational possibilities should be generated incorporating a wide-range of sources. As with the rehabilitation counselor philosophy, this holistic approach is necessary to complete the cultural picture of potential consumers.

During the vocational planning phase of the Crux Model, the rehabilitation counselor and the consumer collaborate on selecting a job that is compatible with the characteristics of the consumer and the job. Once a vocational goal is agreed upon, the steps to getting or maintaining a job need to be addressed. These intermediate steps focus on particular rehabilitation needs that were addressed in the evaluation phase (e.g., level of education, work experience, vocational interests). Fulfilling each need brings the consumer one step closer to becoming a satisfied employee in a suitable environment. Even though the Crux Model focuses on matching an individual to a particular job, the outcome is not obligatory or absolute. Rather, the Crux Model should be used for occupational exploration. The role of the rehabilitation counselor is to help facilitate this exploration and ideally, to help the consumers make their own vocational decision. The role of the rehabilitation counselor not only calls for being a skilled vocational counselor, but also an experienced case manager. Therefore, the process does not end when a vocational decision is reached. Once a vocational decision is reached, the case management process continues into the areas of vocational training, job placement, work accommodations, and eventually, into job analysis and job modifications.[30]

The Crux Model is very comprehensive and provides ample opportunity to gain personal information about the consumer's culture. Advantages are apparent when incorporating the cultural background of all VR consumers. By adding a cultural component, the Crux Model provides the foundation for a long-term relationship between the counselor and the consumer. Time and honesty are needed to foster trust within the counselor-consumer relationship. Time and honesty are vital since many consumers of color enter counseling and the VR system with a certain level of cultural mistrust of the counselor. Cultural mistrust is the tendency for a consumer of color, for example, to mistrust Caucasians (European Americans)—especially in the major areas of government (i.e. education, business and work, interpersonal and social relations, and politics and law).[43] Establishing rapport allows the counselor to create a climate of faith that helps to facilitate the rehabilitation process.

One disadvantage of the Crux Model for persons of color is the need for the consumer to be extremely verbal during the rehabilitation process. For example, depending on the value orientation of a specific culture, the consumer may not be as verbal as the counselor expects or even needs. Information must then be gathered through other entities such as family members. Thus, there may be a likelihood of the VR counselor attaching unnecessary pathology to people of color in the VR system.

THE BROKER MODEL

The Broker Model emphasizes assessing the needs of consumers, treatment planning, and ultimately referring the consumer to other agencies.[11] The Broker Model considers the case manager as a "broker" or negotiator of services who requires the skills to effectively link a consumer's needs with available resources.[11] Once the consumer is connected to needed resources, the case manager's role is completed. In the Broker Model, most of the responsibility is placed on the consumer and the consumer's family. The case manager does not serve in the capacity of an advocate for services. Within this model, the case manager assesses the consumer's needs and identifies what services would be beneficial and available. Ultimately, the Broker Model is extremely limited in its helpfulness in that a long-term consumer-counselor relationship may not be possible.

Those rehabilitation counselors ascribing to the Broker Model must evaluate this model in a cultural context. For example, a Hispanic consumer may expect the rehabilitation counselor to assume most of the responsibility in the rehabilitation process. The Hispanic consumer may view the counselor as the authoritarian and wait on the counselor to initiate needed activities. Using this example, the culturally sensitive counselor must be aware of language barriers that may exist within the Hispanic population. Bilingual consumers are often prematurely terminated based on language barriers. To support this assertion, Moore[20] reported that language barriers are important to understand when working with Hispanic consumers. It is obvious that such barriers with any population may impede the rehabilitation process. Therefore, the rehabilitation counselor must be mindful that they may have to assume a more active role with certain populations than what the Broker Model allows.

In 1995, Rapp did an extensive literature review on the use of case management within the mental health field. Rapp reported results from six studies evaluating the Broker Model, which suggested that for the most part, the model produces few positive effects. Since the Broker Model emphasizes a formal relationship between the consumer and the case manager, Rapp found that more consumers relied on hospitals and did not show an increase in quality of life. Holloway and Carson[13] reported that case managers using the Broker Model were mostly coordinators and brokers of services. These case managers were typically assigned large caseloads, 50:1, and worked a majority of the time directly from their offices. Theoretically, there was a potential strength to this model despite the case manager functioning as a dispassionate broker; the case manager was able to meet the needs of a large population in the most cost-effective way.[13] Obvious weaknesses arose, however, particularly in the assumption that case managers were effectively connecting consumers to appropriate services without direct contact between the managers and the consumers.

Cultural sensitivity is inherently far removed when using this model with non-mainstream consumers. The Broker Model may not be useful when working with a clientele that relies on personal contact and a personal relationship in order to follow through with services. Some populations may consider the counselor who uses the broker system as another person who is giving them the run-a-round. While this perception may be historical in nature, it is these kinds of perceptions that will likely impede the case management and counseling process of the client. It is also obvious that counselors who use this particular model will have to explain upfront what, why, and who during the initial minutes of the intake process. Though there are never guarantees, it is vital to decrease ambiguity early in the case management process when one uses this particular model.

THE REHABILITATION MODEL

The third model is the Rehabilitation Model (Anthony et al., 1988), which is a consumer-centered model. The case manager is responsible for helping the consumer identify individual strengths and weaknesses and teaches skills that may enhance their quality of life. The Rehabilitation Model works toward enriching the consumer's strengths by using planning programs that evaluate areas where the consumer has skill deficits. With this model, there is a strong emphasis on the consumer's preferences (e.g. the type of job the consumer would like to obtain).[30] The Rehabilitation Model is similar to the Bervin assessment model of case management. Bervin's Assessment Model of case management evaluates assessment data using the following three values: assets, limitations, and preferences. Bervin[3] defined assets as particular characteristics of the consumer that help facilitate the attainment of future goals. Limitations were defined as any obstacles that could stand in the way of the consumer and the particular goal(s) of the consumer. As Bervin views it, each consumer has preferences (e.g. interests, needs, fears, likes, dislikes) for safely and effectively reaching future goals. Case managers collect assessment data from all the relevant areas (e.g. medical, vocational, psychological, social) and work closely with the consumer to determine whether an area is an asset, a limitation, or a preference. Once each area is broken down and analyzed, the counselor is able to interpret all the parts as a whole to determine the best plan of action for the consumer.[3] The plan should lead to an effective goal attainment if there is good rapport and collaboration between the counselor and the consumer. The critical element is the counselor's ability to analyze, synthesize, and interpret the assessment data in order to accurately recommend what is best for the consumer.

The assessment phase is critical for the rehabilitation counselor in the Rehabilitation Model. Assessment is a continuous process throughout every stage of the rehabilitation process. It is critical for assessment to continue until a case closes.[30] The Rehabilitation Model, as well as Bervin's Assessment Model, emphasizes the importance of the consumers clearly defining their goals. For the counselor, it is equally important to continually assess the consumer's rehabilitation process, and work on areas of deficiency. Counselors must also work on linking each consumer to a unique service within the community while continuing to monitor the progress. Caseloads within both the Rehabilitation and Bervin Models typically range from 20:1 to 30:1.[13]

The Rehabilitation Model and the Bervin Model possess great utility in providing rehabilitation counseling services for consumers of color. The two models are sufficiently broad to allow the counselor to focus on consumers' specific strengths and weaknesses that may influence the rehabilitation process, rather than culturally biased evaluation measures. Due to the emphasis on consumer's preferences, the Rehabilitation Model heavily relies on the counselor's knowledge of the consumer's preferences within a cultural context. Consumers of color's preferences may not stem from their individual

CHAPTER 9   CASE MANAGEMENT AND VOCATIONAL REHABILITATION COUNSELING

preferences, but from the preferences of their family and other internal support systems. The culturally sensitive counselor must be aware of and sensitive to the factors surrounding the consumer's preference, or lack of preference.

THE ASSERTIVE COMMUNITY TREATMENT (ACT) MODEL

The fourth model is the ACT Model, which is based on Project ACT in Madison, Wisconsin.[38] Work on this model has recently been updated.[44,37] As a backdrop, the ACT Model was developed for individuals who frequently used mental health services. In 1980, Stein and Test[38] sought to empower individuals by moving them out of hospitals and into a supportive local community. Individuals begin to learn and use daily coping skills, which is a strong motivating force in helping consumers form community relationships, live independently, and face daily problems with minimal assistance. In addition, the ACT Model recognizes that circumstances may arise when the individual needs temporary hospitalization.[13]

ACT is based on the principle that services are delivered by an interdisciplinary team, led by a single case manager that works collaboratively with all their consumers. Meetings are scheduled on a regular basis to discuss and evaluate the progress of each consumer. More important to the title of the model, the team typically spends 80% of their time in the community with their consumers. Most of the services are provided by the ACT team, rather than by outside professionals as we observed in the Broker Model. Caseloads are small in the ACT Model due to the amount of fieldwork expected by the team. An optimal caseload ratio is 10:1 and in some areas 15:1.[13]

Several researchers of multicultural counseling emphasize the fact that most people of color ascribe to a "collectivistic" versus an "individualistic" value orientation.[16] Culturally sensitive counselors utilizing the ACT approach may find that they achieve better outcomes because they continuously interface with the consumer's community. Rehabilitation counselors must earn the trust of their consumers of color to be successful. As previously mentioned, many consumers of color enter counseling with a level of cultural mistrust towards the VR counselor. If trust is not perceived, neither the consumer nor the counselor will achieve successful outcomes in the rehabilitation process. To this avail, being a part of the consumer's community allows the counselor to develop better rapport with the consumer, which should lead to better outcomes for both the counselor and the consumer.

THE STRENGTHS MODEL

The final model, the Strengths Model, focuses on the consumer's strengths rather than on the disability. There is a strong importance placed on the counselor-consumer rapport in this model. Initially, counselors work with their consumers to identify their strengths. Next, the counselors create scenarios that the consumer is able to successfully accomplish. This feeling of success boosts the consumer's personal strengths and sense of power and control. As in the

204

role of the rehabilitation counselor, this model seeks to empower consumers with disabilities. Feelings of satisfaction and a sense of power encourage consumers to continue to pursue their goals. The Strengths Model asserts that rehabilitation counselors or case managers must develop four key areas of support: natural, peer, income, and housing.[22] The focus on the consumer's strengths is a very important key in this model.

The Strengths Model also rests on the premise that a consumer's behavior depends largely on the resources available in the community. It has been stated and mentioned in several publications; individuals with disabilities need equal access to community resources to be successful.[30] The Strengths Model has been reviewed in eight studies with consistently positive outcomes in the following areas: hospitalizations, quality of life, social supports, consumer satisfaction, and leisure activities.[18,30] Interestingly, this model functions dually as a service philosophy and a case management model. Some aspects of the Strengths Model have been used in writing mission statements in several case management centers.[23] According to experts using the Strengths Model, the ideal caseload ranges from 10:1 to 20:1.[18]n).

The Strengths Model lends itself to culturally sensitive rehabilitation counseling in that the Strengths Model considers consumers' views of their strengths and goals versus counselors' perception of strengths. In the Strengths Model, the consumer assumes a major role in the rehabilitation process. More specifically, there is ample opportunity for consumers of color to integrate aspects of their culture into the rehabilitation process. The disadvantage of this model in a cultural context is that counselors are not encouraged to assume culturally sensitive skills as they would in other models.

Based on the literature of these five case management models, the relationship between the consumer and case manager is critical, which has always been a fundamental element in traditional rehabilitation counseling. Another essential element in successful case management is the use of teams.[30] Rehabilitation counselors should never be expected to take on all the activities involved in rehabilitation counseling. Teams are needed for planning and monitoring a consumer's goals and progress, as well as supporting each other and offering expertise from each member's own background. Finally, teams benefit from diversity, and collaborating with psychiatrists, social workers, rehabilitation counselors, and nurses enriches the assessment process and the lives of the consumers.[30]

CASE MANAGEMENT STRATEGIES TO ASSIST CONSUMERS WHO ARE RACIALLY DIVERSE

In observing the Parham (2002) model for African American males, we realize that concepts in this model can also be used for a variety of diverse consumers. We have also modified the therapy/counseling model to include the process of case management. In order to gain a complete understanding of the processes involved with the Parham model, one must first be open to changing and modifying one's behavior to increase the chances of a productive outcome for both the consumer and the VR counselor:

- *Connecting with your consumers*: Because there are several ways to connect with consumers, VR counselors may want to consider creating an atmosphere that would facilitate the client being open during the case management process.

- *Assessment*: As Parham[25] noted, there are several techniques that contribute to a counselor's ability to assess what is going on with the client. Understanding cultural strengths and using appropriate clinical instruments are only two tools to consider. Many of the tools that are used to assess the strengths and weaknesses of VR consumers use norms that exclude persons of color. Understanding the instrument limitations based on sample representation, for example, could be helpful when the results of such assessments are used to exclude consumers from receiving certain services.

- *Facilitating Awareness*: Reframing and understanding functional behaviors are two ways to facilitate client awareness during the case management process.

- *Setting Goals*: As Parham[25] noted, the goals that you have during the case management process will chart the course of healing. It is important to respect the need for client distance and examine the client from a culturally centered theoretical basis.

- *Taking Action and Instigating Change*: Empowering, teaching, and becoming a social advocate and engineer on behalf of clients, can assist clients to confront and handle their circumstances in a productive way.

CONCLUSION

While the models and techniques discussed in this chapter are examples of how to use basic case management measures and procedures with culturally diverse populations, the first action must be the willingness of VR counselors to be open to new ways of performing their job functions. As discussed, there are basic strengths and weaknesses to all models. Based on the changing demographics in the United States population, new ways of approaching case management with diverse populations is not only warranted, but critical in continuing to provide services to groups that have typically been served inadequately for many years. This call to the profession must be understood as a call that will help all people with disabilities in the VR system.

REFERENCES

[1]Axelson, J. (1993). *Counseling and development in a multicultural society* (2nd ed.). Pacific Grove, CA: Brooks/Cole.

[2]Anthony, W.A., Cohen, M.R., Farkas, M. & Cohen, B.F. (1988). Clinical care update: the chronically mentally ill. Case management-more than a response to a dysfunctional system. *Community Mental Health Journal, 24,* 1263-1266.

[3]Bervin, N. (1984). Assessment practices in rehabilitation counseling. *Journal of Applied Rehabilitation Counseling, 15* (3), 9-14.

[4]Brill, N.I. (1998). *Working with people: The helping process (6th edition).* White Plains, NY: Longman.

[5]Burnett, P. C. (1999). Assessing the structure of learning outcomes from counseling using the SOLO taxonomy: An exploratory study. *British Journal of Guidance and Counseling, 27*(4), 567-580.

[6]Burnett, P. C., & Meacham, D. (2002). Learning journals as a counseling strategy. *Journal of Counseling and Development, 80*(4), 410-416.

[7]Cohen, R., Phillips, S., & Swerdlki, M. (1996). *Psychological testing and assessment* (3rd ed.). CA: Mayfield.

[8]Dana, R. H. (1998). *Understanding cultural identity in intervention and assessment. Multicultural aspects of counseling series 9.* Thousand Oaks,

[9]Dziekan, K., & Okocha, A. (1993). Accessibility of rehabilitation services: Comparison by racial-ethnic status. *Rehabilitation Counseling Bulletin, 36,* 183-189.

[10]Dworkin, A. G., & Dworkin, R. J. (1999). *The minority report: An introduction to racial, ethnic, and gender relations* (3rd ed.). Fort Worth,

[11]Grech, E. (2002). Case management: a critical analysis of the literature. *International Journal of Psychosocial Rehabilitation, 6,* 89-98.

[12]Giuliano, K. K. & Poirier, C. E. (1991). Nursing case management: Critical pathways to desirable outcomes. *Journal of Nursing Management, 22*(3), 52-55.

[13]Holloway, F. & Carson, J. (2001). Case management: an update. *International Journal of Social Psychiatry, 47*(3), 21-31.

[14]Lee, D. T. F.; Mackenzie, A. E.; Dudley-Brown, S., & Chin, T. M. (1998). *Journal of Advance Nursing. 27*(5), 933-940.

[15]Locke, D. C. (1998). *Increasing multicultural understanding: A comprehensive model* (2nd ed.). Thousand Oaks, CA: Sage.

[16]Kluckhohn, F. R., & Strodtbeck, F. L. (1961). *Variations in value orientations.* Evanston, IL: Row Petersen.

[17]Mahoney, M. J. (1991). *Human change processes.* New York: Basic Books.

[18]Marty, D., Rapp, C. A., & Carlson, L. (2001). The experts speak: the critical ingredients of strengths model case management. *Psychiatric Rehabilitation Journal, 24*(3), 214-221.

[19]Middleton, R. A., Rollins, C. W., Sanderson, P. L., Leung, P., Harley, D. A., Ebener, D., & Leal- Idrogo, A. (2000). Endorsement of multicultural rehabilitation competencies and standards: A call to action. *Rehabilitation Counseling Bulletin, 43*, 219-240.
[20]Moore, C. (2002). Comparative competitive employment levels for Latinos and Non-Latinos without 12 years of education. *Journal of Applied Rehabilitation Counseling, 33*(1), 12-18.
[21]Mullahy, C. (1998). *The case manager's handbook.* Gaithersburg, MD: Aspen.
[22]North Carolina Department of Human Resources, Division of Mental Health, Developmental Disabilities, and Substance Abuse Services (1990). *Approaches to case management with adults with severe and persistent mental illness.* Raleigh, NC.
[23]Onyett, S. (1992). *Case Management in Mental Health.* Chapman & Hall, London.
[24]Organista, P. B., Chun, K. M. & Marín, G. (Eds.). (1998). *Readings in ethnic psychology.* New York: Routledge.
[25]Parham, T. A. (2002). Counseling models for African Americans: The what and how of counseling In T. A. Parham (Eds.), *Counseling Persons of African Descent: Raising the bar of practitioner competence* (pp. 100-118). Thousand Oakes, CA: Sage.
[26]Ponterotto, J. & Casas, M. (1991). *Handbook of racial/ethnic minority counseling research.* Springfield, MA: Charles C Thomas.
[27]Power, P. W. (2000). *A guide to vocational assessment* (3rd ed.). Texas: Pro-Ed, Inc.
[28]Rapp, C. (1995). The active ingredients of effective case management: a research synthesis. In L. Giesler (Ed.), *Case management for behavioral care* (pp. 5-46). Cincinnati, OH: NACM.
[29]Rawlings, S. W., & Saluter, A, F. (1994). Household and family characteristics: U. S. Bureau of the Census, *Current Population Reports*, 20-483.
[30]Roessler, R. T. & Rubin, S. E. (1998). *Case management and rehabilitation counseling: procedures and techniques* (3rd edition). Austin, TX: Pro-ed.
[31]Roessler, R. T. & Rubin, S. E. (1992). *Case management and rehabilitation counseling: procedures and techniques* (2nd edition). Austin, TX: Pro-ed.
[32]Roessler, R. T. & Rubin, S. E. (1979). Diagnostic and planning guidelines for the vocational rehabilitation process. *Rehabilitation Literature, 40*(2), 34-37.
[33]Sandhu, D. S. (1995). Pioneers of multicultural counseling: An interview with Paul B. Rosenthal, D.A., & Berven, N.L. (1999). Effects of client race on clinical judgment. *Rehabilitation Counseling Bulletin, 42*, 243-264.
[34]Rosenthal, D. A., & Kosciulek, J. F. (1996). Clinical judgment and bias due to client race or ethnicity: An overview with implications for rehabilitation counselors. *Journal of Applied Rehabilitation Counseling, 27*, 30-36.

[35]Sue, D. W., Arredondo, P., & McDavis, R. J. (1992). Multicultural counseling competencies and standards: A call to the profession. *Journal of Counseling & Development, 70*, 477-486.

[36]Shaw, L. R.; McMahon, B. T.; Chan, F.; Taylor, D., & Wood, C. (2001). Survey of rehabilitation counselor education programs regarding health care case management in the private sector. *Journal of Rehabilitation, 63* (3), 46-52.

[37]Stein, L. I. & Santos, A.B. (1998). *Assertive Community Treatment of Persons with Severe Mental Illness*. Norton, New York.

[38]Stein, L. & Test, M. (1980). *Alternative* to mental hospital treatment. *Archives of General Psychiatry, 37*, 392-397.

[39]Sue, D. W. (1996). ACES endorsement of the multicultural counseling competencies: Do we have the courage. *Spectrum, 57*(1), 9-10.

[40]Sue, D. W., Carter, R. T., Casas, J. M., Fouad, N. A., Ivey, A. I., Jensen, M., LaFromboise, T., Manese, J. E., Ponterrotto, J. G., Vazqueq-Nutall, E. (1998). *Multicultural counseling competencies: Individual and organizational development* (v 11). Thousand Oaks, CA: Sage.

[41]Sudarkasa, N. (1997). African American families and family values. In H. P. McAdoo (Ed.), *Black families* (pp. 9-40). Thousand Oaks, CA: Sage.

[42]Summers, N. (2006). Fundamentals of case management practice: Skills for the human services (2nd edition). Belmont, CA: Brooks/Cole.

[43]Terrell, F., & Terrell, S. L. (1981). An inventory to measure cultural mistrust among Blacks. *The Western Journal of Black Studies, 5*, 180-184.

[44]Thompson, K.S., Griffith, E. E. H. & Leaf, P.J. (1990). A historical review of the Madison model of community care. *Hospital and Community Psychiatry, 41*, 625-634.

[45]United States Department of Commerce. (2001). *Resident population estimates of the United States by sex, race, and Hispanic origin.* Available: http://www.census.gov/population/estimates/nation/intfile3-1.txt.

[46]Whitney-Thomas, J., Timmons, J. C., Gilmore, D. S., & Thomas, D. M. (1999). Expanding access: Changes in vocational rehabilitation practice since the 1992 Rehabilitation Act Amendments. *Rehabilitation Counseling Bulletin, 43*, 30-40.

[47]Wilson II, C. C. & Gutiérrez, F. (1985). *Minorities and media: Diversity and the end of mass communication.* Newbury Park, CA: Sage.

[48]Wilson, K. B., Harley, D. A., McCormick, K., Jolivette, K. & Jackson. R. (2001). A literature review of vocational rehabilitation acceptance and explaining bias in the rehabilitation process. *Journal of Rehabilitation, 32*, 24-35.

[49]Wilson, K. B., Jackson, R., & Doughty, J. (1999). What a difference a race makes: Reasons for unsuccessful closures within the vocational rehabilitation system. *American Rehabilitation, 25*, 16-24.

[50]Wilson, K. B., Henry, M., Sayles, C., Senices, J., & Smith, D. (2003). Multicultural counseling and counseling competency in vocational rehabilitation. *Journal of the Pennsylvania Counseling Association, 5*, 15-18.

[51]Wilson, K. B. (1999). Vocational rehabilitation acceptance: A tale of two races in a large midwestern state. *Journal of Applied Rehabilitation Counseling 30*, 25-31.

[52]Wilson, K. B. (2002). The exploration of vocational rehabilitation acceptance and ethnicity: A national investigation. *Rehabilitation Counseling Bulletin, 45*, 168-176.

[53]Wilson, K. B., Harley, D. A., & Alston, R. J. (2001). Race as a correlate of vocational rehabilitation acceptance: Revisited. *Journal of Rehabilitation, 67(3)*, 35-41.

[54]Wilson, K. B., Alston, R. J., Harley, D. A., & Mitchell, N. (2002). Predicting vocational rehabilitation acceptance based on race, gender, education, work status at application, and primary source of support at application in the United States. *Rehabilitation Counseling Bulletin, 45*, 132-142.

[55]Wilson, K. B., & Senices, J. (2005). Exploring the vocational rehabilitation acceptance rates of Hispanics and non-Hispanics in the United States. *Journal of Counseling and Development 83(1), 86-96.*

[56]Wilson, K. B., Turner, T., & Jackson, R. J. (2002). Vocational rehabilitation services received after successful closure: A comparison by race. *Journal of Applied Rehabilitation, 33(1), 26-34.*

[57]Woodside, M. & McClam, T. (2003). *Generalist case management: a method of human service delivery (2nd edition).* Pacific Grove, CA: Brooks/Cole.

CHAPTER 10

DIVERSITY ISSUES IN PSYCHOLOGICAL ASSESSMENT

CHOW S. LAM
DEBRA B. HOMA
AMY BUSER

CHAPTER TOPICS

➤ Introduction
➤ Multicultural issues in the assessment process
➤ Issues in the assessment process for persons with disabilities
➤ Conclusion

CHAPTER 10   DIVERSITY ISSUES IN PSYCHOLOGICAL ASSESSMENT

INTRODUCTION

What is psychological assessment? According to the Standards for Educational and Psychological Testing, (American Educational Research Association, American Psychological Association, & National Council on Measurement in Education, 1999), psychological assessment is:

A comprehensive examination of psychological functioning that involves collecting, evaluating, and integrating test results and collateral information, and reporting information about an individual. Various methods may be used to acquire information during a psychological assessment: administering, scoring, and interpreting tests and inventories; behavioral observation; client and third-party interviews; analysis of prior educational, occupational, medical, and psychological records.[p.180]

As stated in the above definition, psychological assessment gathers data from multiple sources, and the clinician analyzes these data within the context of the individual's life history, referral records, and behavioral observations.[52] The purposes of psychological assessment are varied and often depend on the setting in which they are conducted, the needs of the individual, and information requested by the referral source. In a clinical setting, psychological assessments are typically used to assess the individual's current level of psychological functioning, formulate a diagnosis, assist in treatment planning, and assess progress in therapy.[52,2] Psychological assessments may also be conducted to assess cognitive strengths and deficits, diagnose neuropsychological impairment and learning disabilities, assess academic achievement levels, and provide information needed for career decision-making.[2]

Some of the most common tools employed in psychological assessments include the clinical interview, intelligence and aptitude tests, achievement tests, personality tests, and vocational tests. The clinical interview may be structured, semi structured, or unstructured and is generally the first step in a psychological assessment; the interview allows the clinician to elicit important background information from the client and establish rapport.[11] Intelligence tests measure cognitive strengths and limitations as defined by purported constructs of intelligence, often based on theory.[2] In their broadest sense, most intelligence tests are designed to assess capacity for learning[64] and provide a score in the form of the well-known intelligence quotient, or IQ. The most widely used intelligence test for adults in the United States is the Wechsler Adult Intelligence Scale-Third Edition (WAIS-III), considered by Power to be "perhaps the best general adult intelligence test available."[64 p.133] Like intelligence tests, aptitude tests are intended to measure an individual's learning potential but are focused on a specific skill, often with the purpose of determining whether an individual would benefit from training in a particular area.[64]

In contrast, achievement tests assess the knowledge and skills an individual has already acquired through education and training.[64] Achievement tests typically include assessment of academic skills, such as reading, spelling, vocabulary, and mathematics. Personality inventories are designed to measure personal characteristics, such as individual differences in thoughts, feelings, and behavior, based either on theoretically derived constructs or on empirically based factors that are believed to influence an individual's behavior and functioning in various settings.[2] While some personality inventories focus on normal personality functioning, others, such as the Minnesota Multiphasic Personality Inventory (MMPI), are designed to assess maladjustment and psychopathology.[64] Interest inventories assess occupational preferences and are among the most widely used vocational tests. Other types of vocational tests include inventories of work values and needs as well as tests designed to measure career maturity and decision-making.[2]

Although psychological assessment is conducted in a variety of settings and with a wide range of age groups, this chapter will focus on the psychological assessment of adults in clinical and counseling settings and will provide an overview of diversity issues in clinical diagnosis, vocational assessment, and the assessment process, including the clinical interview and testing.

What is a diverse population? As used here, the term diverse populations refers to individuals who fall outside of the mainstream majority culture in the United States, usually designated as "minority groups," which include persons with disabilities and individuals from racial/ethnic groups other than European American. Although assessment issues regarding ethnic minorities and persons with disabilities will be addressed separately, this division is, to some extent, arbitrary. Persons with disabilities represent the largest minority group in the U.S. and share with other minority groups' experiences of discrimination and stigma. Like racial/ethnic minority groups, they have their own culture.[57] This similarity is especially highlighted by deaf individuals, who possess a unique culture and language.

Poverty and race/ethnicity are inter-related and complicate the assessment process of individuals from diverse populations. For example, the 1995 U.S. Census provides the following data regarding poverty rates in the U.S.: 29.3% were African American, 30.3% were Hispanic, 14.6% were Asian and Pacific Islanders, and 14.3% were American Indians[79,32] Race/ethnicity is also associated with disability, lower rates of employment, and low-income levels.[55,57] National data suggest that African Americans and Hispanics are at greater risk than others of incurring physical disabilities.[26] Assessment issues involving ethnicity and disability are, therefore, likely to overlap.

Recognizing the increasing importance of addressing the needs of culturally diverse individuals in service delivery, the American Psychological

Association's Board of Ethnic Minority Affairs established a Task Force in 1988, which developed the American Psychological Association (APA) Guidelines for Providers of Psychological Services to Ethnic, Linguistic, and Culturally Diverse Populations. These guidelines call on psychologists to be culturally responsive to their clients in both assessment and treatment through awareness of ethnic and cultural influences on emotions and behavior and by being respectful of cultural differences in beliefs and worldviews.[4] The Ethical Principles of Psychologists and Code of Conduct[5] stipulate that psychologists be mindful of the impact of race, ethnicity, disability, national origin, and language in both administration and interpretation of assessment results.

MULTICULTURAL ISSUES IN THE ASSESSMENT PROCESS

As mentioned earlier, psychological assessment involves multiple sources from which to gather information on the individual. During the psychological process, attention to special issues is needed when serving persons with a diverse background. The coverage of all areas of assessment issues is beyond the scope of this chapter. We choose several major assessment issues that we believe are essential when considering their application to persons from a diverse background.

CLINICAL INTERVIEW

A most frequent and widely used tool usually is the first step in the assessment process.[11,66] Although the interview is an essential element for obtaining case history information and providing contextual data needed to understand persons from diverse cultures, it is subject to bias and errors arising out of characteristics of both the client and the clinician. Clinicians unfamiliar with an individual's culture, worldview, and language may misunderstand and incorrectly record information needed for appropriate diagnosis.[46] Negative reactions to cultural differences and racial or ethnic stereotypes may also adversely affect clinicians' ability to establish rapport and lead to misdiagnosis. Due to cultural norms, some individuals may be reluctant to divulge personal information to a stranger[66] or may be distrustful of authority figures. Chinese Americans, for example, may be hesitant to initiate conversation out of respect for the clinician's authoritative role and be reluctant to disclose personal difficulties, which should not be misinterpreted as a sign of defensiveness.[15] To counteract the limitations of the interview, clinicians should obtain information from a variety of sources,[43] such as family members, educational and medical records, and persons in the client's community.

When interviewing immigrants, clinicians should obtain information about a number of variables, including age at the time of immigration, generation level, previous occupation, educational background, and acculturation with the new country. Individuals who have recently immigrated experience a period of adjustment, and the process of adapting to a new country may even produce culture shock and a sense of disorientation,[17] which could affect their behavior in the interview. Clinicians must maintain awareness of these issues to help prevent misdiagnosis.

CLINICAL DIAGNOSIS

In a review of the literature, Gray-Little and Kaplan[36] noted a link between ethnicity and diagnoses, finding that "race and ethnicity are sometimes predictive of diagnosis, independent of symptoms."[p. 142]

Studies over a 30-year period indicate that Whites are diagnosed with affective and personality disorders more often than African Americans. Asian Americans are more likely to be diagnosed with affective disorders, and African Americans are more likely to be diagnosed with schizophrenia, even among patients of similar socioeconomic status. The reasons for these findings are not clear. Clinical judgment bias has been implicated as one possible source, though Gray-Little and Kaplan[36] found inconsistent results in their review of the literature, with some studies indicating that ethnic minorities are sometimes over-diagnosed and sometimes under-diagnosed. They concluded that overall, patients' race or ethnicity had an impact on clinical judgment beyond what would be warranted on the basis of symptoms. In the assessment of persons with disability, clinical judgment may be distorted by prejudices and stereotypes, causing clinicians to assume maladjustment and then elicit information from the client that only serves to confirm their prior assumptions, rather than seeking evidence to the contrary; thus resulting in over-diagnosis. In contrast, under-diagnosis may occur due to a process called diagnostic overshadowing, in which the clinician ignores potential signs of psychopathology because they are overshadowed by characteristics of the disability.[57]

Clinical judgment errors may also be caused by the clinician's lack of knowledge of culturally based behaviors and folk beliefs (e.g., beliefs in the presence of spirits, "evil eye," and hexes), which could be misconstrued as symptoms of psychopathology.[60,61] Hays[43] maintains that one of the greatest challenges to the clinician in cross-cultural assessment is to differentiate behaviors and ways of thinking that are culturally normal from those that are pathological. Language differences also may complicate the diagnostic process. In a review of the literature, Paniagua[61] found studies indicating that clients were assigned higher ratings of psychopathology when interviewed in English rather than in their first language.

Numerous studies have also documented cultural variations in how individuals express distress,[84] and one of the most robust findings is that Asian Americans and Hispanic patients are more likely to report physical symptoms when they are depressed, as compared to European Americans.[36] Research of Asian Americans suggests these patterns become more similar to those of

European Americans with increased acculturation.[40] Dana[23] describes five types of psychological distress in multicultural populations (1) disorders that are general and correspond to the categories of the Diagnostic and Statistical Manual of Mental Disorders - IV (DSM-IV),[3] such as 1. depression and schizophrenia, though the symptoms may be expressed differently; 2. culture-bound syndromes; 3. everyday living problems; 4. difficulties caused by societal oppression; and 5. symptoms associated with acculturative stress, that is, difficulties in adapting to the mores and worldviews of the new host culture.[51] Some racial/ethnic groups have had different experiences of discrimination and prejudice that could influence their expressions of distress. African Americans, for example, have had unique experiences compared to other ethnic groups, with a history of oppression accompanied by violence that has generated coping and adaptation strategies needed for survival within a dehumanizing sociopolitical system.[54]

Implications of these culturally based expressions of symptoms are that the DSM-IV's descriptions of symptomotology according to diagnostic categories may not provide an accurate fit for persons from diverse cultures.[36] The fourth edition of the DSM (1994), however, is an improvement over previous versions in that it provides a description of cultural variations of symptoms for some disorders, a listing and description of culture-bound syndromes, and cultural formulation guidelines to help the clinician take into account the client's cultural context. These cultural formulations comprise five categories: cultural identity; cultural explanation of illness; cultural factors related to psychosocial environment and level of functioning; cultural elements of the relationship between the clinician and the client; and overall cultural assessment for diagnosis and care.[61]

PSYCHOLOGICAL TESTING

An important issue in testing involves the cultural equivalence of the traits and abilities test instruments are designed to measure. Just as there are cultural differences in expressions of distress, some research suggests that, through a process of learning and adaptation, the environment influences how individuals' abilities develop from one culture to another. As a consequence, cultures may assign different meanings to various traits and do not necessarily share Western notions of what intelligent behavior is.[38] Sternberg and Grigorenko,[76] for example, noted that their research in Kenya suggested that its inhabitants place more value on social skills as an aspect of intelligence than do individuals in the United States. As Anastasi and Urbina[7] point out, psychological tests represent a sample of behavior, and since behavior is shaped by the culture in which an individual develops, "cultural influences will and should be reflected in test performance."[p.342] This implies a reciprocal association in that standardized tests will measure characteristics that are valued by the majority culture in which the tests are developed[38,71] and may not assess behavior that is characteristic of individuals from minority cultures.[74] In addition, the constructs the tests measure may have different meanings among persons of different cultures.

Standardized testing may present concerns for individuals who received their schooling outside the U.S., especially in a developing country. Some immigrants may have received extremely limited education, or their schooling may have differed significantly from that provided in the U.S. These immigrants are less likely to have had experiences with tests designed to measure cognitive abilities and may be unfamiliar with such tasks. When working with these individuals, clinicians should exercise considerable caution in interpreting test results.[72]

TEST BIAS

Given that most commonly used tests are designed on the basis of European American culture, bias in testing is an issue of concern in the psychological assessment of individuals from diverse cultures who differ from the group upon which the tests were standardized.[58] Even when different racial/ethnic groups are included in a test's standardization group, the sample is often too small and lacks controls regarding acculturation level (Dana, 2000). Test bias refers to whether a test is valid for different groups in a differential way; for example, if it underestimates the future performance of a group.[6,36] Bias may have an impact on test scores in the following ways:

> Construct bias, that is, when a construct has different meanings across cultural groups;

> Item bias, which occurs if individuals respond differently to test items because of cultural variables, even though they have the same amount of the particular trait being measured; and

> Method bias, which may be present in test procedures and administration format.[21,80]

Consequences of test bias include diagnostic errors, such as misdiagnosis,[60] inappropriate educational placements (for example, a disproportionate number of minority students placed in special education programs), and under-prediction of scholastic or occupational potential.

Instruments designed to assess personality and psychopathology have been developed in recent years that include racial and ethnic minorities in standardization samples. The re-standardized edition of the Minnesota Multiphasic Personality Inventory (MMPI-2), for example, was published in 1989 after 10 years of research and gathered a larger normative sample that included proportional representation of diverse populations, based on U.S. Census data.[41] Due to population changes since that time, Hispanics and Asian Americans are now under-represented,[82] Handel and Ben-Porath,[41] in summarizing studies of the MMPI-2 between 1994 and 1998, find that the MMPI-2 appears to be applicable to African Americans in a variety of settings, but more research is needed for other ethnic groups. Other reviews of MMPI-2 research[36,82] note a tendency for Latinos to score higher than White respondents on the L (Lie) scale, one of the validity scales designed to assess test-taking attitudes.[37] This may be interpreted not as a tendency towards deception, but perhaps to present oneself in a socially desirable manner. Individuals from some Latin American countries may have experienced authoritarian and repressive sociopolitical systems[21,19] that, perhaps, could produce a socially desirable response pattern. Clinicians need to be aware that most ethnic groups are not homogeneous[40] and research on many groups, such as Latinos, should be examined as subgroups, rather than as one large category.[41] Acculturation may also have an impact on MMPI-2 results.[40,82] Cuellar[19] suggests that individuals who are less acculturated, especially when combined with a lower socioeconomic status and education, tend to obtain higher scores on measures of psychopathology.

The MMPI-2 may be problematic for individuals with physical disabilities because some clinical scales comprise questions about physical symptoms, and elevations on these scales may reflect realistic consideration of physical concerns rather than psychological difficulties,[26,57] though more research in this area is needed.[43] Rodevich and Wanlass[69] investigated the effects of a T-score correction procedure for the MMPI-2 for individuals with spinal cord injury. They found that before using the correction procedure, the average scores of participants reflected varying degrees of maladjustment or other psychological problems. After using the correction procedure, they found that as a group, the participants would now be seen as being emotionally well adjusted. In a review of studies using the MMPI and MMPI-2 for individuals with vision impairment, Harrington and McDermott[42] noted a tendency toward elevations on Depression and Social Introversion scales that could be attributed to the disability rather than psychopathology, due to bias in test content, and they advised caution in interpreting MMPI results for this population.

The MMPI's usefulness is extremely limited with deaf individuals because its eighth grade-level reading requirements surpass the reading skills of the average deaf high school graduate, and it has biases in content for deaf examinees.[14] Translation into American Sign Language (ASL) of critical items of the MMPI has suggested this to be a promising area for further research into the applicability of a translated version of the MMPI-2.[13] The use of standardized personality tests for deaf individuals is a complex issue, requiring knowledge about deafness, deaf culture, and the individual's case history. Vernon[83] noted the possibility that deafness may affect environmental experiences and produce "an essentially different organization of personality and make normality for a person who is deaf or hard of hearing different from normality for a person with no difficulty hearing."[p.389] Brauer, et al.,[14] describe research findings suggesting that clinicians who were not knowledgeable of deafness and who relied on instruments that were not adapted for use with deaf individuals were more likely to incorrectly diagnose personality aberrations than clinicians who were experienced with this population.

The issue of test bias has been especially controversial regarding cognitive ability testing, as research over a period of many years has indicated significant between-group differences among various racial and ethnic groups. East Asian and Jewish examinees are usually at the top, followed by Caucasians, Hispanics, and African Americans, with the latter groups score often falling one standard deviation below that of Caucasians.[78] The issue has been complicated by the fact that numerous studies to evaluate test bias, usually through regression models comparing intelligence test scores to a criterion such as academic performance, have failed to find evidence of bias. These findings have led many researchers to conclude that, at least on the basis of psychometric data, test bias does not exist because many cognitive ability tests predict various educational and employment performances about equally well for persons from both majority and minority cultures.[16,31,39]

In some instances, studies have suggested that these tests tend to overpredict future performance of diverse populations.[73] In a literature review of studies examining racial/ethnic differences on intelligence tests, Suzuki and Valencia[77] noticed a decline in studies of test bias over the years, perhaps due to a belief that the controversy had been settled. They cite mixed results of previous research and suggest that this issue is not yet resolved. The researchers noted that comparisons between racial/ethnic groups are misleading because the within-group differences are usually greater, with socioeconomic status (SES) often being a major factor in these differences (both within and between groups). Since intelligence tests are more likely to tap experiences and values based on middle-class European culture, ethnic minorities who have grown up in a different cultural environment could be expected to be at a disadvantage.[46] Moreover, the criteria used for assessing predictive validity, such as school performance and occupation may be biased, considering the limitations imposed by society's opportunity structure.[77]

Remedies for test bias will not be easily accomplished. The goal of developing culture-free tests seems elusive thus far and may be impossible to achieve.[45,60] Test developers have attempted for many years to design tests that minimize the impact of culture, usually in the form of nonverbal measures. Even nonverbal test performance has been found to be influenced by culture, perhaps because nonverbal tests involve abstract reasoning skills that are valued in Eurocentric cultures; while persons from other cultures may favor an approach to problem solving that is more contextually based.[7] Developing culture-specific tests and norms for different ethnic groups is a first step in minimizing test bias but has the disadvantage of preventing comparisons across cultures. Cultures are constantly changing, with differing levels of acculturation, so that norms may soon become outdated.[80] Obtaining norms from different ethnic groups may also be impractical. Asian and Pacific

Islanders, for example, represent 28 different countries[43] with marked cultural and language differences between these groups and each having its own unique history.[48] In recent years, advanced test development methods have sought to minimize bias through using expert panels to examine item content, including different racial/ethnic groups in the standardization sample, and applying statistical techniques to examine test performance and differential responding among groups.[78]

Criterion-referenced scores may help minimize the impact of test bias by allowing comparison to a performance standard, rather than to a norm group. Criterion-referenced scores would provide a measure of what the individual knows or can do and determine if this matches the performance standard (for example, math skills required in a particular job). Instead of focusing only on prediction of performance, the criterion-referenced approach would allow clinicians to identify deficient areas and recommend strategies for improvement that would enable the individual to meet the performance standard.[71]

Another solution to test bias has been offered by Cuellar[19] who suggests that data regarding an examinee's acculturation level may be used as a moderator of personality and other psychological assessment measures to correct for test bias. Acculturation data allows the assessor to determine how well psychological test scores predict behavior for persons who are not well represented in standardization samples; using the acculturation score as a moderator, the assessor can raise or lower the individual's score. For example, the Acculturation Rating Scale for Mexican Americans[20,] cited by Zane & Mak, 2003) has been used to correct the tendency of the MMPI to over-diagnose pathology among Latinos. Cuellar[19] proposes applying an Index for Correction of Culture (ICC), which is based on the correlation between the examinee's acculturation score and the criterion for a particular group. The ICC shows how different the examinee is from the normative sample, so that the assessor can adjust test scores accordingly. In practice, however, clinicians rarely have the quantitative data needed to apply this correction procedure and must instead rely on clinical judgment. In addition, in a review of 21 instruments designed to measure acculturation, Zane and Mak (2003) remarked that most were for Hispanic Americans, with only a few designed for Asian/Pacific Islanders and African Americans, thereby limiting clinicians' resources for applying a correction for culture to test results.

TEST TRANSLATION

Test translation involves more than an accurate linguistic translation; it requires determining whether and how the psychological construct is understood across cultures. For example, a concept may be understood differently among different cultural groups or may not be meaningful to a group for whom a test is being translated.[8] To ensure accurate translation, a test should be "back translated," that is, translated back into the original language from the translated version. Achieving high-quality translations can be very costly and, according to Padilla,[58] "few tests are ever translated for use with limited English speakers."[p. 21] An important concept in multicultural assessment is that of "etic" versus "emic" assessment instruments.[22] Etic instruments are those that are developed from outside the culture in which they are being applied; they are often incorrectly assumed to be universally applicable. In contrast, emic instruments are developed from within the culture in which they are being used and, therefore, measure traits that are meaningful to that culture.[49] Instruments must also demonstrate cultural equivalence, which is defined according to four categories 1. functional equivalence, or the role that a behavior or trait plays in different cultures; 2. conceptual equivalence, or the similarities in meaning associated with behaviors and constructs; 3. metric equivalence, a psychometric property requiring that a measurement scale assesses the same trait across cultures; and 4. linguistic equivalence, or appropriate translation of the test.[29,49]

TEST SELECTION

Before selecting tests or procedures to use in the assessment, clinicians should first obtain thorough background information about the client, including medical information, educational background, level of acculturation, English proficiency, and how recently the client immigrated to the U.S.[78] English proficiency by itself may not be sufficient, as clinicians still need to ascertain the client's preferred language for assessment.[81] After gathering this information, they can determine whether or not standardized testing is appropriate. If testing appears to be appropriate, they should proceed cautiously, beginning with a careful reading of the manual for each test being considered. Particular attention should be paid to the examination of norm groups (for example, to see if they include the client's race/ethnic group), and information about validity and reliability. If a test has not been used with diverse populations, clinicians should find out if other tests or procedures would be more suitable.[35] Clinicians also need to ensure that the test does not require skills or behaviors that the examinee has not had the opportunity to perform or learn.[27]

Appropriate test selection is also important in vocational assessment, a common type of psychological testing often used to help individuals make career decisions by providing them with information about their interests, values, aptitudes, and skills.[33] When applied to culturally diverse populations, the counselor needs to keep in mind that vocational counseling is influenced by the values of European American culture with its emphasis on individualism, linear style of decision-making, and success in the competitive labor market.[29] The counselor needs to be aware that these values may be counter to those of clients from diverse cultures and be respectful of these differences.

Vocational tests, such as interest and values inventories, enable counselors to obtain information efficiently and help provide career direction, but they may be subject to bias because they do not represent the experiences of persons from diverse cultures. The career development theories, upon which these tests are based, with their focus on individualism, may not be applicable to persons from collectivistic cultures.[33] Although studies of cross-cultural interest assessment have produced mixed results over the past 20 years,[24] findings in recent years have been positive. In a 1993 review of research on the use of interest inventories across cultures, Fouad[30] noted that, compared to European Americans, African Americans tended to have more Social-Enterprising-Conventional interests (based on Holland's career development model of six occupational themes). Higher scores in sales, social services, business, and verbal-linguistic areas suggest differences in the development and expression of interests. In contrast, in their large sample size (49,450) investigation of the applicability of Holland's model for five racial/ethnic groups, Day and Rounds[24] found similar interest structure among the groups, suggesting that it is universal. Using an ethnically diverse sample of both professionals and students who took the Strong Interest Inventory, Fouad[30] found only a small effect size for race/ethnicity on Holland's occupational themes, with greater within-group differences (due to sex and age) than between-group differences based on ethnicity.

These findings suggested that the Strong Interest Inventory could be useful with diverse populations. In an extensive review of 44 career assessment instruments, including nine interest inventories, Eby and Russell[25] concluded that most of the inventories could be useful for culturally diverse individuals (including persons with disabilities). They cautioned that few of the instruments reviewed provided reliability or validity information regarding diverse populations. In addition, they recommended that more research was needed to validate career assessment instruments for diverse populations as well as to develop instruments for specific groups. Gainor[33] likewise advised caution when interpreting results of interest inventories for individuals from diverse cultures. Results need to be viewed within a cultural context, including the impact of acculturation and ethnic identity.

Interest inventories developed specifically for individuals with physical or mental disabilities are lacking,[64] and few studies have examined the potential impact of a disability on vocational interests. One exception, a 1982 study by Rohe and Athelstan, found that individuals with spinal cord injury tended to have job interests which were inconsistent with their physical limitations, suggesting that clinicians may need to be creative in helping persons with physical disabilities identify vocational options that are congruent with both their interests and capabilities.

TEST-TAKING BEHAVIOR

Cultural factors can influence test-taking behavior[7] and the clinician should take into account the potential impact of cultural factors on test performance.[53] Test-taking performance may be affected by motivation as well as by culture-related behaviors such as work speed, cooperativeness, familiarity with testing, and a tendency to give socially desirable responses (Lonner, 1985). Individuals who received their schooling outside the U.S. in a developing country, or those who received little schooling, may be unfamiliar with testing expectations and common test formats[72] and are likely to be at a serious disadvantage when taking cognitive tests, even those designed to be culture-fair.

Motivation is an important variable in test performance. For many ethnic groups, especially for individuals from a lower socioeconomic level, tests may be seen as a repetition of failure experiences and they may see little likelihood of success.[71] Such expectations may affect motivation to perform well, as research suggests that expectations influence motivation in testing; when individuals believe they have a chance of succeeding if they apply effort, they are more likely to do their best (Katz,[47] cited by Samuda).[71] Smart and Smart[74] suggest that Hispanics may not be acculturated to the assessment process and not understand the relevance of testing, which affects motivation level. Clinicians can promote the motivation of Hispanic clients by explaining the practical usefulness of assessment and its future benefits. Both Hispanics[74] and African Americans[33] may be distrustful of the assessment process due to prior negative experiences with testing and with public institutions. Clinicians can help reduce distrust by being open about this issue, establishing rapport, and trying to understand Hispanics worldview.[1] By taking the time to ensure informed consent, clinicians may also alleviate distrust by fully explaining the assessment process so that clients know what to expect and how the test results will be used.

Fear of failure may also occur, resulting in a tendency to avoid challenging situations, or to give up.[1] Characteristics of the assessment setting itself may have a strong impact on test motivation. Morris,[53] for example, suggests that if African American clients view the setting or clinician as being antagonistic or intimidating, they may "sabotage their own performance during the assessment process."[p. 577] Compounded by fears of failure and negative past experiences, such a setting can generate feelings of anxiety that impair test performance.[71] Cultural stereotypes may also have an impact on motivation and test performance through internalized negative expectations and diminished self-concept.[7,1]

Testing response styles may be strongly influenced by cultural factors. Hispanics may see the clinician as an authority figure, resulting in a tendency to acquiesce and to provide socially desirable responses.[74] Social desirability may also be reflected in test responses of Asian Americans arising from a need not to lose face.[33] Some ethnic groups, especially Hispanics[72] and African Americans,[1] may be at a disadvantage on speeded tests because time is given less emphasis in these cultures than in European American culture. Having different orientations to time, these individuals may work at their own pace with a focus on quality rather than time constraints. This approach results in fewer correct items and thus a lower score, even though most items answered may be correct.[1] Individuals from diverse cultures are also more likely to omit items, rather than guessing.[72] Since omitted items are considered incorrect in many cognitive tests, this response style means that results may not reflect their potential, especially for cognitive tests that have cut-off points after a certain number of incorrect answers. Clinicians can try to reduce these problems by observing clients' response styles during practice sessions for tests or by providing additional practice, when feasible, and by ensuring that clients understand the importance of working quickly and answering as many items as possible.[1]

ISSUES IN THE ASSESSMENT PROCESS FOR PERSONS WITH DISABILITIES

Test fairness and validity, appropriateness of norms, and provision of test accommodations are particular issues of concern in the assessment process of individuals with disabilities. Clinicians cannot assume equivalence of test content if a test requires certain skills that are affected by the disability.[35] Legal requirements, beginning with Section 504 of the Rehabilitation Act of 1973, which stipulate that programs receiving federal assistance to provide accommodations to individuals with disabilities to ensure equality in access and program participation,[63] mandate consideration of test equivalence and fairness for persons with disabilities. These requirements were expanded to the private sector with the Americans with Disabilities Act (ADA) of 1990, which was applicable to employers with more than 15 employees. Provisions of the ADA mandate physical accessibility of assessment programs and test formats that allow persons with disabilities to demonstrate skills and knowledge related to job functions.[67] Assessors should, therefore, provide modifications of tests or test administration, such as time limits, unless these modifications invalidate measurement of the skill the test is designed to assess.[65]

TEST FAIRNESS AND VALIDITY
    Clinicians may need to change how a test is given to ensure test fairness, particularly with regard to test content and the skills needed to perform the test. Deviations from standardized administration, however, can adversely affect test reliability and validity.[65] The key to appropriate accommodation is to provide enhanced access while preserving the validity of test results.[9] A first step in this process is proper test selection; that is, clinicians should consider the skill requirements of the test, such as ability to read, turn pages, and manipulate objects.[65] If a test requires abilities that the individual does not have, then the test is measuring disability, rather than the intended construct. Provision of appropriate test modifications requires clinicians to be knowledgeable about disabilities and the types of accommodations that are available. Smith[75] provides a series of guidelines to assist clinicians in identifying testing accommodations. These include an identification of the client's receptive and

expressive skills (including motoric response), followed by an examination of the receptive and expressive skills required by the selected tests. If these skills do not match, then clinicians should determine what modifications are needed and if these modifications will compromise the validity of test results.

TEST ACCOMMODATIONS

The 1999 Standards for Educational and Psychological Testing (AERA, APA, & NCME) suggest the following strategies for test modifications:

- Presentation format (for example, Braille or large print for individuals with vision impairment and verbal instructions provided in manual communication for persons who are deaf);

- Response format (such as dictating answers to a scribe or into a tape recorder);

- Test timing, such as extended time limits;

- Test setting, such as individual administration instead of group administration for someone with attentional difficulties, and providing special lighting for an examinee with vision impairment;

- Using only portions of tests, for example, selected sections of a cognitive test battery;

- Using substitute tests, such as a test designed specifically for individuals with disabilities.

Extended time is the most frequently used accommodation.[63] Bradley-Johnson and Ekstrom[12] advise clinicians not to use timed tests for individuals with vision impairment, as reading large print takes additional time, and Braille may take two and a half times longer, depending on the person's level of proficiency. Sirici and Geisinger[73] suggest additional accommodations that may be appropriate for persons with learning disabilities as well as for individuals with psychiatric disabilities or metabolic disorders: providing more frequent breaks, presenting instructions or test questions aloud, and allowing use of a computer or calculator.

Due to a lack of research, the impact of test modifications on the assessment of persons with disabilities is largely unknown. One concern is to ensure that accommodated tests provide more accurate results than those that are not accommodated. Modifications may make a test easier or more difficult for the individual with a disability when compared to nondisabled examinees of comparable ability, thus affecting the ability of the test to predict future performance. For example, although extended time may be needed to ensure test fairness, it could also cause fatigue and thereby impair test performance.[65] Certain types of accommodations may hinder clinicians' ability to measure the intended construct of the test, such as reading questions aloud for tests designed to assess reading comprehension and removing or extending time limits for tests in which part of the construct being measured is speed.[73]

The 1999 Standards advise clinicians to "pilot test" modifications when possible, but in reality, this is seldom done. Studies of test accommodations for persons with disabilities are complicated due to 1. small sample sizes, especially for certain disabilities, resulting in a lack of quantitative data[67] 2. group variability, and 3. accommodations variability,[63] which may include a combination of different types of accommodations, such as large print test format and extended time limits. Of the limited research that is available, most studies have examined results of accommodations on high stakes tests, such as the Scholastic Aptitude Test (SAT) or Graduate Record Examination (GRE). These studies were conducted during the 1980s and are described by Willingham, et al.[85] According to Pullin,[67] since that time, there has been "little validity research on modifications to address disabilities."[p. 26]

Lusting and Saura[50] suggest a potential solution to the validity issues raised by test modifications in that they outline a structured procedure for accommodations using criterion-referenced tests. This procedure could be applied in vocational assessment to predict work performance. It would allow the clinician to match test accommodations to the types of accommodations that could be provided in a work setting. With this criterion-based procedure, the client's test performance with accommodations can be compared to the knowledge and skill requirements of a job rather than through comparison to a norm group, which may be invalid, depending on the nature of the test modification.

Another assessment issue involves the debate about whether clinicians should use general or special norms when assessing individuals with disabilities. Comparison of an individual's test scores with a norm group that shares similar characteristics and for which predictive validity is available enables clinicians to make more accurate predictions about future behavior. Most tests, however, do not include persons with disabilities in the normative sample, or if they do, they are small in number.[65] Practical issues may also make development of such norms unlikely, given the problems with sample size and the heterogeneity of individuals with disabilities. This issue becomes especially problematic for individuals with visual impairment because they may require significant test modifications, and individuals with early-onset vision loss may have had different experiences from sighted individuals on whom the norms are based, which could make the norms of ability and personality tests inapplicable for this population.[34] Very few tests provide standardized norms for persons with vision impairment, and those that are available usually are not new, as few have been published within the last 15 years.[12] One recent exception is the Cognitive Test for the Blind, which has shown promise as a useful instrument in assessing the intellectual capabilities of this population.[56]

SPECIAL NORMS

Parker[62] suggests that a solution to the norms problem is to look at test scores as being descriptive, rather than predictive. If clinicians want to describe where a person stands in relation to a norm group, both general and special norms are acceptable. Normative scores become a problem when they are inappropriately used for predictive purposes, as prediction should be based on statistical data, such as regression equations. The purpose of testing will determine norms selection; for example, clinicians may need to compare an examinee's performance to norms of persons without disabilities when this is the context in which the person will be expected to perform, such as an educational or job setting.[65] The 1999 Standards also indicate that regular norms may be used when comparison with the general population is needed. As already noted, test accommodations may substantially alter the test procedures upon which the test is standardized, which could make comparison to standardized competitive norms inappropriate. Competitive norms may underestimate the abilities of persons with disabilities.[10] Some rehabilitation facilities have addressed this problem by developing local client norms, but Berven[10] pointed out that this approach might lead to overestimation of abilities. He proposed a solution that could overcome the disadvantages of using either competitive or local norms: "If clients were followed-up after completing assessment, different client subpopulations could be defined on the basis of training or employment outcomes, and norms could be established for those various subgroups."[p. 61] Such norms would allow comparison to a norm group of similar individuals who experienced successful outcomes in various training programs, jobs, or other areas of concern. Development of these norms, however, would require a sufficiently large group of individuals.

CONCLUSION

We provided a general overview on psychological assessment. As noted, the process of psychological assessment is a multifaceted procedure. The added complexities of understanding an individual who is from a diverse background make psychological assessment a challenging task, especially given the impact of the results and recommendations for clinical and rehabilitation practice. Culturally sensitive rehabilitation professionals should be aware of the limitations of psychological assessment practices, from intakes to the use of standardized assessment instruments[18,44,68] and safeguard themselves from testing bias and misinterpretation of test results. In addition to knowing the "dos" and "don'ts," rehabilitation professionals should be aware of their own worldview and attitudes toward those who are different from them. As pointed out by Fiske[28] there is a tendency, often unconscious, to exaggerate differences between groups and similarities within one group and favor one's in-group over the out-group. This becomes problematic when one group holds much more power than the other group. It is quite common for the in-group to form automatic biases and stereotypic attitudes about people in the out-group.

The American Psychological Association[4] warns that automatic biases and attitudes may lead to miscommunication, since normative behavior in one context may not be necessarily understood or valued in another. Rehabilitation professionals should realize that the responsibility of selecting, administering, and interpreting test results in a culturally sensitive manner remains with themselves. It is our hope that issues and considerations discussed in this chapter would heighten rehabilitation professionals' multicultural awareness and sensitivity and assist them in performing psychological assessments in a culturally sensitive manner.

REFERENCES

[1] Alston, R. J. & McCowan, C. J. (1994). Aptitude assessment and African American clients: The interplay between culture and psychometrics in rehabilitation. *Journal of Rehabilitation, 60* (1), 41-46.

[2] American Educational Research Association, American Psychological Association, & National Council on Measurement in Education (1999). *Standards for educational and psychological testing* (2nd ed.). Washington, DC: American Educational Research Association.

[3] American Psychiatric Association. (1994). *Diagnostic and statistical manual of mental disorders* (4th ed.). Washington D.C.: Author.

[4] American Psychological Association. (1990). Guidelines for providers of psychological services to ethnic, linguistic, and culturally diverse populations. Retrieved March 1, 2003 from http://www.apa.org/pi/oema/guide.html

[5] American Psychological Association. (1992). Ethical principles of psychologists and code of conduct. Washington, DC: Author.

[6] Anastasi, A. (1992). What counselors should know about the use and interpretation of psychological tests. *Journal of Counseling & Development, 70*, 610-615.

[7] Anastasi, A., & Urbina, S. (1997). *Psychological testing* (7th ed.). Upper Saddle River, NJ: Prentice Hall.

[8] Arnold, B. R., & Matus, Y. E. (2000). Test translation and cultural equivalence methodologies for use with diverse populations. In I. Cuellar & F. A. Paniagua (Eds.), *Handbook of multicultural mental health* (pp.121-136). San Diego, CA: Academic Press.

[9] Behuniak, P. (2002). Types of commonly requested accommodations. In R. B. Ekstrom & D. K. Smith (Eds.), *Assessing individuals with disabilities in educational, employment, and counseling settings* (pp. 45-58). Washington, DC: American Psychological Association.

[10]Berven, N. L. (1980). Psychometric assessment in rehabilitation. In B. Bolton & D. W. Cook (Eds.), *Rehabilitation client assessment* (pp. 46-64). Baltimore: University Park Press.

[11]Berven, N. L. (2001). Assessment interviewing. In B. F. Bolton (Ed.), *Handbook of measurement and evaluation in rehabilitation* (3rd ed., pp. 197-213). Gaithersburg, MD: Aspen.

[12]Bradley-Johnson, S., & Ekstrom, R. (1998). Visual impairments. In J. Sandoval, C. L. Frisby, K. F. Geisinger, J. D. Scheuneman, & J. R. Grenier (Eds.), *Test interpretation and diversity: Achieving equity in assessment* (pp.271-295). Washington, DC: American Psychological Association.

[13]Brauer, B. A. (1992). The signer effect on MMPI performance of deaf respondents. *Journal of Personality Assessment, 58*(2), 380-388.

[14]Brauer, B. A., Braden, J. P., Pollard, R. Q., & Hardy-Braz, S. T. (1998). Deaf and hard of hearing people. In J. Sandoval, C. L. Frisby, K. F. Geisinger, J. D. Scheuneman, & J. R. Grenier (Eds.), *Test interpretation and diversity: Achieving equity in assessment* (pp.297-315). Washington, DC: American Psychological Association.

[15]Chan, F., Lam, C. S., Wong, D., Leung, P., & Fang, X. (1988). Counseling Chinese Americans with disabilities. *Journal of Applied Rehabilitation Counseling 19*(4), 21-25.

[16]Cole, N. S. (1981). Bias in testing. *American Psychologist, 36*, 1067-1077.

[17]Comas-Diaz, L., & Grenier, J. R. (1998). Migration and acculturation. In J. Sandoval, C. L. Frisby, K. F. Geisinger, J. D. Scheuneman, & J. R. Grenier (Eds.), *Test interpretation and diversity: Achieving equity in assessment* (pp.231-239). Washington, DC: American Psychological Association.

[18]Constantine, M. (1998). Developing competence in multicultural assessment: Implications for counseling psychology training and practice. *The Counseling Psychologist, 6,* 922-929.

[19]Cuellar, I. (2000). Acculturation as a moderator of personality and psychological assessment. In R. H. Dana (Ed.), *Handbook of cross-cultural and multicultural personality assessment* (pp. 113-1129). Mahwah, NJ: Lawrence Erlbaum Associates.

[20]Cuellar, I., Arnold, B., & Maldonado, R. (1995). Acculturation Rating Scale for Mexican Americans -II: A revision of the original ARSMA scale. *Hispanic Journal of Behavioral Sciences, 17*, 275-304.

[21]Dana, R. H. (2000). Culture and methodology in personality assessment. In I. Cuellar & F.A.

[22]Dana, R. H. (2001a). Multicultural issues in assessment. In B. F. Bolton (Ed.), *Handbook of measurement and evaluation in rehabilitation* (pp. 449-469). Gaithersburg, MD: Aspen.

[23]Dana, R. H. (2001b). Clinical diagnosis of multicultural populations in the United States. In L. A. Suzuki, J. G. Ponterotto, & P. J. Meller (Eds.), *Handbook of multicultural assessment* (2nd ed., pp. 101-131). San Francisco: Jossey-Bass.

[24]Day, S. X & Rounds, J. (1998). Universality of vocational interest structure among racial and ethnic minorities. *American Psychologist, 53*(7), 728-736.
[25]Eby, L. T., & Russell, J. E. A. (1998). A psychometric review of career assessment tools for use with diverse individuals. *Journal of Career Assessment, 6*(3), 269-310.
[26]Elliott, T. R., & Umlauf, R. L. (1995). Measurement of personality and psychopathology following acquired physical disability. In L.A. Cushman & M. J. Scherer (Eds.), *Psychological assessment in medical rehabilitation* (pp. 325-358). Washington, DC: American Psychological Association.
[27]Feist-Price, S., Harley, D. A., & Alston, R. J. (1996). A cross-cultural perspective for vocational evaluation and assessment. *Vocational Evaluation and Work Adjustment Association Bulletin, 29* (2), 48-54.
[28]Fiske, S. T. (1998). Stereotyping, prejudice, and discrimination. In D. T. Gilbert & S. T. Fiske (Eds.), *The handbook of social psychology, Vol. 2* (4th ed., pp.357-411). New York: McGraw-Hill.
[29]Fouad, N. A. (1993). Cross-cultural vocational assessment. *Career Development Quarterly, 42,* 4-13.
[30]Fouad, N. A. (2002). Cross-cultural differences in vocational interests: Between-groups differences on the Strong Interest Inventory. *Journal of Counseling Psychology, 49*(3), 283-289.
[31]Frisby, C. L. (1998a). Culture and cultural differences. In J. Sandoval, C. L. Frisby, K. F. Geisinger, J. D. Scheuneman, & J. R. Grenier (Eds.), *Test interpretation and diversity: Achieving equity in assessment* (pp.51-73). Washington, DC: American Psychological Association.
[32]Frisby, C. L. (1998b). Poverty and socioeconomic status. In J. Sandoval, C. L. Frisby, K. F. Geisinger, J. D. Scheuneman, & J. R. Grenier (Eds.), *Test interpretation and diversity: Achieving equity in assessment* (pp.241-270). Washington, DC: American Psychological Association.
[33]Gainor, K. A. (2001). Vocational assessment with culturally diverse populations. In L. A. Suzuki, J. G. Ponterotto, & P. J. Meller (Eds.), *Handbook of multicultural assessment* (2nd ed., pp. 169-189). San
[34]Gallagher, J. T. & Wiener, W. R. (2001). Assessment of individuals with visual impairment. In B. F. Bolton (Ed.), *Handbook of measurement and evaluation in rehabilitation* (pp. 365-384). Gaithersburg, MD: Aspen.
[35]Geisinger, K. F. (1998). Psychometric issues in test interpretation. In J. Sandoval, C. L. Frisby, K. F. Geisinger, J. D. Scheuneman, & J. R. Grenier (Eds.), *Test interpretation and diversity: Achieving equity in assessment* (pp.17-30). Washington, DC: American Psychological Association.
[36]Gray-Little, B. & Kaplan, D. A. (1998). Interpretation of psychological tests in clinical and forensic evaluations. In J. Sandoval, C. L. Frisby, K. F. Geisinger, J. D. Scheuneman, & J. R. Grenier (Eds.), *Test interpretation and diversity: Achieving equity in assessment* (pp.141-178). Washington, DC: American Psychological Association.

[37] Greene, R. L. (1991). *MMPI-2/MMPI: An interpretive manual.* Needham Heights, MA: Allyn & Bacon.

[38] Greenfield, P. M. (1997). You can't take it with you: Why ability assessments don't cross cultures. *American Psychologist, 52*(10), 1115-1124.

[39] Hale, R. L. (1991). Intellectual assessment. In M. Hersen, A. E. Kazdin, & A. S. Bellack (Eds.), *The Clinical Psychology Handbook* (2nd ed., pp. 374-405). Elmsford, NY: Pergamon Press.

[40] Hall, G. C. N., & Phung, A. H. (2001). Minnesota Multiphasic Personality Inventory and Millon Clinical Multiaxial Inventory. In L.A. Suzuki, J. G. Ponterotto, & P. J. Meller (Eds.), *Handbook of multicultural assessment* (2nd ed., pp. 307-330). San Francisco: Jossey-Bass.

[41] Handel, R. W., & Ben-Porath, Y. S. (2000). Multicultural assessment with the MMPI-2: Issues for research and practice. In R. H. Dana (Ed.), *Handbook of cross-cultural and multicultural personality assessment* (pp. 229-245). Mahwah, NJ: Lawrence Erlbaum Associates.

[42] Harrington, R. G., & McDermott, D. (1993). A model for the interpretation of personality assessments of individuals with visual impairments. *Journal of Rehabilitation, 59*(4), 24-29.

[43] Hays, P. A. (2001). *Addressing cultural complexities in practice: A framework for clinicians and counselors.* Washington, DC: American Psychological Association.

[44] Helms, J. E. (2002). A remedy for the Black-White test-score disparity. *American Psychologist, 57,* 303-304.

[45] Janda, L. H. (1998). *Psychological testing: Theory and applications.* Needham Heights, MA: Allyn & Bacon.

[46] Jenkins, J. O., & Ramsey, G. A. (1991). Minorities. In M. Hersen, A. E. Kazdin, & A. S. Bellack (Eds.), *The Clinical Psychology Handbook* (2nd ed., pp. 724-740). Elmsford, NY: Pergamon Press.

[47] Katz, I. (1968). Factors influencing Negro performance in the desegregated school. In M. Deutsch, I. Katz, & A. Jensen (Eds.), *Social class, race, and psychological developments* (pp. 254-289). New York: Holt, Rinehart & Winston.

[48] Leung, P. & Sakata, R. (1988). Asian Americans and rehabilitation: Some important variables. *Journal of Applied Rehabilitation Counseling 19*(4), 16-19.

[49] Lonner, W. J. (1985). Issues in testing and assessment in cross-cultural counseling. *The Counseling Psychologist, 13*(4), 599-614.

[50] Lusting, D. C. & Saura, K. M. (1996). Use of criterion-based comparisons in determining the appropriateness of vocational evaluation test modifications for criterion referenced tests. *Vocational Evaluation and Work Adjustment Association Bulletin, 29* (1), 15-18.

[51]Marsella, A. J. & Yamada, A. (2000). Culture and mental health: An introduction and overview of foundations, concepts, and issues. In I. Cuellar & F. A. Paniagua (Eds.), *Handbook of multicultural mental health* (pp.3-24). San Diego, CA: Academic Press.

[52]Meyer, G. J., Finn, S. E., Eyde, L. D., Kay, G. G., Moreland, K. L., Dies, R. R., et al. (2001). Psychological testing and psychological assessment: A review of evidence and issues. *American Psychologist, 56*(2), 128-165. -*cultural and multicultural personality assessment* (pp.17-41). Mahwah, NJ: Lawrence Erlbaum Associates.

[53]Morris, E. F. (2000b). Assessment practices with African Americans: Combining standard assessment measures within an Africentric orientation. In R.H. Dana (Ed.), *Handbook of cross-cultural and multicultural personality assessment* (pp.573-603). Mahwah, NJ: Lawrence Erlbaum Associates.

[54]Morris, E. F. (2000a). An Africentric perspective for clinical research and practice. In R.H. Dana (Ed.), *Handbook of cross*

[55]Myers, H. F., & Rodriguez, N. (2003). Acculturation and physical health in racial and ethnic minorities. In K. M. Chun, P. B. Organista, & G. Marin (Eds.), *Acculturation: Advances in theory, measurement, and applied research* (pp. 163-185). Washington, DC: American Psychological Association.

[56]Nelson, P. A., Dial, J. G., & Joyce, A. (2002). Validation of the Cognitive Test for the Blind as an assessment of intellectual functioning. *Rehabilitation Psychology, 47*(2), 184-193.

[57]Olkin, R. (1999). *What psychotherapists should know about disability*. New York: Guilford Press.

[58]Padilla, A. M. (2001). Issues in culturally appropriate assessment. In L. A. Suzuki, J. G. Ponterotto, & P. J. Meller (Eds.), *Handbook of multicultural assessment* (2nd ed., pp. 5-27). San Francisco: Jossey-Bass.

[59]Paniagua (Eds.), *Handbook of multicultural mental health* (pp. 97-120). San Diego, CA: Academic Press.

[60]Paniagua, F. A. (1998). *Assessing and treating culturally diverse clients*. Thousand Oaks, CA: Sage.

[61]Paniagua, F. A. (2000). Culture-bound syndromes, cultural variations, and psychopathology. In I. Cuellar & F. A. Paniagua (Eds.), *Handbook of multicultural mental health* (pp.139-169). San Diego, CA: Academic Press.

[62]Parker, R. M. (2001). Aptitude testing. In B. F. Bolton (Ed.), *Handbook of measurement and evaluation in rehabilitation* (pp. 103-123). Gaithersburg, MD: Aspen.

[63]Pitoniak, M. J., & Royer, J. M. (2001). Testing accommodations for examinees with disabilities: A review of psychometric, legal, and social policy issues. *Review of Educational Research, 71*(1), 53-104.

[64]Power, P. W. (2000). *A guide to vocational assessment.* (3rd ed.). Austin, TX: Pro-Ed.
[65]Pratt, S. I., & Moreland, K. L. (1998). Individuals with other characteristics. In J. Sandoval, C. L. Frisby, K. F. Geisinger, J. D. Scheuneman, & J. R. Grenier (Eds.), *Test interpretation and diversity: Achieving equity in assessment* (pp.349-3371). Washington, DC: American Psychological Association.
[66]Puente, A. E., & Perez-Garcia, M. (2000). Psychological assessment of ethnic minorities. In G. Goldstein & M. Hersen (Eds.), *Handbook of psychological assessent* (3rd ed., pp. 527-551). Oxford: Elsevier Science.
[67]Pullin, D. (2002). Testing individuals with disabilities: Reconciling social science and social policy. In R. B. Ekstrom & D. K. Smith (Eds.), *Assessing individuals with disabilities in educational, employment, and counseling settings* (pp. 11-31). Washington, DC: American Psychological Association.
[68]Ridley, C., Hill, C., & Li, L. (1998). Revisiting and refining the multicultural assessment procedure. *Counseling Psychologist, 6,* 939-947.
[69]Rodevich, M. A., & Wanlass, R. L. (1995). The moderating effect of spinal cord injury on MMPI-2 Profiles: A clinically derived T score correction procedure. *Rehabilitation Psychology, 40*(3), 181-190.
[70]Rohe, D. E., & Athelstan, G. T. (1982). Vocational interests of persons with spinal cord injury. *Journal of Counseling Psychology, 29*(3), 283-291.
[71]Samuda, R. J. (1998). *Psychological testing of American minorities: Issues and consequences* (2nd ed.). Thousand Oaks, CA: Sage.
[72]Scheuneman, J. D. & Oakland, T. (1998). High-stakes testing in education. In Sandoval, J., Frisby, C. L., Geisinger, K. F., Scheuneman, J. D., & Grenier, J. R. (Eds.), *Test interpretation and diversity: Achieving equity in assessment.* Washington, DC: American Psychological Association.
[73]Sireci, S. G. & Geisinger, K. F. (1998). Equity issues in employment testing. In J. Sandoval, C. L. Frisby, K. F. Geisinger, J. D. Scheuneman, & J. R. Grenier (Eds.), *Test interpretation and diversity: Achieving equity in assessment (pp.105-140).* Washington, DC: American Psychological Association.
[74]Smart, J. F. & Smart, D. W. (1993). Vocational evaluation of Hispanics with disabilities: Issues and implications. *Vocational Evaluation and Work Adjustment Association Bulletin, 26* (3), 111-122.
[75]Smith, D. K. (2002). The decision-making process for developing testing accommodations. In R. B. Ekstrom & D. K. Smith (Eds.), *Assessing individuals with disabilities in educational, employment, and counseling settings* (pp. 71-86). Washington, DC: American Psychological Association.

[76]Sternberg, R. J., &: Grigorenko, E. L. (2001). Ability testing across cultures. In L. A. Suzuki, J. G. Ponterotto, & P. J. Meller (Eds.), *Handbook of multicultural assessment* (2nd ed., pp. 335-357). San Francisco: Jossey-Bass.

[77]Suzuki, L. A., & Valencia, R. R. (1997). Race-ethnicity and measured intelligence: Educational implications. *American Psychologist, 52*(10), 1103-1114.

[78]Suzuki, L. A., Short, E. L., Pieterse, A., & Kugler, J. (2001). Multicultural issues and the assessment of aptitude. In L. A. Suzuki, J. G. Ponterotto, & P. J. Meller (Eds.), *Handbook of multicultural assessment* (2nd ed., pp. 359-382). San Francisco: Jossey-Bass.

[79]U.S. Bureau of the Census. (1996). *Poverty in the United States: 1995*. Washington, DC: U.S. Government Printing Office.

[80]Van de Vijver (2000). The nature of bias. In R. H. Dana (Ed.), *Handbook of cross-cultural and multicultural personality assessment* (pp. 87-106). Mahwah, NJ: Lawrence Erlbaum Associates.

[81]Velasquez, R. J., & Callahan, W. J. (1992). Psychological testing of Hispanic Americans in clinical settings: Overview and issues. In K. F. Geisinger (Ed.), *Psychological testing of Hispanics* (pp. 253-265). Washington, DC:

[82]Velasquez, R. J., Ayala, G. X., Mendoza, S., Nezami, E., Castillo-Canez, I., Pace, T., et al. (2000). Culturally competent use of the Minnesota Multiphasic Personality Inventory-2. In I. Cuellar & F. A. Paniagua (Eds.), *Handbook of multicultural mental health* (pp. 389-417). San Diego, CA: Academic Press.

[83]Vernon, M. (2001). Assessment of individuals who are deaf or hard of hearing. In B. F. Bolton (Ed.), *Handbook of measurement and evaluation in rehabilitation* (3rd ed., pp. 385-397). Gaithersburg, MD: Aspen.

[84]Westermeyer, J. (1987). Cultural factors in clinical assessment. *Journal of Consulting and Clinical Psychology, 55*(4), 471-478.

[85]Willingham, W.W., Ragosta, M., Bennett, R.E., Braun, H., Rock, D.A., and Powers, D.E. (1988). *Testing handicapped people.* Needham Heights, MA: Allyn and Bacon. Zane, N., & Mak, W. (2003). Major approaches to the measurement of acculturation among ethnic minority populations: A content analysis and an alternative empirical strategy. In K. M. Chun, P. B. Organista, & G. Marin (Eds.), *Acculturation: Advances in theory, measurement, and applied research* (pp. 39-60). Washington, DC: American Psychological Association.

CHAPTER 11

ADDRESSING THE INDEPENDENT LIVING NEEDS OF ETHNIC/RACIAL MINORITY GROUPS

JOAN LOOBY

CHAPTER TOPICS

- Perceptions of people with disabilities
- The historical roots of the independent living movement
- Independent living and significant social movements of the 1960's and 1970's
- Ethnic/racial minority group and independent living
- Issues impacting ethnic/racial minority group participation in independent living
- Incorporating ethnic/racial minority groups into independent living
- Conclusion

The independent living movement originated in the late 1960's and is often described as a social or civil rights movement involving persons with disabilities, who not only demanded their rights to inclusion in mainstream United States (U.S.) culture and more humane service delivery, but also control for determining the services they require.[8,27,47,64] Title VII of the Rehabilitation Act Amendments of 1978 authorized the addition of, and funding for, independent living rehabilitation programs. This funding was made available through the federal-state rehabilitation programs.[45] The independent living movement has had tremendous impact on redefining traditional notions of disability (the sick/impaired role) and has influenced the development of new service paradigms among disability professionals, researchers, and policy makers. However, more than a quarter century after the Berkeley model had been established by Ed Roberts, independent living services still continue to elude many persons with disabilities and, in particular, persons from ethnic/racial minority groups.

This chapter focuses on independent living. It begins with a brief review of societal perceptions of individuals with disabilities, and legislation that helped to remove critical barriers to their successful integration into mainstream U.S. culture. A historical overview of the independent living movement, the other movements with which it dovetailed, and the legal mandates that gave rise to its inception, are presented. Ethnic/racial minority group participation is discussed, specifically in the context of the four largest minority groups in the United States (Hispanics, African Americans, Asians, and Native Americans). Following this is a comprehensive discussion of issues impacting ethnic/racial minority group participation in independent living. The chapter concludes with suggestions for how independent living can better incorporate racial/ethnic minority groups into its paradigm of services.

PERCEPTIONS OF PEOPLE WITH DISABILITIES

Society has always viewed persons with disabilities as anomalies of nature, evil, God's punishment for a sin, or incapable of making any significant contribution to mankind.[38,44,45,48,52] Such negative perceptions are steeped in history. The Nomads considered people with disabilities useless; the Greeks and Romans specialized in infanticide, murder, and exposure to the elements for children who were disabled. Early Christians pitied people with disabilities and sought to exorcize their conditions through intense ritual and prayer. During the Middle Ages, persons with disabilities were considered evil and often tortured and persecuted. While people with disabilities were institutionalized during the Renaissance, they were subject to horrific treatment and living conditions.[15,27,44,45,46,47]

In America, colonists enacted laws restricting people with disabilities from entering the country. Those born with or who acquired disabilities were sent "away" for treatment, education, or to live elsewhere. For the mentally ill, if one's family was rich, the person was kept at home, but locked in dungeons, cells, attics, and other places, to be kept away from society and others. Those of more tenuous financial circumstances were subjected to inhumane treatment such as whippings, hangings, incarceration, and other cruel, harsh punishment.[9,47]

Near the end of the Nineteenth century, the eugenic movement led to the passage of laws prohibiting persons with disabilities from immigrating to the U.S., marrying, or having children. Eugenics also promoted forced sterilization of people with disabilities, a practice that continued well into the Twentieth century. The rise of the Social Gospel Movement and the American Charity Movement in the 19th century advocated compassion and assistance to persons with disabilities; however, the moral superiority of the helpers, and the moral inferiority of people with disabilities were always underscored.[7,18,23,45,48]

Landmark political, social, and legislative initiatives since the early 1990's, culminating in The Rehabilitation Act of 1973 and its subsequent amendments, and the Americans with Disabilities Act of 1990, have given a voice to persons with disabilities, have helped to remove some critical environmental barriers to their success, and have emphasized their right to self-determination, independence, and choice.[7,27,38,45] As significant as these developments have been, in the 21st century, attitudinal barriers still exclude people with disabilities from equal opportunity and access to society's mainstream.

The independent living movement represented a breaking away from the shackles of confinement imposed by the traditional rehabilitation paradigm to the participation of persons with disabilities in all decisions impacting their lives. However, there has been and continue to be tensions between both philosophies. Mainstream U.S. culture still limits the rights of persons with disabilities, controls their choices, enables their dependency, and continues to embrace the medical model of service delivery as the only model of rehabilitation.[7,45]

THE HISTORICAL ROOTS OF THE INDEPENDENT LIVING MOVEMENT

The independent living movement did not suddenly rise out of the ashes like a Phoenix. It was influenced heavily by the turbulent, socio-cultural milieu of the 1960s and 70s.[8,11,27,29,47]

This was the era of the Vietnam War, where anti-war protests, demonstrations, and marches, particularly by university students, occurred almost daily. This was the time of the Hippie generation who rejected traditional values and advocated sexual freedom, drugs, and rock and roll. This was the time of Black militancy, challenging society, and advocating equality. This was the time of the passage of The Civil Rights Act in 1964. This was also the time of the rise of the Women's Movement. This was the time of the founding of Disabled in Action by Judith Heumann in 1970, and the Physically Disabled Students Program at the University of California Berkeley in 1970, by Ed Roberts and others. The message reinforced by all these events was that turmoil and challenge would produce change.[8]

Frustrated by their second class citizenry, poor service delivery, and lack of opportunity for self-determination, and encouraged by the successes of the civil rights and other movements, persons with disabilities joined together to demand their full participation in the mainstream 70s.[7,8,27,29,46,47] They too felt that they were being denied access to similar services accorded to persons without disabilities. It was in this context that the independent living movement was born. The movement blossomed at a time when several other complementary movements developed, such as the civil rights movement, consumerism, self-help, demedicalization, and deinstitutionalization.[8,11,29,46,47]

INDEPENDENT LIVING AND SIGNIFICANT SOCIAL MOVEMENTS OF THE 1960'S AND 1970'S

THE CIVIL RIGHTS MOVEMENT

The Civil Rights Act of 1964 did not include people with disabilities as a protected class but made vulnerable groups such as persons with disabilities cognizant of their rights to equal societal participation.[8,29,47] The civil rights movement stressed entitlement (vote, trial by a jury of peers, hold political office) and benefits rights (Medicare, attendant care, income assistance), as well as alternative techniques of social protest.[47] The independent living movement's battle for entitlement is manifested in Section 504 of the Rehabilitation Act of 1973 that prohibits various forms of discrimination, and in the provisions of the Americans with Disabilities Act of 1990.[27,45] The movement's fight for benefits is reflected in the Social Security Disability Amendments of 1980, and subsequent revisions in 1986, 1987, and 1990.[27,45] Demonstrations and sit-ins, practices inherent in the civil rights movement, were used effectively by members of the independent living movement to secure their rights.[8]

One of the tenets of the civil rights movement is that racism and prejudice are endemic to American society. Although legislation eliminated many barriers to the equal participation of African Americans in mainstream U.S. culture, it did not change the negative societal perceptions of these individuals. This tenet applies equally well to persons with disabilities. They continue to realize all too frequently that prejudice against disability will continue to thrive in this culture because it glorifies beauty, youth, and able-bodied people, and belittles differences or anomalies.[8,47]

CONSUMERISM

Another movement that influenced independent living was consumerism.[29,47] Its outspoken leader, Ralph Nader, preached consumer sovereignty, that consumers have ultimate control of the choice of goods and services available to them. The independent living movement promoted similar ideology—that persons with disabilities should determine which of their own services they required not professionals. This concept was incorporated into one of the mandates in the Rehabilitation Act of 1973, which stipulated consumer involvement throughout the rehabilitation process, especially in crafting the components of the Individual Written Rehabilitation Plan.[27] If the consumer is deemed ineligible for services, the professional had to stipulate the reasons for such a decision, and the consumer has the right to appeal the ruling.[45] The independent living movement also helped to create a number of advocacy centers offering consumer protection to various groups uneducated about, or who have been denied, their legal rights and benefits.[47]

THE SELF-HELP MOVEMENT

The self-help movement gained momentum in the 1970's with the profusion of self-help literature, and the proliferation of support groups for every conceivable problem imagined.[29,47] Many were modeled after Alcoholics Anonymous whose premise was that sharing with similar others promotes solidarity, support, understanding, and healing.[47] Self-help and group support are hallmarks of the independent living philosophy that places emphasis on people with disabilities assisting each other by virtue of their similar circumstances. Independent living centers, like self-help groups, provide services which may be lacking in traditional helping systems, and allow members to control their own choices.

DEMEDICALIZATION

The voices of many in the independent living movement resonated with support for a shift in paradigm from the traditional medical model of disability as illness and dependency, to individual empowerment and responsibility for ones own health.[29,47] The movement took issue with various aspects of the medical model, such as a continued medical presence despite stability of the disability; emphasis on the sick and dependent roles; acute/restorative care well beyond what is needed; prescribing unnecessary surgery, drugs, and medical care; the physician as the only decision maker; and repeated diagnostics, certification, or treatment services although the person is familiar enough with his or her condition to monitor it effectively.[8] This overarching medical presence in the lives of persons with disabilities runs counter to the independent movement's concept of self-determination.

CHAPTER 11   ADDRESSING THE INDEPENDENT LIVING NEEDS

DEINSTITUTIONALIZATION

Another societal movement that impacted independent living was deinstitutionalization, an attempt to move people out of institutions and back to their communities.[29,47] It was felt that with the right support services, these individuals could live normal, fulfilled lives. This philosophy closely parallels that of the independent living movement that stresses providing community-based services that will ultimately enable people with disabilities to be mainstreamed into everyday life.

MOVERS AND SHAKERS

The philosophy of the independent movement is rooted in self-determination, choice, and consumer control.[34,35,45] Self-determination includes choice, goal setting, optimal control, and responsibility for decision-making while, control implies freedom from coercion, independence, and manipulation of the environment to enable participation in all aspects of the mainstream.[17,51,64]

Berkeley is generally recognized as the birthplace of the independent living movement; however, in 1962, the University of Illinois at Urbana-Champaign pioneered community living for persons with severe disabilities by transferring four disabled students from the campus's nursing facility to a modified home nearby.[8] Its disabled students' program has placed the university as one of the most architecturally accessible institutions of its kind.[8]

The first independent living center was incorporated in 1972 by the efforts of Ed Roberts and a group of severely disabled students who were enrolled at the University of California at Berkeley.[7,8,27,36,38] Roberts, a polio survivor, a quadriplegic, and on a respirator, along with other students with severe disabilities, was housed in the campus hospital because of lack of accessible housing.[38,68] Roberts and his peers organized into a group called the "Rolling Quads", and saw their mission as advocating full community integration for people with disabilities by providing necessary support services to enhance the quality of their lives.[7,38]

The group opened a program office to provide needed support services unavailable elsewhere, and within a year were deluged with so many requests, particularly from the surrounding communities, that they established a Center for Independent Living (CIL) for the community at large.[8,38,45,68] Its basic tenets were that persons with disabilities know the needs of their peers best; service delivery is best provided by people with disabilities; full community integration; services should enhance independence and self-determination; self-determination, independence, and choice.[28,37,38,51,64,68]

Following the successful efforts at Berkeley, CILs were established in Boston, Houston, Columbus, Ann Arbor, and other parts of the country[7,8,27,51] and today over 400 independent living centers operate in the United States.[27,40] Title VII of the Rehabilitation Act Amendments of 1988 stipulate that independent living centers must provide multiple services to persons with a wide array of disabilities; that at least 51% of the policymaking board and the majority of its staff must be persons with disabilities; that consumers with disabilities must be intimately involved in service delivery, program and center design, planning, and training activities, and facilitating consumer and community needs, and that every CIL funded through the Rehabilitation Act must provide information and referral services, advocacy, independent living skills training, and peer counseling.[12,43,45,64]

ETHNIC/ RACIAL MINORITY GROUPS AND INDEPENDENT LIVING

DeJong[8] claimed that at its beginning, the independent living movement garnered its constituency from severely disabled, older adolescents and younger working age adults including those with spinal cord injury, muscular dystrophy, cerebral palsy, multiple sclerosis, and post polio disablement. DeJong believed that this narrow age range was a function of disabling conditions that are more likely to occur during the late teen or early adulthood years. In addition, the movement took root in academic communities. Severely disabled older individuals and ethnic/racial minorities were missing from the group. This is ironic because African Americans as well as other ethnic/racial minority groups including Hispanics and Native Americans have more severe and higher rates of disabling conditions than Caucasians[5,6,31,49,58,63] and the independent living movement drew its impetus from the gains made by African Americans during the civil rights movement.[32]

Since its inception, the constituency of the independent living movement has been Caucasian consumers with disabilities and not ethic/racial minority consumers with disabilities.[8] Although some ethnic/racial minority consumers may have benefited from its outcomes, the numbers pale in comparison to the service delivery benefits of Caucasian consumers. For example, in a national study of independent living centers,[37] found that almost 80% were white consumers and 20% ethnic/racial minority consumers. In a regional study of 32 centers for independent living,[11] reported that, of the 8,000 persons served, almost 90 % were white. To address this problem, a committee established by the National Center for Independent Living recommended that more independent living centers be established in areas with large ethnic/racial minority populations.[39] However, there is not overwhelming evidence that ethnic/racial minority individuals with disabilities are accessing independent living services. The obvious question is, Why not? Answers to this question are provided in the discussion below.

ISSUES IMPACTING ETHNIC/ RACIAL MINORITY GROUP PARTICIPATION IN INDEPENDENT LIVING

Title VII of the Rehabilitation Act Amendments of 1988 stipulate that every center for independent living funded through the Rehabilitation Act must provide the following: (a) information and referral services; (b) advocacy; (c) independent living skills training; and (d) peer counseling.[12,39,43,45,64]

According to Rubin & Roessler[64] *information and referral services* may encompass housing, attendant, adaptive equipment, transportation, community, employment, support group, interpreter and reader, recreational, medical, civil rights, benefits, and other supplementary resource information. *Independent living skills and training* may include instruction in services such as daily survival skills, self- management, social interaction, self- advocacy, community training, utilization of public transportation, pre-vocational training, and other tools necessary for successful independent living. Persons with disabilities serve as role models and mentors by providing *peer counseling* and serving as credible resources for helping persons with disabilities develop autonomy, improve their coping skills, and effectively navigate their place in the community. *Advocacy* services involve individual and community systems; they empower people with disabilities to develop the skills required to achieve their independent living goals and promotes the elimination of barriers and other disincentives that limit full mainstream participation of all persons with disabilities.

The National Center for the Dissemination of Disability Research[32] points out that the key components of the independent living philosophy, however, were ultimately shaped by the norms, beliefs, and values of mainstream U.S. culture articulated through educated Caucasian men with disabilities. Little attempt was made to include other perspectives such as those of ethnic/racial minority groups. Services were often provided in a manner that was inconsistent with their cultural beliefs and values. Therefore, ethnic/racial minority individuals with disabilities did not, and still do not access independent living services as readily as consumers from the mainstream U.S. culture. Another major concern has been the even wider cultural and value differentials between ethnic/racial minorities with disabilities and service delivery personnel. This concern continues to be echoed in the work of rehabilitation researchers and others concerned with diversity in helping professions.[1,2,4,7,19,25,39,41,53,58,60,62,65] Utilization of independent living services by ethnic/racial minority groups is also hampered by a number of barriers specifically related to cultural values and the independent living philosophical orientation. Some of these barriers are articulated below.

DIFFERING WORLDVIEWS

Central to understanding the clash of cultural values that exists between mainstream U.S. culture and ethnic/racial minority groups is the concept of worldview. Sue and Sue[53] define worldview as one's perceptions of his/her relationship to the world via nature, institutions, other people, and things. In other words, it is the lens through which the person discerns and responds to the environment or the person's belief system about how the world works. There is a striking disconnect between the worldview of the four largest ethnic/racial minority groups and mainstream U.S. culture. Individuals from these groups generally tend to be more collectivist in nature and focus on the group, while individuals from mainstream U.S. culture hold worldviews that are more individualistic in nature.[30,35,36,53,55,59] Differences between the worldviews of ethnic/racial minority groups and the mainstream U.S. culture, especially in regards to accessing mental health and other health related services, have been cited frequently in the literature.[3,4,26,39,50,53,26,39,50,53,61,66] Many of these differences directly impact ethnic/racial minority group utilization of independent living services.

INDIVIDUALISM

It is imperative in this discussion to address the concept of "individualism" itself and what it means to individuals from ethnic/racial minority groups. Individualism is one of the most dominant values shaping mainstream U.S. culture, and has directly influenced and shaped rehabilitation service delivery, procedures, rules, and independent living philosophy.[32] As Parkin & Nosek[39] reiterate, individualism stresses achievement of personal goals, self-determination, autonomy, and choice. The notion of individualism fits like a glove in the context of independent living where the individual controls his life, makes decisions, has choices, manages resources, and is an active participant in the independent living community.[34,39] Independent living also means having the resources to achieve the aforementioned goals.

The notion of individualism in the context of the cultural values of ethnic/racial minorities runs counter to their group orientation, interdependence, collectivity, shared decision making, and strong community focus.[32,39,53] For example, many ethnic/racial minority groups define themselves in the context of their family, and view family as a referent point for social economic, emotional, financial, and psychological support.[26,53] The philosophy of independent living, which stresses empowerment, advocacy, personal choice, and independence from others, may negate the importance of family choice and involvement. Family choice and involvement may run counter to the aims of independent living. Therefore, ethnic/racial minority individuals with disabilities may devalue the notion of independence, refuse to access independent living services, and, instead, choose the security of the family.

FAMILY AS REFERENT POINT

The cohesiveness, and security found in ethnic/racial minority families and the sense of collective responsibility for each other may encourage over-protectiveness, paternalism, protection from and distrust of outsiders, and strong sanctions against airing family problems to strangers.[26] In ethnic/racial minority families, family relationships are held sacred, and the family takes precedence over all other matters.[21,10,20,57] Hence, individuals with disabilities may be sheltered from outsiders and are taken care of by family members, or help may be sought from the priest or other significant individuals in the community.[32,50] There is an inherent distrust of outsiders, counselors, and also social service agencies; therefore, if help is sought, it may be done as a last resort.[10,14,16,21,22,57] In Asian families, the preservation of family honor is very important; an individual with a disability may be viewed as bringing shame to the family or perceived as weak and lacking will.[32,53] Asian families may be less comfortable accessing independent living services because this may cause the family to lose face.

RELIGIOUS AND SPIRITUAL PRACTICES

Individuals from ethnic/racial minority groups are firmly grounded in religious and spiritual practices that emphasize some of the following ideas: suffering as a natural consequence of life; that the greater the sacrifice, suffering, and pain one endures, the greater the salvation; that faith in God/a spiritual power is the best medicine for dealing with crisis, turmoil, and illness; that having a disability or illness is God's will, a punishment from God/an offended spirit, something caused by supernatural forces, or as the sins of the parents handed down to their children; that illness results from the failure to live in harmony with nature and the dictates of the culture.[26,30,56,53,67] What logically follows is that these groups believe that having a disability is God's will, and altering or seeking services cannot change the path that God has laid out.[26,53,67]

CAUSES OF DISABILITY

Having a different understanding of the causes of disability may lead individuals with disabilities from ethnic/racial minority groups to seek help through sources other than independent living services. Such systems may include informal and familiar indigenous healing and helping networks.[32] Consequently, accessing independent living services may not be viewed as beneficial.

DEFINITIONS OF DISABILITY

Attitudes about the causes and treatment of disability within mainstream U.S. culture are influenced by the philosophy of individuality and are rooted in the scientific or medical model which views disability as a disease emanating from the individual and treats it in isolation from other aspects of the person.[32] Individuals from ethnic/racial minority groups may define disability differently.

African Americans, for example, view disabilities in a spiritual context, as God's will, hold more varied perceptions of what constitutes "developmental normalcy," and rely heavily on a number of environmental resources for treatment of individuals with disabilities.[32] Hispanics view many disabling conditions as individual differences rather than disabilities, and consider it their duty to care for those family members with disabilities.[50] Although Asians may view disabling conditions as a sign of weakness or bringing shame to one's family, they honor their obligation to care for that person and consider it personal and family shame and dishonor if they are unable to take care of family members.[30] Native Americans have no word for disability in their language, treat each person with respect and dignity, and their belief in the interconnectedness of body and spirit and all things within the universe[6,32] is in direct contrast to the medical model of rehabilitation delivery services.

Consequently, if a service agency advertises itself as serving people with disabilities, it may not reach the consumers it wants to reach because of the differing minority perspectives of what constitutes a disability.[6] These beliefs may help to explain why individuals with disabilities from ethnic/racial minority groups may not access independent living services, and the failure of independent living centers to provide culturally appropriate services to these groups.

INFORMATION AND REFERRAL SERVICES

Information and referral services and independent living skills and training are two mandated domains of independent living centers service delivery. However, there is not overwhelming evidence that individuals with disabilities from ethnic/racial minority populations are accessing these important services. Wright, et al.,[66] conducted a pilot investigation of minority consumers of independent living services via focus groups to determine (a) existing barriers to independent living and their impact on transportation, housing, vocational skills, and health services; and (b) provide recommendations for alleviating said barriers. Participants presented with 17 different disabilities, and included African Americans, Hispanic Americans, Asian Americans, American Indians, and Anglo Americans of varying age ranges.

The researchers reported that specific concerns related to transportation included unreliability, insensitive personnel, little or no attempts to inform consumers about services provided, and inaccessibility in rural areas. Suggestions, such as consumer education and information dissemination, sensitivity training for drivers, and developing a more consumer friendly transit system, were articulated.

Inaccessible and unaffordable housing limited or no attempts to make accommodations for consumers with disabilities, long waiting lists, and financial constraints were mentioned by the researchers as the major obstacles to obtaining suitable housing. Government sponsored initiatives, tax incentives for developers who build accessible housing, ongoing education, and training of landlords about disability, reasonable accommodations, cultural sensitivity, and creating an advertising program focusing on available housing for persons with disabilities, were some proposed solutions.

According to the researchers, participants were also openly critical of the medical community. Frequent complaints included lack of sensitivity and cultural knowledge among providers; negative bedside manner and inadequate medical treatment; limited accessibility to and unaffordable services; and poor medical insurance coverage. Recommendations included major health care changes, employment of culturally competent and sensitive providers, the development of an adequate health network system to address the needs of persons with disabilities, and effective information dissemination systems.

The researchers also indicated that vocational training issues included unsystematic eligibility determination criteria; exclusion from the rehabilitation process; frequent counselor turnover; questionable evaluation methods; prolonged waiting periods for and limited access to services; inadequate testing, training, and placement methods; and a lack of cultural sensitivity among providers. More reliable and efficient testing and training techniques, adherence to the Americans with Disabilities Act (ADA), sensitivity training, and community outreach programs on persons with disabilities were some suggested corrective measures.

The researchers claimed that the most significant responses addressed the inadequacy of independent living services. Participants were not only uninformed, but also unable to access information about available services. Other concerns mentioned, which directly impacted independent living, included little consumer empowerment, inaccessible communities, lack of transportation, restricted opportunities for social relationships and activities, safety concerns, and the inability to access essential survival needs. The authors concluded that ethnic/racial minority consumers with disabilities continue to face many obstacles in their attempts to navigate independent living services.

PEER COUNSELING

One of the services of centers for independent living is to provide peer counseling with individuals with disabilities acting as role models and informational resources, helping consumers develop self sufficiency and autonomy, providing support, and modeling self-sufficiency.[45]

For ethnic/racial minority individuals with disabilities, their support comes from family members who may not have the experience or knowledge of working with disability issues and may or may not define the family member's problem as a disability.[6,32] Family, not outside agencies or individuals, is the referent point for information, teaching coping skills, providing emotional, psychological, economic, and physical support, and the one positive constant in the lives of ethnic/racial minority individuals.[49,50,53,26]

Equally important, asking an individual with a disability from an ethnic/racial minority group to develop autonomy and personal independence may be asking that person to reject cultural and family dictates that emphasize cohesiveness and the importance of the collective over the individual.[53] This may be interpreted as asking the individual to reject important family values and traditions. Because the family prefers to take care of its own, opportunities to interact with other individuals with disabilities may not be frequent because these individuals may not access the system.

ADVOCACY

Self and community advocacy is another core service of independent living centers. This involves learning about and exercising ones right to equal access, to non-discrimination, to appropriate services, and to develop the skills required to achieve independent living goals.[6,45] Self-advocacy involves the individual taking charge of his/her own life and acting in his/her own best interest. This requires having appropriate information, understanding how social agencies function, having the ability to communicate with others, and persistence in the face of denial.[6]

Individuals from ethnic/racial minority groups typically suppress individual interests to the good of the collective or family.[26,39,53] Further, families and other significant persons view their role as supporters and advocates for the needs of the member with a disability.[6] Advocating for one's needs places emphasis on the individual. This may be viewed as being boastful, focusing on self, and disrespecting family rules and dictates, since the needs of the group are priority. Self-advocacy requires persistence with bureaucracy, communicating effectively, and withstanding rejection.[6] Individuals from ethnic/racial minority groups may not choose to subject themselves to this discomfort, especially if it involves violating family values and beliefs.

Looby & Webb[26] claim that individuals from some ethnic/racial minority groups may be introverted and reserved (e.g., Asian); others may not have the language facility to articulate their needs (e.g., Hispanics, Asian Americans); others may honor and value maintaining harmony and acceptance of a particular outcome (e.g. Asians, Native Americans); and others may value respecting authority (e.g. Asians, Native Americans, Hispanics). Therefore, individuals from ethnic/racial minority groups who honor these values may see little benefit in advocacy and may not understand it. When they apply for services and are denied, they may not complain or advocate for their rights because of cultural imperatives which promote maintaining harmony and balance in one's life and with others.[6,53]

CONSUMER CONTROL AND INVOLVEMENT

Consumer control and involvement is another core mandate of independent living centers. The mandate stipulates that the consumer controls and directs the services received and makes major decisions regarding the management of the independent living center.[6] Flowers,[11] conducted a regional survey of cultural diversity within 53 centers for independent living in RSA Region V (Illinois, Indiana, Michigan, Minnesota, Ohio, and Wisconsin). The major focus was on staff diversity and outreach to underserved ethnic minorities.

Responses from 32 of the 53 centers indicated that almost 19% of the directors and 15% of the management staff were racial or ethnic minorities and that they served over 8, 000 persons. Caucasians comprised 89.3% and African Americans 7.02% (9.05 % of the general population in that area was African American) of the consumers utilizing independent living services. Administrators were queried about outreach efforts to increase diversity. Fifty eight percent had no plan; sixty six percent of the centers with plans were unsure of their effectiveness; thirty seven percent had staffing plans in place; twenty five percent felt that their plans were effective; and 19 % did not know if such a plan existed.

The researchers also asked the centers to indicate their specific outreach activities. Activities included direct mailings to organizations, personal visits and presentations to groups, participation in cultural diversity programs and events, and distribution of agency information at sites where persons from ethnic/racial minority groups are served.

The results of the above study seem to indicate that Caucasian consumers with disabilities have more accessibility to independent living centers and services than do individuals with disabilities from ethnic/racial minority groups. Equity of independent living services for persons from ethnic/racial minority groups is mixed. Obviously, without minority consumers, there can be no minority consumer involvement, which is one of the core mandates of independent living.

Research continues to document long-standing problems among ethnic/racial minority groups with disabilities that may or may not be aware of independent living services. These problems include transportation difficulties, limited outreach efforts by social service agencies and rehabilitation service providers, lack of information about services, inaccessibility to rural areas, no community outreach programs, little consumer empowerment, poor finances, limited community resources, and culturally insensitive service delivery.[30,33,39,66]

It is obvious that centers for independent living must engage in a more concerted and comprehensive effort to involve ethnic/racial minority groups in independent living. There are several ways that this may be accomplished.

INCORPORATING ETHNIC/RACIAL MINORITY GROUPS INTO INDEPENDENT LIVING

The following is a list of general recommendations to improve participation of ethnic/racial minority groups in independent living. This list is by no means exhaustive:

- ➢ Include family members and/or significant support entities (individual and community) in consultations with ethnic/ racial minority consumers. Individuals from ethnic/racial minority groups value the importance of family relationships and may not participate in the rehabilitation process without family involvement. Disrespect of the family hierarchy may be interpreted as disrespect for the consumer also, thereby precluding participation in services.

- ➢ Current independent living services and policies reflect the values of mainstream U.S. culture to the exclusion of values of ethnic/racial minority consumers. For example, consideration must be given to critical issues such as the importance of family, communication styles, independence versus the good of the group, definitions of disability, definitions of independence, self sufficiency and dependence, and the significance of guilt and shame in Asian cultures. These concepts serve as guiding principles in the lives of ethnic/racial minority consumers. In order for these individuals to fully participate in independent living, there should be a redefinition of the independent living philosophy to incorporate these and other important cultural values of ethnic/racial minority groups. Perhaps then, ethnic/racial minority consumers may access independent living services.

- ➢ The inability of service providers to network and build alliances with resources existing in ethnic/racial minority communities may prevent minority group participation in independent living. Grass roots, credible, respected individuals from the four ethnic/racial minority groups identified in this chapter can serve as spokespersons to adapt, explain, educate, and even illustrate application of varied components of the independent living mandates in ethnic/racial minority communities. These individuals can be excellent resources for educating service providers and rehabilitation administrators about how to effectively mesh the independent living philosophy with the varied cultural values, practices, and beliefs of ethnic/racial minority groups.

- Recruit and hire ethnic/racial minority service providers with disabilities, and who are bilingual-if possible, and place them in management/decision making roles at the independent living center and on the Board of Directors. These individuals may be better able to articulate the needs of the targeted ethnic/racial minority consumers, serve as role models with whom the consumers can identify, and communicate with them in their native language. These service providers could provide added voices to the concerns of ethnic/racial minority consumers. They could also have an impact on the shaping and development of programs and policies that take into account issues which affect ethnic/racial minority consumer utilization of independent living services.

- Make a more concerted effort to outreach to ethnic/racial minority consumers, especially since research has indicated that they know little about independent living centers and even less about the services provided.[39,66] Outreach efforts should be active, high profile, conducted in ethnic/racial minority communities, and involve all community members, not just those individuals with disabilities. Flowers, et al,[11] feel that outreach efforts should be approached systematically. They suggest that prior to initiating, it is important that independent living centers identify their target group, assess previous efforts, review current policies and procedures, especially recruitment strategies, and then implement their plan/program.

- Given the mistrust that ethnic/racial minority groups may have of strangers and individuals from the "bureaucracy," it is imperative that independent living center staff build personal relationships with members of the ethnic/racial minority group(s) and the community(ies) they wish to serve. Developing relationships with significant community personnel who have been successful in reaching ethnic/racial minority individuals with disabilities can help in a number of ways: making referrals; introduction to other community members and agencies; facilitating entry or outreach to targeted ethnic/racial minority consumers; having an influential and supportive ally; having a respected individual explaining the significance of independent living services to ethnic/racial minority consumers; and adding credibility and trust to the service provider. All of these efforts may serve a critical role in encouraging ethnic/racial minority consumers to access independent living services.

> One of the major findings of the study done by Wright, et al.,[66] and reported by ethnic/racial minority consumers, was a lack of awareness of services provided by independent living centers. To address this problem, multiple methods of communicating and disseminating information should be utilized. For example, word of mouth, providing interpreters, phone calls, mailings, brochures and forms written in the appropriate language of the consumer; pamphlets; flyers; email; newspaper and radio advertisement; mailing lists; setting up booths and displays at events in ethnic/racial minority communities; speaking at churches and other community venues; placing information in local social services, mental health, and other agencies; going from door to door; and placing information in areas populated by ethnic/racial minority consumers with disabilities are some avenues which may be utilized.

> Diversity training as well as training in the Americans with Disabilities Act (ADA) is imperative for effective outreach to ethnic/racial minority populations with disabilities so that they may access independent living services. Staff that are culturally sensitive and educated about rehabilitation mandates, including ADA and independent living, will be able to provide services that are more effective to ethnic/racial minority consumers who want to access independent living services.

> Help to decrease additional existing barriers to independent living for ethnic/racial minority consumers as cited in the Wright, et al.,[66] study. These include, but may not be limited to, transportation, inaccessibility to rural areas, suitable housing, medical treatment, vocational training issues, eligibility determination criteria, dealing with the rehabilitation bureaucracy, advocacy, restricted opportunities for social relationships and activities, safety issues, and accessing basic survival needs.

CONCLUSION

The independent living movement revolutionized rehabilitation and presented a new paradigm within which to view persons with disabilities. This paradigm resulted in considerable social and political changes for persons with disabilities from mainstream U.S. culture. They asserted themselves, demanded access to, and were allowed to participate in mainstream society, became active and capable consumers, and took control of their own lives.

However, the independent living philosophy, though well intentioned, did not take into account the different cultural values and perspectives of individuals with disabilities from ethnic/racial minority groups. As the literature has indicated, today, more than 30 years after the establishment of the first independent living center in Berkeley, California, ethnic/racial minority individuals with disabilities continue to be underserved by independent living centers. As articulated previously, the reasons are varied, but suffice it to say that a major theme has been the differing value systems of individuals from the mainstream U.S. culture and those from ethnic/racial minority groups. This gap can and must be remedied if independent living is to fulfill its mandate for all people with disabilities—full participation in mainstream U.S. society.

REFERENCES

[1] Alston, R. J., & Bell, T. J. (1996). Cultural mistrust and the rehabilitation enigma for African Americans. *The Journal of Rehabilitation, 10*(4), 73-82.

[2] Alston, R. J., & Mngadi, S. (1992). The interaction between disability status and the African American experience: Implications for rehabilitation counseling. *Journal of Applied Rehabilitation Counseling,* 12-15.

[3] Atkinson, D. R. (2004). Counseling *American minorities* (6th ed.). Boston, MA: McGraw-Hill.

[4] Atkinson, D. R., & Hackett, G. (2004). Counseling *diverse populations.* New York, NY: McGraw-Hill (172-187).

[5] Capella, M. E. (2002). Inequities in the VR system: Do they still exist? *Rehabilitation Counseling Bulletin, 45*(3), 143-153.

[6] Clay, J.A. (1992). Native American independent living. *Rural Special Education Quarterly, 11(1),* 41-50.

[7] Conyers, L. M. (2002). Disability: An emerging topic in multicultural counseling. In J. Trusty, E. J. Looby, & D. Sandhu (Eds.), *Multicultural counseling: Context, theory and practice, and competence,* pp. 173-201. New York: Nova Science Publishers.

[8] De Jong, G. (1979). The *movement for independent living: Origins, ideology, and implications for disability research.* East Lansing: University Center for International Rehabilitation, Michigan State University.

[9] Deutsch, A. (1949). The *mentally ill in America* (2nd ed.). New York: Columbia University Press.

[10] Falicov, C. J. (1996). Mexican families. . In M. McGoldrick, J. Pearce, & J. Giordano (Eds.) *Ethnicity and family therapy (*2nd ed.), pp 169-182. New York: Guilford Press.

[11] Flowers, C. R., Edwards, D., & Pusch, B. (1996). Rehabilitation cultural diversity Initiative: A regional survey of cultural diversity within CILs. *Journal of Rehabilitation, 62*(3), 22-28.

[12]Frieden, L. (1983). Understanding alternative program models. In N. M. Crewe and I. K. Zola (Eds.), *Independent living for physically disabled people,* pp. 62-72. San Francisco: Jossey-Bass Publishers.
[13]Frieden, A. (1990). Substance abuse and disability: The role of independent living centers. *Journal of Applied Rehabilitation Counseling, 21*(3), 33-36.
[14]Garcia-Preto, N. (1996). Puerto Rican families. . In M. McGoldrick, J. Pearce, & J. Giordano (Eds.), *Ethnicity and family therapy (*2nd ed.), pp. 183-199. New York: Guilford Press.
[15]Garrett, J. F. (1969). Historical background. In D. Malikin & H. Rusalem (Eds.), *Vocational rehabilitation of the disabled,* pp. 29-38. New York: New York University Press.
[16]Garrett, J.T., & Garrett, M.W. (1994). The path of good medicine. Understanding and counseling Native American Indians. *Journal of Multicultural Counseling and Development, 22,* 134-144.
[17]Giordano, G., & D'Alonzo, B. J. (1994). The link between transition and independent living. *American Rehabilitation, 20*(1), 2-7.
[18]Harber, M. H. (1963). Eugenics*: Hereditarian attitudes in American thought.* New Brunswick, NJ: Rutgers University Press.
[19]Herbert, J. T., & Cheatham, H. E. (1988). Africentricity and the Black disability experience: A theoretical orientation for rehabilitation counselors. *Journal of Applied Rehabilitation Counseling, 19*(4), 50-54.
[20]Herring, R. (1996). Counseling indigenous American youth. In C.C. Lee (Ed.), *Multicultural issues in counseling: New approaches to diversity* (2nd ed.), pp.53-70. Alexandria, VA: American Counseling Association.
[21]Hines, P., & Boyd-Franklin, N. (1996). African American families. In M. McGoldrick, J.Pearce & J. Giordano (Eds.), *Ethnicity and family therapy (*2nd ed.), pp. 66-84. New York: Guilford Press.
[22]Ho, M. K. (1987). *Family therapy with ethnic minorities.* California: Sage.
[23]Judge, M. (1976). A brief history of social services, part I. *Social and* [24]
[25]Leal-Idrogo, A. (1993). Vocational rehabilitation of people of Hispanic origin. *Journal of Vocational Rehabilitation, 3*(1), 27-37.
[26]Looby, E. J., & Webb, T. (2002). Counseling ethnically diverse families.). In J. Trusty, E. J. Looby, & D. Sandhu (Eds.), *Multicultural counseling: Context, theory and practice, and competence,* pp. 144-171. New York: Nova Science Publishers.
[27]Mackelprang, R.., & Salsgiver, R. (1999). Disability*: A diversity model approach in human service practice.* California: Brooks/Cole.
[28]Mathews, R. M. (1990). Independent living as a lifelong community service. *Journal of Head Trauma Rehabilitation, 5*(1), 23-30.
[29]McDonald, G., & Oxford, M. (2003). History of independent living. Article retrieved May 20, 2003, from www.acils.com.

[30]McLaughlin, L., & Braun, K. (1996). Asian and Pacific Islander cultural values: Considerations for health care decision making. *Health & Social Work, 23* (2), 116-126.

[31]McNeil, J. M. (1993). Americans *with disabilities: 1991-92.* U. S. Bureau of the Census Current Population Reports, p. 70-133. Washington, DC: U. S. Government Printing Office.

[32]National Center for the Dissemination of Disability Research. (1999). A review of literature on topics related to increasing the utilization of rehabilitation research outcomes among diverse consumer groups. Article retrieved, April 20, 2004, from www.ncddr.org/du/products/DisabilityDiversity.pdf

[33]Nosek, M. A. (1992). Independent living. In R. M. Parker (Ed.), *Rehabilitation counseling: Basics and beyond* (2nd ed.), pp. 103-133. Austin, TX: Pro-Ed.

[34]Nosek, M. A., Fuhrer, M. J., & Howland, C. A. (1992). Independence among people with disabilities: II. The personal independence profile. *Rehabilitation Counseling Bulletin, 36,* 21-36.

[35]Nosek, M.A., & Howland, C. A. (1992). The role of independent living centers in delivering rehabilitation services to rural communities. *American Rehabilitation, 18*(1), 2-6.

[36]Nosek, M. A., Hughes, R. B. (2004). Navigating the road to independent living. (pp. 172-192). In D. Atkinson, & G. Hackett (Eds.), *Counseling diverse populations,* pp.172-192. New York NY: McGraw-Hill.

[37]Nosek, A. N., Zhu, Y., & Howard, C. A. (1992). The evolution of independent living programs. *Rehabilitation Counseling Bulletin, 35*(3), 175-189.

[38]Olkin, R. (1999). What *psychotherapists should know about disability.* New York: The Guilford Press.

[39]Parkin, E. K., & Nosek, M. A. (2001). Collectivism versus independence: Perceptions of independent living and independent living services by Hispanic Americans and Asian Americans with disabilities. *Rehabilitation Education, 15*(4), 375-394.

[40]Pelka, F. (1993). Fire in the belly: Just how independent is the independent living movement. *Mainstream, 4,* 35-38.

[41]Peterson, G. E. (1996). An analysis of participation, progress, and outcome of individuals with diverse racial and ethnic backgrounds in the public vocational rehabilitation program in Nevada. *Dissertation Abstracts International, 57*(4A), Abstract retrieved December 19, 2000, from Dissertation Abstracts Online: First Search.

[42]Pfeiffer, D. (1994). Eugenics and disability discrimination. *Disability and Society, 9, 481-499.*

[43]Potter, C. G. (1996). After independent living, what next? A primer on independence for people with disabilities, their families, and service providers. *Journal of Applied Rehabilitation Counseling, 27*(2), 36-39.

[44]Preen, B. (1976). Schooling *for the mentally retarded: A historical perspective*. New York: St. Martin's Press.
[45]Rubin, S. E., & Roessler, R. T. (2001). Foundations of the vocational rehabilitation process. (5th ed.). Austin, TX: Pro-Ed.
[46]Shapiro, J. P. (1993). No *pity*. New York: Times Books.
[47]Shreve, M. (1982). The movement for independent living: A brief history. Written under federal grant for an ILC Training Module. Article retrieved May 20, 2003, from www.ilusa.com.
[48]Smart, J. (2001). Disability*, society, and the individual.* Gaithersburg, MD: Aspen Publishers, Inc.
[49]Smart, J., & Smart, D. (1992). Curriculum changes in multicultural rehabilitation. *Rehabilitation Education, 6,* 105-122.
[50]Smart, J. F., & Smart, D. W. (1993). The rehabilitation of Hispanics with disabilities: Sociocultural constraints. *Rehabilitation Education, 7,* 167-184.
[51]Smith, L. W., & Smith, Q. W. (1994). Independent living centers: Moving into the 21st century. *American Rehabilitation, 20*(1), 14-22.
[52]Stein, H. F. (1979). Rehabilitation and chronic illness in American culture: The cultural psychodynamics of a medical and social problem. *Journal of Psychological Anthropology, 2*(2), 153-176.
[53]Sue, D. W., & Sue, D. (2003). Counseling *the culturally diverse: Theory and practice.* New York: Wiley & Sons.
[54]Swedlund, N., Taylor, H. B., & Swank, P. (in press). Self- esteem and women with disabilities. *Social Science and Medicine.*
[55]Triandis, H.C. (1994). *Culture and social behavior.* New York: McGraw-Hill.
[56]Trusty, J., Looby, E. J. & Sandhu, D. (Eds.) (2002). *Multicultural counseling: Context, theory and practice, and competence.* New York: Nova Science Publishers.
[57]Uba. L. (1992). Cultural barriers to health care for southeast Asian refugees. *Public Health Reports, 107,* 544-548.
[58]Walker, S., Akpati, E., Roberts, V., Palmer, R., & Newsome, M. (Eds.). (1986). Frequency and distribution of disabilities among blacks: Preliminary findings. In S. Walker et al (Eds.), *Equal to the challenge: Perspectives, problems, and strategies in the rehabilitation of non-white disabled.* Proceedings of the national conference of the Howard University model to improve rehabilitation services to minority populations with handicapping conditions. (ERIC Education Reproduction Service No. ED 276 198).
[59]Westbrook, M., & Legge, V. (1993). Health practitioners' perceptions of family attitudes toward children with disabilities. A comparison of six communities in a multicultural society. *Rehabilitation Psychology, 38,* 177-185.

[60] Wilson, K. B. (1997). The *relationship between consumer race and vocational rehabilitation services and outcomes*. Unpublished doctoral dissertation, The Ohio State University.

[61] Wilson, K. B. (2002). The exploration of vocational rehabilitation acceptance and ethnicity: A national investigation. *Rehabilitation Counseling Bulletin, 45,* 168-176.

[62] Wilson, K. B., Jackson, R., & Doughty, J. (1999). What a difference a race makes: Reasons for unsuccessful closures within the vocational rehabilitation system. *American Rehabilitation, 25,* 16-24.

[63] Wilson, K. B., Turner, T., Liu, J., Harley, D. A., & Alston, R. J. (2002). Perceived vocational rehabilitation service efficacy by race/ethnicity: Results of a national customer survey. *Journal of Applied Rehabilitation Counseling, 33*(3), 26-34.

[64] Wilson, K. E. (1998). Centers for independent living in support of transition. *Focus on Autism and Other Developmental Disabilities, 13*(4), 246-252.

[65] Wright, T. J. (1988). Enhancing the professional preparation of rehabilitation counselors for improved services to ethnic minorities with disabilities. *Journal of Applied Rehabilitation Counseling, 19*(4), 4-10.

[66] Wright, T. J., Martinez, Y. G., & Dixon, C. G. (1999). Minority consumers of independent living services: A pilot investigation. *Journal of Rehabilitation, 65*(2), 20-25.

[67] Yamamoto, J., & Acosta, F.X. (1982). Treatment of Asian Americans and Hispanic Americans: Similarities and differences. *American Academy of Psychoanalysis, 10,* 585-607.

[68] Zukas, H. (1975). CIL history. Report of the state of the art conference, center for independent living (RSA Grant 45-P-45484/9-01). Berkeley, CA: Center for Independent Living.

CHAPTER 12

HUMAN RESOURCES DEVELOPMENT AND ISSUES IN REHABILITATION

MICHELLE P. POINTER

CHAPTER TOPICS

- Introduction
- Human resources management and development
- Diversity and disability in human resources management
- Human resources management and development in rehabilitation
- Training needs in rehabilitation
- Programs and resources designed to address human resources needs
- Issues for rehabilitation in human resources management and development
- Conclusion

CHAPTER 12   HUMAN RESOURCES DEVELOPMENT AND ISSUES IN REHABILITATION

INTRODUCTION

Resources are crucial to the successful operation of an organization, agency, or business. Although there are different types of resources, it is human resources that are most crucial to organizations. The heart of a business is the group of organized individuals that operate the business. State Vocational Rehabilitation Services Programs provide services to individuals with disabilities. Agencies assess, plan, develop, and provide services "consistent with their strengths, resources, priorities, concerns, abilities, capabilities, interests, and informed choice. (Rehabilitation Act, 1998)$^{Sec.100(a)(2)}$. People are important to the provision of services, and people must be prepared to be effective. These human resources come with varied training and competencies, and from diverse cultures and backgrounds. It is through recruitment, retention, and promotion that human resources development occurs. For purposes of this discussion, human resources development is defined as recognizing and realizing the possibilities and potential for human growth within an agency that make it better and providing avenues for such development/growth.

As diversity has become integral in American society and disability is inherent in life, vocational rehabilitation counselors must be qualified to serve all individuals with disabilities.[59] It is, therefore, imperative that professional counseling be founded on an understanding and appreciation of diversity.[36] Diversity and disability in the workplace, reflective of the vast human resources available today, lends itself to a carefully woven approach to personnel development and is significant during three distinct human resources development phases: recruitment, retention, and promotion. As personnel retention and promotion are considered, issues such as the relationship between knowledge, education, and rehabilitation leadership must be addressed.[47]

In this chapter, human resources development will be examined in the context of multiculturalism and diversity as it is manifested during personnel recruitment, employee retention and development, and promotion. This context is significant as the culture in the 21st century has become increasingly diverse, and pluralism has become the way of society.[36] Lee states, "people who represent diverse cultural backgrounds characteristic of this pluralism will be attempting to develop their abilities and interests within this new social order." [36,p.10] A brief, yet comprehensive discussion of training and development of rehabilitation personnel, reflective of diversity and inclusive of rehabilitation administration and leadership, will also be conducted. Issues that impact the current trends and future direction of rehabilitation will be identified.

As a result of reading this chapter, graduate students are expected to have a more comprehensive understanding of rehabilitation human resources development. Students will also be able to delineate from a multicultural perspective, the complex components of human resource development pertinent to the rehabilitation profession.

A literature review was conducted primarily from a framework of four disciplines: human resources; rehabilitation; diversity and disability; and leadership, which enlarged the pool of available research studies. This chapter will unravel literature and group the information into distinct areas: (1) human resources development and management literature; (2) diversity and disability as it impacts human resources; and (3) human resources in the rehabilitation profession, including both public and private settings. The specific focus of the review will be on diversity, disability, and human resources development, along with related current issues. Implications of the literature review will be drawn.

HUMAN RESOURCES MANAGEMENT AND DEVELOPMENT

Human resources are a valuable commodity, the development of which enhances the continuation of the agency or organization. This development is future-focused, and training and educationally based. It involves planning, managing, and motivating people for the purposes of performance enhancement.[25] Developing employees to carry on the business extends beyond traditional on-the-job-training, focusing more on preparing people for additional responsibilities. Conceptually, human resources development provides for employees' personal growth.[12]

The people who work in the agency are the means to the accomplishment of the agency's purpose and goals, and their competency, growth, and development are necessary. Successful agencies invest in their employees in order to ensure employee growth and agency success. As it relates to human resources management (structural component) and human resources development (growth component), the literature contains various approaches, research findings, and issues. There is, however, agreement on three essential processes that occur: recruitment, retention, and promotion.

Management is the organizational component responsible for acquiring and providing for the employee's growth. It is a mechanism motivated by thought, which seeks, prepares, provides for, and deliberately integrates agency/organizational personnel into its purposeful, goal-directed, and functional operations. Whether it is handled informally or formally, human resources management guides recruitment, retention, and the promotional processes.

Rehabilitation agencies or commissions have separate, dedicated personnel or human resources departments that may be located within the agency or a host organization. For instance, human resources management for VR may be in Education, Labor, Labor and Industry, Family and Social Services, Public Health and Human Services, or Employment and Training. Private and other rehabilitation agencies also have dedicated personnel or HR departments.

Employee development begins with recruitment and leads to retention, and in many cases, promotion.

RECRUITMENT

Practices in recruitment are surprisingly similar cross-nationally[31] as human resource managers are concerned about three general areas: (a) ability/potential to do the job; (b) interpersonal/interorganizational skills; and (c) longevity or return on investment. Employers consider whether a person encompasses the skills, knowledge, and abilities required for the job when reviewing candidates;[12,49] Recruitment initiates the process of human resources development by seeking out and developing a pool of job appropriate applicants. Recruitment has long been a concern of rehabilitation.[44] In a study specific to individuals with disabilities, Keys and Balcazar (2000) reviewed 37 research studies and concluded that even with generally positive employer attitudes and willingness to hire, negative attitudes persisted when specifics (e.g., promotability, accommodation costs) were involved. In another study, Evans,[14] found employers satisfied with the individuals whom they hired but concerned about hiring individuals with specific types of disabilities.

Recruitment efforts vary according to agency and policies. For example, recruitment efforts in VR are guided by federal legislation that requires state rehabilitation agencies to develop a Comprehensive System of Personnel Development (CSPD) and specify its components in the State Plan. One component of the CSPD is the statement of what shall constitute a "qualified" rehabilitation professional in that agency.

Competition among organizations for the most qualified employee is tighter when unemployment rates are lower, and some researchers have suggested using persuasion during interviewing, as well as promoting the agency reputation as a mechanism for obtaining competitive advantage.[15] The outside perception of the agency can be enhanced through the organizational management of diversity. Cross,[11] for example, suggests the use of a social-justice approach where executives explore less oppressive hierarchical and money driven work environments. Thus, the work of executives in more culturally sensitive work settings will impact other areas of employees' lives and will enhance the agency's reputation.

LEARNING STYLES

Recognition of ways individuals work and subsequent utilization of this information in advertising, can positively impact recruitment. Tobias[63] suggested learning style differences are more the cause of employee conflict than culture. Consequently, marketing approaches utilizing the four Gregoric learning styles would most likely appeal to individuals in accordance with their dominant style of learning. In other words, the question to answer when promoting the agency would vary for individuals:

- ➤ Concrete Sequential Dominant learner—What will we accomplish?
- ➤ Abstract Sequential Dominant Learner—What will we learn?
- ➤ Abstract Random Dominant Learner—What difference will we make?
- ➤ Concrete Random Dominant Learner—What makes us unique?

Recruitment can be accomplished internally as well as externally. Internal searches have many benefits. For example, internal searches are good for public relations and organizational reputation, organizational morale, individual ambition, good selection probability, and training mechanisms. They are also less costly. Work on task forces and committees provide experience, training, and promotional exposure for likely candidates. Effectively use personnel files may be sources for internal recruitment. Internal advertisement and subsequent interviews may yield appropriate candidates.

When external searches are utilized, the choice of local, statewide, regional, national, or international advertisement will depend on the scope of the job and the specific knowledge and skills required of the candidates. The modes of communicating vacancies could involve any combination of the following: newspapers; newsletters; Internet postings; web pages; job hotlines; departmental kiosks; employment office listings; job banks; and personnel offices. Announcements may be posted, mailed, emailed, or delivered to schools, colleges and universities, disability and minority organizations, professional organizations, chambers of commerce, churches, civic groups, and other local establishments. Referral sources are many and varied, ranging from employee referrals to placement referral agencies and executive personnel companies.

Diversity is a major concern with recruitment and, in fact, has become a major priority within the Federal government. Specifically, the law states:

> Recruitment efforts within vocational rehabilitation at the level of pre-service training, continuing education, and in-service training must focus on bringing larger numbers of minorities into the profession in order to provide appropriate practitioner knowledge, role models, and sufficient manpower to address the clearly changing demography of vocational rehabilitation.
> Rehabilitation Act, Section 21(a)(4)

Goss[25] explained recruitment as the place where principles of assessment involving judging attributes and abilities, operate. There are three distinct functions: 1. recruitment (e.g., creating a selection pool, evaluating performance needs); 2. selection (e.g., performance potential and succession planning); and 3. appraisal (e.g., reward, performance, career and development planning, and training needs). These three functions directly impact the employee's commitment to the organization.

In order for an organization to continue profitably, employees must invest in it. Whether it is a private or public human services program, its survival, and effectiveness is contingent upon accountability in management.[28] People make investments where there is a commitment to fulfilling their needs. The question in today's multicultural society becomes, how does human resources management recognize, respect, and capitalize on their employees' similarities and differences, and encourage organizational commitment?

RETENTION AND EMPLOYEE DEVELOPMENT

Retention precedes employee development. Employees tend to remain with an agency or organization if the rewards are sufficient. However, rewards are not always monetary. The individual and agency fit is also significant. Both intrinsic (e.g., self-fulfillment, opportunities for growth, job satisfaction) and extrinsic (salary, benefits, work environment) rewards play a role in employee commitment and, ultimately, tenure with the agency.[25,12]

Tenure is impacted by appraisal, although appraisals can be uncomfortable and training may not ease the discomfort. Blankenship and Crimando[6] found no significant correlation between appraisal training and increasing comfort in a study of the effectiveness of performance appraisal among three Illinois community rehabilitation agencies. In another study with community rehabilitation organizations, Mallik and Lemarie[40] examined perceptions of departing community-based rehabilitation program employees as a means to reduce staff turnover. Among other things, they found that employees with a high school, associate, and/or bachelor's degrees reported being in the right job, unlike those with less than a high school diploma and those with a doctoral degree. Overall, employees reported being professionally trained.

BURNOUT

Exhaustion from the work arising from long-term stress and specifically identified as *burnout* is real and has often been explored. Gomez and Michaels[24] observed low to moderate levels of burnout among public and private human service workers. Caseload size was, surprisingly, not significant. It was found that traditional coping strategies were employed. The researchers concluded that increased direct contact with the individuals being served and less paperwork provided more of a sense of personal accomplishment to the human service works.

Stress is especially significant for individuals from minority groups. According to a study by Clark, et al,[8] a stressor for African-Americans is racism; and racism is still very much prevalent today.[13] For example, "Black people have had to re-narrate themselves and re-negotiate their identities as workers...",[67p.352] thus giving an outward appearance of accommodation.

Whether individuals stay, remain in entry positions, become stagnant, grow, and develop, or progress promotionally is influenced by many factors, among which is motivation. Human resources has looked to other disciplines for a theoretical base in the absences of a distinctly human resources theory. Motivational theory is one way to explain human behavior. At this point, a brief discussion of selected theories explaining motivation is warranted.

MOTIVATIONAL THEORY AND HUMAN RESOURCES DEVELOPMENT

Abraham Maslow, Douglas McGregor, Frederick Hertzberg, David McCelland, Stacey Adams, and Victor Vroom are major contributors of motivational theories. Maslow is known for identifying five hierarchical order needs (physiological, safety, belonging, esteem, and self-actualization). McGregor proposed Theory X - Theory Y, which postulated that supervisors viewed human motivation as either negative (Theory X) or positive (Theory Y). On the other hand, Hertzberg proposed motivation hygiene suggesting that motivation was connected to intrinsic and extrinsic factors. Another theorist, McClelland, suggested achievement, affiliation, and power motives were connected to human motivation, and that these were tied directly to situations specific to the work environment (i.e., achievement, affiliation, power). A higher achievement need, for example, is related to higher performance. Adams is recognized for Equity Theory as he examined equity and the impact of perceived inequity in the workplace. Finally, Vroom examined value of effort and reward.[12]

REHABILITATION ACT OF 1973 AS AMENDED

Federal legislation impacting rehabilitation human resources development includes the Comprehensive System of Personnel Development (CSPD) delineated in the Rehabilitation Act. This is a legal requirement for VR agencies and directs an examination of the personnel needs and plan for adequate rehabilitation personnel. In their research on 1996 CSPD state documents, Froehlich, et al.,[19] examined hiring requirements. Recognizing an increase in hiring qualified counselors, they also identified inconsistencies between minimum education requirements and federal law.

The CSPD is specific in requirements and purposes to increase qualified personnel. Guidelines include the following directives: (a) describe procedures and activities that ensure an adequate supply of qualified State rehabilitation professionals and paraprofessionals; (b) specify the number and type of personnel currently needed, and projected to be needed in *five* years; and, (c) delineate a system for the continuing education of professionals and paraprofessionals within VR, especially for the retraining or hiring of personnel consistent with the State's professional requirements. As a result of CSPD, agencies have developed specific plans (incorporated in State Plans) to increase qualified personnel. Collaboration with local colleges and universities has yielded partnerships that lead to paid and unpaid internships, and in some

CHAPTER 12   HUMAN RESOURCES DEVELOPMENT AND ISSUES IN REHABILITATION

instances, direct hires for rehabilitation students from minority and other groups.

A replication study on the Rehabilitation Cultural Diversity Initiative (RCDI) with Region V Centers for Independent Living was conducted by Flowers, et al,[16] Crimando, & Riggar.[10] Their conclusion was that "the way to initiate cultural diversity is to retrain current rehabilitation professionals and to train future professionals in racial/demography of disability"[p.20] using an experiential knowledge approach.

In 1998, the RSA Commissioner reinforced the need to "ensure the quality of personnel who provide VR services and assist individuals with disabilities to achieve employment outcomes through the VR program."[53] RSA has also dedicated funds to enhance the development of Rehabilitation personnel.

AMERICANS WITH DISABILITIES ACT

In 1990, the Americans with Disabilities Act (ADA) made it illegal to discriminate against individuals with disabilities. (United States Equal Employment Opportunity Commission, 1991). The ADA is divided into five titles: Title I, Employment; Title II, Public Services; Title III, Public Accommodations; Title IV, Telecommunications; and, Title V, Miscellaneous. The legislation is especially important to human resources development, as Title I prohibits discrimination by employers in hiring, promotion, and dismissal. The United States Equal Employment Commission (US EEOC) enforces job discrimination, and any discrimination in state and local government programs and activities is enforced by the Department of Justice (DOJ). Workplace accommodations are required by employers with 15 or more employees, according to the Americans with Disabilities Act of 1990. In fact, the ADA specifically prohibits employment discrimination and provides for the hiring of qualified employees who can perform the essential functions of the job with or without reasonable accommodation.

In an effort to examine the conditions that influence accommodations, Geyer and Schroedel[20] conducted a study involving employees who were deaf or hard of hearing. Using a sample of 232 employees, the researchers sought to determine if accommodations were provided more frequently to individuals with higher education, and in more professional and managerial positions. The findings were consistent with their hypotheses. For employees at higher levels, there is greater investment and the employer may "...more readily conclude that these employees perform the types of essential job functions for which an accommodation can be justified."[p.48]

It is also important to consider coworker attitudes regarding individuals with disabilities. Hager[27] reviewed the literature and made recommendations for specific strategies for employers. Suggestions included having a more supportive culture in the work place, plans for career advancement beyond entry level, and assisting employees' social inclusion and mentoring.

DIVERSITY AND DISABILITY IN HUMAN RESOURCES MANAGEMENT

Culture is significant to the work environment, and subsequently to employee commitment and agency retention. Understanding culture is a significant part of HRD and HRM.[11,31,32,7] Recall that people learn differently and consider that they also work differently. In their investigation from a feminist framework of hundreds of papers on HRD,[5] determined that analysis of race, ethnicity, and gender were severely limited in the literature.[62] The fact that people come from diverse racial, ethnic, gender, disability, and cultural backgrounds is significant in understanding human resources development. Individual values, possibly influenced by national culture, influence organizational commitment.[21]

In their study with white counseling students, Evans and Foster[14] concluded that simple multicultural training, although helpful with information processing, might not lead to the complex thinking necessary for moral development. Cross[11] stated "cross-cultural management training has mushroomed, and now includes approaches that take into account patterns of racism, sexism, classism, and anti-immigrant sentiment."[p.62] It can be concluded that managing diversity is multifaceted and involves addressing the ways employees are different and providing fundamental change in the life of the corporation. "Changing the root culture is at the heart of the managing diversity approach."[61,p.26]

The significance of culture in human resource management and development is reflected in the literature. In their examination of international hiring practices, Huo, et al.,[31] determined that as cultures remain different in various countries and regions, and therefore human resources practices vary, there tends to be more divergence of practices as it relates to international recruitment. It is likely that there will be some convergence. Nevertheless, the "...best international human resources management practices ought to be the ones best adapted to cultural and national differences."[p.42]

In another organizational study examining the differences in valuing people across cultures, Jackson[32] identified differences in seven nations regarding the locus of human value and concluded that the West sees people as a means to an end. In a related study on culture, Budwar, and Sparrow[7] saw the need to develop an integrated framework in order to study human resources policies across nations, noting distinctive differences among variables, strategies, and polices.

Minority recruitment is enhanced legislatively through Section 21(a)(4), Rehabilitation Act, 1998). Section 21 findings indicate a disproportionately high rate of disabilities among ethnic and racial minorities and support recruitment equity. If minority recruitment is to succeed, however, diversity in the work place must be a reality. The approach to the management of diversity is more of an attitudinal concept that directs a comprehensive process of creating an atmosphere of inclusion. Organizations committed to managing and facilitating diversity must provide resources and set policies to support and embrace diversity.

There are multiple strategies for rehabilitation human resources to consider to obtain diversity and may include the following initiatives: 1. mentoring programs; 2. diverse focus groups; 3. policy revision sessions inclusive of individuals from minority and disability groups; 4. cultural workshops; 5. shadow days; 6. formal recognition programs; 7. accountability measures; and 8. rewarding creative diversity actions. The American Psychological Association[56] provided awards to three universities for their initiatives with recruitment and retention of ethnic minorities.

HUMAN RESOURCES MANAGEMENT AND DEVELOPMENT IN REHABILITATION

Rehabilitation has grown from an occupation into a profession.[44] In support of this, the concept of a career development tool for educators has been introduced. (Koch, Schultz, and Cusick, 1998). Specifically, this involves the creation of a portfolio for rehabilitation counselors that serve three purposes: (1) educational planning; (2) employment; and (3) career advancement. The rehabilitation profession has historically been synonymous with the State-Federal agency. This is no longer the case[33] as the field has grown tremendously and includes private (for profit and not for-profit) agencies.

All rehabilitation agencies, in order to continue effectively, realize that investing in personnel from all backgrounds has become essential. Strategic planning, goal setting, human resources, and personnel needs assessments similar to American businesses, must be done in the rehabilitation profession to shape its future. (Wright, 1986). Current practices among public rehabilitation agencies reflect acceptable human resources strategies. Vision and mission statements are incorporated in policy and widely distributed. Agencies also recognize and reward performance. Additionally, federal money has been provided for rehabilitation staff training.

ACCEPTING DIVERSITY

Recognizing differences among agency personnel is an important ingredient in agency functioning. For example, Andrew and Robertson[2] found consistency between private sector and public rehabilitation agencies as it relates to expecting computer skills in prospective candidates. However, retention is linked to development that extends beyond initial skills. Equally important is the process of developing diverse individuals within the agency. This requires an understanding of the social structure of the agency as well as how the agency functions, leading to insight into how learning and the acquisition of new skills occurs.

Understanding personal beliefs and attitudes regarding others who are different is a start to "helping people master the intrapersonal and interpersonal awareness needed to apply principles of group dynamics and adult learning to race, gender, and other forms of visible difference."[11p.144] Sensitivity to diversity is crucial to human resources development in the 21st century. Although some individuals simply embrace the richness that emanates from diversity, diversity is a reality and goes beyond choice.[62] The United States Census Projections for 1999 - 2010 indicate a major increase in minority populations in the United States. This increase in population will impact legislation and become a major component of human resources development.

ACCEPTING DISABILITY

Individuals with disabilities are an integral part of the fabric of society; therefore, a significant factor in the human resources development equation. Stigmas still exist, and confidence and success is related to how this is addressed in the work place. Smart (2001) suggests that individuals with disabilities learn to recognize and manage stigmas, acknowledging that although judgments and actions of others may hurt, they do not have to become a part of the individuals' self-concept. Nevertheless, employers have responsibilities.

Employer responsibilities include attention to workplace quality, which impacts employee retention and subsequent organizational commitment. Issues include staff competency, growth, and development. Differences in education, training, abilities, experience, skills, and performance dictate training needs.

TRAINING NEEDS IN REHABILITATION

This section will examine training and preparation using two categories: Rehabilitation specialists; and Rehabilitation administrators and leaders.

REHABILITATION SPECIALISTS

The concept of rehabilitation specialists is inclusive of such professional areas as counseling, vocational evaluation, and job placement. Specific knowledge and skills as well as specific training areas have interested researchers. Over ten years ago, Linkowski, et al.,[39] designed an instrument to validate rehabilitation knowledge standards used in counselor certification. The 57-item instrument included several subscales: 1. Vocational Services; 2. Case Management and Services; 3. Group and Family Issues; 4. Medical and psychological aspects; 5. Foundations of Rehabilitation; 6. Workers Compensation, Employer Services and Technology; 7. Social, Cultural, and Environmental Issues; 8. Research; 9. Individual Counseling and Development; and, 10. Assessment. Subsequently, Szymanski, et al, examined human resources development needs of rehabilitation professionals. Counselor knowledge areas, as well as importance, were examined for validation purposes relative to the practice of rehabilitation counseling.[38]

Rehabilitation counselor and specialist knowledge and responsibilities has been of interest for some time, and efforts to measure these factors has resulted in the development of instruments and inventories.[4,60] The training and preparation of rehabilitation professionals is essential and impacts effectiveness. For example, training and experience with HIV/AIDS significantly impacts counselor knowledge and skills when working with people with the disease.[23]

Research has clearly demonstrated a direct relationship between the level and type of educational degree and competency[55] and Leahy[37] relative to successful closure[9] and this actually varies according to employment settings.[37] One thing that remains consistent is that multicultural competencies are increasingly in demand.[42]

Remaining current is the challenge for the rehabilitation profession, as changes occur rapidly. In fact, several years ago, while counselor education programs tried to keep up with swift legislative shifts, the professional identity and independence of the profession was actually hampered.[30] That is no longer the case and the profession is firmly established and growing with the support of professional organizations.

PROFESSIONAL BODIES AND ORGANIZATIONS

Today there are four major national professional bodies: 1. Commission on Rehabilitation Counselor Certification; 2. American Rehabilitation Counseling Association; 3. Alliance for Rehabilitation; and 4. National Rehabilitation Counseling Association. The rehabilitation code of ethics, which was established in the 1980s, has remained current and alive through revisions.

The Foundation for Rehabilitation Education and Research[18] has identified professional credentialing options as indicated in Table I.

TABLE I

ORGANIZATIONS OFFERING CREDENTIALS RELATED TO REHABILITATION

National Credentials
CCMC	Certified Case Manager (CCM)
CDMSC	Certified Disability Management Specialist CDMS)
CRCC	Certified Rehabilitation Counselor (CRC); Canadian Certified Rehabilitation Counselor (CCRC)
NAADAC	National Certified Addiction Counselor I (NCAC I)
	National Certified Addiction Counselor II (NCAC II)
NBCC	National Certified Counselor (NCC)
	Certified Career Counselor (CCC)
	Certified Clinical Mental Health Counselor (CCMHC)
CCWAVES	Certified Vocational Evaluator (CVE)

State Credentials
(CADAC)	Certified Alcohol and Drug Abuse Counselor
	Licensed Professional Counselor (LPC)

Multicultural Rehabilitation Concerns (NAMRC) and the Council of State Administrators of Vocational Rehabilitation (CSAVR), in which every State Director of Public Vocational Rehabilitation usually maintains membership.

REHABILITATION ADMINISTRATORS AND LEADERS

Leadership is evolutionary and has generally been studied extensively over the years.[58] Some will argue that skillful movement of disciplined, decisive, and responsible risk-takers is how leadership talent enters the pipeline.[35] Others declare a connection between relationships and members of groups, and thereby agree with what Stodgill[58] said:

> Leadership appears to be a working relationship among members of a group, in which the leader acquires status through active participation and demonstration of his [her] capacity for carrying cooperative tasks through to completion.[p. 66]

With the recent focus on transformational leadership and extensive research, many define leadership as transformational. Transformational leaders "use transactional, managerial roles not simply to define, assign, and accomplish tasks and achieve goals, but also to educate, empower, and ultimately transform followers."[54p.20] This is common in public administration. In fact, in a recent study, 97.4% of State VR Directors were found to be transformational leaders.[47]

Public rehabilitation administrators and leaders often develop within the agency and move through internal promotional opportunities. Executive leaders can be appointed, however, and vary substantially in experience and training. Pointer,[47] for example, found 42.3% of respondents to have training fields unrelated to rehabilitation, and State VR Directors were almost equally divided between bachelor and doctoral degrees.

Administrators and leaders have training needs[41] and require training and preparation in management and competencies.[3,17] As leaders must have the ability to influence, energize,[22] lead change,[10] and provide vision, (McFarlane & Griswold, 1992), training and development is also necessary. Due to the nature of rehabilitation, some argue for leader credentialing,[34] as is the case with rehabilitation specialists.

Leadership occurs through preparation and planning and, conversely, succession planning should be considered more as an assessment and human resources development rather than planning for replacement.[35] Nevertheless, diversity remains an area to consider. In her survey of State Directors of VR,[46] found similar demographic characteristics among state leaders, as was found in a study twenty years ago. The leadership in public rehabilitation continues to be predominately white males who have certain dynamics. On the other hand, in instances when the boss is from a minority group (e.g., African American, Latina), other dynamics are inevitable.

In an unrelated agency, research conducted by Embrick[13] with males in lower-level management positions revealed that racial prejudice is alive and there is a bond between white males. Women, especially minority women, in leadership positions are at a disadvantage. Some benefit has been identified with social capital/mentors.[43] In another study, Vianello[66] concluded that although women need more conditions of advantages, once they achieve top positions in public life "they are equal to men in feeling that they exercise power to the same extent as men without the need to be backed by more favorable conditions."

PROGRAMS AND RESOURCES DESIGNED TO ADDRESS HUMAN RESOURCES NEEDS

LONG-TERM AND SHORT-TERM TRAINING PROGRAMS

There are a variety of programs and resources designed to address rehabilitation human resources needs. Colleges and universities with programs accredited by the National Council on Rehabilitation Education (NCRE) exist throughout the nation. Many colleges offer scholarships through federal long-term training grants. Regional Continuing Education Programs and Community Continuing Rehabilitation Programs exist. In addition, there are regional and national rehabilitation leadership programs, all of which can be located via the Internet.

TABLE 2: RESOURCES

SELECTED RESOURCES AVAILABLE TO REHABILITATION ARE INCLUDED IN THIS SECTION.

RSA	Rehabilitation Services Administration	Federal agency that administers the Rehabilitation Act
NCRE	National Council on Rehabilitation Education	The association of rehabilitation educators
NIDRR	National Institute on Disability and Rehabilitation Research	Federal agency that funds disability related research
IRI	Institute on Rehabilitation Issues	Federal program that develops training materials on rehabilitation
NARIC	National Rehabilitation Information Clearinghouse	A clearing house of rehabilitation research and training materials
IARP	International Association of Rehabilitation Professionals	Professional organization focusing on consulting, case management, and expert testimony
CSAVR	Council of State Administrators of Vocational Rehabilitation	Has a standing committee on human resource development

ISSUES FOR REHABILITATION IN HUMAN RESOURCES MANAGEMENT AND DEVELOPMENT

Several issues confront the human services nature of rehabilitation, and they are presented briefly for consideration and professional discussion: 1. *Leadership and qualified rehabilitation specialists pools* are impacted as the massive exit (retirement) of rehabilitation professionals continues; 2. *Funding for training and preparedness* is of concern due to the 2003 reauthorization of the Rehabilitation Act which relaxes legislative control of funds; 3. *Tailored training* as globalization leads to subsequent changes in the nature of work,[52] consumer expectancies of community-based rehabilitation programs (Thomas, Menz, Rosenthal, 2001) and other agencies, and continuous advances in assistive technology[50] 4. *Spirituality and subsequent counselor education;*[26] 5. *Diversity;* 6. *Performance appraisals*; 7. *Job functions and guidelines* in workforce investment centers; and 8. *Education on-line*, as a mechanism to reach diverse and distributed rehabilitation personnel.[22]

CONCLUSION

This chapter has examined human resources development and issues in rehabilitation from a review of the literature. Delineation between management and development of personnel was made. Human resources have been examined within the context of theory and legislation, using an approach of diversity (which includes disability) as the underlying theme within the profession of rehabilitation. Personnel training needs, leadership and succession, and related issues have been explored, and programs and resources identified.

SIGNIFICANCE AND IMPLICATIONS FOR TRAINING, PRACTICE, AND RESEARCH

Guided by the ADA, the Rehabilitation Act, and the CSPD, equity in recruitment, retention, training and development, and promotion is strengthened. Training needs exist at every level of personnel,[41,19,39] and in specific areas.[23] Issues such as succession planning, credentialing, leadership, diversity, funding, on-line education,[22] and spirituality will continue to surface and move to the forefront.

Higher education will be especially challenged as a result of this literature review, as it is significant and has implications for training, practice, performance, and future research. First, there is urgency in training. Recruitment and retention of qualified personnel will be guided by societal, technological, and economic changes, and the applicant pool will reflect increased diversity and disability. Appropriate, continuous upgrading of skills in a cost effective and refined timeframe is necessary. Funding sources for training may become scarce with the 2003 reauthorization changes in the Rehabilitation Act. Consequently, more creative ways to include a larger and more diversified personnel pool will be critical. Finally, transformational leadership will be essential in a global and increasingly diverse environment.

Areas for future research include rehabilitation human resources development, agency leadership, support personnel needs, agency effectiveness, personnel needs in a workforce environment, and differences in human resources development practices.

REFERENCES

[1]Americans with Disabilities Act (1990).

[2]Andrew, J., & Robertson, J. (2001. Private-sector computer skills expectations for rehabilitation counselor job applicants. *Rehabilitation Education, 15*(3), 295-299.

[3]Atkins, D. (1997). Rehabilitation management and leadership competencies. *Journal of Rehabilitation Administration, 21*(4), 249-261.

[4]Beardsley, M., & Rubin, S., (1988). Rehabilitation service providers: An investigation of generic job tasks and knowledge. *Rehabilitation Counseling Bulletin 32*, 122-135.

[5]Bierema, L., & Cseh, M. (2003). Evaluating AHRD research using a feminist research framework. *Human Resource Development Quarterly, 14*(1), 5-21.

[6]Blankenship, C., & Crimando, W. (2003). Effectiveness of a performance appraisal training program in increasing knowledge and decreasing discomfort among rehabilitation supervisors. *Journal of Rehabilitation Administration, 27*(1), 11-22.

[7]Budwar, P., & Sparrow, P. (2002). An integrative framework for understanding cross-national human resource management practices. *Human Resource Management Review, 12*(2002), 377-403.

[8]Clark, R., Anderson, N. B., Clark, V., & Williams, D. R. (1999). Racism as a stressor for African Americans: A biopsychosocial model. *American Psychologist, 54*, 805-816.

[9]Cook, D., & Bolton, G. (1992). Rehabilitation counselor education and case performance: An independent replication. *Rehabilitation Counseling Bulletin, 36*(1), 37-43.

[10]Crimando, W., Riggar, R., Bordieri, J.(1988). Proactive change management in rehabilitation: An idea whose time has been. *Journal of Rehabilitation Administration*, February 1988, 20-22.

[11]Cross, E. (2000). *Managing Diversity: The Courage to Lead*. Connecticut: Quorum Books.

[12]DeCenzo, D. & Robbins, S. (1999). *Human Resource Management. 6th ed.* New York: John Wiley & Sons.

[13]Embrick, D. G. (2005). Race-talk within the workplace: Exploring ingroup/outgroup and public/private dimensions. *The Journal of Intergroup Relations, 32*(51), 3-17.

[14]Evans, K. M. & Foster, V. A. (2000). Relationships among multicultlural training, moral development, and racial identity development of white counseling students. *Counseling and Values, 45*(1), 39-48.

[15]Ferris, G., Berkson, H., Harris, M (2002). The recruitment interview process: Persuasion and organization reputation promotion in competitive labor markets. *Human Resource Management Review, 12*(2002), 359-375.

[16]Flowers, C. R., Forbes, W. S., Crimando, W., Riggar, T. F. (2005). A regional survey of rehabilitation cultural diversity within CILs: A ten-year follow-up. *Journal of Rehabilitation 71*(2), 14-21.

[17]Ford, L. H. (1998). Measuring rehabilitation management and leadership competencies. *Journal of Rehabilitation Administration, 21*(4), 263-272.

[18]Foundation for Rehabilitation Education and Research (2000). *Rehabilitation Counseling: The Profession and Standards of Practice*, Illinois.

[19]Froehlich, Garcia, & Linkowski (1998). Minimum hiring requirements for rehabilitation counselors in states: A comparison across federal regions. *Rehabilitation Education 12*(3), 193-203.

[20]Geyer, P., & Schroedel, J. (1999). Conditions influencing the availability of accommodations for workers who are deaf or hard-of-hearing. *Journal of Rehabilitation 65*(2), 42-50.

[21]Glazer, S. Daniel, S. C., Short, K. M. (2004). A study of the relationship between organizational commitment and human values in four countries. *Human Relations 57*(3), 323-345.

[22]Glenn, M., Danczyk-Hawley, C., & Mann, D. (2000). Rehabilitation leadership on line. *Journal of Rehabilitation 24*(1), 25-35.

[23]Glenn, M., Garcia, J., Li. L., & Moore, D. (1998). Preparation of rehabilitation counselors to serve people living with HIV/AIDS. *Rehabilitation Counseling Bulletin, 41(3),* 190-199.

[24]Gomez, J., & Michaelis, R., (1995). As assessment of burnout in human service providers. *Journal of Rehabilitation,* January/February/March, 23-26.

[25]Goss, D. (1994). *Principles of Human Resource Management.* Routledge: New York.

[26]Green, R. L., Benshoff, J. J., & Harris-Forbes, J., A. (2003). Spirituality in rehabilitation counselor education: A pilot survey. *Journal of Rehabilitation, 67*(3), 55-60.

[27]Hager D. (2003). What we know about preventing and managing coworker resentment or rejection. *Journal of Applied Rehabilitation Counseling 34*(1).

[28]Harley, D. (2002). Book review of management of human service programs. *Journal of Rehabilitation Administration, 26*(3), 193-195.

[29]Hernandez, B., Balcazar. F. (2000). Employer attitudes toward workers with disabilities and their ADA employment rights: A literature review. *Journal or Rehabilitation, 66*(4), 4-16.

[30]Hershenson, D. B. (1988). Along for the ride: The evolution of rehabilitation counselor education. *Rehabilitation Counseling Bulletin, 31,* 204-217.

[31]Huo, P., Huang, H., & Napier, N. (2002). Divergence or convergence: A cross-national comparison of personnel selection practices. *Human Resource Management, 41*(1), 31-44.

[32]Jackson, T. (2002) The management of people across cultures: valuing people differently. *Human Resource Management, 41*(4), 455-475

[33]Jenkins, W. J., Patterson, J. B., & Symanski, E. M. (1992). Philosophical, historical, and legislative aspects of the rehabilitating counseling profession. In R. M. Parker & E. M. Szymanski (Eds.) *Rehabilitation Counseling* (2nd ed.) Texas: Pro-ed.

[34]Jewkes, L. F. (1988). Professional rehabilitation comments and challenges in *Journal of Rehabilitation Administration,* November 1988.

[35]Kesler, G. (2002). Why leadership bench never gets deeper: Ten insights about executive talent development. *Human Resource Planning, 25*(3), 32-44.

[36]Lee, Courtland. (1997). The promise and pitfalls of multicultural counseling. In C. C. Lee (Ed.). *Multicultural Issues in Counseling* (2nd ed.). Virginia: American Counseling Association.

[37]Leahy, M. J., Shapson, P., & Wright, G. (1987). Rehabilitation practitioner competencies by role and setting. *Rehabilitation Counselor Bulletin*, December 1987, 119-130.

[38]Leahy, M., Szymanski, E., & Linkowski, D. L. (1993). Knowledge importance in rehabilitation counseling. *Rehabilitation Counseling Bulletin*, 37(2), 130-145.

[39]Linkowski, D. L., Thoreson, R. W., Diamond, E., E., Leahy, M., J., Szymanski, E. M., & Witty, T., (1993). Instrument to validate rehabilitation counseling accreditation and certification knowledge areas. *Rehabilitation Counseling Bulletin*, *37*(2), 123-129.

[40]Mallik, K. & Lemaire, G. (2003). Assessing departing employee's perceptions may lead to organizational change to reduce staff turnover. *Journal of Rehabilitation Administration, 27*(1), 23-32.

[41]Matkin, R. E., Sawyer, H. W., Lorenz, J. R., & Rubin, S. E.(1982). Rehabilitation Administrators and supervisors: Their work assignments, training needs, and suggestions for preparation. *Journal or Rehabilitation Administration*, 170-187.

[42]Middleton, R., Rollins, C., Sanderson, P., Leung, P., Harley, D., Ebener, D., & Leal-Idrogo, A. (2000) Endorsement of professional multicultural rehabilitation competencies and standards: A call to action. *Rehabilitation Counseling Bulletin, 43*(4), 219-240.

[43]Palgi, M., More, G. (2004). Social Capital: Mentors and contracts. *Current Sociology*, *52*(3), 459-480.

[44]Parker, R., & Szymanski, E. (1992). *Rehabilitation Counseling: Basics and Beyond (*2nd ed.) Texas: Pro-ed.

[45]Pederson, P. (1994). *A Handbook for Developing Multicultural Awareness*, 2nd ed. Virginia: ACA.

[46]Pointer, M. P., (2004). Characteristics and leadership styles of state administrators of vocational rehabilitation. *Journal of Rehabilitation Administration, 27*(3 & 4), 83-93.

[47]Pointer, M. P. (2002). The relationship between transformational leadership, self-reported knowledge, education, educational relevancy, and experience among state vocational rehabilitation directors and rehabilitation rate. *Dissertation Abstracts International*, (UMI No. 3029590).

[48]Powell, G. & Butterfield, D. (2002). Exploring the influence of decision makers race and gender on actual promotions to top management. *Personnel Psychology, Inc.*, *55*, 397-428.

[49]Rehabilitation Services Administration United States Department of Education, (1998). *Rehabilitation Act of 1973 as Amended*, Washington, DC.

[50]Riemer-Reiss, M. Rehabilitation professionals' perceived competencies in assistive technology selection and referral: A preliminary analysis (2003). *Journal of Applied rehabilitation Counseling, 34*(2), 33-36.

[51]Rosenbach, W. E., & Taylor. R. L., (1994). *Contemporary Issues in Leadership 4th ed.* Westview Press.

[52]Ryan, C., (1995). Work isn't what it used to be: Implications, recommendations, and strategies for vocational rehabilitation. *Journal of Rehabilitation* October/November/December, 8-15.

[53]Schroeder, F. (1998). Commissioner's memorandum cm-98-12. *Rehabilitation Services Administration*, Washington, DC.

[54]Sashkin, M. and Rosenbach, W. E. (1993), "A new leadership paradigm", in Rosenbach, W. E. and Taylor, R. L. (Eds), Contemporary Issues in Leadership, Westview, Boulder, CO, pp. 87-108.

[56]Shapeson, P., Wright, G., & Leahy, M. (1987). Education and attainment of rehabilitation competencies. *Rehabilitation Counseling Bulletin*, December 1987, 131-145.

[56]Smith, D. (2000). Psychology departments recognized for ethnic-minority recruitment, retention. *Monitor on Psychology, 31*(11), 14.

[57]Souza, G. (2002). A study of the influence of promotions on promotion satisfaction and expectations of future promotions among managers. *Human Resource Development Quarterly, 13*(3), 325-340.

[58]Stodgill, R. (1948). Personal factors associated with leadership: A survey of the literature. *Journal of Psychology, 25*, 35-71

[59]Szymanski, E., Leahy, M., & Linkowski, D.(1993). Reported preparedness of certified counselors in rehabilitation counseling knowledge areas. *Rehabilitation Counseling Bulletin, 37*(2), 146-161.

[60]Szymanski, E., Linkowski, D., Leahy, M., Diamond, E., & Thoreson, R. (1993). Human resource development: An examination of perceived training needs of certified rehabilitation counselors. *Rehabilitation Counseling Bulletin, 37*(2), 163-181.

[61]Szymanski, E., Linkowski, D., Leahy, M., Diamond, E., & Thoreson, R. (1993). Validation of rehabilitation counseling accreditation and certification knowledge areas: Methodology and initial results. *Rehabilitation Counseling Bulletin, 37*(2), 13-121.

[62]Thomas, R. R. (1991). *Beyond Race and Gender.* New York: AMACOM.

[63]Tobias, C. U. (1995). *The Way We Work: What you Know About Working Styles Can Increase Your Efficiency, Productivity, and Job Satisfaction.* Tennessee: Broadman and Holman.

[64]Wolf, A. W., Wright, G. (1986). Professional perspectives and planning. In T. F. Riggar, D.T. Maki, & A. W. Wolf (Eds.), *Applied Rehabilitation Counseling,* 12-20. New York: Springer.

[65]Valle, M. (1999). Crisis, culture and charisma: The new leader's work in public organizations. *Public Personnel Management, 28*(2) 245-257.

[66]Vianello, M. (2004). Gender differences and power. *Current Sociology, 52*(3), 507-517.
[67]Yancy, G. (2004). Historical varieties of African American labor: Sites of agency and resistance. *Western Journal of Black Studies, 28*(2), 337-353.

Chapter 13

PARTNERING WITH FAMILIES FOR SUCCESSFUL CAREER OUTCOMES

Stacie L. Robertson
Carl R. Flowers

Chapter Topics

- Family models
- Ethnic family development
- Family influence on career success
- Strategies for partnering with families
- Counselor competencies and characteristics
- Conclusion

Family is the foundation from which one learns about the world.[51] Families influence many aspects of an individual's life choices, including education, political views, and in many cases, career choice, and outcomes. In exploring the role of family in successful career outcomes, the importance of family cannot be overstated. Given the important role and influences of family in successful vocational outcomes, it is understandable that programming and services must encompass the whole of an individual's lifestyle, including active involvement of nuclear or traditional family members, in addition to others such as extended family members and a wide variety of community support people. This chapter focuses on considerations and definitions of family explored from various ethnic groups; the role and importance of family in the vocational rehabilitation process; family influences on vocational outcomes; and partnering strategies with clients and families from diverse backgrounds (e.g., African American, Asian American, Hispanic American, and Native American), based on counselor competencies and characteristics.

The notion that disability is a natural part of the human existence has been widely chronicled in the rehabilitation literature.[4,47,56] So too has the idea that family, in various forms and models, is influential in the acceptance, adjustment, and life outcomes of individuals with a disabilities. Power,[40] for example, observed that disability is "a family affair" and that "client performance in vocational rehabilitation is a function of both the person and the family involvement."[p.195] Parke[36] further noted that family members are mothers, fathers, and siblings, who have both direct and indirect influence on one another. As noted above, the notion of family may invoke various images or various definitions, forms, and models. Landesman and Veitz's definition of family as a "social group with whom one resides."[p.61] may be appropriate in some instances; while references to family as people one feels close to and or on whom one tends to depend or rely, may also fit. Another definition, Goldenberg, and Goldenberg[18] observation of family as a system in which a set of rules are in place, where members are assigned ascribed roles and where intricate overt and covert forms of communication are in place, may seem more appropriate.

From a disability standpoint, 2000 census data indicated that more than 20 million (28.1%) families in the United States reported having at least one family member with a disability.[54] Of this group, more than 16% (12 million families) reported that at least one family member reported having a "condition that substantially limits one or more basic physical activities." These data suggest that disability is truly becoming "more common as a larger portion of the U.S. population.[47p.29]

FAMILY MODELS

Hare and Gray[20] (n. d.) observed that the traditional family model (e.g., married couple with their own children, where one parent works outside the home and all family members share a common dwelling) is less common than other familial structures. Data from the 2000 census suggests that this family model is now the *non-traditional* type in the United States, with less than 10% of all American families fitting the definition of a traditional or nuclear family. In its place, other family structure models, including extended, stepfamilies, single-parent families, and alternative families are emerging in the today's society.[7]

Another increasingly common, frequently reported, familial model is the single-parent family. Recent statistics indicate that more than 90% of single-parent households are headed by females.[20] In this pattern, only one parent is responsible for establishing and maintaining family traditions and culture. Another quite common family model is the extended family, where the family unit includes informal kin (who may not be parents and or grandparents), as well as great grandparents, siblings, and other relatives who have maintained relationships with family members. Paniagua[35] served that the extended family often includes both "biologically related individuals as well as non-biologically related individuals"[p.128] where supports (e.g., instrumental, emotional) are provided. The non-biologically related extended family members often include friends, ministers, and healers.

Sue and Sue[51] noted that the extended family plays important roles in decision-making among African Americans, Asians, Hispanics, as well as Native Americans. The influence of the extended family members in decision-making is often based, in part, on the instrumental supports (i.e., financial) and emotional (e.g., advice and counseling) provided.[35] Other family forms include blended families, where families are created by divorce and/or remarriage; and grandparent-led families, in which children are reared by grandparents when the biological parents are no longer able to serve as family leaders, for one reason or another. According to the U.S. Census Bureau,[54] nearly 6 million grandparents were listed as head of households in 2002, and about 4 million youth lived in households headed by a grandparent. Grandparent-headed households have grown by 105 percent since 1970.

Regardless of the family structure, the family influences several aspects of an individual's life choices, including career choice, education, and political views.

ETHNIC FAMILY DEVELOPMENT

AFRICAN AMERICANS

Literature suggests that African American families reflect vast within-group differences, including organizational units, socio-economic status, cultural values, and country of origin.[50] In support, Parke[36] observed that recent literature has shifted toward the African American family being viewed as "resilient,"[p.381] as opposed to previous literature tending to focus on the African American family as being disorganized. This resiliency, the author notes, is characterized by several important areas, including a strong sense of family and familial obligations, willingness to absorb relatives, frequent interaction with relatives, and a system of mutual aid. This strong sense of family or strong kinship bond is highly adaptive for the African-American family in providing support and in combining resources. Also, highly adaptive is the African-American family's ability for role flexibility.[13] This family strength indicates that family members are better able to take on different family roles. This strength, while adaptive in nature, allows for adjustment to the changes in family roles that often come with the onset of a disability. As an example, when compared to other groups, more African American families are headed by single women than any other ethnic group.[54] McCollum's[30] observation that, in many ways, the African American family is defined by the manner in which its members perform "based on the needs within the family itself."[p.220] This supports the view that the African-American family is highly resilient.

ASIAN AMERICANS

In the United States, Asian Americans include populations from nearly 30 countries in the Far East and South Pacific region, including China, Guam, Japan, Korea, the Philippines, and Vietnam. Given the broad variance, Asian American family models tend to be diverse, based on a number of factors, including languages, reasons for immigrating to the United States, and number of familial generations within the country. Ishi-Kuntz, cited in Demo, (Allen, and Fine, 2000) observes that, while within-group diversity is present, one constant is the fact most Asian families are generally viewed as patriarchal. In this population, length of residence in this country is a contributing factor and impacts on how the family is defined.

HISPANIC AMERICANS

The term Hispanic refers to a number of groups of Spanish speaking descent, including individuals from Central America, South America, Cuba, and Mexico.[42] Census data[55] indicate that the Hispanic population experienced more than a 3% increase (14 million) in the United States and continues at a rate (3.6 percent) well above that of other ethnic groups. Regardless of their original country of entry, the Hispanic family unit tends to be a close-knit, family-oriented group, where the larger family (i.e., extended family) unit is common. Observing that Hispanic family members are likely to live in close proximity of one another, Parke[36] explains "there is a high level of cross generational co-residence arrangements and assistance.[p.383]

NATIVE AMERICANS

Given that these populations represent nearly 400 distinct ethnicities and speak more than 200 languages, the literature suggests that it is almost impossible to define the typical family as a group. While different in many familial characteristics, Dykema, et al.[16] and Nelson, and Appleton (1995) suggest that the extended family is one of the "greatest strengths common to American Indian cultures."[p.150] Thomason[52] suggests that at least four family types; Isolated, Traditional, Bicultural, and Acculturated, characterized by where the family lives and the family's participation in traditional within-group activities, are common among this population. The Isolated family usually lives in remote areas of their reservation and retains its preference for use of the native language. This is in contrast to the bicultural family, whose members also lives on the reservation, participates in tribal ceremonies, *and* who prefer speaking English.[52]

As can be seen, the term *family* has many different meanings across cultural populations. Who is considered a family member and how the family is involved in the counseling process, logically, also would differ based on cultural definitions of family? While this chapter offers examples of differences between cultural groups and family involvement in the counseling and career counseling process, multicultural competencies suggest that counselors increase their understanding of cultural differences through further research and involvement with different cultural groups.

FAMILY INFLUENCE ON CAREER SUCCESS

Providing career services to individuals with disabilities from various cultural backgrounds is multidimensional. Cultural differences, the individual's functional limitation, type, level, and onset of the disability, along with numerous other individual factors, may require that career services focus on assisting with independent or interdependent issues (i.e., housing, transportation, personal care assistance) and vocational issues (i.e., decision making skills, vocational development, vocational placement). As an example, an individual with severe mobility impairment, who is unable to drive, may need assistance with personal care and transportation issues before addressing general vocational issues. A holistic point of view is, therefore, necessary for successful career outcomes for individuals with disabilities and their families.

The onset of a disability is, in fact, a family affair.[38,39,41] Often, the family offers assistance with the individual's interdependent needs and influences the individual's vocational decisions. Family influence, therefore, is an important factor in human services and career counseling of individuals with disabilities and is a strong factor in service treatment outcomes for individuals with disabilities. Family influence is especially important when working with those individuals who, based on their cultural beliefs, function in the collective. A collectivist view, inherent in many cultural groups,[46] indicates that disability is a reflection of the entire family as opposed to the individual.[21]

Independent living matters, such as transportation, self-care, housing, and money management skills often are matters of concern for both individuals from various racial/ethnic cultures and individuals with disabilities. Consequently, if the family's cultural values stress the importance of the family unit, an individual with a disability may remain living with the family, regardless of his or her abilities to live independently. Mexican families, for example, may expect a child to live in their home until they are ready to get married and start a family of their own. Within this type of family unit, the family often supports the individual with a disability financially as well as psychologically. In addition to the family unit, the Mexican community is an important factor, and is often seen as family, providing assistance and support to the members of the community.[44] In this situation, the family and community members influence independent or interdependent matters. A Mexican-American with a disability may reside with his or her immediate family members, rely on a family member for personal assistance, and rely on a community member for transportation to and from work. Due to the interdependent nature of various cultural groups, working with the family to develop and implement an interdependent living plan for the person with a disability is vital.

Rehabilitation researchers have historically found that family involvement in the vocational process improves both the quality and quantity of placements.[14,33] Factors such as family background, educational level, occupational attainment, and the family's location in the broader social context (i.e., socioeconomic status and cultural membership) affect vocational development.[25,26,45] The family's influence is apparent with regard to the opportunities provided by the family (i.e., educational, financial, role models, knowledge sources), the family's processes, which may include socialization practices, parent-child relations,[25,26,45] and the family's response to disability.

Family reactions to disabilities in general can significantly factor into the individual's counseling goals and outcomes, including vocational development and placement. This reaction may differ based on the family's cultural beliefs, with definitions of disability differing among cultures.[10,43,49] Causation, along with valued and devalued attributes of disabilities differ across cultures and dictate how disability is defined within the culture and/or the family.[19] Sotnik and Jezewski[49] provide an example:

> ... Southeast Asian beliefs related to disability and its causation range from those that focus on the behavior of the parents, particularly the mother, during pregnancy to sins committed by extended family memberships and reincarnation... A Southeast Asian individual with a disability may be segregated from the community because the disability represents a wrongdoing by the parents or ancestors and is considered a source of disgrace.[p 27]

Taking Southeast Asian cultural beliefs into consideration, the counseling process may be hindered by the family, fearing that inclusion of the individual with a disability into the world of work may highlight the family's disgrace. While the cultural group may espouse a certain belief pertaining to work, beliefs regarding disability may supercede all other traditional beliefs. One individual of Asian decent indicates the following:

> There are many aspects of the way my parents have raised me that would have differed dramatically if I would have been able-bodied. In many ways the situation of me being disabled overshadowed many traditional Asian values they may have held. They did not exert the academic pressures that are common to Asian households, on me. ... I know my parents would have pressured me a lot more to succeed academically if I did not have a disability.[Tsao, 2000]

As noted by Tsao's personal experience, cultural beliefs regarding disability may override cultural beliefs regarding academic and, ultimately, career expectations. As cultural beliefs regarding disability may affect counseling outcomes, so too might cultural beliefs regarding meaningfulness of specific types of work.[21] For some cultural groups, caregiver responsibilities, as they would be assigned to a person with or without a disability, may be considered a positive vocational outcome. With so many family factors influencing counseling and vocational outcomes, it becomes increasingly important to involve the family in the process.

STRATEGIES FOR PARTNERING WITH FAMILIES

Involving the family in vocational rehabilitation can be challenging for all counselors. Rehabilitation counselors, particularly, identify the following as challenges to family inclusion in the rehabilitation process: belief that there is an individual focus inherent in rehabilitation, lack of encouragement for family inclusion by rehabilitation agencies, limited funding, large caseloads, limited counselor time, and lack of training to provide services to families.[1,29] Although this research is specific to rehabilitation, family inclusion is often neglected in other counseling and human service agencies, especially with regard to career counseling. While many roadblocks and challenges to including families in the career counseling process may appear to be present for the counselor, the rewards for inclusion can be tremendous with regard to successful counseling outcomes. Given the various roadblocks to inclusion, it becomes up to the individual counselor to find creative ways in which to include the family.

Issues in working around time limits and caseload size are specific to the individual counselor and agency. There are, however, universal strategies that can assist in enhancing relationships with families who represent various cultural backgrounds. To enhance the relationship with the family, multicultural competencies, and an ability to establish a working alliance with the family, is necessary. Conducting a family assessment to determine the family's ability to assist in the process or to determine if the family is a hindrance to the counseling process can help the counselor to determine strategies on how to involve the family. The remainder of the chapter will review several strategies for partnering with families, including basic competencies and characteristics needed to partner with the family, suggestions on establishing a working alliance with the family, and conducting a family assessment. This chapter concludes by using a rehabilitation model as an example of how families can contribute throughout the counseling process.

COUNSELOR COMPETENCIES AND CHARACTERISTICS

Partnering with multicultural families requires the counselor to possess basic competencies and characteristics. Multicultural competencies, essential when counseling at any level, include counselor knowledge of:

- their own cultural values and biases,
- the client's cultural values and worldview,[51] and
- culturally appropriate intervention strategies.[1]

Multicultural competencies allow the counselor to understand the family's worldview, determine how the counselor's own biases may affect the counseling process, and determine treatment strategies and techniques that will aid in the counseling process.

Counselors with knowledge of their own cultural values and biases are better able to recognize the potential effects or the impact of their values on culturally diverse families[32] and the impact these values may have on the counseling relationship. Knowledge of the family's cultural values and worldviews allows the counselor to determine if the counseling relationship style, techniques, and/or interventions fit with the family's cultural values, beliefs, and worldview. For example, Latino families often value distinct and highly structured family roles and duties. This authority structure of the family often influences how the family views authority in general, indicating that the family respects and may even be most comfortable in hierarchical structures. The counselor who attempts to lessen the power deferential, be less authoritative, more democratic, using indirect and subtle forms of communication may inadvertently alienate, disrespect, and/or confuse the Latino family that values authority structure.[13] Values of importance to counselors that are often placed on the ethnic minority client are independence and achievement, along with self-disclosure and emotional expressiveness.[15,51] Multicultural competency includes knowledge of how these values may come into conflict with a client who values collectivism, cooperation, and 'saving face.'[9]

Inherent in multicultural competencies is the ability to recognize that variations exist within cultural groups, and the ability to avoid stereotyping individuals based on diversity group affiliation.[13,19] As Groce[69] eloquently notes, "no ethnic background wholly explains the way any individual or family will think or act."[p.2] Individuals and families differ in their affiliation with cultural values and beliefs. Individual diversity factors, such as socioeconomic status, may also impact a family's beliefs and values.[19] Knowledge of the variations that are within ethnic/racial groups as they are often categorized within the United States, is necessary. Diller[13] notes that it is common practice in the United States to divide the non-White population into four broad categories (Asian-American, African-American, Latino-American, and Native American). Although there are four broad categories, there is within each of these categories a great deal of variation. For example, the Asian-American category refers to "some twenty-nine distinct subgroups that differ in language, religion, and values." [6,p.195] Establishing a respectful relationship incorporates knowledge of the family's affiliation within their identified cultural group, knowledge of cultural values and beliefs that the family espouses, and knowledge of how these values and beliefs differ from other families or other cultural groups.

Along with multicultural competencies, specific characteristics are requisite to forming collaborative relationships with families. Sohlberg, et al.,[48] note that role release, role replacement, interpersonal communication skills, self-confidence, and being well informed are all characteristics that families in the counseling process regarded favorably. Counselors, who acknowledge the expertise of the family and include the family in the counseling process while sharing their own expertise in counseling, successfully engage in role release and role replacement. Recognizing the expertise of the family along with acknowledging the individual's and the family's strengths and weaknesses[48] increases the likelihood that the family will participate in the counseling process.

As is true for any counseling process, interpersonal communication skills, along with basic counseling skills, are highly regarded in counseling that is inclusive of families. The success of the process is dependent on the counselor's ability to gather information from the family as well as convey information to the family. Equally important, the counselor works as a model to assist the family in developing positive communication within the family constellation.[8] This includes becoming, to the extent possible, a part of the extended family referenced earlier in this chapter.

ESTABLISHING A WORKING ALLIANCE WITH THE FAMILY

The working alliance, or therapeutic relationship, has been found to be one of the most influential aspects of individual and family counseling. A working alliance has been established when the family perceives the counselor as trustworthy and helpful. A collaborative relationship forms when the family believes that they are working together as a team with the counselor.[31] In establishing a working relationship with the family, establishing rapport in a culturally competent manner is vital. In working with culturally different individuals, it may be necessary to alter the standard "getting down to business" attitude customarily adopted in counseling procedures.[13] Alvarez,[3] for example, observed that flexibility and acceptance of different views of time and punctuality are areas of importance when establishing early relationships with clients from differing backgrounds. In altering the standard "getting down to business" attitude, it may be necessary to spend additional time on mutual introductions, counselor self-disclosure, and providing information regarding the helping process.[13]

While not intended as prescriptive, the following are additional considerations for human service professionals when working with families from diverse cultures in developing a working alliance that takes into consideration racial and ethnic diversity. Awareness can be important in achieving successful counseling outcomes. Hispanics, for example, share a common background and culture, and are considered a "family oriented people."[3, p.74] While similar in many aspects, Alavrez[3] observes that it is important to remember that this group also has "various ideas, values, and beliefs that may be different from those of other groups."[p.73] As mentioned previously, recognizing the family's values and how they differ from that of the counselor increases the counselor's multicultural competencies and aids in developing a working alliance. Success with the family, and ultimately the client, is likely to be dependent on the acceptance of the service provider by the family.

Similar to the Hispanic family, knowledge of the values and beliefs of the African American family is also needed to develop a working alliance. Based on a history of discrimination and oppression within the United States, African American individuals and families may be distrustful of counselors and efforts to help.[2,37] Mistrust may also be based on other family members' (i.e., grandparents, siblings, uncles) or community influences and perceptions, along with past racism and prejudice.[58] With African American families, the service provider's acknowledgement and understanding of the realities of racism and oppression can aid in developing a working alliance. Mitigating cultural distrust involves counselors developing their own multicultural competencies, recognizing, and acknowledging differences, and understanding how conflicting values between counselors and families may affect the counseling process. Additional methods of mitigating distrust may include involving trusted members of the community, such as a family minister, into the counseling process.[13]

Thomason[52] observed that because the population is "extremely varied, it is impossible to make general recommendations regarding counseling that apply to all Native Americans."[p.321] In working with the Native American population, Thomason recommends that counselor warmth, caring, and geniuses are important elements in successful outcomes. The counselor's ability to ascertain the client's family and tribal identification (e.g., linkage to tribal culture vs. mainstream culture) can also provide direction on if, how, and when the family might be involved in the client's rehabilitation program and success.

Sue and Sue[51] observed that the admission of family problems or difficulties (e.g., family member seeking/receiving career counseling services) within Asian families is quite uncommon. As a result, gaining the confidence of inner-core family members will be critical to developing a working alliance as well as to the successful participation and outcome in the counseling process.

In many immigrant communities, the extended family is viewed as the norm and determines "where you live, with whom you live, where you work and at what occupation, whom you marry, and where and from whom you seek health care."[19,p.9] In this situation, establishing a trusting relationship with the extended family, and possibly with the community in general, is necessary prior to establishing a relationship with an individual.

Multicultural counseling competencies are imperative during the initial relationship building stage, as well as throughout the counseling process. As mentioned, counselor self-awareness, awareness of the values and beliefs of others, along with an understanding of how values may conflict, assist the counselor in developing a working alliance. Recognizing how to build a relationship that is respectful of cultural values and beliefs allows for the development of a collaborative relationship involving the family.

FAMILY ASSESSMENT

A family assessment can generally aid in determining the family's functioning and to help ascertain the level of involvement the family may have with counseling, goal setting, and planning. Identifying the family's level of disability acceptance, determining the family's strengths and weaknesses, and assessing the family's beliefs about work and/or the family's work ethic all should be part of the family assessment. Bray[8] also suggests assessing the family's power bases, communication patterns, and the effectiveness of the family's communication.

In working with a family from a diverse cultural background, an assessment of acceptance of disability status is warranted for both the family and the individual. The individual and the family may go through similar stages of acceptance, adaptation, or adjustment to the disability, including shock, anxiety, denial, depression, anger/hostility, and adjustment.[23,27,28,34,57] The family's or the individual's stage of acceptance may affect acceptance of diagnosis, degree to which medical and/or psychological treatment is adhered to, and the extent to which the family or individual understands the individual's functional limitations and strengths.[57]

While the family and the individual may go through similar stages of disability acceptance, problematic adjustment behaviors may manifest themselves differently for the family and the individual. Specific to each stage of acceptance are issues that may need to be addressed in counseling. For example, in the denial stage, the individual and/or the family may exhibit a "blatant neglect of medical advice and therapeutic or rehabilitation recommendation."[27] In this situation, a family member in denial may refuse to provide transportation to medical appointments or assistance in personal care needs. Talking with the family, providing medical information, and finding ways to assure that medical needs are taken care of becomes a vital part of the counseling process in this situation.

On the opposite end of the spectrum are those family members whose reaction to disability is to be overprotective of the individual with a disability. Croteau and Dorze[11] define overprotection as the "underestimation of the recipient's capabilities that is manifested in unnecessary help, excessive praise for accomplishments, or attempts to restrict activities."[p.432] This overprotection often has a negative affect on the motivation of the individual in regard to rehabilitation, counseling, and/or employment.[11] In working with families from diverse cultural backgrounds, assessing the family's acceptance of disability will also require knowledge of family roles and how the culture responds to disability. As an example, in many Puerto Rican families, it is the good and caring mother who continues to assist young or disabled children.[19] The counselor who possesses a multicultural awareness will recognize this ongoing assistance as an expected role of the mother, and not an attempt to overprotect or to intentionally discourage self-sufficiency.

Along with an assessment of the family's acceptance of disability and a general family assessment, when working with multicultural families it may prove helpful to assess cultural issues. These issues may include:

➢ the family's cultural identity,

➢ the family's racial salience,[17] that is to say how important the family views race and/or cultural issues, and

➢ the family's and the individual's level of acculturation, or the family's level of adhering to dominate cultural beliefs.

In assessing the acculturation levels of the family and/or individual, the multicultural counselor will also look for any intergenerational conflicts with regard to acculturation and racial salience. Finally, in the family assessment the counselor may find it helpful to identify clients' worldviews and their experiences with prejudice and discrimination, along with how these factors affect the clients' vocational goals and outcomes.[17]

Family assessments can be gained through the use of interviews, observations, and techniques such as the genogram and/or the culturagram. The genogram, an instrument used to examine the internal family relationships, offers the client an opportunity to describe the importance of each family member and the family member's influence on counseling goals or career aspirations.[35] The culturagram, similar to the genogram, is generally used in social work to explore the influence of culture on various aspects of the family's life.[10] The ten areas of discussion addressed in the culturagram are identified in Table 1.

TABLE 1
TEN AREAS OF THE CULTURAGRAM

- Reasons for Relocation (if family is from a different country)
- Legal Status
- Time in Community
- Languages Spoken at Home and in the Community
- Health Beliefs
- Crises Events
- Holidays and Special Events
- Contact with Cultural and Religious Institutions
- Values about Education and Work
- Values About Family-Structure, Power, Myths and Rules

Congress, 2004

FAMILY CONTRIBUTIONS

Specific to vocational rehabilitation, Rubin and Roessler[42] identify various areas in which the family can be included in the career counseling process. While this information is specific to vocational rehabilitation, other human service professionals can adapt the following information to fit within their work setting. Rubin and Roessler[42] divide the vocational rehabilitation process into four phases:

- The evaluation phase,
- the planning phase,
- the treatment phase, and
- the termination phase.

In moving through the vocational process, counselors must be mindful that individuals with disabilities may depend heavily on family for support, knowledge of job and social opportunities, residential and transportation services, and community awareness,[24] to assist the individual through the phases of vocational rehabilitation, or career counseling.

The *evaluation phase* yields information regarding vocational choice options, functional limitations, interests, abilities, and aptitudes.[42] In the evaluation phase, the family's values and beliefs will need to be assessed to determine appropriate vocational choice options and expectations. In this phase, and throughout the process, the family can be a valuable resource. Family members can add to the information gathering process by providing additional information and/or a different perspective with regard to the individual's functional limitations, strengths, interests, and abilities. During the evaluation phase, family members may also assist in a very practical manner through providing transportation, offering support, and assisting the individual in retaining information as it is received throughout this early stage of counseling.

The *planning phase* consists of consolidating information gained in the evaluation phase, determining appropriate counseling objectives, goal setting, and career exploration.[42] Again, the family can provide basic assistance such as transportation to and from meetings, along with financial and residential support. Family input will be needed in determining family and culturally appropriate vocational objectives and goals. As mentioned previously, the family's ownership of the plan and objectives increases the probability of the individual's follow-through. Family members should, therefore, be included in the goal setting process as well as the placement process.

To acquire positive career outcomes, counselors secure and coordinate a variety of services to aid in rehabilitation. These rehabilitation services, as well as job placement itself, make up the *treatment phase* of vocational rehabilitation.[42] Rehabilitation services may include rehabilitation workshops consisting of transitional workshops and/or sheltered workshops, comprehensive rehabilitation centers, and/or work adjustment training. Throughout the treatment process, the individual may work with a variety of service providers, including, but not limited to, medical personnel, psychologist, speech-language pathologist, physical therapist, and occupational therapists. During this phase, the family may assist the counselor in locating culturally appropriate and/or culturally competent facilities and service providers. Similar to the other phases, families may assist in transportation to and from appointments, assure that treatment goals are adhered to, and in assisting the individual in retaining information obtained from service providers.

The treatment phase, by nature, involves a great deal of commitment from the individual with a disability. Family members can provide encouragement and general support, assisting individuals in increasing their belief in their ability to complete the career counseling process. Throughout the process, the family can also provide natural supports, and assist with job search tasks such job search organization, completion of applications, resume writing, and practicing interviewing skills. Family members can provide support through job search networking,[41] as well as socialization skill instructions.

Once an individual is successfully employed, the counselor begins to work toward the termination phases. Counselors, at this time, can provide education to the family in ways in which the family can support the individual in maintaining employment; provide emotional support; as well as residential, financial, and transportation support, if necessary. Family members can be trained by the counselor to provide follow-through support in assisting the individual with a disability in maintaining employment. Counselor commitment to inclusion of the family into the counseling process is an important first step. Counselors are encouraged to find ways to include the family that fit with the counseling goals, the family, and the individual's needs.

CONCLUSION

Successful career outcomes for individuals with disabilities from various cultural backgrounds is inclusive of the family and takes into account family influences on the individual, counseling goals, and outcomes. Partnering with the family involves careful assessment of the individual's definition of family, family influence, cultural factors, and cultural influences. The assessment takes into account the family's influence on the individual's beliefs about work and disability, in general, as well as the individual's career decisions. Through the use of multicultural counseling competencies, the successful counselor establishes a working alliance with the family, remaining flexible to the family's decision-making process. Incorporating the family throughout the various stages of the counseling process assures that the family supports the individual, the career counseling goals, and the process. Often it is this family support that makes for the most successful career outcomes for individuals with disabilities whose cultural heritage values family, the family's influence, and a collective sense of being. While this may be unusual for both the career counselor and the service-providing agency, it is often necessary to obtain successful career outcomes.

REFERENCES

[1]Accordino, M. P., & Hunt, B. (2001). Family counseling training in rehabilitation counseling programs revisited. *Rehabilitation Education, 15,* 255-264.

[2]Alston, R. J., & Bell, T. J. (1996). Cultural mistrust and the rehabilitation enigma for African Americans. *Journal of Rehabilitation, 62,* 16- 20.

[3] Alvarez, L. I. (1998). A short guide in cultural sensitivity training. *Teaching Exceptional Children, 31*(1), 73-77.

[4] Americans with Disabilities Act of 1990, 42 U.S.C. § 12101 et seq.

[5] Arrendondo, P., Toporek, R., Brown, S.P., Jones, J., Locke, D.C, Sanchez, J., & Stadler, H. (1996). Operationalization of the multicultural counseling competencies. *Journal of Multicultural Counseling and Development, 24,* 42-78.

[6] Atkinson, D. R., Morten, G., & Sue, D. W. (1993). *Counseling American minorities: A cross-cultural perspective,* (4th ed.): Dubuque, IA: William C. Brown.

[7] Benshoff, J. J., & Janikowski, T. P. (2000). *The rehabilitation model of substance abuse counseling.* Belmont, CA: Brooks/Cole.

[8] Bray, G. P. (1980). Team strategies for family involvement in rehabilitation. *Journal of Rehabilitation, 46,* 20-23.

[9] Brown, M. T., & Landrum-Brown, J. (1995). Counseling supervision: Cross-cultural perspectives. In J. G. Ponterotto, J. M. Casas, L. A. Suzuki, & C. M. Alexander (Eds.) *Handbook of multicultural counseling* (pp. 263-286). Thousand Oaks, CA: Sage publications.

[10] Congress, E. P. (2004). Cultural and ethical issues in working with culturally diverse patients and their families: The use of the Culturalgram to promote culturally competent practice in health care settings. *Social Work in Health Care, 39,* 249-262

[11] Croteau, C., & Dorze, G. L. (1999). Overprotection in couples with aphasia. *Disability and Rehabilitation, 21*(9), 432- 437.

[12] Demo, D. H., Allne, K. R., & Fine, M. A. (Eds.). (2000). *Handbook of family diversity.* New York: Oxford.

[13] Diller, J. V. (2004). *Cultural diversity: A primer for the human services.* Belmont, CA: Wadsworth Publishing.

[14] Drake, R. E., McHugo, G. J., Becker, D. R., Anthony, W. A., & Clarke, R. E. (1996). The New Hampshire study of supported employment for people with severe mental illness. *Journal of Consulting and Clinical Psychology, 64,* 391-399.

[15] Duncan, L. E. (2005). Overcoming biases to effectively serve African American college students: A call to the profession. *College Student Journal, 39,* 702- 710.

[16] Dykeman, C., Nelson, R. J., & Appleton, V. (1995). Building strong working alliances in American Indian families. *Social Work in Education. 17* (3), 148-158.

[17] Evans, K. M, & Rotter, J. C. (2000). Multicultural family approaches to career counseling. *The Family Journal: Counseling and Therapy for Couples and Families, 8,* 67-71.

[18] Goldenberg, I., & Goldenberg, H. (2004). *Family therapy: An overview* (6th Ed.). Belmont, CA: Wadsworth Publishing.

[19]Groce, N. (2005). Immigrants, disability, and rehabilitation. In J.H. Stone (Ed.). *Culture and disability: Providing culturally competent services* (pp. 1- 14). Thousand Oaks, CA: Sage Publications.

[20]Hare, J., & Gray, L. A. (n.d.). *Non-traditional families: A guide for parents*. Retrieved from http://www.cybernet.org/parent/nontradfam.html.

[21]Hasnain, R., Sotnik, P., & Ghiloni, C. (2003). Person-centered planning: A gateway to improving vocational rehabilitation services for culturally diverse individuals with disabilities. *Journal of Rehabilitation, 69,* 10- 17.

[22]Hayslip, B. & Goldberg-Glen, R., (Eds.) (2000). *Grandparents raising grandchildren: Theoretical, empirical, and clinical perspectives.* New York, NY: Springer Publishing.

[23]Heiber Berns, J. (1980). Grandparents of handicapped children. *Social Work, 25,* 238-239.

[24]Householder, D., & Jansen, D. (1999). Partnerships, families, employers, transition, disabled: Creating the best transition outcomes for moderate and multiply disabled individuals. *Journal of Vocational Rehabilitation, 13,* 51- 55.

[25]Kerka, S. (2000). *Parenting and career development* (Eric Digest No. 214). Columbus, OH: ERIC Clearinghouse on Adult Career and Vocational Education. (ERIC Document Reproduction Services No. ED440251).

[26]Lankard, B. A. (1995). *Family role in career development* (Eric Digest No. 164). Columbus, OH: ERIC Clearinghouse on Adult Career and Vocational Education. (ERIC Document Reproduction Services No. ED389878).

[27]Livneh, H., & Antonak, R. F. (2005). Psychological adaptation to chronic illness and disability: A primer for counselors. *Journal of Counseling and Development, 83,* 12- 20.

[28]Livneh, H., Lott, S. M, & Antonak, R. F. (2004). Patterns of psychosocial adaptation to chronic illness and disability: A cluster analytic approach. *Psychology, Health, and Medicine, 9*(4), 411- 430.

[29]May, K. M., & Hunt, B. (1994). Family counseling training in rehabilitation counseling programs. *Rehabilitation Education, 8,* 348-359.

[30]McCollum, V. J. (1997). Evolution of the African American family: Considerations for family therapy. *Journal of Multicultural Counseling and Development, 25,* 219-229.

[31]McMahon, B. T., Shaw, L. R., Chan, F., & Danczyk-Hawley, C. (2004). "Common factors" in rehabilitation counseling: Expectancies and the working alliance. *Journal of Vocational Rehabilitation, 20,* 101-105.

[32]Middleton, R. A., Rollins, C. W., Sanderson, P. L., Leung, P., Harley, D. A., Ebener, D., & Leal-Idrogo, A. (2000). Endorsement of professional multicultural rehabilitation competencies and standards: A call to action. *Rehabilitation Counseling Bulletin, 43,* 219-240.

[33]Newman, E. (1988). *Barriers to employment of persons with handicaps.* Temple University, 301 University Services Bldg., Philadelphia, PA 19122.

[34]Olney, M. F., & Kim, A. (2001). Beyond adjustment: Integration of cognitive disability into identity. *Disability and Society, 16,* 563-583.

[35]Paniagua, F. A. (1996). Cross-cultural guidelines in family therapy practice. *Family Journal, 4,* 127- 138.

[36]Parke, R. D. (2004). Development in the family. *Annual Review of Psychology, 55*(2), 365-399.

[37]Poston, W. S. C., Craine, M., & Atkinson, D. R. (1991). Counselor dissimilarity confrontation, client cultural mistrust, and willingness to self-disclose. *Journal of Multicultural Counseling and Development, 19,* 65-73.

[38]Power, P. W., & Dell Orto, A. E. (2004). *Families living with chronic illness and disability: Interventions, challenges, and opportunities.* New York: Spring Publishing Company.

[39]Power, P. W., Dell Orto, A. E., & Gibbons, M. B. (1988). *Family interventions throughout chronic illness and disability.* New York: Springer Publishing Company.

[40]Power, P. W. (1988). *Guide to vocational assessment.* Austin, TX: Pro-ED.

[41]Power, P. W., Hershenson, D. B., & Fabien, E. S. (1991). Meeting the documented needs of clients' families: An opportunity for rehabilitation counselors. *Journal of Rehabilitation, 57,* 11-16.

[41]Rogan, P., Banks, & Herbein, M. H. (2003). Supported employment and workplace supports: A qualitative study. *Journal of Vocational Rehabilitation, 19,* 5-18.

[42]Rubin, S. E., & Roessler, R. T. (2001). *Foundations of the vocational rehabilitation process.* Austin, TX: Pro-Ed.

[43]Salas-Provance, M. B., Erickson, J. G., & Reed, J. (2002). Disabilities as viewed by four generations of one Hispanic family. *American Journal of Speech-Language Pathology, 11,* 151-162.

[44]Santana-Martin, S., & Santana, F. O. (2005). An introduction to Mexican culture for service providers. In J. H. Stone (Ed.), *Culture and disability: Providing culturally competent services* (pp. 161-186). Thousand Oaks, CA: Sage Publications.

[45]Schulenberg, J. E., Vonderacek, F. W., & Crouter, A. C. (1984). The influence of the family on vocational development. *Journal of Marriage and the Family, 46,*129-143.

[46]Skowron, E. A. (2004). Differentiation of self, personal adjustment, problem solving, and ethnic group belonging among persons of color. *Journal of Counseling and Development, 82,* 447-456.

[47]Smart, J. F., & Smart, D. W. (2006). Models of disability: Implications for the counseling profession. *Journal of Multicultural Counseling and Development, 84,* 29-40.

[48]Sohlberg, M. M., McLaughlin, K. A., Todis, B., Larsen, J., & Glang, A. (2001). What does it take to collaborate with families affected by brain injury? A preliminary model. *Journal of Head Trauma Rehabilitation, 16,* 498-511.

[49]Sotnik, P., & Jezewski, M. A. (2005). Culture and the disability services. In J. H. Stone (Ed.) *Culture and disability: Providing culturally competent services* (pp. 15- 30) Thousand Oaks, CA: Sage Publications.

[50]Staples, R. (1998). The emerging majority: Resources for non white families in the United States. *Family Relations, 37,* 348-354.

[51]Sue, D. W., & Sue, D. (1990). *Counseling the culturally different: theory and practice* (2nd ed.). New York: Wiley.

[52]Thomason, T. C. (1991). Counseling native Americans: An introduction for non-native-American counselors. *Journal of Counseling and Development, 69,* 321-327.

[53]Tsao, G. (2000). Growing up Asian-American with a disability. Retrieved Aug. 27, 2005 from http://www.colorado.edu/journals/standards/V7N1/FIRSTPERSON/tsao.html.

[54]U.S. Census Bureau (2005). Disabilities and American families 2000: Census 2000 special reports. Retrieved February 15, 200 from http://www.census.gov /prod/2005pubs/censr-23.pdf

[55]U.S. Census Bureau (2005). Hispanic population passes 40 million. Retrieved February 15, 200 from http://www.census.gov/prod/2005pubs/censr-23.pdf

[56]U.S. Department of Education, Office of Special Education and Rehabilitation Services. (2000). *Long-range plan 1999-2003.* Washington DC: Author.

[57]Vincent, K. R. (1990). Coping with disability: The individual or a family member's. *Social Behavior and Personality, 18,* 1-6.

[58]Wilson L., & Stith, S. (1991). Culturally sensitive therapy with Black clients. *Journal of Multicultural Counseling and Development, 19,* 32-42.

REHABILITATION RESEARCH FROM A MULTICULTURAL PERSPECTIVE

Paul Leung
Catherine Marshall
Keith Wilson

CHAPTER TOPICS

- Current status of rehabilitation research and ethnic populations
- The participatory action research model and inclusion of diverse populations
- Relevancy of rehabilitation research to diverse populations
- Evidence based research and diverse populations
- Assets and limitations of using existing databases
- Cultural mistrust and postcolonial traumatic stress

Chapter 14 — Rehabilitation Research from a Multicultural Perspective

The primary purpose of this chapter is to review the current status of rehabilitation research involving diverse ethnic/racial populations, explore the implications of quantitative and qualitative rehabilitation research from a multicultural perspective, and provide some thoughts about what may lie ahead in research related to multicultural rehabilitation. While much has occurred towards a more inclusive approach to rehabilitation research, much more remains to be done.

Over a decade ago, the National Council on Disability held a national conference in Jackson, Mississippi highlighting the "unique needs of minorities with disabilities." The Mississippi conference pointed to a lack of and a need for research related to underserved minority groups. Though that was 1992, that lack of attention to ethnicity and rehabilitation research remains just as relevant today. Any review of rehabilitation research, however cursory, can only lead to the conclusion that there is a long way to go before rehabilitation research can truly mirror the population of the United States. The need is as great today as it was a decade ago for research about diverse ethnic/racial persons who have disabilities.

The theme of this book is a multicultural approach to rehabilitation ad highlights the need for an infusion of multiculturalism into all aspects of the rehabilitation process. This chapter will look at where we are in multicultural rehabilitation research and where we need to go. Strictly speaking, research in the multicultural arena is no different from any other rehabilitation research in considering both qualitative and quantitative approaches. We can assume that any rehabilitation research will involve good methodology and design along with appropriate analysis and interpretation to answer the questions asked. At the same time, this very assumption may be much of the problem. The bottom line is that we may need to rethink the assumption for it may very well be the key to understanding where we are, and what we need to do in multicultural rehabilitation research in order to find solutions that will improve the lives of persons with disabilities who are from diverse populations.

Lila Downs, who is of Mixtec-Indian and Scottish-American heritage, reminds us in her music that she, as are all of us, are creatures of our respective cultures. Though Downs has little to do with rehabilitation research, she directs us to think about who we are. Her message resonates as we think about rehabilitation research as she reminds us that we all are cultural beings. Our culture has an influence on us and on our behavior. This has often been taken for granted and too often ignored. Only recently have we begun the process of looking at culture's impact on research.

Rehabilitation research has drawn primarily on psychology to form our interventions and, as a result, we have tended to focus on the individual. However, given the push of the disability movement, rehabilitation practitioners now realize the importance of the environment and context in understanding disability. We now also accept context and environment as part of the definition of culture. Gergen, et al.,[23] in grappling with the influence of culture on psychology, asked, "To what degree and with what effects is psychological science itself a cultural manifestation? It is immediately apparent that psychology and science are largely products of Western cultural tradition. "Suppositions about the nature of knowledge, the character of objectivity, the place of value in the knowledge generating process, and the nature of linguistic representation all carry the stamp of a unique cultural tradition."[p. 497]

In questioning the relevance of psychology for a changing international world, Mays, et al,[35] shared a similar concern. They wrote that unless U.S. psychology is willing to learn from other nations, "the result will surely be an increasingly fragmented U.S. psychology that is at risk for failing to meet the psychological needs of its own U.S. population, with its rapidly growing multicultural, multinational, and multiracial population."[p.486]

How science is defined and the extent to which science is a "cultural manifestation" depends on one's perspective. This notion mirrors arguments of feminist researchers[18,22] who have long suggested the need to look at things differently. Du Bois,[18] for example, initiated her exploration of science and values by stating that "scienc is *not* 'value-free'; it cannot be. Science is made by scientists, and both we and our science-making are shaped by our culture."[p.105] Dubois further observed that:

> In its conceptions of science and knowing, our society has embraced and reified the values of objective knowledge, expertise, neutrality, separateness, and opposed them to the values of subjective knowledge, understanding, art, communion, craft, and experience. Objectivity and subjectivity are modes of knowing, analysis, interpretation, and understanding. They are not independent of each other and should not be.[p.111]

DuBois[18] went on to write that it is the "*synthesis* of subjectivity and objectivity that is the source of intellectual power and responsibility—and truth."[p.113] Harding[26] argued that we must question the way science is practiced so that there is not to be "an apparent immunity for the scientific enterprise from the kinds of critical and causal scrutiny that science recommends for all the other regularities of nature and social life. If we were to abandon these dogmas of empiricism, we could adopt the alternative view that science is a fully social activity—as social and as culturally specific as are religious, educational, economic, and family activities."[p. 56]

Given that rehabilitation research is a way for us to understand and describe multicultural people with disabilities along with what may assist in improving their lives, rehabilitation's research agenda must be committed to addressing cultural issues using culturally appropriate research design and instrumentation. There is general acceptance in psychometrics that an instrument developed and normed on one population should be used only with great caution with another population. Otherwise, interpretation and conclusions from that instrument have questionable validity and value.[33] However, equal caution is needed as we look beyond assessment and quantitative research "to the extent qualitative researchers carry their own cultural assumptions into the field, they risk imposing a foreign frame of reference in interpreting the experience and meanings of the people they study."[42]

Hughes, et al.,[29] noted "the selection of a research problem is constrained by Western mindscapes" and cautioned that "researchers need to develop culturally anchored methods that avoid ethnocentric biases in research and also take into consideration the role of cultural phenomenon in shaping the outcomes of the research process."[p.689] Hughes, et al.,[29] found that "a culturally anchored perspective draws attention to an ongoing debate regarding the relative utility of qualitative versus quantitative research methodologies."[p.696] They also drew attention to the fact that "qualitative researchers tend to assess behavior in naturalistic settings . . .. Preconceived rules and categories for classifying behavior are de-emphasized: The meaning . . . emerges through inductive analyses of the data themselves."[29, pp. 696-697] While errors associated with inappropriate and culture-bound instrumentation used for measurement may not be the concerns of qualitative research, erroneous culture-bound interpretation of data, such as personal narratives, may be.

CURRENT STATUS OF REHABILITATION RESEARCH AND ETHNIC POPULATIONS

An understanding of multicultural rehabilitation research requires that we briefly look at the current status of social science research related to diverse ethnic and racial populations. Though Sue[38] addressed research and ethnic minority populations from the perspective of psychology, much of what Sue discussed holds true for rehabilitation research. Sue indicated the lack of psychological research on ethnic minority populations is both subtle and systemic. Sue believed "the culprit is how science has been practiced—an effect caused by the selective enforcement of the principles of science."[p. 1070] Sue[38] pointed out the overemphasis on internal validity verses external validity as a basic flaw in how psychological research has been used and interpreted to the detriment of multicultural populations.

Good methodology and design must take into account concepts of culture. Tucker and Herman,[41] in looking at academic needs of African American children, pointed out that theories and interventions are often based on research with mostly European American middle-class samples, and that such theory and research do not advance knowledge about the specific needs of children from other cultural backgrounds. Tucker and Herman[41] make the assertion that not only must research design meet the usual criteria of internal, external, and construct validity, but must also have the added dimension of cultural validity. Rogler[41] argued for using a "continuing and open-ended series of substantive and methodological insertions and adaptations" to "mesh the process of inquiry with the cultural characteristics of the group being studied."[p. 296] Rogler also suggested using pre-testing and planning the collection of data that ensures adaptations to the cultural milieu of the target population and described culturally sensitive research as the "incessant and continuing finely calibrated interweaving of cultural components and cultural awareness into all phases of the research process."[p. 302] In other words, the infusion of culture into research design requires forethought and deliberate action on the part of the researcher.

THE PARTICIPATORY ACTION RESEARCH MODEL AND INCLUSION OF DIVERSE POPULATIONS

The recognition that persons who are the target for research must benefit from that research led the National Institute on Disability and Rehabilitation Research (NIDRR) to promote what NIDRR termed a "new" paradigm. A central focus of this paradigm is Participatory Action Research (PAR) where persons with disabilities are considered an integral part of the research process from inception to completion. The PAR approach requires an active role for individuals with disabilities in defining, analyzing, and solving research issues and problems. PAR is considered a research process that includes both scientists and consumers. Acceptance of the PAR model also implies an acceptance of the role culture plays in behavior, and thus, rehabilitation research as well. PAR implicitly accepts the fact that the environment, including culture, has an influence in defining or describing disability, and that disability is a social construct. Nonetheless, much of current rehabilitation research has followed fairly traditional methodologies utilizing notions and constructs that researchers can readily define using existing instrumentation and accessible participants. As a result, consumers often do not believe that research responds to what they perceive to be important or relevant. Bellini & Rumrill[6] concluded that in rehabilitation research "constructs that are the easiest to measure tend to be less relevant in terms of providing solid findings for practice, whereas constructs that are more complex tend to be those that are most closely related to the valued social outcomes that are important goals for rehabilitation consumers."[p.131] White[47] further elaborated that "in researchers' zeal to create a more robust methodology, they must not neglect the value of their research to those to whom it is often directed—the participants and their peers."[p.438]

Issues of potential bias become even more important when they are intertwined with participants who not only have disabilities but who also are members of diverse ethnic/racial groups. There has been a revisiting in traditional medical research regarding inclusion of diverse populations and the need to be specific about the populations being studied. Under the assumption that researchers must better describe and define participants in their research, the U.S. Dept. of Health and Human Services recently released "Guidance for Industry" regarding the collection of race and ethnicity data in clinical trials.

These guidelines recognize race and ethnicity to be particularly important in the understanding of biological and physiological responses. Though clinical trials are seldom done in rehabilitation research, some of the same issues apply. Rehabilitation researchers need to be specific in their descriptions of the populations they research. There are obvious differences in response to different medical products by racially and ethnically distinct groups that are not only attributable to intrinsic factors, such as genetics, but also to external factors, such as socio-cultural issues or the interaction between the two.

In a discipline closer to rehabilitation, Tucker and Herman[41] found that nearly 40% of published articles in clinical, counseling, and school psychology between 1993 and 1997 did not report the ethnicity of their participants. Perhaps in response to these findings, the American Psychological Association[2] adopted as policy "Guidelines on Multicultural Education, Training, Research, Practice, and Organizational Change for Psychologists." The Guidelines reflect recognition that research may have ignored culture in the past, with culture being seen as a nuisance variable. Culture has now become a "central contextual" variable that explains human behavior. The APA guidelines further indicate that failure to consider "within group" differences to be particularly egregious.[p 39]

RELEVANCY OF REHABILITATION RESEARCH TO DIVERSE POPULATIONS

Even though there has been an increase in culturally diverse participants in rehabilitation research, many studies continue to use predominantly White and middle-class persons as primary participants. These samples, often selected out of convenience, undoubtedly affect external validity as well as the outcomes reported. Thus, rehabilitation research relevancy is affected not only in terms of consumer perception but also in terms of validity.

Other research areas that have application to rehabilitation research and that may assist in moving rehabilitation research toward new areas include other social sciences. Increased knowledge in social psychology and advances in method have facilitated the emergence of several areas in minority research, such as false consensus, perceived group variability, stereotype threat, collective action, the self, perceptions of justice, system justification mechanisms, and coping with stigma. Findings in these domains involve not only research with minority/diverse populations in natural settings, but also experimental research aimed at separating the relative effects of power, status, and group size.

Another issue that is important involves comparing ethnic/racial groups. Much of existing and traditional research with diverse populations portrays these populations in opposition to the majority population for comparison purposes. Ethnic and racial minorities are placed not only in a deficit perspective, but these results may reinforce negative stereotypic images.

Results from these studies may not only be misleading but even counter to the rehabilitation philosophy of focusing on strengths.

EVIDENCE BASED RESEARCH AND DIVERSE POPULATIONS

Attention is currently being given to the use of interventions that are considered evidence or empirically based, i.e., having a "scientific" foundation in the research literature. A primary characteristic of evidence-based intervention involves identified and measured changes, along with evaluating the intervention against an alternate intervention.[13] The problem with evidence-based intervention for diverse populations is that little research data are available, along with the fact that some population groups are numerically quite small. Asian Americans, for example, have essentially been ignored in the literature. As Chwalisz[12] noted, the definition of "evidence" is critical, as is the underlying assumption that "an objective reality exists that can be observed by researchers."[p.499] Chwalisz quoted Sturdee (2001) saying "scientific evidence cannot provide proof; it can only affirm our commitment to the conceptual structures and theoretical constructs provided by the paradigm within which what counts as evidence has already been defined."[p.499] Chwalisz[12] further characterizes psychological treatment evidence as hierarchical, triangulating, and dialectical, whose sources of evidence have been "too narrow to adequately capture the real-world activities of professional psychologists."[p.500] Chwalisz argues for an "expanded view of evidence" and a "philosophical shift in which all sources of evidence have the potential to contribute to the understanding of psychological phenomena."[p.500]

Wampold,[45] commenting on Chwalisz's methodological pluralism, raised a number of questions that provide a foundation for multicultural rehabilitation research. Wampold asked, what is the purpose of collecting evidence? Who evaluates the evidence? What are the theoretical, historical, political, and cultural contexts in which the evidence is embedded? What decisions are made based on the evidence?[p.540] Coleman and Wampold[13] end by advocating processes for determining effectiveness of interventions "that are context driven; respect the interaction among the context, the disorder, and the individual; and systematically use evaluation methods that can capture that complexity."[p. 244]

Given the lack of inclusion of diverse populations in existing research, combined with the difficulty of identifying and locating participants from diverse groups, and especially persons who have disabilities, it is easy to come to a conclusion that it will be some time before enough evidence becomes available upon which to make truly evidence-based decisions. Second, adoption of current evidence-based research in rehabilitation may mean adoption of interventions that may not only be flawed but that may also present ethical dilemmas should they be adopted without further investigation. Sue[38] cited his experience with a task force designated to determine which psychotherapeutic interventions met rigorous criteria to be designated as an empirically validated treatment. The task force found that no studies were ever conducted on the effectiveness of treatment for members of ethnic minority populations. Sue[38] suggested that research is often used to assume generality of findings when it may not be warranted. The difficulty Sue indicated, is "our modus operandi is to assume that the work is universally applicable; the burden of proof is placed on researchers concerned about race, ethnicity, and bias to show that there are ethnic differences."[p.1073] Sue concludes by asking the question, "Whatever happened to the scientific notion of skepticism, where little is taken for granted, where conclusions are drawn from evidence and not from assumptions?"[38,p.1073]

Much of the currently available literature in rehabilitation on different ethnic/racial groups relates to access to rehabilitation services and, in particular, vocational rehabilitation. This area of research has been significant because it calls attention to inequities of access. In addition, research related to underutilization of rehabilitation services by different groups has brought about an emphasis to assure a more consumer-oriented approach benefiting not only individuals from diverse populations but also all persons with disabilities. In part, changes to rehabilitation legislation, such as the Rehabilitation Act, were driven by recognition that diverse ethnic populations did not have equal access to the vocational rehabilitation system.

The majority of research into inequities or unequal treatment has used available databases as primary source documents. The next section will discuss the use of large databases and specifically their relationship to rehabilitation access questions.

ASSETS AND LIMITATIONS ASSOCIATED WITH USING EXISTING DATABASES

Databases are kept by government programs to document their activities and/or populations, and generally contain large amounts of information concerning persons served or those who benefit from activities of the program. Databases of interest to rehabilitation researchers include those kept by the United States Department of Education, Rehabilitation Services Administration (RSA) and the National Institute of Healths (NIH). Such databases contain national samples with similar data available for each state. For example, the national RSA-911 will have similar variables as a state RSA-911 database. To ensure client confidentiality, most databases delete identifying information of individual clients. It is, therefore, not only difficult but also probably impossible to connect database demographics to a particular client or group within the database.

State/national databases are attractive for research for a number of reasons. First, databases generally provide access to large numbers of individuals. This is particularly important when there is need for power with a specific statistical analysis. Many statistics require a minimum number of participants to maintain critical statistical assumptions. Second, large databases can save time and money in identifying and locating participants. Using surveys to gain information on 300 participants, for example, will cost a lot more than using already collected data. The decision to survey participants may mean asking questions such as:

1. What is the cost of a four-page survey?
2. Who will assist with distributing the survey to the participants?
3. Will participants receive a fee for successful completion of the survey?
4. Will the survey be done on the Internet?

Finally, databases usually contain more variables than a survey instrument and, as a result, a researcher can investigate more research questions.

Database research can answer questions limited only by the creativity of the researchers. Using an RSA-911 state or national database, for example, answers can be found for the following types of questions: Are African Americans with disabilities accepted less for VR services than White Americans with disabilities? Is there a difference in successful closures (status 26) among African Americans and White American with disabilities?

At the same time, there are limitations to the use of databases or using recorded data from state and federal government programs. As with ex post facto research designs, independent variables cannot be manipulated or randomly assigned to a treatment group. Thus, cause-and-effect cannot be attributed to the results of studies using databases. For example, the conclusion that an individual who is a White American with a disability will cause that individual to be accepted into the public vocational rehabilitation program cannot be made. It is only possible to say that a correlation exists between the independent and dependent variables. Likewise, a conclusion that being an African American with a disability is the reason for not being accepted into vocational rehabilitation cannot be made. Basically, database results can only conclude there is a possible correlation between both the independent and dependent variables in the study.

Another challenge with using databases is that one can use only the variables that have been collected by the reporting program. The variance explained by the independent variable(s) is quite small for many of the studies exploring the acceptance into vocational rehabilitation at both the state and national levels. Wilson[48] suggested that there are other possible variables that can be used to explain acceptance into vocational rehabilitation besides those variables that are already in the RSA-911 database. Because researchers cannot add to the database, researchers often must speculate about what may have brought about the results. This does not minimize the fact that speculation may provide additional perspectives often validating what is observed in everyday life. Speculation involves questioning and is a needed aspect of research.

ACCURACY OF DATABASE

Agencies and programs often "clean" databases of known errors and to make the database more accurate. The result is that databases presumed to be the same may actually be quite different. The total number of participants may vary, for example, depending on the specific database that is used. Researchers may be using quantitatively different databases for the same year. Using the same procedures (e.g., statistics and sampling) may produce different results. While having quantitatively different database may be unlikely, human error in entry, et cetera, does occur. In an effort to "clean-up" and continuously update the RSA 911 database for accuracy, variables within the database may quantitatively change during this "clean-up" procedure. Researchers need to examine the data closely for possible inconsistencies before using any database. Generally, it helps to ask the particular program about the details of the database and the proper protocol for reporting such inaccuracies. Using checks and balances will ensure results that are more accurate.

INTERPRETATION OF RESULTS

Though the cliché is that numbers do not lie, numbers have meaning that is based on an interpretation by the researcher. Because researchers who are members of the majority population may have a different worldview than African American researchers, we can perhaps not expect White American and African American researchers to be congruent in their interpretations of research findings. While there is nothing wrong with rehabilitation researchers interpreting findings differently, it is important to understand that similar results may produce different meanings depending on who is doing the interpretation.

Interpretations are also accepted or dismissed because of the perceptions and experiences of the persons reading a particular study. For example, results that indicate discrepancies in VR acceptance rates (accessibility) may have different meanings to African American and White American researchers. African American researchers/writers may pay more attention to discrimination in contrast with White Americans researchers who may attend to another possibility. One only has to examine the discussion sections of published research articles by White American and African American authors to see some of these differences. The different opinions expressed by researchers should not be the primary issue. Problems arise only when opinions are expressed that differ from the prevailing views. Perspectives expressed by researchers who are not considered part of the mainstream group tend to be devalued or discounted.

The discounting of positions and opinions based on whether the perspective is part of the mainstream thinking is the crux of the problem. An example of this was the conclusion by an Australian physician that the culprit for gastric ulcers was a bacterium. This was counter to prevailing opinion that gastric ulcers resulted from stress and dietary reasons.[17] Consequently, there was slow acceptance of the bacterial theory and the use of antibiotics for the treatment of gastric ulcers. Well-designed empirically sound research may get the necessary attention needed to add diversity to vocational rehabilitation research, but as noted, there is no consensus about what well-designed empirical research is. This was particularly evident in some of the reactions to studies of the state/federal vocational rehabilitation program.

Given the importance of the VR program to persons with disabilities, including persons from minority racial backgrounds, eligibility, and acceptance into the VR program by minority consumers were among the first multicultural rehabilitation research topics. Vocational Rehabilitation eligibility and race was first explored by Atkins and Wright in 1980. The Atkins and Wright[4] study took a systematic look at vocational rehabilitation (VR) outcomes relative to race. Atkins and Wright reported that African Americans were accepted less for VR services than White Americans in the majority of Rehabilitation Services Administration (RSA) federal regions. As a result, Atkins and Wright generated a lot of controversy in the area of VR research regarding racial and ethnic minorities with disabilities (see the history chapter). Bolton and Cooper[8] challenged the results of the Atkins and Wright study for what they considered to be small percentage differences that existed in VR acceptance between African Americans and White Americans with disabilities.

Since Atkins and Wright,[4] a number of studies on acceptance to Vocational Rehabilitation programs and race have appeared. Herbert and Martinez[28] investigated whether race (Native American/Alaskan Native, Asian/Pacific Islander, African American, or White American) correlated with case service statuses 08 (closed not accepted for VR services), 26 (rehabilitated), 28 (closed other reason after the Individual Plan for Employment [IPE]), and 30 (closed other reasons before the IPE. Herbert and Martinez came to a conclusion similar to Atkins and Wright that African Americans tended to be accepted less for VR services than White Americans.

A year after the Herbert and Martinez[28] study, Dziekan and Okocha[19] looked at the accessibility of VR services with regard to African Americans, Hispanics, Native Americans, Asian Americans, and White Americans. Dziekan's and Okocha's conclusions about African American experiences in VR coincided with those reported by Atkins and Wright and Herbert and Martinez. Two years later, Feist-Price[20] found similar results in examining VR outcomes of another state. Results reported by four of five research teams exploring VR acceptance and ethnicity between 1980 and 1995 strongly suggested that race influences VR acceptance. Although the reasons for discrepancy in VR accessibility are somewhat unclear, many research teams (e.g., Atkins & Wright, 1980; Feist-Price, 1995) believed that prejudice and biased attitudes of White American VR counselors and administrators towards African Americans and people of color in the VR system may play an important role in disparate outcomes of the VR system.

Not long after the Feist-Price[20] study, Wheaton[46] published a study with a conclusion that a significant difference in the acceptance rates among African Americans and White Americans in the VR system did not exist. Likewise, Peterson[38] and Wilson[49] in separate studies came to the conclusion that there was no statistical difference between racial and ethnic minorities and White Americans in VR acceptance. Wilson[49] revisited the notion of VR acceptance and race in response to the need for replication of studies related to VR acceptance and race. Wilson, et al.,[50] replicated the Wilson[49] study and found results similar to earlier research (e.g., Atkins & Wright,[4] Feist-Price,[20] namely that White Americans are more likely to be accepted for VR services than are African Americans with disabilities. These results challenged earlier findings that reported race and VR acceptance as independent of each other.[46,49] What is one to make of these different findings? An answer may lie in the nature of the data, the analysis of the data, the statistical techniques used, as well as in the interpretation of the data.

Addressing limitations of prior VR acceptance studies by using logistic regression, Wilson[48] reported that the primary source of support at referral (entered first) and ethnicity (entered second) were the two variables that emerged as statistically significant in the regression model. Although the methodology in the Wilson[48] study was different than some past studies (for example, Atkins & Wright, 1980), Wilson's results proved analogous with what the majority of studies reported regarding race and VR accessibility—namely, African Americans and other racial and ethnic minorities are less likely to be accepted for VR services when compared to their White American counterparts.

More recently, Wilson[51] found that African Americans with disabilities are more likely to be rejected for VR services when compared with White Americans with disabilities in the United States. In contrast to several other studies on VR accessibility and race, Wilson used a national sample, as did Atkins and Wright[4] to investigate VR accessibility. Thus, the results of studies using large databases by Wilson and Atkins and Wright could be generalized to the entire population of individuals in the VR system rather than just one subset.

There have been other studies that focused on various ethnic/racial groups and the vocational rehabilitation program. For example, Wilson & Senices[53] (in press) compared Hispanics to non-Hispanics (African American, White American, American Indian or Alaskan Native, and Asian or Pacific Islander) in the United States and their VR acceptance rates. Because people who self report as Hispanic are among the fastest growing ethnic group in the United States, attention to Hispanics is a necessary step in the progression of rehabilitation research with racial/ethnic groups. "Hispanics constitute an ethnic group rather than a racial category, and their members may classify themselves as White, Black, or some other race" (Rawlings & Saluter,[39,p. xii]) (also see RSA,[40] & the United States Bureau of the Census, March).[43] Wilson and Senice[53] (in press) found a statistically significant difference between race/ethnicity and VR acceptance of Hispanics and non-Hispanics in the United

States VR system. In particular, Hispanics were more likely to be accepted for VR services than non-Hispanics in the United States. Wilson and Senice (in press) were the first to compare people not only based on race and ethnicity, but also skin color or hue. Most people in the VR system who classify themselves as Hispanic tended to select the White race. Wilson and Senices suggest that people with disabilities who are of a darker hue may be discriminated against because of skin color. Several authors[7,16,21,25,34] support the assertion that discrimination may be based on skin color. Not only are people who classify themselves as racial and ethnic minorities discriminated against in the VR system, but a large part of the discrimination encountered by racial and ethnic minorities occurs as a result of the color of their skin: Specifically, the darker ones' skin the more salient the projected discrimination.[53]

As researchers continue to debate the reasons why racial and ethnic minority groups encounter more Vocational Rehabilitation (VR) ineligibility than other groups[4,8,20,46,] and Wilson, 1997, it is clear that these under-represented groups tend to have different experiences prior to their entry into human services than White Americans[4,25,40] Relative to access to VR services, it is also becoming increasingly apparent that racial minorities also have problems once they enter into the VR system as well.

Once racial minorities are accepted into VR, they may face additional infrastructure barriers that hinder successful rehabilitation outcomes. As part of their study, Atkins and Wright[4] looked at VR case closure patterns among both African Americans and White Americans. Although Atkins and Wright reported that race and reason for closure was statistically significant, it was not clear as to the specific reason for unsuccessful closures after the initiation of the Individual Plan for Employment (IPE) among the participants in their study.

Ross and Biggi[42] looked at access to rehabilitation services at referral while observing outcomes including status 28 (closed after the initiation of the IPE). Ross and Biggi reported that refusal of services emerged as the most cited reason among White American customers for closure when found eligible for VR services, while African Americans were more likely to be closed for failure to cooperate. However, Ross and Biggi[42] did find that unsuccessful outcomes between African Americans and White Americans were not found to be statistically significant.

Herbert and Martinez[28] sought to determine whether race influenced case service outcomes for Statuses 08, 26, 28, and 30. In contrast to the results reported by Atkins and Wright,[4] Ross and Biggi,[42] Herbert and Martinez[28] did not find differences between African Americans and White Americans for Status 28 closure. African Americans and White Americans appeared to differ only slightly in reasons for closures once Individual Plans for Employment (IPE) were initiated. Peterson[38] in a similar study also found no differences in unsuccessful closures after the IPE was initiated.

In an attempt to identify what may account for these differences, Wilson[52] found that African Americans with disabilities were more likely to be categorized "failure to cooperate" while White Americans with disabilities were more likely to appear in the "other" category. Although there is no consensus on reasons for closure after the initiation of the IPE, the fact that more racial minorities are closed "failure to cooperate" may be particularly significant.

REASONS GIVEN FOR VR DISCREPANCIES

Prejudice and bias affect people with disabilities who are racial and ethnic minorities in extraordinarily similar ways; notably, the devaluation of the race or ethnicity of the minority group by White Americans (Olkin, 1999). Considering the extent of diversity and the disproportionate number of unsuccessful racial minorities with disabilities in the VR system, a continued examination of issues related to racial minorities in VR is essential. While much work is needed related to diversity in the VR system, there is room for some optimism regarding outcomes for racial minorities with disabilities.

Wilson, Harley, McCormick, et al.,[54] explored not only the reasons why these particular discrepancies exist but also described the consensus that exists in vocational rehabilitation and human services literature. Wilson, et al., put it this way:

Wilson, et al.,[54] described multiple reasons for VR discrepancies. These reasons included:

1. The differences in worldviews between racial and ethnic minorities and White American counselors,

2. Bias discrimination against racial and ethnic minority clients, and

3. Cultural mistrust by racial and ethnic minority customers towards White American VR counselors, to name a few.

Undoubtedly, discrimination may be unintended but nevertheless real. Not withstanding the intention of discrimination, Wilson, et al.,[54] concluded, "it is apparent that conscious or unconscious discrimination can hamper customers who seek services."[p. 28]

Rehabilitation research has identified issues that interfere with implementation of the basic intent of the Rehabilitation Act. There is need to resolve not only accessibility concerns of racial and ethnic minorities in the VR system but facilitate a more customer friendly milieu for all people with disabilities. There is no doubt of the need for more research that includes a racially and ethnically diverse perspective that will advance a welcoming VR program.

DATA MINING

Another approach to the use of large data sets that has potential in multicultural rehabilitation research has been the adoption of tools long utilized by business and market researchers.[10] Traditionally known as pattern recognition, this approach involves data mining or the "extraction of hidden predictive information from large databases."[p.4] Chan, et al.,[10] used a data mining approach to reexamine effects of demographic variables and acceptance rates of the RSA 911 data sets along with other factors that influence employment rates of vocational rehabilitation consumers who have orthopedic disabilities.

OTHER METHODS OF KNOWING

Qualitative research has been recognized in a number of social science disciplines as having particular value in gathering information from diverse groups that have not had the benefit of research. Lykes[31] wrote about her desire to better understand Guatamalan culture. "It was the concrete problems I confronted in undertaking research with Guatemalan women that enabled me to depart more significantly from the quantitative methods of my training towards a more qualitative participatory model of research that would enable me both to better address the questions I was asking and to engage in research that is consistent with my social goals and commitments."[p.172] Lykes used oral history interviews "as the appropriate method for this study because they are both sensitive to the single individual's experiences, enabling us to look at a woman's understanding of herself and her elaboration of the social meaning of her life, and to the Guatemalan community's long tradition of oral communication."[31, p.172]

Feminists have for some time brought attention to a set of conceptual dichotomies that provide further insight for the need to use different perspectives. Science and epistemology are constructed in dichotomous ways: reason vs. emotion and social value; mind vs. body; culture vs. others; objectivity vs. subjectivity; and knowing vs. being. In each dichotomy, the former often controls the latter lest the latter threaten to overwhelm the former, and the threatening 'latter' in each case appears to be systematically associated with the 'feminine' perspective. Observers of social hierarchies other than that of masculine dominance have pointed to these very same dichotomies as the conceptual scheme that permits subjugation. Harding[27] in *Is Science Multicultural? Postcolonialisms, Feminisms, and Epistemologies* (1998) refers to "the multiplicity of local resources, and their potential for generating knowledge."[p.194] Indigenous communities, such as experienced by Lykes in Guatemala, offer rehabilitation researchers an alternative understanding of "ways of knowing."

In attempting to address disparities of access to health and human services, rehabilitation researchers may need to join others involved with groups where quantitative data are often labeled as "statistically unreliable."[36] To solve this problem, practitioners and researchers often recommend over-sampling,[36,43] and pooling of data,[36,32] as well as other qualitative approaches.[34] Over-sampling is expensive and programs/agencies are often reluctant to do it. In support of qualitative methods, Murray[36] reported that "more research is needed

Chapter 14   Rehabilitation Research from a Multicultural Perspective

on many issues in occupational health and safety, and the health status of workers of color should be given a high priority. This research should use qualitative and ethnographic methods to examine risk [and] evaluate the effectiveness of interventions."[p.224]

Researchers and practitioners across differing fields of work and intervention related to class, ethnically diverse populations, health disparities, access, and appropriate research and evaluation methods are asking similar and sometimes the same questions regarding moving beyond what can be perceived to be a "mafia-type hold" on what is considered rigorous research and ways of knowing. The processes and practices of researchers who work in indigenous communities are influenced by their own cultures as well as those they study. Awareness of this influence and adoption of appropriate research procedures are essential contributions to the validity of research. Yet funding sources and evaluators of "rigorous research" cannot seem to get away from the "gold-standard" of experimental research designs that call for the random assignment of individuals into control groups versus those who receive the intervention. The masses of people on the "lower decks" are telling researchers to consider research methods that are more appropriate to their cultural traditions.

We believe that how we go about knowing in indigenous communities, i.e. how we go about conducting research, is critical if disparities are going to be eliminated in health and human services. This issue is especially critical when a given research design may not be acceptable or appropriate to the community of interest.[15] For example, Linda Tuhiwai Smith[35] (Ngati Awa and Ngati Porou), who works with indigenous people related to health and the author of *Decolonizing Methodologies: Research and Indigenous Peoples* (1999), writes that "story telling, oral histories, the perspectives of elders and of women have become an integral part of all indigenous research."[p.144]

Tutty, et al.,[42] concluded that "good research is good research" and clarified their position by affirming that "fundamental to knowledge acquisition through quantitative and qualitative research studies is the idea that what we think should be *rooted in and tested against good evidence*, and that sound articulated methods—*systematic, disciplined inquiry*—are necessary to bring this about."[p.15] [italics added]) However, what constitutes "good evidence?" Who determines the validity of the evidence? For Inuit whalers, hearing whales breathe constituted good evidence, while the International Whaling Commission's "scientific count" included only those whales that could be seen passing from the edge of the ice. Barreiro[5] reported that while the count resulting from research methods that included hearing whales breathe was initially challenged, the Alaska Eskimo Whaling Commission's "population estimates were verified by successive aerial surveys."[pp.27-28]

Participatory action research calls for persons with disabilities and other community research partners to come together with academic researchers to determine appropriate research strategies.[9] The lesson of the Inuit whalers is that we must learn to trust different views of what constitutes good evidence and how "disciplined inquiry" is to be structured. It may be that too frequently the options for research design rest squarely with academic researchers, and methods that fall below the "gold standard" of traditional experimental designs are suspect and of questionable value in the present political climate of evidence-based intervention.

We need to value the contributions and insights of community partners in research who suggest that research methods that mesh with their cultural traditions and "ways of knowing" may hold particular value in a given community. This was the case in a study involving the needs and resources of families with a relative who had a disability, and involving members of two southeastern American Indian Nations, i.e., the Eastern Band of Cherokee and the Mississippi Band of Choctaw (Marshall & Cerveny, 1994).

Research today tends to be so statistical and numbers-based that many not well versed in interpreting those numbers believe the human element to be missing. Qualitative researchers have to learn and understand that abstract factors not normally included in research design courses, such as communication style and non-verbal communication may be significant. In general, society perceives American Indians as stoic and nonverbal. Yet, qualitative data show the opposite (Marshall & Cerveny, 1994). Qualitative methodology can allow investigators to reach a personal level with research participants; however, for some, this may be too difficult, too draining, potentially lethal—a catharsis. On the one hand, telling one's story is difficult and painful, yet the irony here is that this is the way history, help, and medicine have been passed on for generations with Indian people. Some researchers may consider qualitative research as too simple, yet such techniques transcend the past and can be a comfortable means of learning and explaining.[34] It is only through understanding history and culture, as well as appreciating different ways of knowing, that rehabilitation researchers enter into authentic partnerships in participatory research.[14]

CULTURAL MISTRUST AND POSTCOLONIAL TRAUMATIC STRESS

Indigenous or native people often expect that rehabilitation researchers have an understanding of their culture, including history and environment, as part of the participatory research process. Stone,[37] a researcher and a member of the Blackfeet Nation, has written, "that in order to do ethical and moral research in the First Nations community, we must be aware of the postcolonial stress impact as an issue."[p.114] Understanding the history and trauma of Native peoples is a responsibility of the researcher. The researcher must understand the impact of the dispossession, biological warfare, the boarding school era, termination, and federal government attempts at acculturation through urban relocation programs. Rehabilitation researchers must be concerned with how an indigenous, colonized, or low-income community might view the investigator as an oppressor "because it is the oppressor who defines the problem, the nature of the research, and, to some extent, the quality of interaction between him and his subjects."[30, p.77] Stone[37] believes it is both naïve and inappropriate for researchers to present themselves to a Native family that may be already carrying a psychological burden and say, "Hey, trust me. Throw yourself open for research. Let me interview you. Let me give you this questionnaire. Oh, do not worry. It will not hurt. It is for your own good. I'm here to help you."[p.114] Similar examples can be found in African American rehabilitation research.[1]

Rehabilitation researchers are in communities in order to help. While qualitative research and participatory strategies may give us an important opportunity for developing research procedures that are both culturally sensitive and result in valid conclusions, ultimately the goal is a "culturally grounded knowledge base"[29, p. 699] that allows us to document needs, to intervene when appropriate, and to better serve people with disabilities. Our objective is to achieve culturally grounded knowledge, and that requires that we constantly check our research strategies and our data interpretations along with soliciting feedback from colleagues, from community research partners, and from research participants. This objective requires that we stay informed of both the history and the present social, cultural, and political circumstances of those we hope to help.

REFERENCES

[1]Alston, R. J. & T. Bell (1996) Cultural mistrust and the rehabilitation enigma for African Americans. J. of Rehabilitation, 62(2) 11-15.

[2]American Psychological Association (2002) Guidelines on Multicultural education, training, research, practice, and organizational change for psychologists. Washington, D.C.

[3]Angel, R. & Gronfein, W. (1988) The use of subjective information in statistical models, American Sociological Review 53, 464-473

[4]Atkins, B. J., & Wright, G. N. (1980). Three views: vocational rehabilitation of Blacks: The statement. *Journal of Rehabilitation, 46*, 40, 42-46.

[5]Barreiro, J. (1992). The search for lessons. *Akwe:kon Journal, 9*, 18-39.

[6]Bellini, J. & Rumrill, P. (2002) Contemporary insights in the philosophy of science: implications for rehabilitation counseling research. *Rehabilitation Education 16*(2) 115-134.

[7]Bennett, C. (1995). *Comprehensive multicultural education: Theory and practice* (3rd ed.). Needham Heights, MA: Allyn & Bacon.

[8]Bolton, B., & Cooper, P. G. (1980). Three views: Vocational rehabilitation of [9]

[9]Bruyere, S. M. (1993). Participatory action research: Overview and implications for family members of persons with disabilities. *Journal of Vocational Rehabilitation, 3* (2), 62-68.

[10] Chan, F., Wong, D., Rosenthal, D.A., Kundu, M., & Dutta, (2004) A. Eligibility rates of traditionally underserved individuals with disabilities revisited: a data mining approach. Journal of Applied Rehabilitation Counseling 36(3) 3-10.

[11] Chan, F. Cheing, G., Chan, J. Y., Rosenthal, D., Chronister, J. (2005). Predicting Employment Outcomes of Rehabilitation Clients with Orthopedic Disabilities: A CHAID Analysis. Disability and Rehabilitation, 28(5) 257-270.

[12] Chwalisz, K. (2003) Evidence-Based practice: a framework for twenty-first-century scientist-practitioner training. *The Counseling Psychologist 31*(5) 497-528.

[13] Coleman, H. K. K. and B.E. Wampold (2003) Challenges to the development of culturally relevant, empirically supported treatment in Pope-Davis, D.B, Coleman, H. L. K., Liu, W. M., & Toporek, R. L. (eds) Handbook of multicultural Competencies, Sage Publications: Thousand Oaks.

[14] Davis, J. D., Erickson, J. S., Johnson, S. R., Marshall, C. A., Running Wolf, P., & Santiago, R. L. (Eds.). (2002). *Work Group on American Indian Research and Program Evaluation Methodology (AIRPEM), Symposium on Research and Evaluation Methodology: Lifespan Issues Related to American Indians/Alaska Natives with Disabilities*. Flagstaff: Northern Arizona University, Institute for Human Development, Arizona University Center on Disabilities, American Indian Rehabilitation Research and Training Center.

[15] Davis, J. D., & Keemer, K. (2002). A brief history of and future considerations for research in American Indian and Alaska Native communities. In J. D. Davis, J. S. Erickson, S. R. Johnson, C. A. Marshall, P. Running Wolf, & R. L. Santiago, (Eds.), *Work Group on American Indian Research and Program Evaluation Methodology (AIRPEM), Symposium on Research and Evaluation Methodology: Lifespan Issues Related to American Indians/Alaska Natives with Disabilities* (pp. 9-18). Flagstaff: Northern Arizona University, Institute for Human Development, Arizona University Center on Disabilities, American Indian Rehabilitation Research and Training Center.

[16] Devine, P. G., & Elliot, A. J. (1995). Are racial stereotypes really fading? The Princeton trilogy revisited. *Personality and Social Psychology Bulletin, 21*, 1139-1150.

[17] DuBois, A (1995) Spiral Bacteria in the Human Stomach: The Gastric Helicobacters http://www.cdc.gov/ncidod/eid/vol1no3/dubois.htm April 26, 2004

[18] Du Bois, B. (1983). Passionate scholarship: Notes on values, knowing and method in feminist social science. In G. Bowles and R. D. Klein, *Theories of women's studies* (pp. 105-116). Boston: Routledge and Kegan Paul.

[19] Dziekan, K. I., & Okocha, A. G. (1993). Accessibility of rehabilitation services: Comparison by racial-ethnic status. *Rehabilitation Counseling Bulletin, 36, 183*-189.

[20]Feist-Price, S. (1995). African Americans with disabilities and equity in vocational rehabilitation services: One state's review. *Rehabilitation Counseling Bulletin, 39*, 119-129.

[21]Freud, S. (1938). *The Basic Writings of Sigmund Freud.* Trans. By A. Brill. New York: Modern Library.

[22]Gatens-Robinson, E., & Tarvydas, V. (1992). Ethics of care, women's perspectives and the status of mainstream rehabilitation ethical analysis. *Journal of Applied Rehabilitation Counseling, 22*(4), 26-33.

[23]Gergen, K. J., Gulerce, A., Lock, A., & Misra, G. (1996). Psychological science in cultural context. *American Psychologist, 51*(5), 496-503.

[24]Graves, W. (1991, September). Participatory action research: A new paradigm for disability and rehabilitation research. *ARCA Newsletter*, pp. 8-11.

[25]Hacker, A. (1995). *Two nations: Black and White, separate, hostile, unequal.* New York, NY: Macmillan.

[26]Harding, S. (1986). *The science question in feminism.* Ithaca, NY: Cornell University Press.

[27]Harding, S. (1998). *Is science multicultural?: Postcolonialisms, feminisms, and epistemologies.* Bloomington: Indiana University Press.

[28]Herbert, J. T., & Martinez, M., Y. (1992). Client ethnicity and vocational rehabilitation case service outcome. *Journal of Job Placement, 8*, 10-16.

[29]Hughes, D., Seidman, E., & Williams, N. (1993). Cultural phenomena and the research enterprize: Toward a culturally anchored methodology. *American Journal of Community Psychology, 21(6)*, 687-703.

[30]Ladner, J. A. (1987). Introduction to tomorrow's tomorrow. In Harding, S. (Ed.) (1987). *Feminism and methodology.* Bloomington: Indiana University Press and Milton Keynes: Open University Press.

[31]Lykes, M. B. (1989). Dialogue with Guatemalan Indian women: Critical perspectives on constructing collaborative research. In R. Unger (Eds.), *Representations: Social constructions of gender*, pp. 167-184. Amityville, NY: Baywood Publishing Co.

[32]Marshall, C. A. & Largo, H. R., Jr. (1999). Disability and rehabilitation: A context for understanding the American Indian experience. *The Lancet, 354*, 758-60.

[33]Marshall, C. A., Leung, P., Johnson, S.R., & Busby, H. (2003). Ethical practice and cultural factors in rehabilitation. *Rehabilitation Education, 17*(1), 55-65.

[34]Marshall, C.A., Sanders, J. E., & Hill, C. R. (2001). Family voices in rehabilitation research. In C. A. Marshall (Ed.), *Rehabilitation and American Indians with disabilities: A handbook for administrators, practitioners, and researchers* (pp. 219-234). Athens, GA: Elliott & Fitzpatrick, Inc.

[35]Mays, V. M., Rubin, J., Sabourin, M., & Walker, L. (1996). Moving toward a global psychology: Changing theories and practice to meet the needs of a changing world. *American Psychologist, 51*, 485-487.

[36]Murray, L. R. (2003). Sick and tired of being sick and tired: Scientific evidence, methods, and research implications for racial and ethnic dispariteis in occupational health. *American Journal of Public Health, 93*(2) 221-226.

[37]*NIH Policy on Reporting Race and Ethnicity Data: Subjects in clinical research* Release Date: August 8, 2001 NOTICE: NOT-OD-01-053 National Institutes of Health.

[38]Peterson, G. E. (1996). *An analysis of participation, progress, and outcome of individuals from diverse racial and ethnic backgrounds in the public vocational rehabilitation program in Nevada.* Unpublished doctoral dissertation, University of Northern Colorado.

[39]Rawlings, S. W., & Saluter, A, F. (1994). *Household and family characteristics: U. S. Bureau of the Census, Current Population Reports*, P20-483.

[40]Rehabilitation Services Administration (RSA). (1995). *Reporting manual for the case service report (RSA-911)* (RSA-PD-95-04). Washington, DC: Rehabilitation Services Administration.

[41]Rogler, L. H. (1989) The meaning of culturally sensitive research in mental health. *American Journal of Psychiatry 146*(3) 296-303.

[42]Ross, M. G., & Biggi, I. M. (1986). Critical vocational rehabilitation service delivery issues at referral (02) and closure (08, 26, 28, 30) in serving select disabled persons. In S. Walker, F. Belgrave, A. M. Banner, & R. W. Nicholls (Eds.), *Equal to the challenge: Perspective, problems, and strategies in the rehabilitation of the nonwhite disabled: Proceedings of the National Conference* (pp. 39-50). Washington, DC: The Center for the Study of Handicapped Children and Youth, School of Education, Howard University. (ERIC Document Reproduction Service No. ED 276 198).

[43]Schacht, R. M., White, M., Daugherty, R., LaPlante, M., & Menz, F. (2003). *An analysis of disability and employment outcome data for American Indians and Alaska Natives.* Flagstaff: Northern Arizona University, Institute for Human Development, Arizona University Center on Disabilities, American Indian Rehabilitation Research and Training Center. (Available from the American Indian Rehabilitation Research and Training Center, Institute for Human Development, Northern Arizona University, PO Box 5630, Flagstaff, AZ 86011) National Institute on Disability and Rehabilitation Research. (1998, October). NIDRR 1999-2004 Long-Range Plan. Washington, DC: Author.

[34]Schulman, K. A., Berlin, J. A., Harless, W., & Kerner, J. F., Sistrunk, S. Gersh, B., Dubé., R., Taleghani, C., Burke, J., Williams, S., Eisenberg. J. M., & Escarce, E. (1999). The effect of race and sex on physicians' recommendations for cardiac catheterization. *The New England Journal of Medicine, 340*(8) 618-628.

[35]Smith, L. T. (1999). *Decolonizing Methodologies: Research and Indigenous Peoples.* London: Zed Books, Ltd.

[36]Steinbeck, J., and Ricketts, E. F. (1971) [originally published in 1941]. *Sea of Cortez: A leisurely journal of travel and research.* Mamaroneck, NY: Paul P. Appel, Publisher

[37]Stone, J. (2002). Focus on cultural issues in research: Developing and implementing Native American postcolonial participatory action research. In J. D. Davis, J. S. Erickson, S. R. Johnson, C. A. Marshall, P. Running Wolf, & R. L. Santiago, (Eds.), *Work Group on American Indian Research and Program Evaluation Methodology (AIRPEM), Symposium on Research and Evaluation Methodology: Lifespan Issues Related to American Indians/Alaska Natives with Disabilities* (pp. 98-121). Flagstaff: Northern Arizona University, Institute for Human Development, Arizona University Center on Disabilities, American Indian Rehabilitation Research and Training Center. (Available at http://www.wili.org/docs/AIRPEM_Monograph.pdf)

[38]Sue, S. (1999). Science, ethnicity, and bias. *American Psychologist, 54*(12), 1070-1077.

[39]Szymanski, E. M. (1993). Research design and statistical design. *Rehabilitation Counseling Bulletin, 36*(4), 178-182.

[40]Thomas, A., & Sillen, S. (1972). *Racism and psychiatry.* New York: Carol Publishing Group.

[41]Tucker, C. M & Herman, K. C. (2002) Using culturally sensitive theories and research to meet the academic needs of low-income African American children *American Psychologist 57*(10) 762-773

[42]Tutty, L. M., Rothery, M. A., & Grinnell, R. M., Jr., (1996). *Qualitative research for social workers: Phases, steps, & tasks.* Boston: Allyn and Bacon.

[43]United States Census Bureau (2001). Residential segregation of Hispanics or Latinos: 1980 to 2000. Census 2000 news releases [On-line]. http://www.census.gov/hhes/www/housing/resseg/ch6.html [2002, November. 27].

[44]Walker, M. L. (1993). Participatory action research [editorial]. *Rehabilitation Counseling Bulletin, 37,* 2-5.

[45]Wampold, B. E. (2003) Bashing positivism and revering a medical model under the guise of evidence. *The Counseling Psychologist, 31*(5) 539-545.

[46]Wheaton, J. E. (1995). Vocational rehabilitation acceptance rate for European Americans and African Americans: Another look. *Rehabilitation Counseling Bulletin, 38,* 224-231.

[47]White, G. (2002) Consumer participation in disability research: the golden rule as a guide for ethical practice. *Rehabilitation Psychology 47*(4) 438-446.

[48]Wilson, K. B. (2000). Predicting vocational rehabilitation eligibility based on race, education, work status, and source of support at application. *Rehabilitation Counseling Bulletin, 43,* 97-105.

[49]Wilson, K. B. (1999). Vocational rehabilitation acceptance: A tale of two races in a large Midwestern state. *Journal of Applied Rehabilitation Counseling 30,* 25-31.

[50]Wilson, K. B., Harley, D. A., & Alston, R. J. (2001). Race as a correlate of vocational rehabilitation acceptance: Revisited. *Journal of Rehabilitation, 67*(3), 35-41.

[51]Wilson, K. B. (2002). The exploration of vocational rehabilitation acceptance and ethnicity: A national investigation. *Rehabilitation Counseling Bulletin, 45,* 168-176.

[52]Wilson, K. B. (2003). Vocational rehabilitation eligibility and unsuccessful closures after the initiation of the individual plan for employment (IPE): Are there really differences? *Journal of the Pennsylvania Counseling Association, 5, 2, 13-23.*

[53]Wilson, K. B., & Senices, J. (2005). Exploring the vocational rehabilitation acceptance rates of Hispanics and non-Hispanics in the United States. *Journal of Counseling and Development 83(1),* 86-96.

[54]Wilson, K. B., Harley, D. A., McCormick, K., Jolivette, K. & Jackson. R. (2001). A literature review of vocational rehabilitation acceptance and explaining bias in the rehabilitation process. *Journal of Rehabilitation, 32,* 24-35.